The
[Un]Documented
Mark Steyn

The
[Un]Documented
Mark Steyn

Don't Say You Weren't Warned

MARK STEYN

REGNERY
PUBLISHING
A Salem Communications Company

Library of Congress Cataloging-in-Publication Data

Steyn, Mark.
  The undocumented Mark Steyn : don't say you weren't warned / Mark Steyn.
    pages cm
  Summary: "He's brash, brilliant, and drawn to controversy like a moth to a flame. Mark Steyn is America's most brutally honest columnist, ready to sound off on every hot issue in the news-and always ready to ruffle feathers. Prepare to be shocked and entertained by this curated compendium of Steyn's most provocative, hilarious, and thought-provoking columns"-- Provided by publisher.
  ISBN 978-1-62157-318-0 (hardback)
  I. Title.
  PN4913.S766A25 2014
  814'.54--dc23
                              2014032955

Published in the United States by
Regnery Publishing
A Salem Communications Company
300 New Jersey Ave NW
Washington, DC 20001
www.Regnery.com

Distributed to the trade by
Perseus Distribution
250 West 57th Street
New York, NY 10107

Manufactured in the United States of America

10 9 8 7 6 5 4 3 2 1

Books are available in quantity for promotional or premium use. For information on discounts and terms, please visit our website: www.Regnery.com.

CONTENTS

INTRODUCTION
Me and My Little Black Dress ix

I: UP, DOWN, OVER AND OUT
Viagra Nation 1
Decaffeinated 6
Unsung Songs 9
Oh, Say, Can You See? 14

II: SPIRITS OF THE AGE
Life Class 23
E Pluribus Composite 26
Sheet Music 32
Did the Earth Summit Move for You? 36
The Media's Maternal Instincts 40
Living Large 44

III: THE REPUBLIC OF MANNERS
Potpourri Roasting on an Open Fire 51
Last Dance 55
We've Figured It Out 58
The Audacity of Grope 62
In the Absence of Guns 67
Arms Are for Dining 73

IV: THE BUREAU OF COMPLIANCE
Signs of the Times 79
Carried to Extremes 84

Illegally Admiring the King's Deer 87
Ninjas vs. Turtles 91
The Butt Stops Here 99

V: HOMELAND SECURITY

Priorities 105
Choc and Awe 109
The All-Seeing Nanny 112
The Paramilitarized Bureaucracy 117

VI: THE STORIES WE TELL

Meeting Mr. Bond 123
Boy, Meats, Girl 128
Look Where Your Stories Have Landed You 134
Cover Story 141
When Harry Met Hillary 145

VII: IMPERIAL ECHOES

Keeping It 151
Queer Theory 156
Son of Empire 160
The People's Queen 166
Celebrity Caesar 170
The Footstools of Camelot 174

VIII: SEPTEMBER 12

History's Calling Card 179
The Brutal Afghan Winter 181
The Brutal Cuban Winter 186
The Limits 191
Too Big to Win 194
Drone Alone 202

A National Disgrace 205
The Man at the Border.................................. 209

IX: THE WAR ON WOMEN
My Sharia Amour 217
Barbie in a Burqa...................................... 223
How Unclean Was My Valley 228

X: MYSTIC CHORDS
Sounds of the Rude World 235
Decoration Day 240
Say, It Ain't So Joe 244
Happy Birthday, Mister Bob 249
We Aren't the World 253
The Parliament of Euro-Man 258
Changing His Tune 263
Changing His Words 267
Moon River and Me 270

XI: AFTER WORK
The Aristorockracy 279
The Waste of People.................................... 282
A Town with Pity...................................... 285
The Post-Work Economy................................ 290
Tribal America.. 294

XII: BIRTH OF TOMORROW
Post-Modern Family 301
Only the Clonely...................................... 305
Stork Report.. 309
The Right to Choose 314
How Weird How Soon?................................. 317

XIII: CURTAINS

Double Act 323
Croc of Gold 328
Every Dog Should Have His Day 333
The Seventy-Year Itch 339

XIV: LAST LAUGHS

Joking Aside 347
The Pinkshirts 351
Little Stasi-on-Avon 357
"There Is No More Molly" 362
The Unsafe Space 369

XV: LENGTHENED SHADOWS

Footsteps in the Desert 377
Sex at Sunset 381
A Stroll at Twilight 384

XVI: AGAINST THE GRAIN

Dutch Courage 389
The Uncowardly Lioness 393
The Reformation of Manners 397

POSTSCRIPT: EVERYONE'S A CRITIC

Throwaway Line 403
My Favorite Wahhabi 405
Of All the Gin Joints in All the Towns in All the World 409
Laying It on the Line 411

ACKNOWLEDGMENTS 417
INDEX 419

INTRODUCTION

ME AND MY LITTLE BLACK DRESS

A DECADE OR SO back, early in the 2004 presidential election season, a publisher took me to lunch and pitched me a book. She wanted me to write a John Kerry election diary. Easy gig. All I had to do was follow him around and mock him mercilessly. Well, I hemmed and hawed and eventually she got the picture and said, "Okay, what would you like to write a book about?"

And so I replied, "Well, I've got this idea for a book called *The End of the World*."

And there was a pause and I could feel her metaphorically backing out of the room, and shortly thereafter she literally backed out of the room. But not before telling me, somewhat wistfully, "You know when I first started reading your stuff? Impeachment. Your column about Monica Lewinsky's dress was hilarious." She motioned to the waiter. "Check, please!" And I got the distinct impression she was feeling like the great pop guru Don Kirshner when the Monkees came to him and said they were sick of doing this bubblegum stuff and they needed to grow as artists. My "Monica's dress" column appeared in Britain's *Daily Telegraph* in 1998, although it was, in fact, datelined two decades later—August 22, 2018:

> She is older now, her once dazzling looks undeniably faded, her famous beauty worn and creased.
>
> "Sorry about that," she says. "I was supposed to get ironed yesterday."

Yes, it's "that dress"—the dress that, 20 years ago this month, held the fate of a presidency in her lap. It has been two decades since the day she gave her dramatic testimony to the grand jury and then promptly disappeared into the federal witness protection program. Even as she recalls her brief moment in the spotlight, she looks drawn. But that's because, following extensive reconstructive surgery, she's been living quietly as a pair of curtains in Idaho.

"What do you think?" she says, saucily brushing her hem against the sill as her pleats ripple across the mullions. "It cost less than Paula Jones' nose job."

To be honest, I was lucky to get the interview. The dress was supposed to be doing the BBC—the full sob-sister treatment, Martin Bashir, the works—but, to protect her identity, they wanted to do that undercover secret-location protect-your-identity trick with the camera that makes part of the screen go all fuzzy and blurry.

"Are you crazy?" she yelled at them. "It'll look like I've still got the stain."

The Nineties were a lot of fun for a columnist. A third Clinton term and I could have retired to the Caribbean. But then came the new century and the new war, and I felt like Ingrid Bergman in *Casablanca* when she tells Bogey, "I put that dress away. When the Germans march out, I'll wear it again." I put Monica's dress away. When the jihadists march out, I'll wear it again.

My apocalyptic tome came out in 2006 (courtesy of the publisher of the book you're holding right now) as *America Alone: The End of the World as We Know It*—jihad, demographic decline, the death of Europe, all the fun stuff. I followed it with *After America: Get Ready for Armageddon*—debt, doom, decadence, societal meltdown, total civilizational collapse, all the even more fun stuff. I don't know whether the Monkees in their serious-artist phase ever felt it might be nice to sing "Daydream Believer" occasionally, but, after a decade of apocalyptic despair, I've found myself passing the closet and eyeing Monica's dress wistfully. All jihad and no play can get to you after a while, so, in the interests of a balanced diet, what follows runs the gamut from Clinton's boxer shorts to Barbie's burqa.

The old artistic trade-off—"Do you want it good or do you want it Friday?"—doesn't really apply to jobbing columnists: Your editors want it Friday. Good is an extra. But if you're lucky, a few of them hold up over the decades—not because you were aiming to say anything profound, but because in that snapshot of whatever was happening that particular Friday you alighted upon a small close-up that illuminates the big picture: The story of Deena Gilbey's post-9/11 torments by the federal bureaucracy that facilitated the murder of her husband is still a perfect encapsulation of the near suicidal stupidity of America's immigration regime. The coverage of the Million Mom March is a textbook case of the U.S. media's willingness to serve as the court eunuchs of the Democratic Party. The new federally-mandated street signs in Barre, Vermont, explain why this country is the Brokest Nation in History. Over the years, I've written on a lot of different subjects: I was "Musical Theatre Correspondent" for *The Independent* in London, and obituarist for *The Atlantic* over here. And I've included a bit of movie criticism, literary disquisition, musical analysis, showbiz arcana, mostly, as above, for the larger truths they exemplify.

There are politicians here, of course, although both Clinton, staggering pantless through American feminists' defense of him, and Obama, running on biography but one full of entirely invented friends and family, seem more interesting to me as cultural phenomena. Sadly, there's still no "John Kerry election diary," although not because I didn't enjoy valuable "face time" with the great man during his campaign for the White House. In 2003, I was at a campaign event in Haverhill, New Hampshire (for more on Haverhill, see this book's postscript), chatting with two plaid-clad old-timers:

The Senator approached and stopped in front of us. The etiquette in primary season is that the candidate defers to the cranky Granite Staters' churlish indifference to status and initiates the conversation: "Hi, I'm John Kerry. Good to see ya. Cold enough for ya? How 'bout them Sox?" Etc. Instead, Senator Kerry just stood there nose to nose, staring at us with an inscrutable Botoxicated semi-glare on his face. After an eternity, an aide stepped out from behind him and said, "The Senator needs you to move."

"Well, why couldn't he have said that?" muttered one of the old coots.

Why indeed? But then again—from another campaign stop, a year later, at the popular burger emporium Wendy's:

Teresa Heinz Kerry pointed to the picture of the bowl of chili above the clerk's head: "What's that?" she asked. He explained that it was something called "chili," and she said she'd like to try a bowl. The Senator also ordered a Frosty, a chocolate dessert. They toyed with them after a fashion and then got back on the bus.... He may not enjoy eating at Wendy's, but his faux lunch order captures the essence of his crowd-working style: chili and Frosty. If I were the Wendy's marketing director, I'd make it the John Kerry Special from now through Election Day.

Nothing wrong with that. But I feel like Bob Hope must have felt flipping through his best Coolidge jokes during the Dukakis campaign. As I write, people keep asking me whom I favor for the nomination in 2016. Well, as a resident of a New Hampshire township with more than thirty-seven people, I don't have to seek out presidential candidates; they're there at the inn and the general store and the diner and the Grange. And, over the period covered by this book, I've seen enough next-presidents-of-the-United-States for several lifetimes: Phil Gramm, Pete Wilson, Bob Dornan, Bob Dole, Elizabeth Dole,

Orrin Hatch, Gary Bauer, Lamar Alexander, Tom Tancredo, Tommy Thompson, Alan Keyes....

Would it have made any difference to the country had any of these fine upstanding fellows prevailed? Or would we be pretty much where we are anyway? Aside from a trade agreement here, a federal regulation there, I'd plump for the latter. You can't have conservative government in a liberal culture, and that's the position the Republican Party is in. After the last election, I said that the billion dollars spent by the Romney campaign on robocalls and TV ads and all the rest had been entirely wasted, and the Electoral College breakdown would have been pretty much what it was if they'd just tossed the dough into the Potomac and let it float out to sea. But imagine the use all that money and time could have been put to out there in the wider world.

Liberals expend tremendous effort changing the culture. Conservatives expend tremendous effort changing elected officials every other November—and then are surprised that it doesn't make much difference. Culture trumps politics—which is why, once the question's been settled culturally, conservatives are reduced to playing catch-up, twisting themselves into pretzels to explain why gay marriage is really conservative after all, or why thirty million unskilled immigrants with a majority of births out of wedlock are "natural allies" of the Republican Party.

We're told that the presidency is important because the head guy gets to appoint, if he's lucky, a couple of Supreme Court judges. But they're playing catch-up to the culture, too. In 1986, in a concurrence to a majority opinion, the Chief Justice of the United States declared that "there is no such thing as a fundamental right to commit homosexual sodomy." A blink of an eye, and his successors are discovering fundamental rights to commit homosexual marriage. What happened in between? Jurisprudentially, nothing: Everything Chief Justice Burger said back in the Eighties—about Common Law, Blackstone's "crime against nature," "the legislative authority of the State"—still applies. Except it doesn't. Because the culture—from school guidance counselors to sitcom characters to Oscar hosts—moved on, and so even America's Regency of Jurists was obliged to get with the beat. Because to say today what the Chief Justice of the United States said twenty-eight years ago would be to render oneself unfit for public office—not merely as Chief Justice but as CEO of a private company, or host of a cable home-remodeling show, or dog-catcher in Dead Moose Junction.

What politician of left or right championed gay marriage? Bill Clinton? No, he signed the now notoriously "homophobic" Defense of Marriage Act. Barack Obama? Gay-wise, he took longer to come out than Ricky Martin. The only major politician to elbow his way to the front of the gay bandwagon was Britain's David Cameron, who used same-sex marriage as a Sister-Souljah-on-steroids moment to signal to London's chattering classes that, notwithstanding his membership of the unfortunately named "Conservative Party," on everything that mattered he was one of them.

But, in Britain as in America, the political class was simply playing catch-up to the culture. Even in the squishiest Continental "social democracy," once every four or five years you can persuade the electorate to go out and vote for a conservative party. But if you want them to vote for conservative *government* you have to do the hard work of shifting the culture every day, seven days a week, in the four-and-a-half years between elections. If the culture's liberal, if the schools are liberal, if the churches are liberal, if the hip, groovy business elite is liberal, if the guys who make the movies and the pop songs are liberal, then electing a guy with an "R" after his name isn't going to make a lot of difference. Nor should it. In free societies, politics is the art of the possible. In the 729 days between elections, the left is very good at making its causes so possible that in American politics almost anything of consequence is now impossible, from enforcing immigration law to controlling spending.

What will we be playing catch-up to in another twenty-eight years? Not so long ago, I might have suggested transsexual rights. But, barely pausing to celebrate their victory on gay marriage, the identity-group enforcers have gone full steam ahead on transgender issues. Once upon a time there were but two sexes. Now Facebook offers its 1.2 billion patrons the opportunity to select their preference from dozens of "genders": "male" and "female" are still on the drop-down menu, just about, but lost amid fifty shades of gay—

"androgynous," "bi-gender," "intersex," "cisfemale," "trans*man," "gender fluid"....

Oh, you can laugh. But none of the people who matter in American culture are laughing. They take it all perfectly seriously. Supreme Intergalactic Arbiter Anthony Kennedy wields more power over Americans than George III did, but in a year or three he'll be playing catch-up and striking down laws because of their "improper animus" and wish to "demean" and "humiliate" persons of gender fluidity. Having done an impressive job of demolishing the basic societal building block of the family, the ambitious liberal is now moving on to demolishing the basic biological building block of the sexes. Indeed, taken in tandem with the ever greater dominance of women at America's least worst colleges and, at the other end of the social scale, the bleak, dispiriting permanence of the "he-cession," in twenty-eight years' time we may be fairly well advanced toward the de facto abolition of man, at least in the manly sense. That seems to me at least as interesting a question as whether the Republicans can take the Senate with a pick-up in this or that swing state. Culture is the long view; politics is the here and now. Yet in America vast cultural changes occur in nothing flat, while, under our sclerotic political institutions, men elected to two-year terms of office announce ambitious plans to balance the budget a decade after their terms end. Here, again, liberals show a greater understanding of where the action is.

So, if the most hawkish of GOP deficit hawks has no plans to trim spending until well in the 2020s, why not look at what kind of country you'll be budgeting for by then? What will American obesity and heart-disease and childhood diabetes rates be by then? What about rural heroin and meth addiction? How much of the country will, with or without "comprehensive immigration reform," be socioeconomically Latin-American? And what is the likelihood of such a nation voting for small-government conservatism?

There's a useful umbrella for most of the above: The most consequential act of state ownership in the twentieth-century western world was not the nationalization of airlines or the nationalization of railways or the nationalization of health care, but the nationalization of the family. I owe that phrase to

Professor R Vaidyanathan at the Indian Institute of Management in Bangalore. He's a bit of a chippy post-imperialist, and he's nobody's idea of a right-winger, but he's absolutely right about this. It's the defining fact about the decline of the west: Once upon a time, in Canada, Britain, Europe, and beyond, ambitious leftists nationalized industries—steel, coal, planes, cars, banks—but it was such a self-evident disaster that it's been more or less abandoned, at least by those who wish to remain electorally viable. On the other hand, the nationalization of the family proceeds apace, and America is as well advanced on that path as anywhere else. "The west has nationalized families over the last 60 years," writes Vaidyanathan. "Old age, ill health, single motherhood—everything is the responsibility of the state."

When I was a kid and watched sci-fi movies set in a futuristic dystopia where individuals are mere chattels of an unseen all-powerful government and enduring human relationships are banned and the progeny of transient sexual encounters are the property of the state, I always found the caper less interesting than the unseen backstory: How did they get there from here? From free western societies to a bunch of glassy-eyed drones wandering around in identikit variety-show catsuits in a land where technology has advanced but liberty has retreated: how'd that happen?

I'd say "the nationalization of the family" is how it happens. *That's* how you get there from here.

But I see I've worked my way back to all that apocalyptic gloom I came in with at that long-ago publisher's lunch. So you'll be relieved to hear there's some lighter stuff along the way—Viagra, potpourri, Marilyn Monroe, Soviet national anthem rewrites....

Finally, a note on what Daffy Duck, in a livelier context, called "pronoun trouble": I wound up living in New Hampshire through the classic disastrous real estate transaction. I walked into the realtor intending to buy a little ski place I could use for a couple of winter weekends and a week at Christmas, and walked out with a two-hundred-year-old farmhouse needing two hundred years of work on it. In those days, I wrote mainly on music and film and other showbizzy subjects, and gradually my editors in London and elsewhere became aware that I was doing all this showbizzy stuff from some obscure corner of America. And so they started to ask me to write on this or that political story. Most foreign correspondents in America are based in New York, Washington, or Los Angeles, so I like to think I came at the subject from a different angle (again, see this book's postscript for more on my whereabouts).

But, as I said, it can lead to Daffy-style pronoun trouble. Writing for publications in Britain, Canada, Australia, and elsewhere, I used to be very careful about my pronouns. Then I discovered that for the previous six months some malicious Fleet Street sub-editor at *The Daily Telegraph*, in my more contemptuously hectoring surveys of the London scene, had been taking out every dismissive "you snotty Brits" and replacing it with "we." A while later, I got a barrage of emails from Canadians sneering at me as a wannabe American along with even more emails from aggrieved Americans huffing at my impertinence at claiming to speak on behalf of their country. It turned out some jackanapes of a whippersnapper at *The New York Sun* had been removing all my "you crazy Yanks" and replacing it with "we." The same thing happened to my compatriot Michael Ignatieff, who returned to Canada from a lucrative gig at Harvard intending to become Prime Minister only to find that his opponents dredged up every *New York Times* column of his in which he'd used the word "we" as shorthand for "we Americans." Mr. Ignatieff led the Canadian Liberal Party to their worst defeat in history and is now back at Harvard.

When the Internet took off, someone commented that my colleague David Frum wrote for Americans as an American and for Canadians as a Canadian. And someone else responded that I'd taken it to the next level: Steyn wrote for Americans as an American, Canadians as a Canadian, and Britons as a Briton. And then a third person chipped in that, no, it was subtler than that: Steyn wrote for Britons as a Canadian, for Canadians as an American, and for Americans as a Briton.... Well, I don't know about that, but throughout my time writing for *The Chicago Sun-Times* and Canada's *National Post* and Britain's *Spectator* and *The Australian* and *The Irish Times*, I do think it helps sometimes to view one society through the lens of another:

Two pieces here on welfare as viewed from Britain's "housing estates" and Canada's Indian reservations offer lessons for Americans too.

And, whatever Michael Ignatieff feels about it, for my own part I generally use "we" to mean "western civilization," which could use a few more friends on the pronoun front. Left to my own devices, I'd probably write just about music. But the Taliban banned music. And Sayyid Qutb was so disgusted by hearing "Baby, It's Cold Outside" at a church dance in Greeley, Colorado, that he went back to Egypt and became the intellectual driving force behind the Muslim Brotherhood.

Which is to say that even the smallest pleasures have to be earned, and defended. So ultimately, if you like "Baby, It's Cold Outside" or even the Monkees, you need to pitch in on this clash-of-civilizations thing, too.

I

UP, DOWN, OVER AND OUT

VIAGRA NATION

Pfizer's chemists at their research facility in Sandwich, England, originally synthesized sildenafil to help with angina. In clinical trials, it did little for patients' chest pain, but along the way someone noticed that it caused a pronounced reaction somewhat lower down. On March 27, 1998, the FDA approved it as a treatment for erectile dysfunction, and in the weeks thereafter America talked of little else.

The Wall Street Journal, May 12, 1998

"HI, I'M WALTER, your waiter, and today's special is Linguine Viagra."

"Mmmm," said my date appreciatively. "That's what I call *al dente*."

I'm beginning to feel like the guy who was out of town the day the coup happened. You spend a quiet month ice fishing in Queen Maud Gulf and return to find the country changed beyond all recognition. Everywhere you turn, the Viagrafication of America proceeds apace. Even in the tiny portion of the news that isn't devoted to Viagra, it seems implicitly present—the surging Dow, El Niño, the rush to megamergers. I quote from memory: "The First National Bank of Little Snakc, Nevada, announced today that it is merging with New Mexico's Banco Flaccido to form ViagraBank, the world's biggest financial institution ever. In other news, Hurricane Viagra swept through a Florida trailer park, leaving 53 double-wides up-ended."

Forget Microsoft; Viagra now commands 98 percent of the metaphor market—and Congress isn't doing a thing about it. Frank Luntz has polling data showing that 83 percent of soccer moms want Republicans to use more Viagra imagery ("education vouchers will be the Viagra of our nation's SAT scores"). Al Gore's minders are already working up self-deprecating Viagra jokes: "Okay, Mr. Vice President, all you have to say is, 'Recently. I was. Proud.

1

To take. Viagra.' Then you simply stand there, completely stiff from head to toe, same as always, and just say in your usual monotone, 'Whoops. Guess I. Took one. Too Many.'"

As the only guy in the country not taking the tablets, I wasn't sure I knew enough about the subject. So my pal Earl and I repaired to Starbucks after lunch, where I told him I was writing a column on Viagra.

"*Grrrrrreattt!!*" he said, slapping my back somewhat over-heartily. "I write all my columns on Viagra. Guess you've finally figured it out, amigo: The milquetoast pantywaist Andy Williams Prozac era is over. I used to be like you, cranking out reasonable on-the-one-hand-on-the-other-hand wimpsville stuff for *Harper's*. Now, thanks to the little blue diamonds, I'm a ferocious right-wing bastard with my own column in *The American Spectator*! That'll put the lead back in your pencil, buddy boy." He glanced at the menu. "Hey, what's the flavor of the day?"

"Viagraccino," said Kelli. "One cup and you'll be up all night."

Earl is, of course, not his real name. His real name is Chuck. He just called to make sure I mention it. Chuck Malmquist, 57 Elm Street, Apartment B. Second left after the Citgo station. Chuck says it saves a whole lot of time if the chicks already know you're on Viagra.

Presumably that's why every medical correspondent on every American magazine has no problem lining up on-the-record testimonials from "Tom Cannata, a 43-year-old accountant from Springfield, Mass" and "Ronald Marrocco, a 55-year-old diabetic from St. Petersburg, Fla," both eager to disclose their prodigious intake to any passing reporter. My favorite to date—I mean my favorite so far, not my favorite to go to dinner and a movie with—is Irving Mesher, described as "a 73-year-old retired New York City firefighter, who currently lives at a family-owned nudist resort in Pennsylvania's Pocono mountains." Mr. Mesher, according to *Time*, has sex "three or four times a week with several girlfriends in their twenties." He is planning "a Viagra party."

I suppose it was too much to expect American men to take an impotence pill without advertising the fact. After all, the U.S. not only has more women with breast implants than any other country on the planet, but also more women happy to tell you they have breast implants—see Pamela Lee, Jenny McCarthy, Jane Fonda. This is in the same fine tradition of full disclosure as the cereal packet: "Grandma's Country Kitchen Old-Time Vermont Maple Oatmeal. Made in Wisconsin entirely from artificial ingredients." But, contemplating a society in which artificially aroused men pursue ever more artificially enhanced women, I wonder if we aren't in danger of unnecessarily complicating the whole business.

Does America need more seventy-three-year-old nude firemen? It's bad enough with the old coot down the street standing under our window with his ukulele every night serenading the missus with "Viagra Con Dios." After my month away, my lovely bride was looking forward to my return, but I couldn't help noticing on my first evening back that she seemed vaguely...dissatisfied.

"Well, it was okay," she said after some prompting, "but why can't you be more like Bob Dole?"

"Bob Dole?" I scoffed. I was laughing so much I rolled off the bearskin rug, and got rather a nasty splinter. It was only later that I discovered that the test group for the new impotence pill had included the Republican presidential candidate—ex officio, one assumes. Doubtless the congressional leadership made up the rest of the group. But Bob Dole's endorsement does make you wonder about other possible side effects—a sudden urge to dive off the stage, a tendency to refer to yourself in the third person. I asked my pal Earl—sorry, Chuck—if he was worried.

"Chuck Malmquist's not worried," he said. "Chuck Malmquist's gonna pop a couple of Viagras, head downtown. It's about America, leadership, babes, whatever."

As I understand it, although Viagra dramatically improves sexual performance, it can also cause headaches, impaired vision, rashes, and diarrhea. Chuck was unperturbed. "Sure, the first time was a problem," he conceded. "I was in the bar putting the moves on Tina when I suddenly had to rush for the men's room. By the time I got back, the impaired vision had kicked in, so I went to the wrong table and put my arms around Norm from accounting.

He wouldn't have minded, but my face was breaking out, so he fled screaming."

"Good grief, that's terrible," I said.

"Not really. By then I had a jackhammer of a headache, so I just wanted to go home anyway. But I'm on top of it now. First, I take two Viagra, then one Arret for the diarrhea plus another Viagra to counter the side effects of the Arret, then half a dozen Children's Motrin, followed by Vagisil for the rash plus a couple of Rogaine. . . ."

"But Rogaine's for baldness. . . ."

"Hey, don't knock it. My new back hair covers the rash. Then I take another Viagra to counter the potential libido-depressing effect of the Rogaine, followed by two Lipitor to lessen my risk of heart attack."

"But you're not at risk of heart attack. . . ."

"You try doing the mambo with thirty pounds of tablets in your pocket."

As Chuck roared off in his new Chevy Agra—the sport-utility vehicle with the world's largest cup holder—I reflected on how far we've come in just a few weeks. I can dimly recall hearing something about Viagra on the radio a month or so back, but assumed it was just an obscure African dictatorship, the latest stop on the Clinton Apology Tour:

"The President today apologized to the people of Viagra. 'The United States has not always done the right thing,' said Mr. Clinton. 'We discriminated against the Viagran people for no other reason than that their skin was different—slightly flushed, with a bead of sweat on the upper lip and an agitated look in the eyes. As President, I would be calling for a national conversation on Viagra, if we weren't already talking about nothing else.'"

Last week, it was announced that Viagra will soon be available in wafer form, bringing our social evolution full circle. A century and a half ago, Sylvester Graham, nutritionist, reformer and author of *The Young Man's Guide to Chastity*, invented the Graham Cracker as an aid to diminishing the male sex drive. Today, the Graham cracker must yield to the Viagra wafer, an idea whose time has come. The Clinton presidency has at last stumbled on its rendezvous with history: While Ronald Reagan and George Bush presided over the fall of Communism, Mr. Clinton presides over the rise of Viagra. It may not be true that any young boy can grow up to be president. But at least, thanks to Viagra, any young boy can grow up to be this president.

Graham Cracker, anyone?

DECAFFEINATED

National Review, July 4, 2011

THIS FALL MARKS the centenary of William Mitchell. You may not have heard of him, but in his day he was a big cheese. Indeed, he was a big processed cheese, with what's now Kraft Foods. Mitchell invented Cool Whip and quick-set Jell-O and powdered egg whites for cake mix. He was in the grand tradition of American entrepreneurial energy: Henry Ford made travel faster, Alexander Graham Bell made communication faster, Bill Mitchell made Jell-O even faster. When he died, I wrote an appreciation and noted his one great miscalculation, late in life. He noticed the dahlias growing on his daughter's land, came up with the idea of roasting their tubers, and created a brown substance with a coffee-like taste that he called Dacopa.

It flopped. The fearless pioneer of convenience foods had failed to foresee that in his final years coffee would become the ultimate inconvenience food. Where once you'd say, "Gimme a cuppa joe, Darlene," and the waitress would slide it across the counter, now you stand around for twenty minutes as the "barista" juices the espresso, froths up the milk, lathers on the foam, gives it a shot of caramel flavoring, sprinkles it with cinnamon, adds a slice of pepperoni and a soupçon of aubergine coulis, and instead of two bits charges you $5.95.

It's getting on for two decades since I first did a world's-slowest-coffee routine on the BBC with the great Bonnie Langford, West End child star and Doctor Who's perkiest sidekick. Jackie Mason was also on the show, and asked me who our writer was. I felt it would make me look like a loser to say I'd written it myself, so I promised to pass on any message. "Tell him he may be on to something," growled Mason. A few years later, I opened up *The American Spectator* to find the comic genius had worked up a Starbucks routine all his own.

At the time, I thought the ever more protracted java jive was an anomaly—the exception that proved the rule. Now I can see it was a profound insight: America's first slow-food chain was an idea whose time had come. Who knew you could make people stand in line (long *long* lines at city outlets in rush hour) for a cup of coffee? Don't tell me it's a Continental thing. I like my *café au lait* in Quebec, and it takes a third of the time of all the whooshing and frothing south of the border. Same in a Viennese *Kaffeehaus*. But I was at a "fair trade" Vermont coffee joint the other day, and there was no line at all, and it still took forever. And, as I began to get a little twitchy and pace up and down, I became aware of the handful of mellow patrons scattered about the easy chairs looking up from their tweets as if to scold: "What's with the restless energy, dude?"

I felt like the fellow in *Invasion of the Body Snatchers*: Everybody else in town had fallen asleep…and then stayed asleep. This is a paradox for our times: the somnolent coffee house. I had a strange urge to yell, "Wake up, we're trillions of dollars in debt! The powder keg's about to blow!," but I could feel the soporific indie-pop drifting over the counter, so I took my espresso to go, and worked off my torporphobic rage by shooting iPods off the tailgate of a rusting pick-up in the back field for the rest of the day.

"You just don't get coffee culture," sighed a friend. What "culture"? The coffee houses of seventeenth-century England were hives of business: They spawned the Stock Exchange and Lloyd's of London. The coffee houses of eighteenth-century Paris were hives of ideas: At Café Procope, Voltaire, Rousseau, and the gang met to thrash out the Enlightenment. The coffee houses of twenty-first-century America have spawned the gingerbread eggnog macchiato and an accompanying CD compilation. Unless, that is, there's something else going on: One is mindful of Number Two's briefing (in *Austin Powers*) to the recently defrosted Dr. Evil on what he's been up to while the evil mastermind bent on world domination has been in orbital cryostasis. "I seized upon the opportunity to invest in a small Seattle-based coffee company several years ago," he informs the doctor. "I believe if we shift our resources away from world domination and focus on providing premium-quality coffee drinks, we can increase our gross profits fivefold."

That's not such a good bet these days—Starbucks has closed a thousand outlets since 2008—but, on the other hand, world domination–wise, the espresso era does seem to have presided over a transformation in the dominant cultural aesthetic. Inertia has never been cooler. It's seeped out of the coffee house to stalk the land. I mean Barack Obama barely even bothers to pretend he's got a plan for debt "reduction" or Medicare "reform," does he?

I don't go in for as much pop sociology as, say, David Brooks. But, for the sake of argument, let's say he got it right on the general sensibility of a decade ago in *Bobos in Paradise: The New Upper Class and How They Got There.* Would you put money on his contemporary American elites to rouse themselves before catastrophe strikes? Or is somnolent, myopic complacency unto the end the way to bet?

Bit of a downer to end on, I know. But have a Dacopa. Unlike a soy peppermint chai frappuccino, it might perk you up.

UNSUNG SONGS

Maclean's, October 8, 2007

WHAT'S THE DIFFERENCE between Fred Thompson, actor and presidential candidate, and people fluent in the Amurdag language?

Well, let's start with what they have in common: they both turned up in the news cycle a few days ago. *National Geographic* made the headlines with a report that half the world's seven thousand languages will disappear by the end of the century. Languages are vanishing faster than at any time in human history. In Australia alone, researchers for the Living Tongues Institute for Endangered Languages could identify only three speakers each of Yawaru and Magati Ke. As for the Amurdag tongue, I use the singular advisedly: they were able to find just one man with rudimentary knowledge of the language. On the other hand, given that Amurdag was already thought to be extinct, his lone tongue may portend a stunning comeback for the lingo, the first shoots of a new Amurdag spring.

For *National Geographic* types, the tragedy is "the loss of knowledge about the natural world." "Most of what we know about species and ecosystems is not written down anywhere," says Professor David Harrison of Swarthmore College in Pennsylvania. "It's only in people's heads."

Big deal. The species and the ecosystem will, despite the sterling efforts of SUV drivers, still just about be around for folks to figure out. The real loss is more elusive and more profound. For generations there have been Yawaru and Magati Ke songs: no one will sing them ever again. There are stories of Yawaru and Magati Ke heroes and scoundrels: no one will know them, no one will tell them. And no one will care, because only a handful of anthropologists will be aware they ever existed. The extinction of Yawaru and Magati Ke not only obliterates their future but their past.

The death of even the smallest, meanest culture is a humbling event.

Which brings us to Fred Thompson. The other day, Senator Thompson was on the campaign trail and told his audience: "This country has shed more blood for the liberty of other countries than all other countries put together."

More than "all other countries put together"? As I told our American friends, I'm the most pro-American non-American on the planet, but if that's the new default braggadocio, include me out. *The Washington Post's* attempt to refute Thompson by championing the Soviets was as predictable as it was absurd—the Reds certainly shed a lot of blood but not obviously in the cause of liberty. Yet slightly more startling was the number of pro-Fred American conservatives who sent me scornful emails belittling the efforts of the Commonwealth.

As old-timers will tell you at Royal Canadian Legion halls, the Dominion "shed more blood" proportionately than the United States in the Second World War. Newfoundland—not yet part of Canada—had a higher per-capita casualty rate than America. No surprise about that: Newfs and Canucks sailed off to battle two years ahead of the Yanks. And, if we're talking hard numbers, almost as many Britons died in the war as Americans, despite the latter having thrice the population.

To this, my U.S. correspondents responded that that was all very well but these chaps were fighting for King and Empire rather than engaging in a selfless campaign of global liberation for noble reasons. Arguing the respective motivations of a dead Canuck on Juno Beach and a dead Yank on Omaha is a shrill and unworthy argument, and anyway I generally incline to Patton's line that the object isn't to die for your country but to make the other sonofabitch die for his. But imagine what the state of liberty in the world would be like had the British Empire not decided to soldier on alone, against all the odds and all the expert advice, after the fall of France in 1940.

Here's another thought experiment: imagine no Pearl Harbor, no casus belli to draw in the Americans. And yet somehow the mangy old British lion and its loyal cubs in the dominions managed to win all by themselves, and at all those war cemeteries on the Continent there was no Old Glory, just Union Jacks and Red Ensigns. Fred Thompson would not be able to make his claims to American über-exceptionalism über alles because the romance of America the Liberator would not exist. *Saving Private Ryan* would be about some bloke from the Cheshire Regiment, or maybe even the Princess Patricias. Hollywood would be forced to do as it did up to the Thirties: its tales of derring-do on far-flung shores would be mostly British—the Bengal Lancers et al.

Instead, by 1945 Hollywood was making films like *Objective: Burma*, in which what was in real life an Anglo-Aussie campaign became onscreen an all-American one. British public opinion resented that enough to chase the movie out of the country. Fifty-five years later, the film *U-571* told the story of a critical episode in the Battle of the Atlantic—the capture of a German submarine's Enigma cipher machine by the Allies. In humdrum reality, it was a British operation. In Hollywood, it was left to...well, guess who? By this stage, British public opinion just gave a shrug, and left the picture to flop all on its ownsome.

The Americans entered the war, and they won it, and they won big, unlike the Brits and Canadians. So it's theirs to mythologize, as Senator Thompson did. And there's no point anybody complaining about it. The rest of the Allies are not quite in the designated Magati Ke role, but they're almost there. The Thompson crack and the *National Geographic* line are both about cultural victory and cultural eclipse.

A year ago I gave a speech down under at the Sydney Conservatorium of Music. Sell-out audience, standing room only. So many folks that, blinking out across the footlights, I couldn't really discern midst the great tide of humanity any particular demographic characteristics. But the excitable Aussie pundit Antony Loewenstein did. Evidently he felt like a hip-hopper at a tea-dance: "The crowd largely consisted of old, white males," he wrote. "Steyn and his fellow travelers speak eloquently about western civilization on the verge of collapse, but the kind of world they imagine is not one that I either recognize or want. Thankfully, his 'vision' is likely to die with the Bush Administration. Likewise the elderly types at last night's event probably still fondly remember the White Australia [immigration] policy. They'll be dead soon enough."

Oh, I don't know. Leaving aside the question of whether the bloom of youth has faded from my own cheeks, I was introduced on stage by Dr. Janet Albrechtsen, who's a brainy gal but also quite a hottie. At the end of the evening, I posed for photographs with several gorgeous young sheilas, even if too many of them did tend to offer the somewhat dispiriting line that their mothers are really big fans of mine. Greg Lindsay, of the Centre for Independent Studies, which organized the event, responded that 10 percent of the audience were students, another third were under forty, a third were female, etc.

But that's not really what Loewenstein means. When someone deploys the "old white men" crack, they're saying you are the past, and your bitterness and prejudice is little more than a side effect of your decrepitude. Whereas we are the forces of progress, and therefore by definition we're young and healthy and full of vigor. So many of the most deeply ingrained assumptions about a culture are predicated on a youthful dynamism. We love the young because the young are the future—not just in pop songs and movies but in everything. As the blond blue-eyed Aryan boy in the Hitler Youth get-up sings in *Cabaret*, "Tomorrow belongs to me." It's his youth that makes the scene seductive and dangerous. If he were an "old, white male" like me or Noam Chomsky or Neil Young or Gloria Steinem, it would be merely pathetic.

I may, indeed, be "dead soon enough," as Mr. Loewenstein devoutly wishes. But so will the greying Sixties boomers whose ancient pieties provide so much of his cobwebbed progressivism. And to whom then will tomorrow belong? On my Australian tour, I was speaking mainly on demographic decline—on the failure of Spaniards, Italians, Russians, Japanese, and, yes, Canadians to have enough children to sustain not just their welfare programs but their societies and culture. That blond blue-eyed apple-cheeked Aryan lad from *Cabaret* is now an elderly Berliner wondering why he hasn't got any grandchildren. By the end of this century, the Yawaru and Magati Ke languages will be extinct. But there'll be little reason to learn German or Japanese either.

And the last Belgians and Italians, like the Kallawayan people of Bolivia, will make their accommodations with the future. "Children are little barometers of social prestige," says Professor David Harrison. "They understand implicitly that if they live in an environment where two languages are spoken, one of them is less valued than the other, and they will speak the more valued language."

That applies to broader cultural choices, too. If you're Nada Farooq, raised by moderate Muslim immigrants in Mississauga, Ontario, educated at Meadowvale Secondary School, what's "more valued"? Your "fellow Canadians" who gave their lives at Normandy? Or the fallen Chechen jihadist for whom you named your newborn son? In much of the west, "cultural eclipse" would seem to be a given. The only question is what comes next.

OH, SAY, CAN YOU SEE?

How many politicians does it take to change a light bulb?

Answer: Three hundred and fourteen members of the House of Representatives, plus eighty-six out of one hundred senators, and one president—Bush by name, who signed into law on December 19, 2007, something called the Energy Independence and Security Act.

The act doesn't do anything for energy "independence," although it does dramatically reduce yours. Likewise your "security." And it also outlaws one of the great icons of the Age of Invention—U.S. Patent Number 223,898, granted on January 27, 1880, to Thomas Edison: the incandescent light bulb.

By law, the electric bulb as we have known it is history, as America joins Canada, Australia, and the European Union in punching your lights out. The approved replacement is the CFL. You may have seen it already in certain environmentally conscious households poking out from under ceiling fixtures like a yogurt-coated curly fry (it's about 25 percent longer than the old bulb). That's what CFL stands for: Curly Fry Lightbulb.

Or you may not have seen it, not if you happened to be visiting in the evening when the lights are "on" but everything seems a bit sort of blurry. Edison's soon-to-be-illegal bulb concentrates its light. The new improved bulb diffuses it. And, if you drop one, you could be diffusing it all over the entire municipal sewage system. Guest-hosting America's Number One

*radio show, I found myself reading out the official advice on
what to do if you break a CFL:*

The Rush Limbaugh Show, December 30, 2010

ACCORDING TO THE cheery cut-out 'n' keep guide from the pro-CFL *U.S.
News & World Report,* "The bulbs must be handled with caution. Using a
drop cloth might be a good new routine to develop when screwing in a light
bulb."

That's not such a big deal, is it? You can get a drop cloth at Home Depot
for a couple bucks. Just be sure to keep it handy when you need to change a
light bulb—and in a well-lit area where you won't have to wait so long for the
CFL to warm up before you can see where the drop cloth is. And, if while
installing the new light bulb you have to drop something, drop the drop cloth
rather than the CFL.

But, if you do drop the CFL, which contains "a small amount of mercury,"
there's no need to panic. "We encourage people not to panic if they break a
light bulb," says Scott Cowger, Director of Outreach and Communications,
for Maine's Department of Environmental Protection.

Phew, thank goodness for that. You mean I can just scoop it up and toss
it in the trash? Whoa, hold on. This is the official advice from the State of
Maine Department of Environmental Protection's Bureau of Remediation
and Waste Management:

What if I accidentally break a fluorescent lamp in my house?
The lamp contains a small amount of mercury, but you can
clean this up yourself if you do the following:
Do not use a vacuum cleaner to clean up the breakage. This
will spread the mercury dust and vapor throughout the area, and
could potentially contaminate the vacuum cleaner.

Okay, I can't just pick the broken light bulb up and stick it in the trash, and I can't use my vacuum cleaner either.

> Keep people and pets away from the breakage area until the cleanup is complete.

Great, got it, my pooch starts snuffling around it, and the dog's gonna die.

> Ventilate the area by opening windows and leave the area for fifteen minutes before returning to begin the cleanup. Mercury vapor levels will be lower by then.

Okay, so ventilate the area. Open the windows. Leave it for fifteen minutes, get your pets out so they don't go snuffling around in all the mercury from the light bulb. Got it. So I take me, grandma, the pets, get us all out of the house, open the windows for fifteen minutes.

> For maximum protection, and if you have them, wear rubber gloves to protect your hands from the sharp parts.

Fine. So after fifteen minutes with grandma and the pets outside, I have to go inside and find the rubber gloves to throw away the light bulb.

> Carefully remove the larger pieces, place them in a secure closed container, preferably a glass container with a metal screw top lid and seal, like a canning jar.

Right. So I need rubber gloves and a canning jar when I reenter the premises.

> Next, begin collecting the smaller pieces and dust. You can use two stiff pieces of paper such as index cards or playing cards to scoop up pieces.

Okay, so I need rubber gloves, a canning jar and a set of playing cards when I reenter the contaminated premises.

> Pat the area with the sticky side of duct tape, packing tape, or masking tape to pick up fine particles. Wipe the area with a wet wipe or damp paper.

Gotcha. When I reenter the premises, I need rubber gloves, I need a canning jar, I need a pack of playing cards, and I need duct tape and wet wipes.

> Put all waste and materials into the glass container including all materials used in the cleanup as well.

Ah. So you have to throw away your playing cards and your gloves and your duct tape and the canning jar, too.

> Tape and label the container as "universal waste: broken lamp." Remove the container with the breakage and cleanup materials. Continue ventilating the room for several hours. Wash your hands and face. Take the glass container with the waste material to a facility that accepts universal waste.

So you can't toss it in the trash, you can't toss it in your regular town dump, you have to take it to a special facility.

> When a break happens on carpet, homeowners may consider removing throw rugs or the area of the carpet where the breakage occurred as a precaution, particularly if the rug is in an area frequented by infants, small children, or pregnant women.

So now aside from getting the gloves and the canning jar and the set of playing cards, you've got to have a pair of scissors to cut up and remove the contaminated carpet from your floor. See how simple it is? Just fourteen easy steps. With Edison's light bulb, if you break it, it's one cumbersome step—you toss it in the trash. But according to the Maine Department of Environmental Protection, with the Curly Fry Lightbulb it's just fourteen easy steps. All you need to keep handy are duct tape, playing cards, a canning jar, a sticky label to put on it. Who doesn't have those within easy reach of every electrical outlet?

If you've got a mason jar but it's still got your pickles and berries in it, the Bureau of Remediation and Waste Management adds:

You may need to empty it into another container before using it.

Don't ask me why. Are they just stating the obvious? Or will the mercury mutate with the content to create some giant toxic pickle that will rampage up the Maine coast all the way Down East to Campobello Island, where it will pick up the Roosevelt summer retreat and crumple it like matchsticks and hurl it across the Bay of Fundy to Nova Scotia?

This is the official State of Maine advice on what to do if you break a light bulb in America in the twenty-first century, culminating with: Don't forget to empty any pickled tomatoes or persimmon jelly you may have into another mason jar.

So that's now two mason jars you need if you break a light bulb. If you don't have another mason jar available, just empty the pickled tomatoes or the persimmon jelly on to the carpet, because, as the Bureau of Remediation also tells us, you're going to have to throw the carpet out anyway and any other fabrics that come into contact with the Curly Fry Lightbulb. Throw away your carpet, throw away your canning jar, throw away your playing cards....

Oh, and throw away your clothes. You can't stick any contaminated clothes in the washer because, says the Environmental Protection Agency, mercury fragments in the clothing will contaminate the machine and pollute the sewage system. Got that? So, even if you do everything right, the li'l ol' lady next door who's eighty-seven and perhaps isn't up to speed on the Curly Fry Lightbulb, maybe she'll just break a light bulb and she'll put the drop cloth in the washer and it'll contaminate the entire sewage system.

So only one thing can be said with certainty: the ensuing kidney and brain damage caused by this is going to make one hell of a class action lawsuit circa 2030.

This is Big Government at work. It solved a problem that didn't exist. There's nothing wrong with Edison's light bulb: it's the great iconic American invention, the embodiment of American dynamism of the nineteenth century. And what did we do in the twenty-first century? We banned it! If it ain't broke, don't fix it. But we fixed it anyway. And as a result, every time you break it, you now need to have a mason jar, you need to have a set of playing cards, you need to have rubber gloves, you need to have throw mats, you need to empty out your persimmon jelly onto the contaminated carpet, and you're going to be at risk from a polluted sewage system....

Oh, and the list on the State of Michigan light-bulb disposal site is even longer than Maine's. It's not just a convenient fourteen-step disposal plan for your Curly Fry Lightbulb, they've got an eighteen-step disposal plan. You don't just need the drop cloth and the baby wipes and the pack of playing cards and the two mason jars and the new carpet, you also need additional items—like an eye dropper. You know—an eye dropper, for putting drops in your eyes?

You need an eye dropper just to throw out a light bulb—the new light bulb they're making us all install because they banned the old light bulb that doesn't require you to have a pack of playing cards, two mason jars, a new carpet, and an eye dropper handy when you happen to break them.

For a century, Edison's light bulb was regarded as a beacon of American genius; then it became a "climate criminal." That transformation is American decline in a nutshell.

Mark Steyn in for Rush. More to come....

II

SPIRITS OF THE AGE

LIFE CLASS

This column was an attempt to convey to British readers something of the flavor of high-school graduation, a ritual largely unknown across the Atlantic and one at odds with the basic organizing principle of English education: The continual assurances by commencement speakers that yours is the most awesome generation ever to walk the earth ring a little odd if you're a survivor of some grim Dotheboys Hall where the prevailing educational philosophy was to lower your "self-esteem" to undetectable levels by the end of the first week.

The Daily Telegraph, June 20, 1998

THERE IS A reassuring tedium to "commencement," the annual high school graduation ceremonies, at least in my corner of northern New England, where nothing much changes about these occasions: The students all wear gowns and mortarboards and conclude with a mass display of synchronized tassel-twirling. The school band always plays "Pomp and Circumstance"—and not in the nerds'-night-out sense of "Land of Hope and Glory" at the Proms, either.[1] These guys mean it.

Then come the zillions of student awards, some time-honored, like Randolph High's Daughters of the American Revolution Award, which went to Charlotte Phillips; some of more recent vintage, like Rochester High's Go For It Award, which went to Rachel Stringer; and some, usually with names like

---

1 "Land of Hope and Glory" is A. C. Benson's lyric (largely unknown in the United States) to Elgar's "Pomp and Circumstance March No. 1." A hymn to England ("mother of the free"), it is sung in gusto by an audience in patriotic dress at the last night of the annual Sir Henry Wood Promenade Concerts at the Royal Albert Hall. It is also used as England's national anthem at the Commonwealth Games.

The Steadfast Award, are frankly just to ensure that even the class thicko wins something. At Rochester, the Roxanne Curtis-Bowen Award went to Bobbi-Jo Bowen, presumably for being the Best Bowen of the Year. As for the speeches, the approved metaphors involve doors, thresholds, crossroads, and bridges, although exceptions are permitted: at Vermont's Chelsea High, the Class of '98 were "caterpillars emerging as butterflies," according to valedictorian Kelly MacCarthy, winner of the L. B. Bowen and Bertha Bowen Award, an award apparently open to non-Bowens.

Someone always says that life is not a rehearsal. This year it was Mary Burnham of Waits River Valley School. "Life's not a rehearsal," she said. "This is it." If life were a rehearsal, Mary's speech would be cut before the first out-of-town preview. The starrier the guest speakers, the more pitiful their attempts to ingratiate themselves with pupils: over the border in New Hampshire, former Governor Steve Merrill cited Madonna as a fine role model because she's in the gym every day at 5 a.m. "Madonna understands commitment," he told Woodsville High Graduates.

Of course, in these non-elitist times, the very idea of a star speaker is suspect. For the commencement address at Whitcomb High in Bethel, the graduating class, instead of choosing a state senator or some other local worthy, invited John Hubble, a "member of the high school maintenance staff"—i.e., the janitor. With all those metaphors about thresholds and new doors opening, it makes sense to ask the guy with a full set of keys. "Always try your best," Mr. Hubble told them, "but don't take things too seriously."

Naturally, a little controversy is to be expected. For example, class valedictorian Kate Skidmore declared that it was time "to tell the truth" about Woodsville. "Look around you!" she cried. "There are gay people everywhere in Woodsville." This seems unlikely: Woodsville is named for a man called Woods, who went into the woods business and started a sawmill. It's populated by scrawny, leathery, stump-toothed guys in plaid and their somewhat more expansive wives. I've spent hours looking for a decent gay disco and no one's ever said: "Oh, sure. Second left after the lumber yard and the woodchipper rentals. I was just heading over there myself."

Alas, such genial provocations have now been swept aside by Kate Logan, late of the Long Trail School in Dorset, Vermont. Hitherto, Dorset has principally been known as the site of America's first marble quarry, in 1785. Today it's famous for young Kate, who seems to have lost her marbles completely. At last week's commencement, the eighteen-year-old stepped to the podium, warmed up with some traditional guff about her "journey on a road less traveled," moved on to thank the school for challenging and inspiring her, and then threw off her cap, let her white graduation robe slip to the floor, and finished her speech completely naked.

"Without expectations, feeling the limitless directions, to open myself completely," continued Kate, as students, teachers, friends, and family took in every dimple of her five-foot, six-inch, 140-pound form, "for it is only then, when I am open and free, that truth and wisdom will reveal themselves." As you'll have gathered, Miss Logan's public speaking style can use all the visual aids it can get.

Afterwards, Kate said she'd given the last half of her speech nude to celebrate her graduation on a "spiritual level." "When you're moving through a place of truth and being yourself," she said, "it's always going to work out right."

The school, meanwhile, has released a statement saying "the incident was overwhelmingly inappropriate and is not reflective of our student body."

As *The Burlington Free Press* noted, it was certainly reflective of one student body.

Heigh-ho. Life, as someone said, is not a rehearsal. Or, anyway, not a dress rehearsal.

E PLURIBUS
COMPOSITE

Syndicated column, May 5, 2012

HAVE YOU DATED a composite woman? They're America's hottest new demographic. As with all the really cool stuff, Barack Obama was doing it years before the rest of us. In *Dreams from My Father*, the world's all-time most unread bestseller, he spills the inside dope on his composite white girlfriend, after an off-Broadway play prompts an agonizing post-show exchange about race.

> When we got back to the car she started crying. She couldn't be
> black, she said. She would if she could, but she couldn't. She could
> only be herself, and wasn't that enough....

Not for Barack's literary imagination, it wasn't: His humdrum real white girlfriend never saw the play, and no such conversation ever took place. But, even if she could be herself, that's never going to be enough in the new composite America. Last week, in an election campaign ad, Barack revealed his latest composite girlfriend—"Julia."[1] She's even more useless than the old New York girlfriend. Not only can't she be herself, she can't be *anything* without massive assistance from King Barack's beneficent government every step of the way, from his "Head Start" program at the age of three through to his Social Security benefits at the age of sixty-seven. Everything good in her life

---

1 "The Life of Julia" was a new Obama campaign ad, showing "Julia" going from birth to retirement with Big Government assisting her every step of the day. For conservatives, it was as hideous a hymn to lifelong dependency as one could wish, but progressives insisted that women could "relate" to it.

she owes to him. When she writes her memoir, it will be thanks to a subvention from the Federal Publishing Assistance Program for Chronically Dependent Women but you'll love it: *Sweet Dreams from My Sugar Daddy*. She's what the lawyers would call "non composite mentis." She's not competent to do a single thing for herself—and, from Barack's point of view, that's exactly what he's looking for in a woman, if only for a one-night stand on a Tuesday in early November.

Then there's "Elizabeth," a sixty-two-year-old Democratic Senate candidate from Massachusetts. Like Barack's white girlfriend, she couldn't be black. She would if she could, but she couldn't. But she could be a composite—a white woman and an Indian woman, all mixed up in one! Not Indian in the sense of Ashton Kutcher putting on brownface make-up and a fake-Indian accent in his amusing new commercial for the hip lo-fat snack Popchips. But Indian in the sense of checking the "Are you Native American?" box on the Association of American Law Schools form, which Elizabeth Warren did for much of her adult life. According to her, she's part Cherokee and part Delaware. Not in the Joe Biden sense, I hasten to add, but Delaware in the sense of the Indian tribe named in honor of the home state of Big F**kin' Chief Dances with Plugs.

How does she know she's a Cherokee maiden? Well, she cites her grandfather's "high cheekbones," and says the Indian stuff is part of her family "lore." Which was evidently good enough for Harvard Lore School when they were looking to rack up a few affirmative-action credits. The former Obama special adviser to the Consumer Financial Protection Bureau and chairperson of the Congressional Oversight Panel now says that "I listed myself in the directory in the hopes that it might mean that I would be invited to a luncheon, a group, something that might happen with people who are like I am," and certainly not for personal career advancement or anything like that. Like everyone else, she was shocked, shocked to discover that, as *The Boston Herald* reported, "Harvard Law School officials listed Warren as Native American in the '90s, when the school was under fierce fire for their faculty's lack of diversity."

And so the same institution at which young Barack was "the first African-American president of *The Harvard Law Review*" notched up another famous first: As *The Fordham Law Review* reported, "Harvard Law School hired its first woman of color, Elizabeth Warren, in 1995." To the casual observer, Mrs. Warren, now the Democrats' Senate candidate, might seem a 100 percent woman of non-color. She walks like a white, quacks like a white, looks whiter than white. She's the whitest white since Frosty the Snowman fell in a vat of Wite-Out. But she "self-identified" as Cherokee, so that makes her a "woman of color." Why, back in 1984 she submitted some of her favorite dishes to the *Pow Wow Chow* cookbook, a "compilation of recipes passed down through the Five Tribes families."

The recipes sent in by "Elizabeth Warren—Cherokee" include a crab dish with tomato mayonnaise. Mrs. Warren's fictional Cherokee ancestors in Oklahoma were renowned for their ability to spear the fast-moving Oklahoma crab. It's in the state song:

> *Ooooooklahoma!*
> *Where the crabs come sweepin' down the plain....*

But then the white man came and now the Oklahoma crab is extinct, and at the Cherokee clambakes they have to make do with Mrs. Warren's traditional Five Tribes recipe for Cherokee Lime Pie.

A delegation of college students visited the White House last week, and Vice President Biden told them: "You're an incredible generation. And that's not hyperbole either. Your generation and the 9/11 generation before you are the most incredible group of Americans we have ever, ever, ever produced." Ever ever ever ever! Even in a world where everyone's incredible, some things ought to be truly incredible. Yet Harvard Law School touted Elizabeth "Dances with Crabs" Warren as their "first woman of color"—and nobody laughed.

Because, if you laugh, chances are you'll be tied up in sensitivity-training hell for the next six weeks.

Because in an ever more incredible America being an all-white "woman of color" is entirely credible.

But, with the impertinent jackanapes of the press querying the bona fides of Harvard Lore School's first Native American female professor, the Warren campaign got to work and eventually turned up a great-great-great-grand-mother designated as Cherokee in the online transcription of a marriage application of 1894.

Hallelujah! In the old racist America, we had quadroons and octoroons. But in the new post-racial America, we have—give me a minute to fish out my calculator—duoettrigintaroons! Martin Luther King dreamed of a day when men would be judged not on the color of their skin but on the content of their great-great-great-grandmother's wedding-license application. And now it's here! You can read all about it in Elizabeth Warren's memoir of her struggles to come to terms with her racial identity, *Dreams from My Great-Great-Great-Grandmother.*

Unfortunately, the actual original marriage license does not list Great-Great-Great-Gran'ma as Cherokee, but let's cut Elizabeth Fauxcahontas Crockagawea Warren some slack here. She couldn't be black. She would if she could, but she couldn't. But she could be 1/32nd Cherokee, and maybe get invited to a luncheon with others of her kind—"people who are like I am," 31/32nds white, and they can all sit around celebrating their diversity together. She is a testament to America's melting pot, composite pot, composting pot, whatever.

Just in case you're having difficulty keeping up with all these Composite-Americans, George Zimmerman,[2] the son of a Peruvian mestiza, is the embodiment of endemic white racism and the reincarnation of Bull Connor, but Elizabeth Warren, the great-great-great-granddaughter of someone who

---

2　A few weeks earlier, George Zimmerman, a Neighborhood Watch coordinator in Florida, had fatally shot a black youth, Trayvon Martin. Wishing to present the case as an example of white-on-black violence, *The New York Times* was eventually obliged to file Mr. Zimmerman under the hitherto unknown category of "white Hispanic."

might possibly have been listed as Cherokee on an application for a marriage license, is a heartwarming testimony to how minorities are shattering the glass ceiling in Harvard Yard. George Zimmerman, redneck; Elizabeth Warren, redskin. Under the Third Reich's Nuremberg Laws, Mrs. Warren would have been classified as Aryan and Mr. Zimmerman as non-Aryan. Now it's the other way round. Progress!

Coincidentally, the Equal Employment Opportunities Commission last week issued an "Enforcement Guidance" limiting the rights of employers to take into account the criminal convictions and arrest records of job applicants because of the "disparate impact" the consideration of such matters might have on minorities. That's great news, isn't it? So Harvard Law School can't ask Elizabeth Warren if she's ever held up a liquor store because, if they did, the faculty might be even less Cherokee than it is.

My colleague Jonah Goldberg wrote the other day about Chris Mooney, author of *The Republican Brain*, and other scientific chaps who argue that conservatives suffer from a genetic cognitive impairment that causes us to favor small government. In other words, we're born stupid. In that case, shouldn't we be covered by the Americans with Disabilities Act and the Equal Employment Opportunities Commission?

Aw, don't waste your time. Elizabeth Warren will be ahead of you checking the "Are you a right-wing madman?" box on the grounds that she had a great-great-great-grandfather who voted for Benjamin Harrison. And "Julia" will be saying she was born conservative but thanks to Obama's new Headcase Start program was able to get ideological reassignment surgery. And Barack's imaginary girlfriend will be telling him that she'd be left if she could, but she's right so she can't, but she'd love to be left. So he left her.

In the new Composite America, you can celebrate diversity all by yourself.

❅   ❅   ❅

Regarding Elizabeth Warren's contributions to that cookbook Pow Wow Chow *(a "compilation of recipes passed down through the Five Tribes families"), a few days after my column appeared, it was reported that Mrs. Warren's crab dish passed down from her Cherokee ancestors actually came from an upscale Manhattan restaurant on Fifty-fifth Street across from the St. Regis Hotel.* Noah Glyn of National Review:

> *Two of the possibly plagiarized recipes, said in the* Pow Wow Chow *cookbook to have been passed down through generations of Oklahoma Native American members of the Cherokee tribe, are described in a New York Times News Service story as originating at Le Pavilion, a fabulously expensive French restaurant in Manhattan. The dishes were said to be particular favorites of the Duke and Duchess of Windsor and Cole Porter.*

As the blogger Pundette wondered: "Were they Cherokee, too?"

Why not? As Broadway's first Native American composer, Cole Porter wrote about his Indian blood in his famous song, "I've Got Sioux under My Skin."

Actually, that last line quoted above briefly made me wonder if writing about American liberalism isn't a threat to one's sanity. Some societies are racist, some societies work hard to be non-racist, but only in America does the nation's most prestigious law school hire a 100 percent white female as its first "woman of color" on the basis that she once mailed in the Duke of Windsor's favorite crab dish to a tribal cookbook. If the House of Windsor is now one of the five tribes, all America has to do is restore the monarchy, and the Queen will be your first "woman of color" in the Oval Office.

Before he ascended to the throne, the Duke inspired a hit song of reflected celebrity: "I Danced with a Man Who Danced with a Girl Who Danced with the Prince of Wales." That seems to be how Harvard Law's identity-group quota-filling works. I'm confident that, if this issue re-emerges during Elizabeth Warren's campaign to be the first Native-American president, she'll be able to prove she danced with a man who danced with a girl who danced with someone who once changed planes at a municipal airport accidentally built on a Cherokee burial ground.

SHEET MUSIC

Maclean's, October 1, 2007

IN THE GOLDEN AGE of Hollywood, actresses had no known position on toilets. If Myrna Loy or Ginger Rogers, Norma Shearer, or Mary Astor had opinions on bodily fluids, they kept them to themselves.

In the Seventies, when it was put about that Sarah Miles drank her own urine every day, it got her marked down as a kook. You don't remember Sarah Miles? She starred in *Ryan's Daughter*, very memorably, but not apparently as memorable as her formidable urine intake. Thirty years on, it's understood in Fleet Street that whenever you pitch an interview with Miss Miles to your editor you'll be expected to bring up the pee-swigging. She usually replies that she hasn't touched a drop in years.

But après Sarah le déluge. The other day, W magazine ran an admiring profile of Cate Blanchett: "Green before it was hip, she cites Al Gore and David de Rothschild as heroes and believes that leaf blowers 'sum up everything that is wrong with the human race,'" etc. In the midst of these effusions, the elegant Aussie revealed that, in order to give her new mansion as small an environmental footprint as possible, she requested that the plumbing be constructed to "allow them to drink their own waste water." Miss Blanchett isn't some dippy loopy Milesy fringe goofball. She's the most acclaimed actress of her time. She's the star of *The Golden Age*—no, no, silly; nothing to do with micturition, it's about Elizabeth I. In November, Todd Haynes's new film will star her as Bob Dylan. Bob Dylan? "Haynes became convinced that Blanchett was the right woman for the job while watching her perform in a 2006 production of *Hedda Gabler* at the Brooklyn Academy of Music," writes Jenny Comita. Of course!

This isn't like the old-school Sarah Miles urine-chugging. Miss Blanchett and her husband have paid their architect thousands of dollars to design a system whereby the bodily waste goes down the toilet, gets whisked by pipeline through the walk-in closet, over the balcony, down the wall, back in through the rec room, and up into the wet bar directly into the soda siphon. As her fellow Antipodean, the Aussie wag Tim Blair, observed: "Not exactly Pickfair, is it?"—Pickfair being the legendary mansion of Douglas Fairbanks and Canada's own Mary Pickford. But who's to say Pissfair won't become the norm in the new Hollywood?

Sheryl Crow, meanwhile, recently proposed that when it comes to, ah, other waste products, her environmentally conscious fans should use only a single sheet of bathroom tissue per visit. I fell asleep three minutes into Al Gore's Live Earth extravaganza, so I don't know whether she turned up to perform some new consciousness-raising song on the theme—sheet music, as they say in Mexico—but a celebrity fundraising cover of "All We Are Saying Is Give One Piece a Chance" is surely a project all Hollywood can get behind.

As it turns out, Miss Crow is a bit of a paper tiger on the eco-bathroom front. In 2005, MTV got Cameron Diaz to host a series called *Trippin'*, in which she and her A-list chums went to Tanzania, Honduras, Nepal, and the like and praised the environmental friendliness of village life. "I aspire to be like them," Drew Barrymore told viewers after spending a few days in a remote Chilean community unburdened by electricity or indoor plumbing. "I took a poo in the woods hunched over like an animal. It was awesome." Does a Barrymore crap in the woods? Not in John, Ethel, and Lionel's day. You can understand why Cate Blanchett's so opposed to leaf blowers if they're blowing any leaves from round Drew's stomping grounds.

By now, you're probably wondering: oh, come on, Steyn, you're not going to do lame jokes about modish celebrities' latest obsession for the rest of the column, are you? Well, I just might. But let me slip in a serious point first: a big chunk of so-called "progress" is, in fact, just a matter of simple sanitation and hygiene.

Take, for example, America's quartet of murdered presidents: Lincoln, Garfield, McKinley, and Kennedy. You could reduce that mortality rate by 25 percent just by washing and rinsing. James Garfield was shot at the Baltimore and Potomac Railway Station on July 2, 1881, and took two and half months to expire, which is almost as long as he'd been in office before he set off to catch the train. It's now accepted that he died not from the gunshot wound but from the various medical personnel poking around inside him looking for the bullet with dirty hands and unsterilized instruments. Joseph Lister's ideas on antisepsis had become standard in Britain but not yet in the United States. Within three years of the President's death, Dr. William S. Halsted opened America's first modern operating room at Bellevue. So if Garfield was shot today, he'd be home in three days.

But you don't have to be targeted for assassination to reap the benefits of hygiene. Do you know the expression "getting hold of the wrong end of the stick"? It comes from the public latrines of ancient Rome. They were very agreeable design-wise—marble benches and so forth. And at the end of the bench was a bucket of salt water with a stick in it. On the end of the stick was a sponge. The patron would use the stick to sponge his person in the relevant areas, then put it back in the bucket for the next customer. It doesn't really matter whether you get the wrong end of the stick: the right end was good enough to spread all manner of diseases.

Almost every setback suffered by man in the next couple of millennia has some connection to human fecal matter: more crusaders were done in by dysentery than by the enemies' scimitars; America's Civil War soldiers were twice as likely to die in camp racked by disease as in combat. Today, what Drew Barrymore regards as an "awesome" experience is one reason the teeming shantytowns of West Africa have infant mortality rates approaching one in three. Male life expectancy in Côte d'Ivoire: forty-two. Liberia: forty-one. Sierra Leone: thirty-seven. And the Sheryl Crow one-piece rule would do a lot to help the developed world's statistics head in the same direction.

But, beyond the data, there's something very curious about a culture whose most beautiful women, the beneficiaries of every blessing this bountiful society can shower upon them, are so eager to flaunt their bodily waste in the public prints. And even more bizarre is their conviction that one of the most basic building blocks of modern life—hygiene—is now an example of western consumerist excess. Perhaps it will catch on. Perhaps ten years from now there will be a Peebucks on every corner selling entirely recycled beverages: a venti urinatte for $6.29, but only "fair trade urine," in which the peasant has been paid a living wage for his specimen, a guarantee symbolized by a logo—a new Golden Arches, say.

And after that who knows where we'll go? As George Monbiot, the bestselling doom-monger from Britain's *Guardian*, writes: "It is impossible not to notice that, in some of the poorest parts of the world, most people, most of the time, appear to be happier than we are. In southern Ethiopia, for example, the poorest half of the poorest nation on earth, the streets and fields crackle with laughter. In homes constructed from packing cases and palm leaves, people engage more freely, smile more often, express more affection than we do behind our double glazing, surrounded by remote controls." In Ethiopia, male life expectancy is 42.88 years. George was born in 1963. If the streets and fields are crackling with laughter, maybe it's because the happy peasants are reading his syndicated column in *The Gamo Gofa Times-Herald*. No wonder they're doubled up and clutching their sides. It's not just the dysentery from the communal latrine.

Every civilization eats its own but rarely quite so literally. The western world worries about "the environment" as if we are trespassers upon it. If so, it won't be for much longer. On the fast depopulating plains of eastern Germany, municipal sewer systems are having to adjust to the problem of declining use. Rural communities are emptying out so dramatically there are too few people flushing to keep the waste moving, and to get it flowing again they're having to narrow the sewer lines at great expense. For the demographically dying west, it's not a question of "sustainable growth," but of sustainable lack of growth. One can talk breezily about western civilization being flushed down the toilet of history, but it turns out even that's easier said than done. Long before Sheryl Crow's celebrity pals have squeezed their last Charmin, it will be clear that the job of "saving the planet" is one the west has bequeathed to others.

DID THE EARTH SUMMIT MOVE FOR YOU?

The Daily Telegraph, August 31, 2002

"THE WORLD SUMMIT kicks off in Johannesburg today, aiming to tackle poverty and protect the environment.... It will consume a huge amount of resources and create as much pollution in ten days as 500,000 Africans manage in a year."—*The Daily Record*

"Caviar and Call Girls Find Their Place at the Earth Summit"—*The Times*

I'm glad I made the effort to attend the opening gala of the Earth Summit, truly a night to remember. The banqueting suite of Johannesburg's Michelangelo Hotel was packed as Bob Mugabe warmed up the crowd with a few gags: "I don't know about you," he said, "but I'm starving...." Pause. "... millions of people!"

What a master of timing! The canned laughter—an authentic recording of happy Ethiopian peasants clutching their bellies and corpsing—filled the room.

After the chorus of native dancers clad only in packing cases and palm leaves, Natalie Cole came on to sing her famous anthem to industrial development, "Unsustainable / That's what you are," and sixty-five thousand of the world's most eligible bureaucrats, NGO executive council members, and BBC environmental correspondents crowded the dance floor to glide cheek to cheek under a glitter ball of premium ox dung specially flown in from Bangladesh. It glittered because of the 120,000 flies buzzing around it, their gossamer wings dappling the transnational activists below in a myriad of enchanting shadows.

And then I saw her. She was wearing a low-cut dress and had the most fabulous pair of melons. "Holy cow!" I gasped, as she approached my table. "They've gotta be genetically modified!"

"No," she said, sliding into the chair opposite and giving me a good look at them. "They're all natural." She tossed them to Kofi Annan. "They're for his organic juggling routine." I had to laugh. Sabine Arounde is the Belgian delegate to Unescam, the United Nations Expensive Summits & Conferences Agenda Monopolizers, and, lemme tellya, when she's in a room the rising temperatures are nothing to do with fossil fuel emissions.

"We met at Durban," I reminded her.

"Oh, yeah," she said. "The conference on world health."

"Racism," I corrected her.

"Whatever," she said. "This one's more my bag. I'm very into S & M."

"Come again?"

"S and M. Sustainable Alternative Natural Development Mechanisms," said Sabine.

We were interrupted by the waiter, as oleaginous as a tanker spill. "Will sir and madam be having the Beluga caviar, foie gras, lobster, and magnum of champagne?"

"Certainly not!" I snapped. "The papers back home are full of stories about how we're all scoffing the caviar and chugging down the bubbly while just a mile down the road the locals are holding the Distended Belly of the Week competition. In compliance with Foreign and Commonwealth Office guidelines, I'll just stick with Set Menu B."

"An excellent choice," he said. "Would sir prefer the mako shark soup or the black rhino confit on a bed of Amazonian mahogany leaves?"

"I'll have the rhino," I said, "followed by the lightly poached panda with a goldenseal salad and two green-cheeked parrot's eggs over easy."

"And would sir like to see the wine list?"

"Just bring me a Scotch and humpback whale oil on the rocks."

As Sabine ordered, she looked coolly into my eyes and Natalie Cole's voice wafted across the room to capture the moment:

Like a cloud of smog that clings to me
How the thought of you does things to me....

The orchestra pit had been converted into an authentic replica of a Rwandan latrine and, even as Natalie sang the line, it sprang to life in a hundred dancing fountains of E coli-infected martini.

"There's something heady in the air tonight," I murmured.

"It's the CO_2," purred Sabine.

Four hours later, the exhausted UN lovely, her spent body glistening with the heat of passion, lay back on the shards of her shattered headboard. "Wow!" she whimpered, struggling for breath. "Now that's what I call sustainable growth. You are incredible!"

"UN seen nothin' yet, baby," I said.

Yet, to my extreme annoyance, who should burst through the door but everybody's favorite *Guardian* columnist. "You know, of course, George Monsanto," said Sabine, hastily pulling the tigerskin bedspread around her.

"Monbiot!" I exclaimed. "I thought you were running away from *The Guardian* to join the gaily pealing fields of Gamo Gofa, where the rude peasant existence is so much more fulfilling than life in the west."

"I am," he said. "I'm on my way to Ethiopia right now. But I just wanted to stop in and thank you for coming here, eating the caviar, drinking the champagne, sucking the praline-flavored centers out of the individually wrapped Belgian chocolates on your king-sized bed, and blowing all the billions of western taxpayers' dollars. Without your sacrifice, those poor industrialized chumps would have even more money to spend on consumer goods and home improvements, making their pathetic lives even more worthless and hollow."

"You're right," sighed Sabine. "But I don't know how much longer I can sustain this level of sustainable development conferencing."

"Then why not come with me?" said George. "Be a happy, laughing Ethiopian field hand."

"Okay, I will!" said Sabine.

She had me just for a moment, and then we both exploded in guffaws and ordered another bottle of the Château Margaux.

THE MEDIA'S
MATERNAL
INSTINCTS

The National Post, May 15, 2000

BACK IN THE SIXTIES, when he held one of Britain's oldest Cabinet posts, Edward Heath, the Lord Privy Seal, was greeted by a foreign dignitary as "Lord Heath." Mr. Heath explained that, though Lord Privy Seal, he was neither a lord nor a privy nor a seal.

Likewise, yesterday's Million Mom March: there were neither a Million, nor did they March, and while most were Moms, or anyway female, their mommyness was not their defining characteristic. Instead of marching, they milled on Washington's Mall, listening to keynote speaker Rosie O'Donnell. Instead of a million, the Moms themselves downgraded expectations to a hundred thousand. I see my friends at *The Sunday Telegraph* in London persist in referring to the "so-called Million Mom March," but no such niceties trouble the U.S. media. Perhaps like Heinz's "57 varieties" the formulation is now so familiar that only a boorish literalist would require it to be accurate. But at least, when the Reverend Louis Farrakhan started this thing with his Million Man March, the old race-baiter and wacky numerologist was insistent that one million living, breathing, countable African-Americans would be present.

There weren't. But a deluded nutcake crazy enough to believe he can draw a crowd has more integrity than the Moms' last-minute attempt to pre-spin their low turnout.

As to their maternal status, Wednesday's *Washington Post* put it this way: "The Million Mom March was conceived last August in a suburban New

Jersey mother's living room." Donna Dees-Thomases "called a few friends, and they called a few friends, and within a week they had an idea."

Ah, citizen activism, you can't beat it. According to ABC's Elizabeth Vargas, she's "a typical mom." According to Diane Sawyer, Ms. Dees-Thomases has "never really organized anything larger than a car pool." According to NBC's Lisa Myers, she's "a suburban mom, too busy with her two daughters and a part-time job to pay much attention to politics."

Car pool, 'burbs, daughters, Jersey: you get the idea. In fact, Ms. Dees-Thomases used to pay quite a bit of attention to politics: she was a staffer to two Louisiana Democrat senators, Russell Long and Bennett Johnston. How many "suburban moms" have been staffers to not one but two senators? Perhaps she snoozed her way through those jobs, spending most of her time on the phone organizing car pools for fellow soccer moms. But she's been paying enough attention to politics in recent months to be a contributor to Hillary Clinton's Senate campaign.

Still, maybe she was just helping out a family member: Her sister-in-law, Susan Thomases, is Hillary's closest political advisor.

And, just to round things out, even that reference to "a suburban New Jersey mother's living room" is only technically accurate. Although Ms. Dees-Thomases is "a suburban New Jersey mother," the living room in question was in her other home on Fire Island, the hedonist playground long favored by fetching young men of a certain persuasion.

If there's anywhere that could use less gun control, it's Fire Island. The last time I was there you could barely find a leaf within nine feet of the ground: the deer population had grown beyond the ability of the local vegetation to sustain it. But unfortunately this is not hunting country: for Fire Island's menfolk, the thrill of the chase lies elsewhere. So the trees have been defoliated as high as the whitetail can reach and many of the poor beasts now look as emaciated as the louche chaps lounging on the beach listening to their Bette Midler CDs.

But "The Million Mom March was conceived last August in a gay resort community by a Hillary Clinton donor who's never organized anything larger than a Democratic senator's office" doesn't have quite the same ring, does it?

And why should ABC, NBC, *The Washington Post*, and *The New York Times* be expected to know any of this? Just because half her surname might have rung a vague bell is no reason to leap to conclusions and assume she's connected with Susan Thomases—any more than it would be wise to assume from the other half of her name that she's related to Rick Dees and his Cast of Idiots, whose "Disco Duck" was a Number One hit in 1976.

But, speaking of Casts of Idiots, what about CBS? By now, you may be curious about that "part-time job," as NBC coyly referred to it. A couple of waitressing shifts? A little secretarial work for the school district?

No, Donna is a part-time publicist for David Letterman's *Late Show*.

Before that, she was a full-time publicist for CBS news anchor Dan Rather.

CBS This Morning, which is part of the same news division as Dan's nightly broadcast, was one of the first news shows to report the Million Mom March movement last September, when Hattie Kauffman interviewed Donna.

"What," asked Hattie, "turns a mild-mannered suburban mom into an anti-gun activist?"

The correct answer is: "A leave of absence from my employer, CBS, which, by remarkable coincidence, is also your employer, Hattie."

But that's not what Donna said. Only in the last week has CBS News begun disclosing that she's one of theirs. As to Ms. Dees-Thomases' work for those two Dem senators, not one U.S. newspaper or TV network has mentioned them, with the exception of Rupert Murdoch's Fox News Channel. Mr. Murdoch, as we know, is a malign influence seeking to use his media outlets to further his sinister personal agenda.

Try it the other way round: "Barbara Bush was a typical Maine housewife with no interest in politics until she decided to start Housewives for Massive Tax Cuts. 'As a typical housewife,' she says, 'I know what it's like when an ordinary working stiff like George comes home every night and says, Geez, Barb. Not Cheez-In-A-Can on a second-hand Pop Tart again.'"

Or: "Canada's Moms for Monarchy Movement was conceived last August by Elizabeth Windsor, a typical mother of four struggling to balance the needs of her family with the pressures of work. Liz, who's never organized anything larger than a Royal Tour, says she'd always been too busy signing bills into law and giving Throne Speeches to pay much attention to constitutional matters."

Every year, tens of thousands of pro-life women descend on Washington on the anniversary of the landmark *Roe v. Wade* decision. And every year they're buried at the foot of the "Local News Briefs" on page E29. When you remark on the contrast between their perennial obscurity and the delirious coverage of the Milling Mall Moms, the news honchos say, "Ah, well. That's because the Million Moms are so much more media-savvy."

What kind of kinky post-modern response is that? Don't worry, we're not biased, we're just easily manipulated, and who better to manipulate us than Dan Rather's press agent?

I believe Dan when he says "liberal media bias" is one of the great myths. Although various recent polls show that half of all Americans live in households with guns, think Dubya is better on gun control than Al Gore, and have a positive opinion of the NRA, I'm willing to accept that no one who works in the CBS newsroom knows anyone who belongs to that half of the populace. But what happened with Donna Dees-Thomases goes beyond "bias": In essence, America's major news outlets colluded in the perpetration of a fraud on their audiences.

Well, the non-March is over now, and the non-Millions are relaunching themselves today as a political lobby group. Good luck to them. But yet again those old Soviet hardliners can only marvel: They spent decades smashing presses and jamming transmitters in an effort to shut down the flow of information. America's achieved that happy state just by leaving it to ABC, CBS, and NBC.

LIVING LARGE

Syndicated column, January 18, 2013

I WAS OUT of the country for a few days and news from this great republic reached me only fitfully. I have learned to be wary of foreign reporting of U.S. events, since America can come off sounding faintly deranged. Much of what reached me didn't sound entirely plausible: Did the entire U.S. media really fall for the imaginary dead girlfriend of a star football player?[1] Did the President of the United States really announce twenty-three executive orders by reading out the policy views of carefully pre-screened grade-schoolers ("I want everybody to be happy and safe")? Clearly, these vicious rumors were merely planted in the foreign press to make the United States appear ridiculous.

Meanwhile, hot from the fiscal-cliff fiasco, the media are already eagerly anticipating the next in the series of monthly capitulations by Republicans, this time on the debt ceiling. While I was abroad, a Nobel Prize–winning economist, a Harvard professor of constitutional law, a prominent congressman, and various other American eminences apparently had a sober and serious discussion on whether the United States Treasury could circumvent the debt constraints by minting a trillion-dollar platinum coin. Although Joe Weisenthal of *Business Insider* called the trillion-dollar coin "the most important fiscal policy debate you'll ever see in your life," most Democrat pundits appeared to favor the idea for the more straightforward joy it affords in sticking it to the House Republicans. No more tedious whining about spending from GOP congressmen. Next time Paul Ryan shows up in committee demanding to know about deficit-reduction plans, all the Treasury Secretary has to do is

---

1   Manti Te'o had recently been praised for continuing to play stellar football for Notre Dame while mourning his late girlfriend, Lennay, who had died in a car accident while battling Leukemia. Lennay turned out not to exist.

pull out a handful of trillion-dollar coins from down the back of the sofa and tell him to keep the change.

The trillion-dollar-groat fever rang a vague bell with me. Way back in 1893, Mark Twain wrote a short story called "The Million Pound Bank Note," which in the Fifties Ronald Neame made into a rather droll film. A penniless American down and out in London (Gregory Peck) is presented by two eccentric Englishmen (Ronald Squire and Wilfrid Hyde-White) with a million-pound note which they have persuaded the Bank of England to print in order to settle a wager. One of the English chaps believes that simple possession of the note will allow the destitute Yank to live the high life without ever having to spend a shilling. And so it proves. He goes to the pub for lunch, offers the note, and the landlord explains that he's unable to make change for a million pounds, but is honored to feed him anyway. He then goes to be fitted for a suit, and again the tailor regrets that he can't provide change for a million pounds but delightedly measures him for silk shirts, court dress, and all the rest. I always liked the line Mark Twain's protagonist uses on a duke's niece he's sweet on: He tells her "I hadn't a cent in the world but just the million pound note."

That's Paul Krugman's solution for America as it prepares to bust through another laughably named "debt limit": We'd be a nation that hasn't a cent in the world but just a trillion-dollar coin—and what more do we need? As with Gregory Peck in the movie, the mere fact of the coin's existence would ensure we could go on living large. Indeed, aside from inflating a million quid to a trillion bucks, Professor Krugman's proposal economically prunes the sprawling cast of the film down to an off-Broadway one-man show with Uncle Sam playing every part: A penniless Yank (Uncle Sam) runs into a wealthy benefactor (Uncle Sam) who has persuaded the banking authorities (Uncle Sam) to mint a trillion-dollar coin that will allow Uncle Sam (played by Uncle Sam) to extend an unending line of credit to Uncle Sam (also played by Uncle Sam).

This seems likely to work. As for the love interest, in the final scene, Paul Krugman takes his fake dead girlfriend (played by Barack Obama's composite girlfriend) to a swank restaurant and buys her the world's most expensive bottle of champagne (played by Lance Armstrong's urine sample).

Do you ever get the feeling America's choo-choo has jumped the tracks? Joe Weisenthal says that the trillion-dollar coin is the most serious adult proposal put forward in our lifetime "because it gets right to the nature of *what is money*." As Weisenthal argues, "we're still shackled with a gold-standard mentality where we think of money as a scarce natural resource that we need to husband carefully." Ha! Every time it rains it rains trillion-dollar pennies from heaven. I believe Robert Mugabe made a similar observation on January 16, 2009, when he introduced Zimbabwe's first one-hundred-trillion-dollar bank note. In that one dramatic month, the Zimbabwean dollar declined from 0.0000000072 of a U.S. dollar to 0.0000000003 of a U.S. dollar. But that's what's so great about being American. Because, when you're American, one U.S. dollar will always be worth one U.S. dollar, no matter how many trillion-dollar coins you mint. Eat your heart out, you Zimbabwean losers. As Joe Weisenthal asks, what is money? Money is American: Everybody knows that.

Whether the world feels this way is another matter. For Paul Krugman, the issue is the insanity of the Republican Party, as manifested in their opposition to automatic debt-ceiling increases. By contrast, the contrarian Democrat Mickey Kaus thinks Republicans ought to be in favor of the trillion-dollar coin as an easy short-term fix to prevent them from getting screwed over by Obama and the media for the second time in a month. But out there, in what the State Department maps quaintly call the rest of the world, nobody cares about Democrats or Republicans, and the issue is not the debt ceiling but the debt. Forty-four nations voted at Bretton Woods to make the dollar the world's reserve currency. If they were meeting today, I doubt they'd give that status to a nation piling on over a trillion in federal debt per year, 70 percent of which its left hand (the U.S. Treasury) borrows from its right hand (the Federal Reserve) through the Nigerian-e-mail equivalent of Paul Krugman's trillion-dollar groat.

Meanwhile, I see the Bundesbank has decided to move three hundred tons of German gold from the Federal Reserve in New York back to Frankfurt.

It's probably nothing. And what's to stop the Fed replacing it with three hundred tons of Boston cream donuts and declaring them of equivalent value? Or maybe three hundred imaginary dead football girlfriends, all platinum blondes.

Memo to John Boehner and Paul Ryan: No one will take you seriously until you find some photogenic second-graders and read out their cute letters. "I want everybody to be happy and safe and fithcally tholvent." They may have to practice.

III

THE REPUBLIC OF MANNERS

POTPOURRI
ROASTING ON AN
OPEN FIRE

Maclean's, December 25, 2006

I'M ONE OF THOSE FELLOWS who tends to leave the old Yuletide preparations until around 2 p.m. on Christmas Eve only to discover that half the stores closed early at 1 p.m. and those still open have nothing left except for massive storewide clearances on Hannukah wrapping paper. Yet for a fly-by-the-seat-of-my-Santa-suit-pants kind of guy, I seem to have acquired over the years an enormous number of books on how to have the perfect Christmas. There's *Checklist for a Perfect Christmas* by Judith Blahink and *How to Have a Perfect Christmas* by Helen Isolde and *The Absolutely without a Doubt Most Fantastically Perfect Christmas Ever* by Evelyn Minshull and *Creating the Perfect Christmas: Stylish Ideas and Step-By-Step Projects for the Festive Season* by Antonia Swingson and Sania Pell, because there's nothing you need around this time of year more than a multi-step project. The more steps the merrier, I always say. One stands agape before those folks who not only have their own seasonal celebrations under scheduled-to-the-second control but also find time to write a bestseller with a faintly hectoring title like *It's Beginning to Look a Lot Less Like Christmas than It Should Considering It's Already the Second Week of September.*

For the most part, these authors seem to have no existence beyond the holiday season. The two-female co-author combo is a particular favorite, both of them on the back in cozy sweaters looking like extras from *The Andy Williams Christmas Show.* Is there really an "Antonia Swingson" or "Sania Pell"? Their names sound alarmingly like their home-making tips: "For fun on

Christmas morning, why not cut up the gift tags and randomly assemble them into holiday-advice-book author-pseudonyms?" "Judith Blahink"? Isn't the blahinks what Scrooge has when they find him face down in the mulled cider? Christmas? Blah-hink-humbug.

I don't want to give the wrong impression. A lot of the stuff in these tomes is very intriguing. Each year, for example, I dig out my old pal Martha Stewart's entry in the field—*Martha Stewart's Christmas*—and find myself strangely drawn to the phrase "coxcomb topiary." The thing's huge. It starts out as a misshapen lump like a hobbit that's fallen into a trash compactor but that's before Martha's got to work "studding" it with—to pluck at random—"tiny pomegranates dusted with clear glitter." Who would have thought the English language would ever have need for those words assembled in that order? Every third week of December, I read them and marvel. And then I drive to Walmart.

"Coxcomb" is the perfect *Perfect Christmas Book* word. Not all perfect Christmas authors are hip to that. Some think you can eschew "coxcomb" and get away with "potpourri," which your run-of-the-mill generic mediocre *Most Fantastically Perfect Christmas Ever* book throws around the joint like, well, potpourri. But what is it the Fool tells King Lear? "If thou follow him, thou must needs wear my coxcomb." Or I am thinking of his codpiece? I always did get them mixed up at school. Codpiece topiary would also add a distinctive touch to one's holiday, although perhaps a livelier talking-point than one might want in a Christmas centerpiece. But the point is, if thou followest Martha, thou must needs wear her coxcomb. Also her persimmon, another great *Perfect Christmas Book* word. If I were ever to write my own seasonal advice book, I would do so under the *nom de plume* (or, indeed, *nom de plume pudding*) of Persimmon Coxcomb.

In *Old-Fashioned Country Christmas* by Vickie and Jo Ann of the Gooseberry Patch, Joan Schaeffer is more off-hand: "Snip herbs and tie in small bundles to dry. During the winter when the fireplace is in use, toss a bundle of herbs into the crackling fire for a wonderful scent." I like the insouciance of that "toss." But it's a very useful tip. A blazing hearth of oregano helps tone down the overpowering stench of cinnamon that can otherwise so easily predominate at this time of year. Still, the truly perfect preparing-for-Christmas book eschews Schaefferesque nonchalance, preferring an artful balance of massive effort and minimal reward. Nothing sums up the genre more succinctly than the two words "non-alcoholic wassail," for which cup of cheerlessness one can find a recipe in *Christmas 101* by Rick Rodgers.

As the title suggests, Mr. Rodgers, the author of *Thanksgiving 101*, sticks with the basics. "Organization is a skill I developed as a caterer," he begins. Without organization, you're screwed. You're Baghdad beyond the Green Zone. But, with organization, you'll be your very own Red-and-Green Zone, and Mr. Rodgers is the go-to guy. Before you can organize your Christmas it's important to organize the organization of your Christmas, and a useful aid to organization is something called a "list." That's why, like many seasonal advice-givers, he has a section called—wait for it!—"Making a List and Checking It Twice." This isn't his line. He got it from the lyric for a song called "Santa Claus Is Coming to Town." Did you know that seasonal music can often add an appealingly seasonal touch to the seasonal atmosphere at this seasonal time of the seasonal season? Why not teach yourself vocal arranging and work up your own a cappella multi-part medley of "In the Bleak Midwinter" and "I Wonder as I Wander" for cousin Mabel's kids to distract Gran'pa with on Christmas morning as you're putting the final touches of clear glitter on the tiny pomegranates?

But I'm getting ahead of myself. Before you can organize anything, you have to organize your list. As Rick Rodgers says, "A series of lists will help you breeze through the process."

And don't worry, it's not boring! As Rick Rodgers also says, "Every time you mark a chore off the list, you will get a rewarding sense of accomplishment."

But what if your list is simply too extensive? As Rick Rodgers further counsels, "If you look at a list and feel overwhelmed, pick up the phone and get a friend to give you a hand!"

But, by this stage, Rodgers knows he may be pushing the joys of list-making a tad too far and that it's time to get on to the actual lists. "Here," he writes, "are the lists that I use again and again."

And the first one is... "Guest List"! "If you are having a large holiday season party, send out invitations as early as possible." But when should one have a holiday season party? A good tip is to hold it during the holiday season. "We usually give our holiday party the week between Christmas and New Year's," reveals Mr. Rodgers.

Ha! What a piker! The true secret of successful Christmas planning is not to schedule it in December. As Vickie and Jo Ann recommend in *Old-Fashioned Country Christmas*: "Rather than having your annual party in December when you're too overwhelmed to enjoy it, host a cookout in July with a Christmas theme, everything red and green!" Bright red watermelon, green salad, but with Christmas decorations! "White twinkling lights, Christmas napkins and a small artificial tree decorated with take-home ornaments make for a very festive atmosphere." And in Canada in July we may even have real snow!

Christmas in summer, huh? That doesn't sound much like an "old-fashioned country Christmas," unless the country in question is Australia. Yet it makes perfect sense, and not just because nothing says "dreary convention-bound loser" like holding your Christmas party at Christmas. After all, if you schedule your holiday season for July, it'll free up a lot of time in late December to work on your coxcomb topiary.

LAST DANCE

The Wall Street Journal, April 11, 1997

LIONEL BART, COMPOSER of *Oliver!*, once told me that he did so many drugs in the late 1960s that he came round in the early 1980s and realized that he didn't have a single memory of the 1970s. "Did I miss anything?" he asked.

"Not really," I replied. For Lionel and the similarly situated, Anthony Haden-Guest's *The Last Party: Studio 54, Disco, and the Culture of the Night* (Morrow) and John Heidenry's *What Wild Ecstasy: The Rise and Fall of the Sexual Revolution* (Simon & Schuster) are here to fill in the missing gaps.

If you can remember the Sixties, so the old gag goes, you weren't really there; if you can remember the Seventies, chances are you aren't here. For Mr. Haden-Guest, researching his "culture of the night" is now an act of archeology: Deep in the basements of Manhattan warehouses, you can discern traces of the physical landscape, but the witnesses are gone. Steve Rubell, Studio 54's presiding genius, is dead of AIDS; so's his onetime partner's some-time lover, Roy Cohn; so are celebrity regulars like Halston and Nureyev; so are their paramours like "the notorious livewire of Nightworld" Victor Hugo— no relation to the author of *Les Misérables*, though in his final days he wound up sleeping in a park.

In Mr. Heidenry's account of landmark victories in the sexual revolution, most of the freedom fighters end the same way: Michel Foucault, the French philosopher and S&M devotee, is dead of AIDS; so's Franco Rossellini, pro-ducer of *Caligula*, the "first sexually explicit first-run movie in history"; so's John ("Johnny Wadd") Holmes, the gifted star of a hundred lesser epics.

But before it shriveled away to an emaciated cadaver of its former self, what a world it was! Sometimes it seems to blur into one composite haze, involving copious use of Quaaludes and grottoes. There were those so eager to get back to the nonstop party that they'd leap from bed and get an early breakfast at four in the afternoon.

Once upon a time, there were famous concert pianists and novelists and impresarios, but the heyday of hedonism blended such distinctions into one homogenized category of "celebrity": The photographs of Studio 54's celebrity couples are like a computer breakdown at a dating agency—"William Burroughs and Madonna," "Regine and Salvador Dali," "Margaret Trudeau on the floor with marijuana importer Tom Sullivan."

What happened during the Seventies can be neatly encapsulated by the career of one Linda Boreman. Miss Boreman fell in with Chuck Traynor, an abusive gun-toting pimp who put her to work servicing business clients who liked to spank and whip. One day Mr. Traynor landed her a starring role in a film where she was mounted—there is no delicate way to put this—by a German shepherd (by which I mean a dog, not a shepherd). On the strength of this effort, she was signed for another film, called *Deep Throat*, for which she changed her name to Linda Lovelace. The movie earned the first ever "100" rating from *Screw* magazine, but even more surprisingly *Time* magazine and other mainstream publications ran stories on it, and the film took off—a porn film for Mr. and Mrs. America. The star was invited on *The Tonight Show*, shot a cover for *Esquire*, and turned up at Hollywood parties.

Linda Lovelace's translation from involuntary prostitute to celebrity darling exemplifies the more general trend—of how the dark fringes of society crept into the centrality of our culture. Celebrities were decadent in the Twenties, but they kept it to themselves; in the Seventies, they came out of the closet, trailing nightclubbers and swingers with them. But Miss Lovelace's original film moniker fits better: In this world, there's little lace, less love, but it is a bore, man. Mr. Haden-Guest calls it "the last good time," but look at those snapshots again: Baryshnikov and Jagger and Liza, all dead-eyed. "Grace Jones came in naked. Quite a few times," says a doorman. "Probably more than she should have. Because after a while it became boring."

Mr. Haden-Guest's is the more elegant read: An urbane Englishman, he descends to the lowest depths of New York's Hellfire Club but always gives the impression he's just passing through—Haden-Guest as Hades guest. Mr. Heidenry is more earnest, as you'd expect from a former editor of *Penthouse Forum*, and he mourns the lost Arcady of America's cities, "where once tourists could obtain both topless and bottomless shoeshines." For him, the final nail in the coffin was that big 1994 survey showing that the Americans who get the most sex are…monogamous married couples.

Neither author questions the assumptions underlying the excesses, but then those assumptions are probably the sexual revolution's most lasting legacy. The Me Decade is over, but its philosophy—hey, man, whatever's your bag, it's cool—endures, no matter if it kills you and your friends and even some uptight squares as well. Both books contain vivid portraits of Seventies nightlife—of basement floors invisible under a writhing mass of interchangeable bobbing heads and thrusting members. There is no joy, no passion. Mr. Heidenry writes of a group called the Sexual Egalitarian and Liberation Festival, a revealing acronym: SELF. At "the last party" the floor was always full, but ultimately everyone danced alone.

WE'VE FIGURED
IT OUT

The Spectator, February 3, 2001

WHAT DO WOMEN WANT? Who cares? Nick Marshall knows what he wants. Raised in Vegas, Nick is now a Chicago ad executive with a fabulous pad that's great for nailing chicks. Unfortunately, life is about to get more complicated.

Nancy Meyers's film *What Women Want* opens with a bleary Nick on the morning after. Happily, last night's piece of tail was obliging enough not to stick around for breakfast, leaving only the flimsiest of undergarments for Nick's indulgent housekeeper to tidy away. Although Nick is played by Mel Gibson, he's really Dino in the Matt Helm movies, or Tony Franciosa, or Jack Lemmon in *How to Murder Your Wife*, which has an identical opening, except that the babe—Virna Lisi—is still there and the sassy Hispanic housekeeper is a stiff-upper-lipped English valet played by Terry-Thomas. But, accessories aside, Nick is a Sixties swinger updated to the Oughts, and Mel plays him with a finger-snappy Rat Pack cool. As Sinatra observed in "Come Blow Your Horn":

> *In civilized jungles*
> *The females adore*
> *The lions who come on swingin'*
> *If you wanna score*
> *Roar!*

Of course, it was easier in Frank's day. And something of the problem with this film's concept is indicated by the fact that, in order to establish what passes for Nick's character, the soundtrack relies exclusively on Sinatra, Sammy Davis, Bobby Darin, etc. Indeed, there are moments when the picture teeters dangerously on the brink of Austin Powers played straight. Anyway, when Nick gets to the office, there's bad news. The booze and car ads that made the agency the king of the Eighties don't work anymore: female-angled advertising is where the big bucks are, and so a hotshot woman has been brought in as Nick's boss to reorient company strategy. Nick instantly picks up on what's needed. "I gotta think like a broad," he says. And a broad is another country: they do things differently there. The new creative director, Darcy (Helen Hunt), sends him home with a bunch of female products whose accounts are up for grabs: lipstick, leg wax, push-up bra, pantyhose, etc.

Flicking through the channels, Nick despairs. "There's way too much estrogen on TV. The perfect antidote to estrogen is Frank. I need some Frank." He puts on Sinatra's "I Won't Dance" and twirls joyfully around the room, although one can't help feeling this represents a fundamental misreading of the Sinatra oeuvre: Frank was the first male pop singer to get in touch with his feminine side and sing women's torch songs, and, as to whether or not he knew what women want, he is by my reckoning the only celebrity all of whose ex-wives speak well of—go on, ask Mia Farrow.

But let that pass. After his shot of Frank, Nick puts on the lipstick; tries out the leg wax—ouch!; pulls up the pantyhose—more shtick, efficient enough; spills the pills for PMT, HRT, whatever they are, slips on them, falls in the bath, electrocutes himself, and somehow the combination of the electric shock and the feminine personal products results in him waking up with the ability to hear what women are thinking.

This is a mixed blessing. He discovers that every woman in his office is only pretending to like him—they think he's a jerk, a dog, a schmuck, a pig, a boor.... Even his sexual confidence is dented, as he hears his bedmate absent-mindedly musing to herself in mid-congress, "Is Britney Spears on Leno tonight?" The only exceptions are his two assistants, played by lovely Valerie Perrine and Delta Burke, who dote on him uncritically. His mind-reading powers don't work on them, because apparently they don't have minds to read. This is a rather patronizing joke on the part of Ms. Meyers and her writers, and a reminder that women can be as crudely insensitive to women as any man. Incidentally, if you were able to read my mind right now, you'd know I'm thinking about when Val Perrine, back in the Seventies, had an affair with Bob Fosse, performed a little bit of seasonal topiary on her pubic hair for Valentine's Day, and then walked nude into Fosse's room saying "Look, I have a heart on for you."

But that's what guys want. What do women want? Well, it turns out that what they want is—stop me if you've heard this before—a man who'll listen. To them, that is. As the movie progresses, Helen Hunt and full supporting cast marvel ever more deliriously at Mel's amazing ability to listen!

So all women want is a man who'll "listen" except for throwing in the odd flight of faux-sensitive psychobabble? Nancy Meyers's solitary insight has been the conventional wisdom for two generations, and boils down to little more than flattery dressed up as pseudo-analytical sensitivity as general in its application as a tabloid horoscope. And because men have been told that's what women want for thirty years they've got very good at faking it because it's a surefire way to get 'em into bed. Any guy who doesn't know that what women want is a guy who'll listen is a guy who's managed to avoid listening to a quarter-century bombardment on the subject from chick flicks, Oprah, radio call-ins—in which case he's probably clinically deaf, not merely chauvinist. Even us clapped-out old sexists have got hep to the listening angle. It's painless enough: just nod sympathetically every now and again, and lie back and think of England. The 2001 equivalents of those Sixties swingers Mel digs are the hordes of guys out every night faking listening to the way women fake orgasm.

So the surprising thing about *What Women Want* is how little they want. Nonetheless, Nick embarks on the inevitable transformation into a born-again feminist, and the equally inevitable realization that he's falling for Darcy. In the traditional male-makeover sex comedy, Rock Hudson would be reformed by the steely determination of Doris Day. But here Mel Gibson's miscast leading lady is little more than a bundle of insecurities: *What Women Want* really wants is a strong woman's role to go mano a mano with Mel. Instead, the somewhat programmatic script just delivers him from one setpiece scene to another, letting the central romance fall a little flat.

Still, in his first romantic comedy, Mel gives a masterful performance, full of wonderful touches: I like the way, as he passes his female colleagues and hears how they despise him, just a flicker of hurt crosses his face. But that's another oddity: the uncomplicated chauvinist hound dog Nick seems far more of a rounded character than the sensitive listening Nick. When you compare the buoyancy of his "I Won't Dance" dance to his new-man smooch with Helen Hunt, you can't help noticing that Mel's character seems far deeper when he's shallow and at his shallowest when he's being deep. This may be a useful insight if Ms. Meyers wants to make a sequel about What Men Want.

THE AUDACITY OF GROPE

The Spectator, April 4, 1998

DURING THE GULF WAR, a United States pilot was captured by Iraqi troops. As luck would have it, she was a female pilot, so the Iraqis raped and sodomized her. Safely back home, the plucky gal declared that this was all just part of combat risk.

"Combat risk": there's a lot of it around at the moment. In the ongoing war between women and the phallocratic tyranny, Gloria Steinem recently clarified the rules of engagement. For months now, conservative women have been assailing feminist spokespersons for their inconsistency with regard to, on the one hand, Anita Hill and, on the other, Paula, Monica, Kathleen, a former Miss America, a former Miss Arkansas, a couple of stewardesses on the '92 Clinton campaign plane, etc. Those of us in the phallocratic tyranny have mostly had to twiddle our thumbs in the members-only cocktail lounge with a martini in one hand and a showgirl in the other while the little ladies slugged it out. But in *The New York Times*, Ms. Steinem has now issued a definitive ruling: "It's not harassment and we're not hypocrites."

The founder of *Ms.* magazine and the National Women's Political Caucus says "for the sake of argument" she's willing to believe all the President's female accusers. But, even so, what's the big deal? After considering both Kathleen Willey (a "reckless pass at a supporter during a low point in her life") and Paula Jones ("he asked her to perform oral sex and even dropped his trousers"), Ms. Steinem comes to the same conclusion: "It never happened again. In other words, President Clinton took 'no' for an answer." He showed a fine understanding of "the commonsense guideline to sexual behavior that came out of the women's movement 30 years ago: no means no; yes means yes."

I confess I didn't notice the piece at first; I was too busy drooling over the *Playboy* Implants of the Month centerfold. But a pal pointed it out to me and my reaction was as immediate as his: as the eponymous swinger of *Austin Powers, International Man of Mystery* would say, "Shagadelic, baby! Let's shag!!" It turns out we'd both completely misread "the commonsense guideline to sexual behavior that came out of the women's movement." For years, the more straightforward feminists have stomped around in fierce T-shirts demanding, "What Part of NO Don't You Understand?" Quite a big part, it seems. I didn't realize "No" includes one complimentary grope with optional pants-drop and positioning of feminist hand on aroused male genital area. If she doesn't go for it, well, no hard feelings (except on your part): just extricate your fingers from her underwiring and move on to the next broad. Your feminist credentials are impeccable: you didn't rape her, so give yourself a pat on the back and the next one a pat on the butt.

Frankly, I was skeptical. "It's too easy," I said to the guys after reading Ms. Steinem's column. "There must be a catch."

But we went through it again, and there isn't. If this is feminism, hey, let's have more of it!

At this point, I ought to declare an interest: I've met Ms. Steinem just once, on the eve of the 1993 presidential inauguration. She told me an interminable anecdote about coming across a turtle in the middle of the road, moving it to the shoulder, only to see the turtle waddle back onto the asphalt again—I think the turtle was meant to represent the American people, or the Democratic Party, or maybe Jimmy Carter. Anyway, my mind wandered and, like most predatory males, I found myself undressing her with my eyes, Ms. Steinem being one helluva looker, as many of these feminist babes are. If only I'd been au courant with feminist orthodoxy, I'd just have lunged straight for her bazongas.

Nor is it just Ms. Steinem. Anita Hill, the distinguished former University of Oklahoma law professor, enthusiastically endorsed the new feminist line on the President's behavior: "We aren't talking about sexual harassment," she declared. But, in that case, what *does* constitute sexual harassment? In her recent book, *Speaking Truth to Power*, Professor Hill offers some specific examples, like the revealing uniforms waitresses at the Hooters restaurant chain are forced to wear. Shocking.

This is, as legal scholars say, an "evolving" area. According to a survey in *Working Woman* magazine, over 60 percent of respondents claimed to have been sexually harassed. Presumably the remaining 40 percent are just women who've been at the receiving end of one of the President's "consoling hugs." But in theory, there are seventy million women out there waiting to bring sexual harassment lawsuits. They can't all be Hooters waitresses. One who did sue was the woman who objected to a colleague displaying a photo of his wife in a bathing suit on his desk. Others include the college students in Houston who are suing their drama professor because, by teaching Shakespeare, Molière, and other sexist oppressors, he's creating a "hostile work environment." He, in turn, is suing the university for sexual harassment because, by supporting the students' suit, they've created a hostile work environment for him. At the University of Pennsylvania, a woman in a short skirt complained of a "mini-rape" because some fellow strolling past observed, "Nice legs." If only he'd thought to drop his pants and invite her to "kiss it."

In such a world, many of us potential rapists have found it easier to stay indoors and finish that novel or concerto we've always meant to write— although even then our sins will find us out. Beethoven's Ninth Symphony, according to feminist musicologist Susan McClary, reveals "the throttling murderous rage of a rapist incapable of attaining release." As they say at the Vienna Conservatory, "What part of *Nein* don't you understand?"

Happily, in this minefield of confusion, Ms. Steinem has now simplified the rules. In the dark ages, senior executives would simply sidle up to the new girl in the typing pool and utter boorish, chauvinist, intimidating cracks like, "Why, Miss Jones, you're beautiful without your glasses." Today, under Ms. Steinem's "commonsense guideline," the sensitive Clintonian New Man can instead say, "Why, Ms. Jones, you're beautiful without my pants on." I think I speak for most unreconstructed old sexists when I say that we'll gladly tear up the offensive snaps of the missus, willingly forswear insulting remarks about nice legs, lay off allusions to that misogynist Shakespeare, and swap that rapist stuff by Beethoven for something more enlightened ("Yo, bitch, sit on this") if in return we can solicit fellatio from every well-stacked chick in the accounts department.

There's just one thing that bothers me. As I arrived at the office with my boxers round my ankles, I couldn't help thinking: this new revised feminism is great for guys, but what's in it for women? I mean, I know Monica Lewinsky was the only White House intern to land a full-time job with the federal government, but, for most other women, Ms. Steinem's license to grope could mean a lot of unwanted traffic across their brassieres and a lot of executive penises being waved in their faces. What does the sisterhood get in return?

Well, as Gloria sees it, it's an acceptable "combat risk." "For one thing," she writes, "if the President had behaved with comparable insensitivity toward environmentalists, and at the same time remained their most crucial champion and bulwark against an anti-environmental Congress, would they be expected to desert him?"

Indeed. If, say, he'd signed the Kyoto treaty, would they overlook his own excessive emissions? Absolutely. "If President Clinton were as vital to preserving freedom of speech as he is to preserving reproductive freedom, would journalists be condemned as 'inconsistent' for refusing to suggest he resign? Forget it."

By "reproductive freedom" Ms. Steinem means abortion. Indeed, the most sensible interpretation of her strategy is that it's an excellent way of drumming up business for her favorite industry: if every man is to be allowed one free pass at every female subordinate or job interviewee, the law of averages suggests a lot more women will find themselves exercising their right to "reproductive freedom." This is what the leadership of the women's movement has been reduced to: defending a man's right to trouser-drop in order to protect a woman's "right to choose." Of America's 1.6 million annual abortions, only fifteen thousand are for any kind of fetal abnormality; less than 1 percent of all pregnancies are due to rape. That leaves over one in four healthy fetuses voluntarily terminated as a cumbersome form of belated contraception. Leaving aside the individual consequences—variously traumatizing, dehumanizing, or physically harmful, the real "women's health issues" that feminists never talk about—what is it exactly that women are choosing?

Some women have been embarrassed at the apparent contradictions of Ms. Steinem's thumbs-up to unwanted breast-fondling and fellatio-demanding. But in fact it's a logical harmonic convergence between the first move—the initial lunge—and the last resort—the abortion: Ms. Steinem has constructed defenses of both sexual harassment and "reproductive freedom" that boil down to... party time for guys! There's a bumper sticker popular with feminists: "I'm Pro-Choice and I Vote!" Now we men can get one of our own: "I'm Pro-Choice and I Grope!"

IN THE ABSENCE OF GUNS

The American Spectator, June 2000

CELEBRITY NEWS FROM the United Kingdom:

In April, Germaine Greer, the Australian feminist and author of *The Female Eunuch*, was leaving her house in East Anglia, when a young woman accosted her, forced her back inside, tied her up, smashed her glasses, and then set about demolishing her ornaments with a poker.

A couple of weeks before that, the eighty-five-year-old mother of Phil Collins, the well-known rock star, was punched in the ribs, the back, and the head on a West London street, before her companion was robbed. "That's what you have to expect these days," she said, philosophically.

Anthea Turner, the host of Britain's top-rated National Lottery TV show, went to see the West End revival of *Grease* with a chum. They were spotted at the theatre by a young man who followed them out and, while their car was stuck in traffic, forced his way in and wrenched a diamond-encrusted Rolex off the friend's wrist.

A week before that, the ninety-four-year-old mother of Ridley Scott, the director of *Alien* and other Hollywood confections, was beaten and robbed by two men who broke into her home and threatened to kill her.

Former Bond girl Britt Ekland had her jewelry torn from her arms outside a shop in Chelsea; Formula One Grand Prix racing tycoon and Tony Blair confidant Bernie Ecclestone was punched and kicked by his assailants as they stole his wife's ring; network TV chief Michael Green was slashed in the face by thugs outside his Mayfair home; gourmet chef to the stars Anton Mosimann was punched in the head outside his house in Kensington....

Rita Simmonds isn't a celebrity but, fortunately, she happened to be living next door to one when a gang broke into her home in upscale Cumberland Terrace, a private road near Regent's Park. Tom Cruise heard her screams and bounded to the rescue, chasing the attackers for three hundred yards, though failing to prevent them from reaching their getaway car and escaping with two jewelry items worth around $140,000.

It's just as well Tom failed to catch up with the gang. Otherwise, the ensuing altercation might have resulted in the diminutive star being prosecuted for assault. In Britain, criminals, police, and magistrates are united in regarding any resistance by the victim as bad form. The most they'll tolerate is "proportionate response"—and, as these thugs had been beating up a defenseless woman and posed no threat to Tom Cruise, the Metropolitan Police would have regarded Tom's actions as highly objectionable. "Proportionate response," from the beleaguered British property owner's point of view, is a bit like a courtly duel where the rules are set by one side: "Ah," says the victim of a late-night break-in, "I see you have brought a blunt instrument. Forgive me for unsheathing my bread knife. My mistake, old boy. Would you mind giving me a sporting chance to retrieve my cricket bat from under the bed before clubbing me to a pulp, there's a good chap?"

No wonder, even as they're being pounded senseless, many British crime victims are worrying about potential liability. A few months ago, Shirley Best, owner of the Rolander Fashion boutique whose clients include the daughter of the Princess Royal, was ironing some garments when two youths broke in. They pressed the hot iron into her side and stole her watch, leaving her badly burned. "I was frightened to defend myself," said Miss Best. "I thought if I did anything I would be arrested."

And who can blame her? Shortly before the attack, she'd been reading about Tony Martin, a Norfolk farmer whose home had been broken into and who had responded by shooting and killing the teenage burglar. He was charged with murder. In April, he was found guilty and sentenced to life imprisonment—for defending himself against a career criminal in an area where the police are far away and reluctant to have their sleep disturbed. In the British Commonwealth, the approach to policing is summed up by the motto of Her Majesty's most glamorous constabulary: The Mounties always get their man—i.e., leave it to us. But these days in the British police, when they can't get their man, they'll get you instead: Frankly, that's a lot easier, as poor Mr. Martin discovered.

Norfolk is a remote rural corner of England. It ought to be as peaceful and crime-free as my remote rural corner of New England. But it isn't. Old impressions die hard: Americans still think of Britain as a low-crime country. Conversely, the British think of America as a high-crime country. But neither impression is true. The overall crime rate in England and Wales is 60 percent higher than that in the United States. True, in America you're more likely to be shot to death. On the other hand, in England you're more likely to be strangled to death. But in both cases, the statistical likelihood of being murdered at all is remote, especially if you steer clear of the drug trade. When it comes to anything else, though—burglary, auto theft, armed robbery, violent assault, rape—the crime rate reaches deep into British society in ways most Americans would find virtually inconceivable.

I cite those celebrity assaults not because celebrities are more prone to wind up as crime victims than anyone else, but only because the measure of a civilized society is how easily you can insulate yourself from its snarling underclass. In America, if you can make it out of some of the loonier cities, it's a piece of cake, relatively speaking. In Britain, if even a rock star or TV supremo can't insulate himself, nobody can. In any society, criminals prey on the weak and vulnerable. It's the peculiar genius of government policy to have ensured that in British society everyone is weak and vulnerable—from Norfolk farmers to Tom Cruise's neighbor.

And that's where America is headed if "gun control" makes any headway in Washington: Less guns = more crime. And more vulnerability. And more Americans being burgled, and assaulted, and raped. I like hunting, but if that were the only thing at stake with guns, I guess I could learn to live without it. But I'm opposed to gun control because I don't see why my neighbors in New Hampshire should have to live the way a friend of mine does in old

Hampshire—in a comfortable manor house in an extremely prosperous part of rural England, lying awake at night listening to yobbo gangs drive up, park their vans, and test her doors and windows before figuring out that the little old lady down the lane's a softer touch.

Between the introduction of pistol permits in 1903 and the banning of handguns after the Dunblane massacre in 1996, Britain has had a century of incremental gun control—"sensible measures that all reasonable people can agree on." And what's the result? Even when you factor in America's nutcake jurisdictions with the crackhead mayors, the overall crime rate in England and Wales is higher than in all fifty states, even though over there they have more policemen per capita than in the U.S. on vastly higher rates of pay installing more video surveillance cameras than anywhere else in the western world. Robbery, sex crimes, and violence against the person are higher in England and Wales; property crime is twice as high; vehicle theft is higher still; the British are 2.3 times more likely than Americans to be assaulted, and three times more likely to be violently assaulted. Between 1973 and 1992, burglary rates in the U.S. fell by half. In Britain, not even the Home Office's disreputable reporting methods (if a burglar steals from fifteen different apartments in one building, it counts as a single crime) can conceal the remorseless rise: Britons are now more than twice as likely as Americans to be mugged; two-thirds will have their property broken into at some time in their lives. Even more revealing is the divergent character between UK and U.S. property crime: In America, just over 10 percent of all burglaries are "hot burglaries"—committed while the owners are present; in Britain, it's over half. Because of insurance-mandated alarm systems, the average thief increasingly concludes that it's easier to wait till you're home, knock on the door, and punch your face in. Your home-security system may conceivably make your home more secure, but it makes you less so.

Conversely, up here in the New Hampshire second Congressional district, there are few laser security systems and lots of guns. Our murder rate is much lower than Britain's and our property crime is virtually insignificant. Villains are expert calculators of risk, and the likelihood of walking away uninjured with an eighty-dollar TV is too remote. In New Hampshire, a citizen's right to defend himself deters crime; in Britain, the state-inflicted impotence of the homeowner actively encourages it. Just as becoming a drug baron is a rational career move in Colombia, so too is becoming a violent burglar in the United Kingdom. The chances that the state will seriously impede your progress are insignificant.

To a North Country Yankee it's self-evident that, when a burglar breaks into your home, you should have the right to shoot him—indeed, not just the right, but the responsibility, as a free-born citizen, to uphold the integrity of your property. But in Britain and most other parts of the western world, the state reserves that right unto itself, even though at the time the ne'er-do-well shows up in your bedroom you're on the scene and Constable Plod isn't: He's some miles distant, asleep in his bed, and with his answering machine on referring you to central dispatch God knows where.

These days it's standard to bemoan the "dependency culture" of state welfare, but Britain's law-and-order "dependency culture" is even more enfeebling. The Conservatives' big mistake between 1979 and 1997 was an almost willfully obtuse failure to understand that giving citizens more personal responsibility isn't something that extends just to their income and consumer choices; it also applies to their communities and their policing arrangements. If you have one without the other, you end up with modern Britain: a materially prosperous society in which the sense of frustration and impotence is palpable, and you're forced to live with a level of endless property crime most Americans would regard as unacceptable.

We know Bill Clinton's latest favorite statistic—that twelve "kids" a day die from gun violence. In reality, five-sixths of those 11.569 grade-school moppets are aged between fifteen and nineteen, and many of them have had the misfortune to become involved in gangs, convenience-store hold-ups, and drug deals, which, regrettably, have a tendency to go awry. If more crack deals passed off peacefully, that "child" death rate could be reduced by three-quarters. But away from those dark fringes of society, Americans live lives blessedly untouched by most forms of crime—at least when compared with supposedly more civilized countries like Britain. That's something emotionally inclined gun-banners might consider, if only because in a gun-free America women and the elderly and gays and all manner of other fashionable victim groups will be bearing the brunt of a much higher proportion of violent crime than they do today. Ask Phil Collins or Ridley Scott or Germaine Greer.

ARMS ARE FOR DINING

The National Post, May 25, 2000

GIVE THE NATIONAL RIFLE ASSOCIATION credit for audacity. At its annual convention last weekend it announced plans to build a theme restaurant in Times Square," reported *The New York Times* yesterday. The NRA Sports Grille will feature "a wild game menu and fresh mineral waters from around the world."

The news that the NRA's getting into the theme-restaurant business came as no surprise to my old friend Armand Croissant, New York's top theme-restaurant consultant. "I've been working on it for months, darling!" he told me excitedly. "It was my idea to put the 'e' on the end of the 'Grill.' Like spelling caliber 'calibre.' Makes it more sophisticated. More European. Gourmet dining. Cordon bleu."

"Gordon blew what?" said his NRA liaison man Bud, skimming *Guns & Ammo* as he waited for Armand to finish ordering the flower arrangements. "Gordon blew away a couple of punks who wanted to shake him down for drug money?"

"Cordon bleu," sighed Armand. "Or, as I like to think of it, Carbine Bleu. It's a whole new concept: Fine dining for gun nuts."

"A gun restaurant, Armand?" I said, frankly unpersuaded. "Planet Hollywood, the Hard Rock Cafe, that's one thing. But surely this is a bit controversial at a time when politicians are calling for mandatory trigger locks."

"We have trigger lox," he beamed. "Served on a poppyseed bagel with an avocado dip. But it's not mandatory. It's just one of many exciting menu options." He suggested we wander over and take a look at the restaurant itself.

But Bud raised his hand. "Hold it right there, boys. You know they won't let you in if you're not wearing an ammo belt."

"This is my favorite bit," giggled Armand, as Bud fitted us out with a couple of stylish bandoliers from his couturier. As we strolled over, my old pal, one of New York's shrewdest trend-spotters, explained his thinking. "The celebrity restaurants are all played out. The big growth area in theme eateries now is political lobby groups. I've just been pitching the idea of a restaurant to the National Organization of Women."

"And what did they say?"

"Well, to be honest, they said, 'Spend all day and night slaving over a hot stove? Typical bloody men. Try cooking it yourself, you sexist bastard.' Then they hung up."

We were in Times Square now, and, as we entered the NRA Grille, a grisly sight confronted us. At the very first table, two couples lay sprawled in their chairs, their faces spattered with red, their shirts turning a dark, remorseless crimson. The men were screaming, the women wailing in agony.

"Oh, my God!" I cried. "This is exactly what the gun-control groups are talking about!"

"It's their own fault," said the waiter. "I warned them: Never shake a full ketchup bottle." As the stricken diners were helped to the bathroom—or, as the NRA calls it, the powder room—Armand and I were shown to our banquette.

"Hi, I'm Earl and I'll be your shooter today. I mean, your server. Can I interest you in a beverage option?"

Armand was in a generous mood, so he ordered a .22 magnum of champagne.

"What's your special today?" I asked.

"It's the Saturday Night Special."

"But it's Wednesday lunchtime."

"Sorry, but that's the special every day," said Earl. "Oh, and just so you won't be embarrassed, it's our policy to have one standard tip."

"And what's that?"

"'Always sleep with a firearm under your bed.'"

"But we're in a restaurant," I pointed out.

"In that case, always sleep with a firearm under your bed of lettuce."

As we waited for our beverages, Armand kept a close eye on his latest venture, the Bureau of Alcohol, Tobacco, and Firearms' new federal theme restaurant across the street. "It's a sidewalk café called the Steakout!" he said. I looked out the window and, sure enough, behind a screen of protective shrubbery, the pavement was lined with attractive wrought-iron tables, underneath which several federal agents were lying on the ground staring directly at us while enjoying a rib eye with mashed potato.

Armand had the gun rack of lamb. I ordered the sea bass in a red pepper sauce served on arugula. But apparently I'd misheard: it turned out to be sea bass in a red pepper sauce served on a Ruger. "You know this is rather good," I told Armand, thinking I might review the place for *The National Post*. "Has the chef been recommended by any magazines?"

"No, but several magazines have been recommended by the chef." He snapped his fingers and Earl reappeared with a tray of assorted ammunition clips.

"For dessert," he said, "may I recommend the assault trifle?"

"What's that?" I asked.

The kitchen door swung open and four sous-chefs sprayed us with whipped cream, custard, and sponge. Then it was time for coffee and a complimentary Soldier Of Fortune Cookie. "Care for a reload?" asked Earl, topping up the cup.

"What a great place," I said as we left. But Armand was already on to his latest project, for the Trial Lawyers Association.

"What is it?" I asked. "A bar and grill?"

"It's The Bar," he said, huffily. "And they don't grill, though they will cross-examine you lightly for a modest four-figure fee. It's the hottest restaurant in New York." And he was right: when we reached the door, the maître d' refused to admit us. "I'm sorry," he said. "But you can't come in without a suit."

IV

THE BUREAU OF
COMPLIANCE

SIGNS OF THE TIMES

National Review, November 9, 2011

WHENEVER I WRITE about the corrosive effect of Big Government upon the citizenry in Britain, Canada, Europe, and elsewhere, and note that this republic is fairly well advanced upon the same grim trajectory, I get a fair few letters on the lines of: "You still don't get it, Steyn. Americans aren't Euro-pansies. Or Canadians. We're not gonna take it."

I would like to believe it. It's certainly the case that Americans have more attitude than anybody else—or, at any rate, attitudinal slogans. I saw a fellow in a "Don't Tread on Me" T-shirt the other day. He was at LaGuardia, and he was being trod all over, by the obergropinführers of the TSA, who had decided to subject him to one of their enhanced pat-downs. There are few sights more dismal than that of a law-abiding citizen having his genitalia pawed by state commissars, but having them pawed while wearing a "Don't Tread on Me" T-shirt is certainly one of them.

Don't get me wrong. I like "Don't Tread on Me." Also, "Don't Mess with Texas"—although the fact that 70 percent of births in Dallas's largest hospital are Hispanic suggests that someone has messed with Texas in recent years, and fairly comprehensively.

In my own state, the Department of Whatever paid some fancypants advertising agency a couple of million bucks to devise a new tourism slogan. They came up with "You're Going to Love It Here!," mailed it in, and cashed the check. The state put it up on the big "Bienvenue au New Hampshire" sign on I-93 on the Massachusetts border, and ten minutes later outraged Granite Staters were demanding it be removed and replaced with "Live Free or Die." So it was. Americans are still prepared to get in-your-face about their in-your-face slogans.

No other nation has license-plate mottos like "Live Free or Die." No other nation has songs about how "I'm proud to be a Canadian" or "Australian" or "Slovenian"—or at least no songs written in the last twenty years in a contemporary pop vernacular. And yet, underneath the attitudinal swagger, Americans are—to a degree visiting Continentals often remark upon—an extremely compliant people.

For example, if you tootle along sleepy two-lane rural blacktops, the breaks in the solid yellow line are ever farther apart. One can drive for miles and miles without an opportunity to pass. Motoring around Britain and Europe, I quickly appreciate being on a country lane and able to see the country, as opposed to admiring rural America's unending procession of bend signs, pedestrian-approaching signs, stop signs, stop-sign-ahead signs, stop-sign-ahead-signs-ahead signs, pedestrian-approaching-a-stop-sign signs, designated-scenic-view-ahead signs, parking-restrictions at the-designated-scenic-view signs, etc. It takes me a little longer to get used to the idea that I'm free to pass other cars pretty much whenever I want to, as opposed to settling in behind Granny for the rest of the day as the unbroken yellow lines stretch lazily down broad, straight, empty rural blacktop, across the horizon and into infinity. Want to pass on a blind bend in beautiful County Down or the Dordogne? Hey, it's your call. Your decision. Fancy that.

Italian tanks may have five gears for reverse and only one for forward, but in a Fiat the size of your cupholder it's a different story. The French may plant trees on the Champs-Élysées because the Germans like to march in the shade, but they'll still pass you at 120 on the Grande Corniche. When you've done your last cheese-eating surrender-monkey crack, that cloud in your windshield is a dinged deux chevaux leaving your fully loaded SUV for dust. Continentals would never for a moment tolerate the restrictive driving conditions of the United States, and they don't understand why Americans do. Mon dieu, is not America the land of the car chase?

Gitcha motor running
Head out on the highway

Looking for adventure....

Actually, America is the land of the car-chase movie. Off-screen, it's a more sedate affair. Gitcha motor running, head out on the highway, shift down to third gear as there's a stop-sign-ahead sign ahead. At dinner in Paris, I listened to a Frenchman and an Italian while away the entrée chortling at how docile and deferential Americans are.

Most of all they were amused by the constant refrain from the American right that if the nation doesn't change course it will end up as mired in statism as Europe. "Americans love Big Government as much as Europeans," one chap told me. "The only difference is that Americans refuse to admit it." He attributed this to our national myth-making—"I'm proud to be an American, where at least I know I'm free." Yet, on that two-lane blacktop, unlike the despised French surrender monkeys, Americans are not to be trusted to reach their own judgment on when it's safe to pull out and leave Gran'ma eating dust. Odd.

But these days what *can* Americans be trusted with? The U.S. has more highway signs than almost any other country: not just mile markers but fifth-of-a-mile markers; not just "Stop" signs, but four-way "Stop" signs. America also has the worst automobile fatality rate in the developed world, in part because there's so much fascinating reading material on the shoulder. Our automobile fatality rate is three times that of the Netherlands, about the same as Albania's, down at sixty-second in the global rankings, just ahead of Tajikistan and Papua New Guinea. President Obama warns that unless we "invest" more in roads, we risk becoming "a nation of potholes"—just like Albania. Except that there'll be federally mandated "Pothole Ahead" signs in front of each one.

You may have noticed those new lime green pedestrian signs sprouting across the fruited plain, in many cases where no pedestrian has been glimpsed in years. Some new federal regulation requires them to be posted wherever pedestrians are to be found, or might potentially be found in the years ahead. I just drove through Barre, Vermont, which used to be the granite capital of the state but, as is the way, now offers the usual sad Main Street of vacant storefronts and non-profit community-assistance joints. For some reason, it has faded pedestrian crossings painted across the street every few yards. So, in full compliance with the Bureau of Compliance, those new signs have been stuck in front of each one, warning the motorist of looming pedestrians, springing from curb to pavement like Alpine chamois.

The oncoming army of lurid lime signs uglies up an already decrepit Main Street. They dominate the scene, lining up in one's windshield with the mathematical precision of Busby Berkeley's chorines in *Gold Diggers of 1935*. And they make America look ridiculous. They are, in fact, double signs: One lime green diamond with the silhouette of a pedestrian, and then below it a lime rectangle with a diagonal arrow, pointing to the ground on which the hypothetical pedestrian is likely to be hypothetically perambulating. The lower sign is an exquisitely condescending touch. A nation whose citizenry is as stupid as those markers suggest they are cannot survive. But, if we're not that stupid, why aren't we outraged?

What's the cost of those double signs—three hundred bucks per? That's the best part of four grand wasted on one little strip of one little street in one small town. It's not hard to see why we're the Brokest Nation in History: You can stand at almost any four-way across the land, look in any direction, and see that level of statist waste staring you in the face. Doesn't that count as being trod on? They're certainly treading on your kids. In fact, they've stomped whatever future they might have had into the asphalt.

A variant of my readers' traditional protestation runs like this: "Americans aren't Europeans, Steyn. We have the Second Amendment, and they don't." Very true. And Vermont has one of the highest rates of firearms ownership in the nation. And Howard Dean has a better record on gun rights than Rudy Giuliani. Or Chris Christie. But one would be reluctant to proffer the Green Mountain State as evidence of any correlation between gun rights and small government. And Continentals don't see a gun rack in your pickup as much consolation for not being able to pass for the next twenty-eight miles.

If I've sounded a wee bit overwrought in recent columns, it's because America is seizing up before our eyes. And I'm a little bewildered by how many Americans can't see it. I think about that chap at LaGuardia with "Don't Tread on Me" on his chest, and government bureaucrats in his pants. And I wonder if America's exceptional attitudinal swagger isn't providing a discreet cover for the withering of liberty. Sometimes an in-your-face attitude blinds you to what's going on under your nose.

CARRIED TO
EXTREMES

National Review, February 16, 2010

"IT'S 'ELF 'N' SAFETY, mate, innit?"

You only have to spend, oh, twenty minutes in almost any corner of the British Isles to have that distinctive local formulation proffered as the explanation for almost any feature of life.

The signs at the White Cliffs of Dover warning you not to lean over the cliff?

It's Health & Safety, mate.

Primary schools that forbid their children to make daisy chains because they might pick up germs from the flowers?

Health & Safety, mate.

The decorative garden gnomes Sandwell Borough Council ordered the homeowner to remove from outside her front door on the grounds that she could trip over them when fleeing the house in event of its catching fire?

Health & Safety.

The fire extinguishers removed from a block of flats by Dorset building-risk assessors because they're a fire risk?

Health & Safety. Apparently the presence of a fire extinguisher could encourage you to attempt to extinguish the fire instead of fleeing for your life.

In December a death in the family brought me face to face with Health & Safety. I don't mean the deceased expired because he tripped over a garden gnome or succumbed to a toxic daisy chain: He died of non–Health & Safety–related causes. A funeral just before Christmas is always a logistical nightmare, and I didn't really start grieving until the car pulled into the churchyard. It was a picture-perfect English country setting: The old part of the church dates from the ninth century, and the new part from the tenth century. I felt a mild pang of envy at such a bucolic resting place: Mossy gravestones, the shade of a yew tree, cattle grazing across the church wall.

Ahead of us, the pallbearers emerged from the hearse, very sober and reserved. And at that point they produced a contraption halfway between a supermarket cart and a gurney. "What's that?" asked someone. Funeral directors are immensely finicky, and, in the course of a thousand-and-one questions about the size of this, the color of that, nobody had said anything about a shopping cart.

"Oh, that's to roll the coffin in on," replied one of the pallbearers.

"Hang on," I said. "You're pallbearers. Aren't you going to carry the coffin?"

"Not allowed, mate. 'Elf 'n' Safety. The path's uneven." He motioned to the worn gravel track leading from the church gate to the door.

"The path's been uneven for a thousand years," I pointed out, "but it doesn't seem to have prevented them holding funerals."

"It's not me, it's 'Elf 'n' Safety," he said, sullenly. "They'd rather we wheeled it in in case one of us slipped. On the uneven path."

We conferred. The ladies were unhappy about the Walmart cart. "Screw this," said my brother-in-law gallantly. "We'll carry it in." He motioned to me and a couple of other male relatives.

"You can't do that," protested the head pallbearer. "You're not licensed pallbearers."

"So what?" I said. "As you've just explained, a licensed pallbearer is explicitly licensed not to bear palls."

"You can't just pick up the coffin and take it in!" he huffed. It was now the undertakers' turn to confer. Inside the church, the organist was vamping the old Toccata & Fugue and wondering where everyone was. I had a vague feeling we were on the brink of the more raucous moments of the Ayatollah Khomeini's funeral, with rival mobs tugging his corpse back and forth.

The pallbearer returned. "We'll carry it," he informed us, "but you blokes have to help us. That way, if 'Elf 'n' Safety complain, we can say you made us do it, and they can take it up with you."

"I don't believe New Hampshire would extradite for that," I said confidently. And we made a rather moving and solemn sight as we proceeded stiffly down the dangerously uneven path that villagers had trod for over a millennium until we reached the even more dangerously uneven ancient, worn flagstones of the church itself.

As they say over there, it's Health & Safety gone mad, innit? Or as a lady put it after the funeral, as we were discussing the fracas, "There's only one thing that annoys me more than Health & Safety gone mad, and that's when people say, 'Ooo, it's Health & Safety gone mad!'"

I know what she means. In Britain, the distillation of any daily grievance into a handy catchphrase seems to absolve one of the need to do anything about it. As long as they can grumble the agreed slogan, they'll put up with ever more absurd incursions on individual liberty. No state can ensure its citizenry against all risks, although in Nanny Bloomberg's New York City and hyper-regulated California they're having a jolly good go. And that's the point: The goal may be unachievable, but huge amounts of freedom will be lost in the attempt. The right to evaluate risk for oneself is part of what it means to be a functioning human being.

Meanwhile, back at the headquarters of the Health & Safety Executive itself, it was reported in 2007 that staff are forbidden to move chairs lest they do themselves an injury. Instead, a porter has to be booked forty-eight hours in advance, which makes last-minute seating adjustments at staff meetings somewhat problematic. "Pull up a chair"? Don't even think about it.

It's good to know that at their own HQ the ever more coercive tin-pot bureaucrats don't just talk the talk, they walk the walk. Even if they won't push the push.

ILLEGALLY ADMIRING THE KING'S DEER

Syndicated column, October 11, 2013

IF A GOVERNMENT shuts down in the forest and nobody hears it, that's the sound of liberty dying. The so-called shutdown is, as noted last week, mostly baloney: Eighty-three percent of the supposedly defunded government is carrying on as usual, impervious to whatever restraints the people's representatives might wish to impose, and the eight hundred thousand "non-essential" workers have been assured that, as soon as the government is once again lawfully funded, they will be paid in full for all the days they've had at home.

But the one place where a full-scale shutdown is being enforced is in America's alleged "National Park Service," a term of art that covers everything from canyons and glaciers to war memorials and historic taverns. The NPS has spent the last two weeks behaving as the paramilitary wing of the DNC, expending more resources in trying to close down open-air, unfenced areas than it would normally do in keeping them open. It began with the war memorials on the National Mall—that's to say, stone monuments on pieces of grass under blue sky. It's the equivalent of my New Hampshire town government shutting down, and deciding therefore to ring the Civil War statue on the village common with yellow police tape and barricades.

Still, the NPS could at least argue that these monuments were within their jurisdiction—although they shouldn't be. Not content with that, the NPS shock troops then moved on to insisting that privately run sites such as the Claude Moore Colonial Farm and privately owned sites such as Mount Vernon were also required to shut. When the Pisgah Inn on the Blue Ridge Parkway declined to comply with the government's order to close (an entirely illegal order, by the way), the "shut down" Park Service sent armed agents and vehicles to blockade the hotel's driveway.

Even then, the problem with a lot of America's scenic wonders is that, although they sit on National Park Service land, they're visible from some distance. So, in South Dakota, having closed Mount Rushmore, the NPS storm troopers additionally attempted to close the *view* of Mount Rushmore— that's to say a stretch of the highway, where the shoulder widens and you can pull over and admire the stony visages of America's presidents. Maybe it's time to blow up Washington, Jefferson & Co. and replace them with a giant, granite sign rising into the heavens bearing the chiseled inscription "DON'T EVEN THINK OF PARKING DOWN THERE."

But perhaps the most extraordinary story to emerge from the NPS is that of the tour group of foreign seniors whose bus was trapped in Yellowstone Park on the day the shutdown began. They were pulled over photographing a herd of bison when an armed ranger informed them, with the insouciant ad-hoc unilateral lawmaking to which the armed bureaucrat is distressingly prone, that taking photographs counts as illegal "recreation." "Sir, you are recreating," the ranger informed the tour guide. And we can't have that, can we?

They were ordered back to the Old Faithful Inn, next to the geyser of the same name, but forbidden to leave said inn to look at said geyser. Armed rangers were posted at the doors, and, just in case one of the wily Japanese or Aussies managed to outwit his captors by escaping through one of the inn's air ducts and down to the scenic attraction, a fleet of NPS SUVs showed up every hour and a half throughout the day, ten minutes before Old Faithful was due to blow, to surround the geyser and additionally ensure that any of America's foreign visitors trying to photograph the impressive natural phenomenon from a second-floor hotel window would still wind up with a picture full of government officials. The following morning the bus made the two-and-a-half-hour journey to the park boundary but was prevented from using any of the bathrooms en route, including at a private dude ranch whose owner was threatened with the loss of his license if he allowed any tourist to use the facilities.

At the same time as the National Park Service was holding legal foreign visitors under house arrest, it was also allowing illegal immigrants to hold a rally on the supposedly closed National Mall. At this bipartisan amnesty bash, the Democrat House minority leader, Nancy Pelosi, said she wanted to "thank the President for enabling us to gather here," and Republican congressman Mario Diaz-Balart also expressed his gratitude to the Administration for "allowing us to be here."

Is this for real? It's not King Barack's land; it's supposed to be the people's land, and his most groveling and unworthy subjects shouldn't require a dispensation by His Benign Majesty to set foot on it. It is disturbing how easily large numbers of Americans lapse into a neo-monarchical prostration that few subjects of actual monarchies would be comfortable with these days. But then in actual monarchies the king takes a more generous view of "public lands." Two years after Magna Carta, in 1217, King Henry III signed the Charter of the Forest, which despite various amendments and replacement statutes remained in force in Britain for some three-quarters of a millennium, until the early Seventies. If Magna Carta was a landmark in its concept of individual rights, the Forest Charter played an equivalent role in advancing the concept of the commons, the public space. Repealing various restrictions by his predecessors, Henry III opened the royal forests to the freemen of England, granted extensive grazing and hunting rights, and eliminated the somewhat severe penalty of death for taking the King's venison. The NPS have not yet fried anyone for taking King Barack's deer, but they are putting you under house arrest for taking a photograph of it. It is somewhat sobering to reflect that an English peasant enjoyed more freedom on the sovereign's land in the thirteenth century than a freeborn American does on "the people's land" in the twenty-first century.

And we're talking about a lot more acreage: Forty percent of California is supposedly federal land, and thus two-fifths of the state is now officially closed to the people of the state. The geyser stasi of the National Park Service have in effect repealed the Charter of the Forest. President Obama and his enforcers have the same concept of the royal forest that King John did. The

Government does not own this land; the Park Service are merely the janitorial staff of "we the people" (to revive an obsolescent concept). No harm will befall the rocks and rivers by posting a sign at the entrance saying "No park ranger on duty during government shutdown. Proceed beyond this point at your own risk." And, at the urban monuments, you don't even need that: It is disturbing that minor state officials even presume to have the right to prevent the citizenry walking past the Vietnam Wall.

I wonder what those Japanese and Australian tourists prevented from photographing bison or admiring a geyser make of U.S. claims to be "the land of the free." When a government shutdown falls in the forest, Americans should listen very carefully. The Government is telling you something profound and important about how it understands the power relationship between them and you.

The National Park Service should be out of the business of urban land marks, and the vast majority of our "national" parks should be returned to the states. And, after the usurpation of the people's sovereignty this month, the next President might usefully propose a new Charter of the Forest.

NINJAS VS. TURTLES

These days I write often about what the militia guy below calls "the militarization of the police," and what I usually refer to as "the paramilitarization of the bureaucracy." Because in America everybody's the police: Every rinky-dink pen-pusher at the Department of Paperwork can execute a warrant, and dispatch his agency's personal Delta Force—from the IRS to the Department of Agriculture.

If I sound a little naïve in the piece below, it's because a lot of this stuff— the whole money-no-object flood-the-zone approach of U.S. policing—was still new to me, as it was to many Americans back then. These days, the three-in-the-morning knock from what I've come to call "the full Robocop" is a far more routine feature of American life.

The Spectator, September 1, 1995

"AT ONE TIME," says Scott Stevens of the White Mountain Militia, "these federal agents couldn't act without the consent of the states. Now they go where they like—like in Communist Russia: they take a Ukrainian guy and send him to keep an eye on people in Moldavia."

Hmm.

To America's mainstream media, the scrawny, mustachioed Stevens is a paranoid whacko talking through his hat, which in a sense he is, as his hat is proudly emblazoned "Live free or die with the White Mountain Militia." "What we're seeing," he insists, "is the militarization of the police." We're in a diner, and Stevens's voice carries, and I'm faintly embarrassed. But the waitress shoveling us hot cakes and sausage and muffins and coffee refills nods her head in agreement with practically everything he says.

It's not just Scott Stevens and the White Mountain Militia who talk like this. Groups from the National Rifle Association to the Northwest Imperative "white flight" movement routinely issue warnings about federal agents out of control—or "jackbooted government thugs," to quote the NRA press release which prompted former president George H. W. Bush to resign his membership. To the gun kooks, "Waco" and "Ruby Ridge" are names that resonate as deeply as "Stonewall" and "Kent State" do to gays and hippies. In my neck of the woods, where the only federal agent in town is the postmistress, Waco and Ruby Ridge seemed even less relevant to our lives than the O. J. trial. Waco, you'll remember, was the Branch Davidian loony commune who got fried two years ago; Ruby Ridge, in Idaho, is the other "controversial" federal raid, in which Randy Weaver's young son and wife wound up dead, the latter shot in the back of the head by an FBI sniper as she was cradling her baby. The first of these targets was a southern religious cult, the second was a western survivalist one, and the members of both were blithely dismissed as the sort of obvious fruitcakes bound to end up blinking at the world through the other end of a fed's gun sights.

But it's a funny thing: however wacky the militia sound, these days whenever you meet someone who's been through a federal raid, it's the feds who come over as the fruitcakes.

Take Will Hunter. He's a former Vermont state legislator, Harvard Law graduate, and lunch companion of Peregrine Worsthorne.[1] That last bit, which admittedly his recent profile in *The Valley News* neglected to dwell on, came about when Hunter was a Rhodes Scholar at Oxford and rented digs from the Conservative MP Sir Philip Goodhart. Under the onerous tax regime prevailing in Britain in the late Seventies, Sir Philip found it more advantageous to collect his monthly rent in whisky, and, in return, Hunter and his roommates were occasionally invited up to the main house for lunch with his visiting grandees.

---

1   Sir Peregrine is a columnist, former editor of *The Sunday Telegraph*, and the second person to say the F-word on British television (after Kenneth Tynan, but before the Sex Pistols).

After Oxford, Hunter could have had his pick of America's big city law firms. Instead, he returned to Vermont and became a country lawyer, defending those sad, straggle-bearded losers with rusting pick-ups who live anonymous lives in tar-paper shacks on the edge of White River Junction—until they're picked up on sex abuse or dope charges. For a hotshot attorney willingly to choose those clients over O. J. or Exxon probably does look suspicious when fed into a government computer, even before you throw in associations with dangerous subversives like Peregrine Worsthorne.

Even so, the events of Friday, June 9, came as a surprise. At three o'clock a.m. on a sleepy back road in the Black River valley, the Hunters were woken by a pounding on the door and the entrance of seven agents from the Drug Enforcement Administration in bullet-proof vests. The next day, Vermonters heard from DEA man James Bradley that Hunter had been fingered for laundering drug proceeds: "It is clear from the testimony of a cooperating informant that Sargent and Hunter had worked together to launder Sargent's money." No "allegedlys" there, no "helping police with their inquiries,"[2] no presumption of innocence. Just "It is clear."

In Chicago's Cabrini Green housing projects or the livelier quartiers of south Florida, drug raids are the urban equivalent of chirruping cicadas, part of the soothing lullaby of the night. But Vermont is the second most crime-free state in the Union, and the village of Cavendish is sleepy by Vermont standards. (Its only notable resident hitherto was one Alexander Solzhenitsyn, who selected the township for his western exile but last year announced at Town Meeting that he's heading home to post-Soviet Russia.) To Vermonters, the Hunter raid was unprecedented. Disappointingly for the DEA, which seized hundreds of files and four computers (including those of *Vermont Law Week*, which Hunter publishes from his basement), no one else seems to think he's laundering anything.

The line taken by the crusty old Yankee at the store is that Hunter can't even launder his pants, which, unlike the DEA statement, has the merit of

---

2   The customary euphemism of Her Majesty's constabulary.

being a proved fact. His clothes come from the annual Weathersfield rummage sale, and he greets me at the door without shoes—the first barefoot lawyer I've ever met.

My initial reaction is to say, "Wow! The feds really tore the place apart," but on closer inspection, it turns out that most of the debris in his cheerfully disheveled home-cum-office is the kids' toys, the pet turtles, and the other detritus from the Hunters' unlaundered life: the neighbors deeded them an adjoining ten-foot strip of land, but on condition they keep that side of the lot clear of junk. Hunter makes twenty thousand dollars a year and, taking a leaf out of Sir Philip's book, will accept payment in cheese and maple syrup—and in one case a tie-dyed cummerbund, which he wore at his wedding.

It's the clash of cultures you're struck by: the DEA men shone flashlights on Hunter's kids and in-laws, and demanded to know where he kept his weapons; his wife, April, was more preoccupied in getting the feds to keep the basement door shut so that the cats wouldn't get out and savage the chicks in her daughter's bedroom. "I suppose, if you're a DEA agent, Vermont isn't the most exciting posting," she says sympathetically, showing me, as she showed her nocturnal interrogators, the turtles in the bathtub. Happily, in defiance of the prevailing trend when federal agents come a-callin', in this instance they left behind no dead women or children, or even turtles.

What impressed the locals was, as at Waco and Ruby Ridge, the sheer lavishness of the operation: Branch Davidians, Rocky Mountain white separatists, eccentric Vermont lawyers—they may all be nuts, but you marvel at the number of sledgehammers federal law enforcement can muster to crack them. In this neighborhood, public service is local and voluntary. Across the border in New Hampshire, my town can afford one cop whose accounts are scrupulously mailed to every resident:

Item 4: Cruiser Usage
Miles driven: 9,881
Gasoline consumption: 761.5
Average miles per gallon: 13.5.

In towns like Cavendish, the fire department consists of volunteers. The townsfolk of a neighboring municipality turned out in force this month to erect—like an old-fashioned barn-raising—a new fire station. Yet the federal government apparently can afford to pay a fully-armed DEA team, accompanied by a U.S. attorney and two customs officers, presumably all on overtime, to swoop down in the middle of the night on a small-town lawyer. Let's assume Hunter's guilty: you can guarantee that the money he's laundered will be significantly smaller than the cost of the raid.

That's the history of the Drug Enforcement Administration in a nutshell: in the two decades since President Nixon declared the "war on drugs," the DEA have been given more and more money, more and more resources and more and more powers—and the net result is that we have more and more drugs, and more and more drugs-related crime. By any standards, the DEA must be considered the most spectacular failure—yet they're less accountable than my town's one-man police department.

"I didn't even know there were Vermont DEA agents before this happened," says Hunter. "They're not part of the community, they're like flotsam on the pond, unconnected to anything. Who's this guy Bradley who slammed me in the papers? Who does he answer to? If it were some local cop, you could call up the chief and say, 'Hey, this guy's totally off base.' I don't know who to call about this...."

It's true, the DEA isn't listed in Hunter's book. I try Vermont directory assistance and get some Justice Department automated touch-tone "press four if you want to visit Canada" junk. Then I try again.

"Bradley," answers Bradley. Good grief. James Bradley, DEA agent-in-charge for Vermont and a mere hundred miles upstate from Cavendish. It's that easy. And, after an obligatory "no comment," he proceeds to comment away merrily.

So why, I ask, didn't the DEA go round at nine a.m. instead of three in the morning? Make it less of a "raid," more of an "appointment"?

"That's not the way we do things," he says.

So the DEA doesn't distinguish between raiding coke barons in Miami and a family home in rural Vermont? It's all the same—bullet-proof vests and all?

"Mark, it was perfectly proper," sighs Agent Bradley.

Even the vests?

"They wore those uniforms because they were on their way from another raid."

I ask him why, almost two months after she wrote, Hunter's wife has had no reply to her letter to Janet Reno, head of the Justice Department.

"If someone in England wrote to the Queen," says Agent Bradley, "would they get a reply?"

Well, from a secretary, an acknowledgement or something....

"Mark, she sent it to Janet Reno, Senator Leahy, Congressman Sanders, the head of the DEA, the head of U.S. Customs, she sent it to everyone in the world. Do you take a person like that seriously?" The letter is lying on his desk and he starts to quote from it.

But wait a minute: The Justice Department's official position, as stated on CBS Television, is that they never received any letter....

Over the telephone, Agent Bradley is charming and a lot chattier than his British equivalent would be. But you can hear in his answers the assumption that Mrs. Hunter, who's the local representative on the state environmental commission, is some kinda flake. Even if she were, would that justify not answering her letter? I'm struck by how government officials seem to take pleasure in smearing ancillary targets of their attention. Chit-chatting with the Hunters, I mention federal claims that the Waco cult was a hotbed of sex 'n' substance abuse. The day after the conflagration, President Clinton commented gravely that all Americans would be "shocked by the depravity of what was going on in that compound."

"Yeah, right," says Mrs. Hunter scornfully. "There's children being abused in there, so let's go in and put a stop to it by killing them."

"If they whack someone, they're going to cover themselves by smearing the guys they've whacked," says Scott Stevens back in the militia booth at the diner. When discussing Waco, he eschews the word "compound" and prefers "homestead," which, in truth, whenever you see it burning on television, is what it looks like. "With Randy Weaver, they were bugging him for days, trying to get him to sell them a sawn-off shotgun. So eventually he did. Then, when they said they were ATF [Alcohol, Tobacco, and Firearms agents], he said it was entrapment. That's why he wouldn't appear in court. So they besiege his property, and this one agent, Lon Horiuchi, 'accidentally' kills the guy's wife with a specially outfitted sniper rifle at only two hundred yards." Stevens laughs. "You ever shot anyone accidentally with such a sophisticated outfit?"

"Well, no," I laugh back, trying to approximate the chortle of someone who only shoots people at two hundred yards deliberately. But I get his drift.

"These people in Drug Enforcement and Alcohol, Tobacco, and Firearms," says Will Hunter, "wrap the shroud of national security around them. There isn't any Communist threat anymore, so it's not the military and the CIA, but the feds are the Nineties equivalents: they have this mission that they're on, and they think they can do whatever they want."

Leaving his house, I take a deep gulp of cool Vermont air and savor the still of the rural night. In the next valley, no doubt, one of those hippie draft-dodgers who scrammed to Vermont back in the Sixties is lighting up a joint. I dislike drugs and regard them as one of the most pitiful features of contemporary existence. But, if I had to choose, I'd say that the corrosive, corrupting force here is national policing waging its "war." Intentionally or not, it reduces everything to the worst-case scenario, so that, for a few hours one Friday morning, it policed small-town Vermont as if it were drug-infested Miami. "Reds under the beds" was supposedly McCarthyite paranoia. But feds under the beds? They're there.

✳   ✳   ✳

Three years after the above piece, Will Hunter pleaded "guilty" to one count of "mail fraud," which, like "wire fraud," is one of the boundlessly metastasizing catch-alls of federal justice intended to let Washington prosecute anything it wants: "Mail fraud" means we lack jurisdiction to prosecute the actual crime, so we'll get you on the covering letter. That "one count" is characteristic, too: One of the most disreputable features of federal justice is the way they bulk up the counts in order to lessen the likelihood of acquittal and therefore lean on you to settle. As The Boston Globe put it in 2013:

> *By stacking charges as high as possible and wielding the threat of mandatory sentencing laws, the argument goes, prosecutors intimidate defendants and make it all but impossible to turn down their offers.*

Indeed. The federal justice system wins 97 percent of its cases without going to trial, a success rate unknown to all but the most neurotic and insecure dictatorships—and even there they usually feel obliged to go through the motions of a show trial. So the DEA ninjas in the full Robocop staged a three a.m. raid on a small Vermont cape—and made it stick on one count of mail fraud.

When I run for president with my authentic Hawaiian birth certificate downloaded from the Internet, reforming the federal "justice" system will be high on my agenda.

THE BUTT STOPS HERE

Syndicated column, November 8, 2013

AT A TIME when over four million people have had their health insurance canceled, it's good to know that some Americans can still access prompt medical treatment, even if they don't want it. David Eckert was pulled over by police in Deming, New Mexico, for failing to come to a complete halt at a stop sign in the Walmart parking lot. He was asked to step out of the vehicle, and waited on the sidewalk. Officers decided that they didn't like the tight clench of his buttocks, a subject on which New Mexico's constabulary is apparently expert, and determined that it was because he had illegal drugs secreted therein. So they arrested him, and took him to Gila Regional Medical Center in neighboring Hidalgo County, where Mr. Eckert was forced to undergo two abdominal X-rays, two rectal probes, three enemas, and defecate thrice in front of medical staff and representatives of two law-enforcement agencies, before being sedated and subjected to a colonoscopy—all procedures performed against his will and without a valid warrant.

Despite their best efforts, Mr. Eckert's bottom proved to be a drug-free zone, and so, after twelve hours of detention, he was released. If you're wondering where his lawyer was during all this, no attorney was present, as police had not charged Mr. Eckert with anything, so they're apparently free to frolic and gambol up his rectum to their hearts' delight. Deming police chief Brandon Gigante says his officers did everything "by the book." That's the problem, in New Mexico and beyond: "the book."

Getting into the spirit of things, Gila Regional Medical Center subsequently sent Mr. Eckert a bill for six thousand dollars. It appears he had one of what the President calls those "bad apple" health plans that doesn't cover anal rape. Doubtless, under the new regime, Obamacare navigators will be happy to take a trip up your northwest passage free of charge. That's what it is, by the way: anal rape. The euphemisms with which the state dignifies the process—"cavity search"—are distinctions that exist only in the mind of the perpetrator, not the fellow on the receiving end. Fleet Street's *Daily Mail* reports that this is at least the second anal fishing expedition mounted by local authorities. Timothy Young underwent a similar experience after being fingered by the same police dog, Leo, who may not be very good at sniffing drugs but certainly has an eye for a pert bottom. At the time of Mr. Young's arrest, Leo's police license had reportedly expired a year-and-a-half earlier, but why get hung up on technicalities?

Messrs Eckert and Young may yet win their cases. But one notes that the Supreme Court has dramatically circumscribed Fourth Amendment protections against unreasonable search and seizure when it occurs at America's border, and post–9/11 the "border" has been redefined to mean anywhere within one hundred miles of the actual frontier. Many European countries are not one hundred miles wide in their entirety. A hundred-mile buffer zone from Belgium's northern border, for example, would be well south of the southern border and deep into France. But Deming falls within the hundred-mile Fourth Amendment–free zone, and so, I note, between the seacoast and the Quebec border, does the whole of my own state of New Hampshire. It would be prudent perhaps for Granite Staters to affect a loose-buttocked saunter when strolling around the White Mountains.

Of course, even with millions of canceled health care policies freeing up medical staff, it is unlikely that the authorities could ever give the full Deming PD treatment to the bulk of the populace. Perhaps that's why Americans do not seem to get terribly exercised by these cases. There are over three hundred million people, and the chances of Leo taking a fancy to one's own posterior are relatively remote. Yet tyranny is always capricious, and the willingness of police and compliant doctors and nurses to go along with it ought to disturb a supposedly free people, no matter how comparatively rare it may seem.

Meanwhile, an unarmed woman was gunned down on the streets of Washington for no apparent crime other than driving too near Barackingham Palace and thereby posing a threat to national security. As disturbing as Miriam Carey's bullet-riddled body and vehicle were, the public indifference to it is even worse. Ms. Carey does not appear to be guilty of any act other than a panic attack when the heavy-handed and heavier-armed palace guard began yelling at her. Much of what was reported in the hours after her death seems dubious: We are told Ms. Carey was "mentally ill," although she had no medications in her vehicle and those at her home back in Connecticut are sufficiently routine as to put millions of other Americans in the category of legitimate target. We are assured that she suffered from post-partum depression, as if the inability to distinguish between a depressed mom and a suicide bomber testifies to the officers' professionalism. Under DC police rules, cops are not permitted to fire on a moving vehicle, because of the risk to pedestrians and other drivers. But the Secret Service and the Capitol Police enjoy no such restraints, so the car doors are full of bullet holes. The final moments of the encounter remain a mystery, but police were supposedly able to extract Ms. Carey's baby from the back of a two-door vehicle before dispatching the defenseless mother to meet her maker.

Did I mention she was African-American? When a black teen dies in a late-night one-on-one encounter with a fellow citizen on the streets of Sanford, Florida,[1] it's the biggest thing since Selma. But when a defenseless black woman is gunned down by a posse of Robocops in broad daylight on the streets of the capital, the Reverend Jesse Jackson and the Reverend Al Sharpton and all the other bouffed and pampered grievance-mongers are apparently cool with it.

This isn't very difficult. When you need large numbers of supposedly highly trained elite officers to kill an unarmed woman with a baby, you're doing it wrong. In perhaps the most repugnant reaction to Ms. Carey's death, the United States Congress expressed their "gratitude" to the officers who killed her and gave them a standing ovation. Back in the Eighties, the Queen

---

1　This is the Trayvon Martin shooting referred to in "E Pluribus Composite."

woke up to find a confused young man at the end of her bed. She talked to him calmly until help arrived and he was led away. A few years later, Her Majesty's Canadian Prime Minister, Jean Chrétien, was confronted by an aggrieved protester. As is his wont, he dealt with it somewhat more forcefully than his sovereign, throttling the guy, forcing him to the ground, and breaking his tooth, until the Mounties arrived to rescue the assailant from the PM. But, had the London and Ottawa intruders been gunned down by SWAT teams, I cannot imagine for a moment either the British or Canadian Parliament rising to applaud such an outcome. This was a repulsive act by Congress.

Miriam Carey is already forgotten, and the lawyer her family hired has now, conveniently, been jailed for a bad debt. I am not one for cheap historical analogies: My mother spent four of her childhood years under Nazi occupation, and it is insulting to her and millions of others who know the real thing to bandy overheated comparisons. But there is a despotic trend in American government. Too many of our rulers and their enforcers reflexively see the citizenry primarily as a threat. Which is why the tautness of one's buns is now probable cause, and why in Congress the so-called people's representatives' first instinct is to stand and cheer the death of a defenseless woman.

* * *

In 2014, the city of Deming and Hidalgo County settled with Mr. Eckert for $1.6 million. After nine months of federal obfuscation, Ms. Carey's family launched a wrongful-death suit against the Secret Service and the Capitol Police.

V

HOMELAND SECURITY

PRIORITIES

The National Post, July 29, 2002

EVERY SO OFTEN, the name of Deena Gilbey crosses my radar screen.

Who's Deena Gilbey? Well, she's one of several hundred non-U.S. citizens widowed on September 11, 2001. Her husband, Paul, was a trader with Euro-Brokers on the eighty-fourth floor of the World Trade Center and that Tuesday morning he stayed behind to help evacuate people. He was a hero on a day when America sorely needed them, having been thoroughly let down by those to whom the defense of the nation was officially entrusted. Mr. Gilbey was a British subject on a long-term work visa that allowed his dependents to live in America but not to work themselves. The Gilbeys bought a house in Chatham Township and had two children, born in New Jersey and thus U.S. citizens. All perfectly legal and valid.

But then came September 11. And a few days afterwards Mrs. Gilbey received a form letter from the Immigration and Naturalization Service[1] informing her that, upon her husband's death, his visa had also expired and with it her right to remain in the country. She was now, they informed her, an illegal alien and liable to be "arrested and deported."

Think about that. On the morning of Wednesday, September 12, some INS departmental head calls the staff into his office and says, "Wow, that was a wild ride yesterday. But the priority of the United States Government right now is to find out how many legally resident foreigners have been widowed and see how quickly we can traumatize them further."

And maybe someone says, "Well, you know, boss, maybe leaning on Deena Gilbey really isn't where we ought to be concentrating our energies

---

1   The INS was dismantled by the Homeland Security Act of 2002, and in 2003 its responsibilities were divided among three agencies of the new Department of Homeland Security.

right now. I mean, we did after all issue visas to every single one of those nineteen terrorists. Given that the fellows we let in then went on to murder Mrs. Gilbey's husband, should we really be adding insult to the great injury we've done her?"

But, if anybody did say that, he was presumably put on sick leave, and the rest of the feds went back to business as usual.

As on September 11 itself, when the FBI, INS, FAA, and the other hotshot money-no-object acronyms flopped out big time, it was the local guys who came through. The Police Chief of Chatham, New Jersey, was outraged by the Government's harassment of Mrs. Gilbey, and the British press picked it up, and eventually it came to the attention of the President, who in late October signed special legislation for the hundreds of law-abiding widows and children in Mrs. Gilbey's position.

And then a week or so back, it all came up again. It turned out that the President's special legislation designed to cover Mrs. Gilbey's situation did not, in fact, cover it. The U.S.A. Patriot Act allows foreign-born widows and children of 9/11 to apply for permanent residency—the famous "Green Card." But Mrs. Gilbey was told by the INS she didn't qualify because "her paperwork had not reached a certain level of the process."

Look at that phrase. Cut it out. Enlarge it. Pin it to the wall. Suspend it from the ceiling, lie on the carpet, and try to figure out what it means. It is, as they say in Mrs. Gilbey's native land, bollocks. It is bollocks forward, sideways, and back-to-front. It is bollocks on stilts. It does not address the reality of the situation—that Mrs. Gilbey is the mother of American citizens, that her husband died saving the lives of American citizens, that he is buried in a vast mass grave on American soil, that his relict is no threat to anyone, and that the sensible thing to say is, "Oh, let's just stamp the thing and give it to her. Every minute we waste on Deena Gilbey is a minute we could be devoting to the guys we should really be looking into."

It is the kind of bollocks that makes you wish that Mohammed Atta, to whom the United States Government did give a visa, had hung a left at the last minute and ploughed through whichever office the INS twerp who wrote that letter was working in.

The reason "the paperwork had not reached a certain level" was because, after applying for his Green Card way back in 1994, Paul Gilbey had then changed jobs—which meant he had to go to the back of the line and start from scratch. At the INS, having different U.S. companies competing for your services is cause for punishment. Regular folks don't change jobs every decade, they join a government agency when they're twenty-one and stay there for the next four decades until they retire on lavish benefits at taxpayer expense. So the Gilbey paperwork, having painstakingly climbed to the second level of the INS ladder, was now back down the garbage chute at the bottom.

Facing deportation yet again, Mrs. Gilbey this time lined up the support of not just the Chatham Police Chief but also New Jersey Senator Jon Corzine, Tony Blair, and even Hillary Rodham Clinton. And so last week it was announced that, barring the INS discovering further pretexts for deporting her, she'll be allowed to stay.

Meantime, while Mrs. Gilbey has been frantically petitioning senators and prime ministers, Saudi citizens have been enjoying the benefits of a service called "Visa Express," under which they can be processed for admission to the United States without having to be seen by any U.S. consular official. Instead, they are, to all intents and purposes, approved by their Saudi travel agent. Fifteen out of nineteen of the September 11 terrorists were Saudis. Yet ten months after September 11 this program was still up and running, still shoveling out pre-approved visas.

Visa Express was a pilot program, unique to Saudi Arabia. But, even before September 11, why would you pilot a fast-track admissions program in a country profoundly anti-American, anti-Christian, anti-Semitic, anti-western? What do the American people gain by it?

The State Department now claims to have shut the program down, but not before revealing the surreal immigration preferences of the United States Government: Give them the best part of a decade and they cannot complete

Paul Gilbey's Green Card application, but give 'em two minutes and the word of a Saudi travel agent and they're happy to issue fast-track visas to three of Mr. Gilbey's murderers—Salem al-Hamzi, Khalid al-Mihdar, and Abdul Aziz al-Omari. Mr. Gilbey's widow needs to go through CIA clearance to remain in the country, but no such burdens weigh on the compatriots of his murderers. Indeed, the Deputy Secretary of State Richard Armitage said on June 10, 2002, that even if the Foreign Terrorist Tracking Task Force believes "the applicants may pose a threat to national security," that's "insufficient to permit a consular official to deny a visa."

You can fly a jet at full speed into the bureaucratic mindset but it just bounces off, barely felt. The INS has no real idea who's within America's borders. One reason they have no idea is because it takes them a decade to process a routine Green Card application by a highly-employable, high-earning, law-abiding citizen of America's closest ally. That's a joke, and it brings the entire system into disrepute. But that's big, sprawling, inefficient, your-paperwork-has-not-reached-a-certain-level government for you. The INS failed to get Messrs al-Hamzi, al-Mihdar, and al-Omari, but they did get Deena Gilbey. Congratulations, guys.

We talk about government "intelligence failure" as if it's something to do with misreading satellite intercepts between Peshawar and Aden. But the "intelligence failure" of September 11 is more basic than that, a failure of intelligence in the moderately-competent grade-school sense.

And nothing we've learned in the last ten months—from Mohammed Atta's posthumous flight-school visa issued by the INS six months after he'd reduced the World Trade Center to rubble to last week's very belated suspension of the Saudi fast-track—suggests that federal officialdom has changed or is even willing to change. Paul Gilbey is buried in the dust of Ground Zero. At the very least America should also bury with him the bureaucratic inertia symbolized by his decade-long Green Card application.

CHOC AND AWE

The Corner, April 24, 2011

I AM LOOKING this bright Easter morn at a Department of Homeland Security "Custody Receipt for Seized Property and Evidence." Late last night, crossing the Quebec/Vermont border, my children had two boxes of "Kinder Eggs" ("Est. Dom. Value $7.50") confiscated by U.S. Customs and Border Protection.

Don't worry, it's for their own safety. I had no idea that the United States is the only nation on the planet (well, okay, excepting North Korea and Saudi Arabia and one or two others) to ban Kinder Eggs. According to the CBP:

> Kinder Chocolate Eggs are hollow milk chocolate eggs about the size of a large hen's egg usually packaged in a colorful foil wrapper. They are a popular treat and collector's item during holiday periods in various countries around the world, including those in Europe, South America and even Canada. A toy within the egg is contained in an oval-shaped plastic capsule. The toy requires assembly and each egg contains a different toy. Many of the toys that have been tested by the Consumer Product Safety Commission in the past were determined to present a choking hazard for young children.

And yet oddly enough generations of European and Latin American children remain unchoked. The very name "Kinder" is German for "children." (There was a BBC telly series a couple of decades back called *Die Kinder*—"the children"—whose title initially confused me because I assumed it was some sort of *Die Hard* sequel, with Bruce Willis re-tooled for the caring Nineties.)

Gotta love that "even Canada," by the way: Is that an implied threat that Kinder Egg consumption is incompatible with participation in NORAD or membership of NAFTA?

> The Food and Drug Administration has issued an import alert for Kinder Eggs, because they are a confectionery product with a non-nutritive object imbedded in it. As in years past, CBP, the Food and Drug Administration and CPSC work in close collaboration to ensure the safety of imported goods by examining, sampling and testing products that may present such import safety hazards. Last year, CBP officers discovered more than 25,000 of these banned chocolate eggs. More than 2,000 separate seizures were made of this product.

Let's see—CBP, FDA, CPSC. I'm impressed it takes a mere three agencies from the vast alphabet soup of federal regulation to keep us safe from the menace of confectionery products with non-nutritive embeds. As Janet Napolitano would say, the system worked. I hope America's chocolate soldiers are enjoying their seized eggs this Easter.

Bonus prediction: What's the betting that the first jihadist to weaponize a Kinder Egg makes it on to the plane?

P.S.: My kids asked the CBP seizure squad if they could eat the chocolate in front of the border guards while the border guards held on to the toys to prevent any choking hazard—and then, having safely consumed the chocolate, take the toys home as a separate item. This request was denied, and, indeed, my ten-year-old was informed that by proposing it he was obstructing a federal official in the course of his duties.

Could have been worse. Could have been a three-hundred-dollar fine, plus a $250 fee for seized-egg storage.

P.P.S.: The real choking hazard is the vise-like grip of government.

＊　＊　＊

In the years since, the Kinder Egg Orange Alert has become an Easter tradition in my family. In 2014, heading back from Montreal late one night a couple of days before Good Friday, I pulled up in front of the guard on the U.S. side of the Quebec/Vermont border. He asked the usual questions, and then said, "Are you bringing anything back from Canada?"

"Oh, just some Easter eggs," I said, breezily—and instantly regretted it.

The hitherto somewhat lethargic agent sprang visibly alert. "Easter eggs?" he said, with a palpable menace in his voice.

"Not Kinder Eggs," I replied, trying very hard not to roll my eyes. "Just regular home-made Québécois Easter chocolate."

He de bristled, and waved us through. "Close call, Dad," said my daughter.

Indeed. I'd smuggle in a dirty nuke before I'd risk another Kinder Egg in the car. My children are older now, and can take or leave them. But, precisely because of that CBP guard, they make a point of always eating some whenever we're north of the border. I'm worried that, by making Kinder Eggs cool and transgressive, the Department of Homeland Security has increased the exposure of my children to this "choking hazard." Maybe I can get in on a class-action law suit against DHS....

THE ALL-SEEING NANNY

Maclean's, September 3, 2009

TO PASSING TOURISTS, catching yet another government poster apprising you of electronic surveillance looming in the distance, the initials "CCTV" can be oddly reminiscent of "CCCP," the Cyrillicized abbreviation for the USSR. In fact, CCTV is the United Kingdom's ubiquitous acronym. Nobody needs to be told what it stands for. It accompanies you as you make your way to work, whether by car, bus, train, or taxi. And it's there waiting for you at the end of your shift, as you go to buy your groceries or head to the movies. Last year, when David Davis resigned from the shadow cabinet because of the remarkably bipartisan insouciance about the "erosion of fundamental British freedoms," he claimed there was "a CCTV camera for every fourteen citizens." The British, according to another well-retailed line, are apparently the most video-monitored people in the world other than the North Koreans. In an aside in his new novel *The Defector*, the American author Daniel Silva lays out the background:

> "So how are the British so certain about what happened?"
>
> "Their little electronic helpers were watching."
>
> Navot was referring to CCTV, the ubiquitous network of 10,000 closed-circuit television cameras that gave London's Metropolitan Police the ability to monitor activity, criminal or otherwise, on virtually every street in the British capital. A recent government study had concluded that the system had failed in its primary objective: deterring crime and apprehending criminals.

Only three per cent of street robberies were solved using CCTV technology, and crime rates in London were soaring.

Embarrassed police officials explained away the failure by pointing out that the criminals had accounted for the cameras by adjusting their tactics, such as wearing masks and hats to conceal their identities.

Apparently, no one in charge had considered that possibility before spending hundreds of millions of pounds and invading the public's privacy on an unprecedented scale. The subjects of the United Kingdom, birthplace of Western democracy, now resided in an Orwellian world where their every movement was watched over by the eyes of the state.

All true, except for the "10,000" cameras, which is certainly an underestimate. By some calculations, they're now approaching five million (public and private) across the country. On this side of the Atlantic, closed-circuit television is mostly confined to banks and a select few other locations, and they still look like cameras. Not on the streets of London, where ever smaller boxes mounted ever more discreetly to the clutter of curbside signage betray no clue as to their purpose. Not that the authorities are embarrassed by them. Quite the contrary. Jolly promotional placards advertising that you're in their reassuring presence are almost as frequent as the cameras. Strolling down Piccadilly the other day, I lost count of the number of signs emblazoned "WESTMINSTER CCTV: KEEPING OUR STREETS SAFE," complete with a cute little CCTV logo that they paid some marketing firm to hire a graphic artist to cook up. Any day now the government will surely unveil some lovable anthropomorphized cartoon figure—Carlton Camera or some such— who'll appear in public service announcements saying he's just popped up to keep an eye on you.

But perhaps I overestimate the modern security state's need to soft-soap its purposes. A couple of years back, London Transport unveiled a poster called

"SECURE BENEATH THE WATCHFUL EYES" showing the iconic red double-decker bus making its way across a Thames bridge protected by a sky filled with giant all-seeing eyes. "CCTV & Metropolitan Police on buses," explained the caption, "are just two ways we're making your journey home more secure." The draftsmanship was beautiful, the image a strange conflation of classic London Underground poster art and 'tween-wars Continental Fascist propaganda. You would have thought that anyone who had…well, not even read but was just dimly aware of the vague gist of Orwell's *1984* could not possibly have approved such a campaign. But London Transport did, and Londoners more or less accepted it.

If you're a novelist, it's impossible to write a story set in Britain without taking CCTV into account. In his new book *The Ghosts of Belfast*, Stuart Neville writes of his protagonist: "The truth was he'd slept very little the previous night. It took him an hour and a half to work his way through the streets, avoiding CCTV cameras on his way home."

Easier said than done. Daniel Silva captures the scale of the enterprise:

> "Were you able to trace the car's movements with CCTV?"
>
> "It turned left into Edgware Road, then made a right at St. John's Wood Road. Eventually, it entered an underground parking garage in Primrose Hill, where it remained for 57 minutes…. After leaving the garage, it headed northeast to Brentwood, a suburb just outside the M25. At which point, it slipped out of CCTV range and disappeared from sight."

Did you tell your wife you were kept late at the office but you were in fact parked outside your mistress's flat at 27b Lucknow Gardens? There's an electronic record of that somewhere in a government database. Maybe that's nothing to worry about, maybe no one will ever have cause to dig it out. But it's in there.

So now the country with the most CCTV cameras in the "civilized" world also has the most hooded youths. On a dismal ride back up to London on a

CCTV-fitted train through the Oxfordshire countryside the other Sunday afternoon, I was joined, in an otherwise empty carriage, by three persons in large feature-concealing hooded sweatshirts. In an idle moment while the train was stalled outside a tunnel, I found myself reflecting that, even after an hour in their company, I'd have a job picking them out of a police lineup.

"Er, well, he was wearing a hooded sweatshirt, officer."

"Did the shadow on his upper chest indicate any other features, such as the length of his nose, or an unusually hirsute mole?"

"It might have, but I couldn't tell, as the sweatshirt was black."

"Hmm. A black sweatshirt. Well, that narrows it down a bit."

Happily, the lads graciously declined to stab me. Not all hooded youths are criminal, but the larger percentage who aren't favor the garb in part because it flips the finger at the surveillance state. It is, thus, a CCTV-generated fashion statement, and now so widespread that, in the twilight of his premiership, with his usual control-freak instincts, Tony Blair mused on the possibility of banning hooded sweatshirts in order to prevent "anti-social behavior" and restore "respect on our streets."

But "respect" is a two-way street. And on Britain's two-way streets, where the government cameras whir 24-7, the security state signals its contempt for the citizen. And, needless to say, if the Big Blairite Brother had banned "hoodies," British youth could easily have adopted the burqa as the uniform of alienated youth, and Her Majesty's Government wouldn't have done a thing about it. Mr. Blair's one-time deputy, an Old Labour bruiser called John Prescott, was once approached at a motorway caff by a gang of hooded yoofs anxious to beat him up and (in a touch of artistic symmetry) videotape the encounter: in a sense, they were proposing to demonstrate their "respect" for CCTV Britain by shooting their own CCTV footage.

So CCTV isn't simply a new "technique," as, say, fingerprinting once was. It makes a larger statement about what's happened to a land that was once, as Daniel Silva acknowledges, the crucible of liberty. Henry Porter's new novel *The Dying Light* is set mainly in an English market town in Shropshire that feels as claustrophobic as Communist East Germany, a land in which rural coppers badger you for such amorphous offenses as "failing to account for your intentions in a designated area." Returning to her native sod from a job in New York, the heroine can't help noticing that there's "more surveillance than I thought possible in a free country," and yet the citizenry are quiescent. The Prime Minister is struck by Oliver Cromwell's choice of job description, "Great Lord Protector": "That is exactly what you feel leading the country: an acute desire to protect the people"—for the best of motives.

Earlier this year, Greater Manchester Police introduced "Smart Cars"— little bubble vehicles equipped with rotating cameras on twelve-foot poles poking through their roofs. As the BBC reported, "Anyone seen driving while distracted—eating at the wheel, playing with the radio or applying makeup for instance—is filmed by the cameras." Shortly thereafter, they get a letter and a fine.

Henry Porter's political thriller nudges that on just a wee bit: unmanned four-camera mini-drones sail the skies, tracking the wayward "citizen" even in the remotest thickets of the country. What next? CCTV in private homes? Ah, but we're already there. This month the "Secretary of State for Children" (another Orwellian touch) announced that twenty thousand "problem families" would be put under twenty-four-hour CCTV supervision in their homes. As The Daily Express reported, "They will be monitored to ensure that children attend school, go to bed on time and eat proper meals."

Orwell's government "telescreen" in every home is close to being a reality, although even he might have dismissed as too obviously absurd a nanny state that literally polices your bedtime.

THE PARAMILITARIZED BUREAUCRACY

National Review, August 28, 2012

I FLEW IN to Montreal from an overseas trip the other day and was met by a lady from my office, who had kindly agreed to drive me back home to New Hampshire. At the airport she seemed a little rattled, and it emerged that on her journey from the Granite State she had encountered a "security check" on the Vermont-Quebec border. U.S. officials had decided to impose temporary exit controls on I-91 and had backed up northbound traffic so that agents could ascertain from each driver whether he or she was carrying "monetary instruments" in excess of ten thousand dollars. My assistant was quizzed by an agent dressed in the full Robocop and carrying an automatic weapon, while another with a sniffer dog examined the vehicle. Which seems an unlikely method of finding travelers' checks for twelve thousand dollars.

Being a legal immigrant, I am inured to the indignities imposed by the United States Government. (You can't ask an illegal immigrant for ID, even at the voting booth or after commission of a crime, but a legal immigrant has to have his Green Card on him even when he's strolling in the woods behind his house.) And indeed, for anyone familiar with the curious priorities of officialdom, there is a certain logic in an agency that has failed to prevent millions of illegal aliens from entering the country evolving smoothly into an agency that obstructs law-abiding persons from exiting the country.

But my assistant felt differently. A couple of days later, I was zipping through a DVD of *The Great Escape*, trying to locate a moment from that terrific wartime caper that I wished to refer to in a movie essay. While zapping back and forth, I chanced on a scene after the eponymous escape in which Richard Attenborough and Gordon Jackson are trying to board a small-town bus while Gestapo agents demand "Your papers, mein Herr." My assistant walked in in the middle, and we exchanged some mordant cracks about life under the Nazis. "It's almost as bad as driving from Lyndonville to Lac Brome for lunch." Etc. Her family have lived blameless and respectable lives in my North Country town for a quarter-millennium, and she didn't like the idea of having to clear an armed checkpoint on a U.S. highway in order to make a day trip to Canada.

But, if you don't care for the Third Reich comparisons, consider more recent European ones: The capital flight from Greece, Spain, Italy, and elsewhere as the euro zone approaches breaking point. Greek bank deposits dropped 16 percent in the year to this April; according to a Credit Suisse analysis, capital outflows from Spain are currently running at about 50 percent of GDP. Most of these Mediterranean euros have found safe haven in German banks. You can do that on the Continent, not just because of the common currency but because of the free movement of people within the so-called Schengen area. So, if a Greek figures that now's the time to load up the trunk with "monetary instruments" and drive them to a bank in Munich before the whole powder keg goes up, there's no gauntlet of machine guns and sniffer dogs to run. My friend's experience suggests that, come the collapse of the U.S. dollar, Washington is going to be far less sanguine about your tootling what's left of your 401(k) up to the Royal Bank of Canada.

In fact, it already is. On January 1, 2013, the FATCAT Act (technically, it's FATCA, but we all get the acronymic message) imposes a whole new bunch of burdensome regulations and punitive fines on Americans with non-U.S. bank accounts. Not just Mitt and his chums with the numbered accounts in Zurich, but ordinary Americans teaching abroad at, say, the International School in Accra, or doing regular business in Ireland, or with an old family hunting camp in Quebec for which they've always had a small checking account just to pay grocery and fuel bills when they're up there. Americans now enjoy less financial freedom than Canadians, Swedes, and Italians. When

I mentioned this on National Review Online recently, I received a fair few emails from readers saying they have no plans to work abroad or buy a second home, so why should they care?

Here's why: Because Washington is telling you something important about how things are likely to go when things get even worse. Which is the way to bet. American government is not noted for its sense of proportion. This is a bureaucracy whose Fish and Wildlife agents fine an eleven-year-old Virginia schoolgirl $535 for the crime of rescuing a woodpecker from a cat and nursing him back to health; whose National Oceanic and Atmospheric Administration agents threaten a marine biologist with twenty years in jail over whistling at a whale; whose Food and Drug Administration agents want a hundred grand in fines from some onanistic weirdo in Fremont who gives away his sperm to infertile couples. If you're wondering which of the Food and Drug Administration's twin responsibilities semen counts as, don't waste your time: Whether your deposit belongs at a Swiss bank or a sperm bank, it's all federally regulated.

By the way, I use the word "agents" rather than "officials" because, in the developed world, the paramilitarized bureaucracy is uniquely American. This is the only G7 government whose education minister has his own SWAT team—for policing student-loan compliance. The other day, the Gibson guitar company settled with the feds over an arcane infraction of a law on rare-wood importation—after their factories were twice raided by "agents" bearing automatic weapons. Like the man said, don't bring a knife to a guitar fight. Do musical-instrument manufacturers have a particular reputation for violence? Akin to that of female marine biologists and sixth-grade schoolgirls?

As American insolvency grows and the dollar dies and the real value of household wealth shrinks, is it likely that Washington will share Athens', Madrid's, and Rome's insouciant attitude to capital mobility? Or will exit controls on I-91 become as familiar a sight as TSA pat-downs? The United States has the most powerful government, with the longest reach, of any nation in history. It is also the Brokest Nation in History. Resolving that contradiction is unlikely to be pretty.

VI

THE STORIES WE TELL

MEETING MR. BOND

Maclean's, December 1, 2006

HIS FIRST DRAFT would have been good enough for most of us:

> Scent and smoke and sweat hit the taste buds with an acid thwack
> at three o'clock in the morning.

But he wasn't happy and tried again:

> Scent and smoke and sweat can suddenly combine together and
> hit the taste buds with an acid shock at three o'clock in the morn-
> ing.

Still not quite there. So he rewrote once more, and this time he skewered
it precisely:

> The scent and smoke and sweat of a casino are nauseating at three
> in the morning. Then the soul-erosion produced by high gam-
> bling—a compost of greed and fear and nervous tension—becomes
> unbearable and the senses awake and revolt from it.
> James Bond suddenly knew that he was tired.

It was January 15, 1952, and Ian Fleming—a middle-management newspaper man—had sat down in his study at Goldeneye, his home in Jamaica,
opened up a brand new typewriter (gold-plated), and begun the first chapter
of his first book. Conceived as a bestseller, *Casino Royale* effortlessly tran-
scended such unworthy aims. Today, its protagonist is up there with Count

Dracula and Batman and a handful of other iconic A-listers. Fleming did not anticipate what to me is always the dreariest convention of the celluloid Bond blockbuster—the final twenty minutes in which 007 and the girl run around a hollowed-out mountain or space station or some other supervillain lair shooting extras in BacoFoil catsuits while control panels explode all around them and Bond looks frantically for the big red on/off button that deactivates the nuclear laser targeting London, Washington, Moscow, and/or Winnipeg. But, that oversight aside, it's remarkable how much of the 007 architecture the novelist had in place so quickly. In *Casino Royale*, the roulette table shows up on page one, M on page three, Moneypenny on page thirteen, the Double-Os on fourteen, the CIA's Felix Leiter on thirty-one, the first dry martini, shaken not stirred, on page thirty-two. "Excellent," pronounces Bond on the matter of the last, "but if you can get a vodka made with grain instead of potatoes, you will find it still better."

So five chapters in and Fleming's invented most of the elements propping up the formula for the next five decades. That's not to say he was formulaic. *Au contraire*, that's the big difference between the Bond books and the Bond films: Fleming eschewed formula. Sometimes he put 007 up against evil megalomaniacs bent on world domination; but he also wrote *The Spy Who Loved Me*, a tale of small-time hoods told by a young woman (*une jolie Québécoise*, as it happens) in which Bond doesn't turn up until halfway through; and *From Russia with Love*, with its unhurried Bond-free Soviet prologue; and a dozen or so short stories, one of which—"Quantum of Solace"—is little more than a dinner-party anecdote told to Bond by a colonial civil servant. Fleming had such confidence in his character's adaptability to form it's a wonder he didn't put him in *Chitty Chitty Bang Bang*.

By contrast, the films settled into their groove early and were disinclined to depart therefrom. So we've had four decades of the pre-credits sequence, the song, the titles with the naked girls morphing into pistols and harpoons, Q saying "Oh, grow up, 007," the double entendres ("I'm afraid something's come up"), etc. Whether it's a smart move to dump it all, as the new *Casino*

Royale does, remains to be seen. But, as with the allegedly stale formula, almost all the "new" gritty, tough Bond comes direct from Fleming.

Not that he gets much credit either way. In his anthology of espionage fiction, Alan Furst explains that "there were two standards for the selections in *The Book of Spies*: good writing—we are here in the literary end of the spectrum, thus no James Bond—and the pursuit of authenticity."

My, that's awfully snooty. It's not clear to me that Fleming is any less "authentic" than, say, John le Carré. Certainly, an organization such as SPEC-TRE seems more relevant to the present globalized alliances between jihadists, drug cartels, and freelance nuke salesmen than anything in *The Russia House.* Indeed, to assume the murky moral ambiguity of Cold War wilderness-of-mirrors spy fiction must be "authentic" indicates little more than political bias. There's no evidence the vast majority of MI6, the CIA, or the KGB saw it like that, and as to the general glumness of pre-swinging London, Fleming's far more evocative than the "authentic" chaps:

> He thought of the bitter weather in the London streets, the grudg-ing warmth of the hissing gas-fire in his office at Headquarters, the chalked-up menu on the pub he had passed on his last day in London: "Giant Toad and 2 Veg."
> He stretched luxuriously.

As for "good writing" at the "literary end," Furst is on thin ice here with his cringe-makingly clunky sex scenes in which (speaking of literary ends) characters "ride each other's bottoms through the night," which makes them sound like Paul Revere fetishists. For all his famously peculiar tastes, Fleming had a careless plausibility in this area: I like his line that "older women are best because they always think they may be doing it for the last time." Like the best Fleet Streeters of his generation, he was an extremely good writer, at least in the sense that he was all but incapable of writing a bad sentence. Do you know how rare that is in this field? The bestselling author David Baldacci, for example, is all but incapable of writing a good sentence, though it doesn't seem to make any difference to sales of *Absolute Power*, etc.

It's essential for thriller writers to skewer the details precisely: in *Casino Royale*, one notes, the wire transfers are effected via the Royal Bank of Canada. But it was never about the numbingly nerd-like annotation of the "pursuit of authenticity." With his fanatical insistence on ritualized cocktails, and cigarettes (Morland) and breakfast menus (Cooper's Vintage Oxford Marmalade), Bond prefigured much of today's brand-name fiction. Consumer name-dropping was a novelty in the drab British Fifties, and, of course, unlike chick lit and Hollywood soft porn, there's something pleasingly goofy about a fellow who spends so much time getting beaten and tortured by cruel men in the shadows and then gets hung up not only about which caviar and which Bollinger, but which strawberry jam (Tiptree "Little Scarlet") and which nightshirt ("Bond had always disliked pyjamas and had slept naked" until in Hong Kong he had discovered "a pyjama-coat which came almost down to the knees"). Fleming's 007 is a paradox: he prizes habit but dreads boredom. As he muses to himself in *Casino Royale*:

> He found something grisly in the inevitability of the pattern of each affair. The conventional parabola—sentiment, the touch of the hand, the kiss, the passionate kiss, the feel of the body, the climax in bed, then more bed, then less bed, then the boredom, the tears and the final bitterness—was to him shameful and hypocritical. Even more he shunned the mise en scène for each of these acts in the play—the meeting at a party, the restaurant, the taxi, his flat, her flat, then the weekend by the sea, then the flats again, then the furtive alibis and the final angry farewell on some doorstep in the rain.

That's beautifully poised: "then more bed, then less bed." It's all the better because Bond thinks he means it. Fleming understood the sleight of hand involved in each book—the strange disquisitions on short men or American road signs or the ghastliness of tea that glide you over the not quite convincing plot twist and on to the next magnificent set piece. He kept it up almost to the end, until sickness and boredom ground him down.

But, as an exercise in sheer style, the Fleming of *Casino Royale* is hard to beat. It's not about the plot. Unlike almost any other thriller writer, he can be read over and over and over.

BOY, MEATS, GIRL

Until middle age, Mike Ockrent was one of many British directors of his generation eking out a living in fringe theatre and bulking up his bank account with the occasional West End transfer. And then lightning struck: He revived and reshaped a forgotten local musical called Me and My Girl, *and one of those rare but wonderful showbizzy things happened. "This would close in its first 20 minutes on Broadway," Alan Jay Lerner, writer of* My Fair Lady, *scoffed to me on its London opening. But it didn't. It transferred to New York, and was a smash—and made Ockrent a player in American theatre. The interview below took place shortly before the opening of his Gershwin revival,* Crazy for You. *Not only was he a big man on Broadway, but he'd found love there, too: The choreographer on the show was the prodigiously talented Susan Stroman.*

They married in 1996, and for Ockrent it seemed like one of those musical-comedy endings, in which love and showbiz success, the whole magilla, all come together. And then he was hit by leukemia. He died in 1999, at fifty-three, having just started work on his latest project—a stage version of Mel Brooks's film The Producers. *Instead, his wife and choreographer, Miss Stroman, found herself shepherding Broadway's biggest turn-of-the-century hit through to opening night, and then to the big screen.*

There have been many times in the years since when I've been watching some play or movie, and something Ockrent said to me decades ago pops into my head. He was a very gifted man, and I think this interview conveys something of his enthusiasm—for his work and for America. But he's also very good here on how even frothy nonsense is better for having some big idea underpinning it. He was an old Labour "luvvie"—a theatrical leftie—but what he has to say about storytelling applies whatever your politics:

The Independent, March 3, 1993

IN MIKE OCKRENT's novel *Running Down Broadway*, the musical theatre correspondent of *The Independent* goes to interview the director of a big American musical and throws up over his carpet. Two years later, life imitates art—up to a point: Mike Ockrent is now the director of a big Broadway musical, although, sadly, despite three vindaloos and fourteen pints of lager, I find myself unable to disgorge on his carpet. But, in Ockrent's home, it's not only the rugs that remain untainted. The whole apartment looks like the way you dream of doing your pad if you ever make it big in showbiz—except that, if you ever do make it big in showbiz, you're usually too jaded and cynical to go in for such wholesome memorabilia as Ockrent displays. There's a large photograph of some black kids breakdancing under the marquee of *Me and My Girl* (his first New York smash), while yellow cabs and neon billboards and burger joints scream across the background—the sort of sweetly naïve acceptance of the hip-hooray and ballyhoo of Broadway that hard-boiled Great White Way wiseacres would scoff at.

Something of the same quality colors his novel. As a study of an arts writer on *The Independent*, it's uncannily accurate: the musical theatre critic is a total loser, a bedsit deadbeat, a sexual inadequate with suicidal tendencies— "although, unlike you, he lives in Willesden," adds Ockrent, reassuringly. But, as a portrait of Broadway, it's slightly quaint—you can sort of tell it was written by an Englishman whose introduction to this world was backstage movies: for example, producers still scream "You schmuck!" at their directors, as opposed to "You c**ksucker!"

Yet here he is: the toast of New York, the slick superstager of *Crazy for You*, the show that brought the Gershwins back to Broadway and, according to *The New York Times*, heralded the exhilarating triumphant re-birth of the American musical. "Frank Rich's piece was basically, 'Thank God, it isn't British.' But he does another review the next day on WBJR...."

You mean WQXR?

"Is it? If it's not called Melody Radio or BBC2, it's a mystery to me. But he did mention then, almost apologetically, that I was British."

Ockrent had had hits before—*Passion Play, Educating Rita*—but it was his overhaul of *Me and My Girl* that first brought him to the attention of the Americans. In the 1930s, it had been a strictly local hit that, like most British musicals of the period, never traveled. Half a century later, Ockrent and Stephen Fry exhumed the piece. At the West End press call, the director overheard a photographer say, "I don't give this six weeks." Ockrent bet him a cheeseburger it would run at least seven. It did: seven years (though he's still owed the burger). "We just did it because we thought it would be fun as a Christmas show at the Leicester Haymarket. . . ." But it played Broadway, Tokyo, is still touring Britain, and made Ockrent the obvious choice when the producer Roger Horchow decided he wanted to revive another Thirties property, the Gershwins' *Girl Crazy*.

In their original forms, these musicals were harmless pieces of fluff for the tired-businessman crowd. Today, they come riddled with subtext. I mention to Ockrent that, a few years ago, when I'd described *Me and My Girl* as a musical comedy about a Cockney who inherits an earldom, he'd pointed out that, in fact, he'd taken a neo-Brechtian line on the material.

"That's right," he says.

Er, just remind me: what was the neo-Brechtian line again?" Like most of the audience, I find the Brechtian line less easy to recall than the line about "Aperitif?" "No, thanks, I've brought my own.

"Well, it's all sorts of notions about class, British imperialism. . . ." He recalls how he'd been very taken by some prince interviewed by Robert Lacey on a TV series about European aristocracy, and how he'd wanted to raise the subject of ancestor worship, which is what gave the prince an advantage over a fellow like himself, who could only trace his family one-and-a-half generations back to somewhere in Mitteleuropa, and how he carefully selected the ancestors of the Cockney earl to represent different stages in imperial history since the twelfth century. . . . "And out of that sprang the number 'Men of Hareford,' where the ancestors come out of their paintings and start tapping. . . ."

But it's the tapping you remember. . . .

"Yes, but I think it was Hal—" (Ockrent is one of the few Britons who can plausibly first-name drop Hal Prince, director of *Cabaret*) "—or maybe it was Steve—" (And Stephen Sondheim, composer of *Sweeney Todd*) "—who said whenever you're working on a musical that appears to be light and fluffy, it's crucial to have a really important thought that underpins the thing. It's not just Fred meets Sally, Sally loses Fred, then they get together. That isn't enough today. That's the big difference between what we're doing in the Nineties and the way it used to be. We've all come out of university. . . ."

So it's just to salve your conscience?

"Well, the people working on it have to get some satisfaction. And, in the end, it isn't satisfying to whip up a soufflé if you haven't cooked the venison just before it."

In the old non-red-meat days of 1930, Girl Crazy *was about a Jewish cabbie who goes west and becomes a mayor, or maybe it was a Jewish mayor who goes west and becomes a cabbie. Venison-wise, what's* Crazy for You *about?*

"Well, the venison is about cultural renewal. The soufflé is 'Let's put on a show, let's do up the theatre, and everybody lives happily ever after.' But the meat of it is that this is a town, Deadrock, that has died; the culture is dead; everybody's asleep, nobody does anything. Then in comes this guy with enormous energy who wants to be a dancer, who wants to have rhythm, and he enthuses this town with a whole new life: he gives them rhythm, he gives them their culture back."

So it's a metaphor for the state of American showbiz?

Ockrent looks at me scornfully: I'd mistaken his haunch of venison for a soggy quarter-pounder. "It's a metaphor for the state the world is in. Look at us here: we're cutting back on our grants and our subsidies, we never believe culture is important, we never support it, and, if you don't have a culture, you have no life. . . ."

So this glossy sappy-happy song'n'dance bonanza is, in fact, an argument for increased state subsidy of the arts?

"Absolutely. Philip Hedley of the Theatre Royal, Stratford East,[1] would be happy with it."

As it happens, *Crazy for You* is the first of Ockrent's hits not to originate in the subsidized theatre, while his productions for commercial managements have proved considerably less commercial: *Look! Look!* was a short-lived play about the audience that never found one of its own; *Follies* was a textbook definition of a *succès d'estime*—a success that runs out of steam. "*Follies* said a lot about marriage and hopes dashed, and that's an important topic. But if it's something called *Follies* at the Shaftesbury, you expect to see a traditional follies. If it had been called *Middle-Aged Spread....*"

You'd expect Ray Cooney?

"Okay, *Middle-Aged Dread*. But the point is you'd know not to take Gran'ma for an undemanding night out."

He doesn't accept the easy précis of his career, as a division between splashy hits and more ambitious but less lucrative works. There are, he reckons, just as many important intellectual threads running through *Crazy for You*. Moreover, his approach to this show is no different from his early productions at the Traverse in Edinburgh, when he was heavily influenced by Peter Stein of Berlin's Schaubühne Theatre and worried, in his dramaturge C. P. Taylor's phrase, about "the paucity of modern philosophy."

Today, there's no paucity of philosophy about Ockrent. Indeed, whenever you enquire about a specific lyric or even a throwaway joke, he inevitably expands it into a discussion on geopolitical socioeconomic trends post-Thatcher. In his novel, *The Independent*'s musical theatre loser-schmucko plans his suicide while listening to Streisand singing Sondheim: "Jesus, I love musicals!" he moans. Ockrent loves 'em, too, but, a physicist by training, he needs to know why.

"I do love Broadway, it's consummately professional, it's enthusiastic. When you cast the chorus here, you say, 'We'd love you to be in the show,' and

---

1   The Theatre Royal, Stratford East, is an East End theatre run by the Theatre Workshop, whose productions include *Oh, What a Lovely War* and *A Taste of Honey*.

they nod quietly and go, 'Uh-huh.' 'We're going to start rehearsals on September 21st.' 'Uh-huh.' 'So we'll see you then.' 'Okay.' And off they go: all very cool, very English. You do the same thing in America and they go, 'Wow! Yo!' There's no pretending that it doesn't mean much. On *Crazy for You* here, we've been working on the accents and I've been trying to explain that it's more than the accents: it's the way sentences are structured, even the body language is different—you come *forward* to talk. We hate display, we believe children should be seen and not heard—and where's it got us? It's got us in the worst recession, we're a third-rate power...."

Like the fourteenth chorus of an Ockrent first-act finale, the sheer exuberance is infectious. "So what you're saying," I ask, "is that Britain wouldn't be such a depraved hellhole if we all went around as if we were auditioning for a musical comedy on Broadway?"

But even Ockrent knows when you've gone too far.

"Er, no, Mark. I wouldn't say that. I wouldn't agree with that at all...."

LOOK WHERE YOUR STORIES HAVE LANDED YOU

On Valentine's Day 1989, Ayatollah Khomeini took out a fatwa on a Brit-
ish subject for writing a novel. Here's a near contemporary column, by way
of illustrating how, at the time, I missed the bigger picture. Then again so
did his defenders, who insisted on presenting this affair as one that "raised
questions" about "the role of literature in society." Phooey. It was a would-
be Sharia mob hit in the cause of Islamic imperialism, and perhaps, if we'd
understood it as that, we wouldn't have seen so many others in the decades
since. I've warmed up to Sir Salman over the years, and I'm not sure I'd
write this piece this way if I were doing it today. But he's changed too, from
the Rushdie of the 1980s—reflexively leftist, anti-Thatcher, the works. The
old line—a neoconservative is a liberal who's been mugged—goes tenfold
for him. He's not just a liberal mugged by reality; he's a liberal whom real-
ity has spent a quarter-century trying to kill. I still have difficulties with
his novels, not least the one that got him into all the trouble, but in his col-
umns and essays he has outgrown his illusions. Anyway, here's my thoughts
on Rushdie's first major post-fatwa interview, in October 1990 from The
Independent, *followed by the author's response:*

The Independent, October 1, 1990

A FEW YEARS back, on the street in New York, I was stopped by an opinion
pollster and asked who I wanted to win the Iran-Iraq War:

(a) Iran

(b) Iraq

(c) Neither of the above

I plumped for (c). Like most people (I suspect), I feel pretty much the same way about "the Rushdie affair." Despite Norman Tebbit's[1] best efforts, the novelist is no villain. But nor is he, as Harold Pinter,[2] Fay Weldon,[3] and Co. would have us believe, any kind of hero. On *The Late Show* last year, Michael Ignatieff[4] flayed Geoffrey Howe[5] for saying on the World Service that he didn't much care for *The Satanic Verses*. But Sir Geoffrey, if you study his remarks in full, got it absolutely right: Rushdie is entitled to the protection of the state not because he is a "great writer" but because he is a British subject. To append to the dispute any crusade about the right to free speech or the role of literature in society is ridiculous. Rushdie is only in his present predicament because literature—or at least the metropolitan English novel—has become so remote from society that it no longer has any role. To read the original reviews of the book, in which the offending passages went without comment, is to enter a sort of strange sunlit conservatory, comfortably insulated from the real world. Unfortunately for Rushdie, it was, alas, not perfectly insulated. "The pen is mightier than the sword" is one of the most illusory refuges there is: the mob's reaction to an articulate man's powers of persuasion has invariably been to kill him.

Last night, Rushdie enjoyed as close an approximation of his old Hampstead dining haunts as he's likely to see for some time—in the form of a genial

---

1   Norman Tebbit, a Thatcher loyalist, had resigned from the Government to care for his wife, who was left permanently disabled by the IRA's bombing of the Tory conference at Brighton in 1984.

2   The late Mr. Pinter was a successful playwright and ferociously anti-American.

3   Miss Weldon is an English novelist.

4   Mr. Ignatieff, now at the Kennedy School at Harvard, was formerly a BBC TV host, leader of the Liberal Party of Canada, and Leader of Her Majesty's Loyal Opposition in the House of Commons at Ottawa.

5   Sir Geoffrey was then Chancellor of the Exchequer in the British Government.

conversation with Melvyn Bragg[6] on *The South Bank Show*. The author's choice of interrogator for his first TV appearance and its timing—to coincide with the publication of his new book—was presumably a deliberate strategy by Rushdie to show that it was business as usual: just another author on the plug circuit. But instead it had the effect of reminding you that the world of English letters is far too trivial to be at the eye of such a great socio-historical geo-political storm. Even a man with as inexhaustible a taste for blood as the Ayatollah Khomeini should have understood that.

In his own way, Rushdie came close to admitting as much: "You know the old Chinese curse which says, 'May you live in interesting times.' Well, here I am—living in interesting times. Writers shouldn't have lives this interesting. It gets in the way of your work." There was a wry chuckle after this—one of several self-deprecating mannerisms the author seems to have acquired in hiding—but there was no doubt that he meant it. It was an understandable plea just to be left to get on with it. Yet it was at odds with everything he, Bragg, Harold Pinter, Lady Antonia Fraser, and the other members of the 20th June Group of writers[7] have been peddling for years—that the artist is an important figure in society whose views on politics and the wider world we ought to pay attention to. It is the theory which has underpinned broadcasting in this country for years: a successful businessman's views on anything are unlikely to be sought by TV producers unless his factory closes, but if you've been nominated for the Booker Prize you're apparently qualified to go on BBC2 and twitter on about Eastern Europe and the Gulf Crisis (Fay Weldon on *The Talk Show with Clive James* was the apotheosis of this philosophy). The notion that literature should be left alone to be literature recurred throughout the program and was, if not an absolute admission of defeat, the most telling indicator of Rushdie's despair.

"I feel very sad for my book," he said quietly. "All these other languages, whether they're political or religious or sociological or whatever, have been

---

6　Lord Bragg is a longtime Brit telly and radio host, and a prominent Labour Party supporter.

7　An association of left-wing writers, roundly mocked by conservatives, formed in 1987 to protest the policies of Mrs. Thatcher's Ministry. Rushdie was a member.

used to talk about what is after all a work which doesn't respond to being talked about in those languages—I mean, not just my novel, any novel...." Not surprisingly, his new book is "at one level about what is the nature of fiction." "Look where stories have landed you now," says one of the characters. "You'd have done better to keep your feet on the ground, but you had your head in the air."

Perhaps it's unfair to have expected Bragg to press Rushdie on some of these points. After all, for someone who's endured what he has, it must have been enormously therapeutic and reassuring to be swaddled once again in the snug parameters of arts criticism. "After your first book," began Melvyn, "which was not particularly well-received...."

At such points, the gentility of the encounter took on a surreal quality. If only Rushdie could return once more to a world where he had no more to fear than not being particularly well-received. Chubbier and erubescent, his physical appearance could almost be some sort of political metaphor: the sinister Bombay exotic atop Mr. Tebbit's diatribe in *The Independent Magazine* appeared to have metamorphosed into an amiable Julian Critchley type.[8] Only those unnerving eyes gave him away—more heavily hooded than ever before, rolled upwards with the upper half of the irises permanently invisible. It was like watching some sort of intermediate stage between life and death.

Nobody deserves to go through what Rushdie has suffered. But it seemed unclear by the end just what he had drawn from the experience. He likes his Special Branch protectors, he says, although it might have been more illuminating to know what they made of him. "I keep pointing out," he chuckled, "that there's not a lot of left-wing writers who find out this much about the British secret police." It's possible that he was using these terms ironically, but I don't think so—and it illustrates why Rushdie is such a non-starter as an epic hero. Is "British secret police" really an accurate description of the Special

---

8   Sir Julian was an affable, clubbable Tory "wet," as Mrs. Thatcher liked to say—i.e., hopeless on policy, but genial company. His memoir was called *A Bag of Boiled Sweets*, and is a breezier read than most of the Rushdie oeuvre.

Branch, or is it just cheaply emotive? Is Rushdie even "left-wing" in anything other than a sentimental socializing sense, or is he like most of his friends and confrères so far out as to be off any workable political landscape, untroubled by such trifles as mortgage rates, inflation, and the ERM of the EMS?

Mr. Tebbit was wrong to criticize Rushdie on political grounds for his comparison of Britain with Nazi Germany and for his crude insults for Mrs. Thatcher. But they're certainly contemptible on literary grounds. In his overheated abuse of contemporary Britain, Rushdie so devalued his own currency—language—as to render himself completely impotent. It's a shame the angry Muslims can't see that. But, if it hadn't caused the deaths of so many, from Pakistani demonstrators to an imam in Belgium, the whole affair would be the reductio ad absurdum of the English novel. It may well be that the novelist's most enduring contribution to the English language is the introduction, for which he is indirectly responsible, of the word "fatwa."

*　*　*

A few days later, Mr. Rushdie (as he then was) wrote to our letters page. If he'd been on the ball, he'd have rightly taken me apart for downplaying the whole free speech thing. As I've had cause to learn myself in recent years, when some goons want to kill you over a book, the merits of the book are not the issue; the goons are. Instead, Rushdie defended himself on the charge of being "anti-British":

> *Sir: The canard about my "comparison of Britain with Nazi Germany", repeated by your TV critic Mark Steyn ("Life in the Hampstead archipelago", 1 October), needs to be nailed once and for all. Last year, Sir Geoffrey Howe suggested that The Satanic Verses likened Britain to Hitler's Germany. Even though Mr. Steyn thinks that Sir Geoffrey "got it absolutely right", there is nothing remotely resembling such an assertion anywhere in the novel. Since then,*

Norman Tebbit has made a similar allegation in your pages. It is important to set the record straight.

In 1982, I gave a talk about racism in Britain on the Channel 4 programme Opinions. The text of this talk was printed in New Society, and can be checked by anyone who cares to do so.

This is how it began:

"Britain is not South Africa.... Nor is it Nazi Germany. You may feel that these two statements are not exactly the most dramatic of revelations. But it's remarkable how often they, or similar statements, are used to counter the arguments of anti-racist campaigners...."

Later in the same talk, I said:

"Let me repeat what I said at the beginning. Britain isn't Nazi Germany. The British Empire wasn't the Third Reich. But in (postwar) Germany... attempts were made by many people to purify German thought and the German language of the pollution of Nazism. But British thought... has never been cleansed of the filth of imperialism."

This is strong language. It may not be to the taste of Messrs Howe, Tebbit, Steyn et al. It is deliberately polemical. I did, and do, find the ideology of imperialism poisonous. Its remnants and recrudescences in present-day Britain are likewise unlovely. But it is, to say the least, bizarre that a piece in which I repeatedly distinguished between British racism and other, more extreme forms of racial prejudice should have given rise to the notion that I said the exact opposite.

Mr. Steyn says that "in his overheated abuse of contemporary Britain, Rushdie so devalued his own currency—language—as to render himself completely impotent". Mr. Steyn may think it bad form to get angry about racial bigotry, but he ought at least to study what a man actually said before calling him "contemptible". When

*such accusations arise out of ignorance, they have a way of rebound-
ing upon the accuser.
    Yours faithfully,
    Salman Rushdie*

*The novelist mailed that in from his secure location. My editor, Andreas
Whittam Smith, stopped me in the stairwell and demanded to know whether I'd
sent him a reply. "No," I said. "I don't have his address."*

*However, I didn't think it much of a response—and all that stuff about the
"purifying" of thought sounds positively totalitarian. Indeed, wasn't the Ayatollah merely attempting to "purify" literature of Rushdie's "filth"? As for "the filth
of imperialism," in 2007, the novelist was knighted by the Queen, but I see he
was made a Knight Bachelor, rather than a Knight Commander of the imperi-
alistically filthy Order of the British Empire, so in that sense I suppose he's stayed
true to the position articulated in his letter.*

COVER STORY

Syndicated column, June 23, 2012

COURTESY OF DAVID MARANISS'S new book, we now know that yet another key prop of Barack Obama's identity is false: His Kenyan grandfather was not brutally tortured or even non-brutally detained by his British colonial masters. The composite gram'pa joins an ever-swelling cast of characters from Barack's "memoir" who, to put it discreetly, differ somewhat in reality from their bit parts in the grand Obama narrative. The best friend at school portrayed in Obama's autobiography as "a symbol of young blackness" was, in fact, half Japanese, and not a close friend. The white girlfriend he took to an off-Broadway play that prompted an angry post-show exchange about race never saw the play, dated Obama in an entirely different time zone, and had no such world-historically significant debate with him. His Indonesian step-grandfather supposedly killed by Dutch soldiers during his people's valiant struggle against colonialism met his actual demise when he "fell off a chair at his home while trying to hang drapes."

David Maraniss is no right-winger, and can't understand why boorish non-literary types have seized on his book as evidence that the President of the United States is a Grade A phony. "It is a legitimate question about where the line is in memoir," he told Soledad O'Brien on CNN. My Oxford dictionary defines "memoir" as "an historical account or biography written from personal knowledge." And if Obama doesn't have "personal knowledge" of his tortured grandfather, war-hero step-grandfather, and racially obsessed theater-buff girlfriend, who does? But in recent years, the left has turned the fake memoir into one of the most prestigious literary genres: Oprah's Book Club recommended James Frey's A Million Little Pieces, hailed by Bret Easton Ellis as a "heartbreaking memoir" of "poetic honesty," but subsequently revealed to be heavy on the "poetic" and rather light on the "honesty." The "heartbreaking memoir" of a drug-addled street punk who got tossed in the slammer after brawling with cops while high on crack with his narco-hooker gal-pal proved to be the work of some suburban Pat Boone type with a couple of parking tickets. (I exaggerate, but not as much as he did.)

Oprah was also smitten by *The Education of Little Tree*, the heartwarmingly honest memoir of a Cherokee childhood which turned out to be concocted by a former Klansman whose only previous notable literary work was George Wallace's "Segregation Forever" speech. *Fragments: Memories of a Wartime Childhood* is a heartbreakingly honest, poetically searing, searingly painful, painfully honest, etc., account of Binjamin Wilkomirski's unimaginably horrific boyhood in the Jewish ghetto of Riga and the Nazi concentration camp at Auschwitz. After his memoir won America's respected National Jewish Book Award, Mr. Wilkomirski was inevitably discovered to have been born in Switzerland and spent the war in a prosperous neighborhood of Zurich being raised by a nice middle-class couple. He certainly had a deprived childhood, at least from the point of view of a literary agent pitching a memoir to a major publisher. But the "unimaginable" horror of his book turned out to be all too easily imagined. Fake memoirs have won the Nobel Peace Prize and are taught at Ivy League schools to the scions of middle-class families who take on six-figure debts for the privilege (*I, Rigoberta Menchú*). They're handed out by the Pentagon to senior officers embarking on a tour of Afghanistan (Greg Mortenson's *Three Cups of Tea*) on the entirely reasonable grounds that a complete fantasy could hardly be less credible than current NATO strategy.

In such a world, it was surely only a matter of time before a fake memoirist got elected as President of the United States. Indeed, the aforementioned Rigoberta Menchú ran as a candidate in the 2007 and 2011 presidential elections in Guatemala, although she got knocked out in the first round—Guatemalans evidently being disinclined to elect someone to the highest office in the land with no accomplishment whatsoever apart from a lousy fake memoir. Which just goes to show what a bunch of unsophisticated rubes they are.

In an inspired line of argument, Ben Smith of the website BuzzFeed suggests that the controversy over *Dreams from My Father* is the fault of conservatives who have "taken the self-portrait at face value." We are so unlettered and hicky that we think a memoir is about stuff that actually happened rather than a literary *jeu d'esprit* playing with nuances of notions of assumptions of preconceptions of concoctions of invented baloney. And so we regard the first member of the Invented-American community to make it to the White House as a kinda weird development rather than an encouraging sign of how a new post-racial, post-gender, post-modern America is moving beyond the old straightjackets of black and white, male and female, gay and straight, real and hallucinatory.

The question now is whether the United States itself is merely the latest chapter of Obama's fake memoir. You'll notice that, in the examples listed above, the invention only goes one way. No Cherokee orphan, Holocaust survivor, or recovering drug addict pretends to be George Wallace's speechwriter. Instead, the beneficiaries of boring middle-class western life seek to appropriate the narratives and thereby enjoy the electric frisson of fashionable victim groups.

And so it goes with public policy in the west at twilight.

Thus, Obama's executive order on immigration exempting a million people from the laws of the United States is patently unconstitutional, but that's not how an NPR listener looks at it: To him, Obama's unilateral amnesty enriches stultifying white-bread America with a million plucky little Rigoberta Menchús and their heartbreaking stories. Eric Holder's entire tenure as Attorney-General is a fake memoir all by itself, and his invocation of "executive privilege" in the Fast & Furious scandal is preposterous, but American liberals can't hear: Insofar as they know anything about Fast & Furious, it's something to do with the government tracking the guns of fellows like those Alabama "Segregation Forever" nuts, rather than a means by which hundreds of innocent Rigoberta Menchús south of the border were gunned down with weapons sold to their killers by liberal policymakers of the Obama Administration. If that's the reality, they'll take the fake memoir.

Similarly, Obamacare is apparently all about the repressed patriarchal white male waging his "war on women." The women are struggling thirty-year-old

Georgetown Law coeds whose starting salary after graduation is 140 grand a year, but let's not get hung up on details. Dodd-Frank financial reform, also awaiting Supreme Court judgment, is another unconstitutional power grab, but its designated villains are mustache-twirling, top-hatted bankers, so likewise who cares?

One can understand why the beneficiaries of the postwar west's expansion of middle-class prosperity would rather pass themselves off as members of way cooler victim groups: It's a great career move. It may even have potential beyond the page: See Sandra Fluke's dazzling pre-Broadway tryout of *Fake Memoir: The High School Musical*, in which a wealthy law student approaching middle age passes herself off as the Little Rigoberta Hussein Wilkomirski of the Rite Aid pick-up window. But transforming an entire nation into a fake memoir is unlikely to prove half so lucrative. The heartwarming immigrants, the contraceptive-less coeds, the mustache-twirling bankers all provide cover for a far less appealing narrative: an expansion of centralized power hitherto unknown to this republic. In reality, Obama's step-grandfather died falling off the chair while changing the drapes. In the fake-memoir version, Big Government's on the chair, and it's curtains for America.

WHEN HARRY MET HILLARY

Hillary Clinton's book, Living History, *was published in June 2003 a few days before J. K. Rowling's latest Harry Potter blockbuster. For some reason, my* Daily Telegraph *column managed to get these two quite distinct authors confused:*

The Daily Telegraph, June 21, 2003

WELL, THE BIG DAY is here! Around the world this morning, bookstores opened their doors and millions of customers who'd spent the night waiting patiently in long lines eagerly stampeded to the counter and said, "Here's the copy of *Living History* I bought last week. I'd like my money back, please."

Sadly, the publisher's returns policy, conveniently footnoted on page 523 of the book, makes that impossible. But already industry observers are hailing the brilliant marketing strategy of ensuring that no details of the fictional bestseller were allowed to leak out until the checks for advance orders had cleared. It's that kind of sophisticated media campaign that has helped make its multimillionaire creator, J. K. Rodham, the world's most widely unread author.

It's hard to imagine now, but just a few years ago Rodham was financially dependent on the government, living in dreary public housing in an obscure part of Little Rock, and separated from her husband for a few hours while he was over at his brother's testing the new hot tub with a couple of cocktail waitresses. It was then that the soon-to-be-world-famous author came up with her incredible plot: the story of an adolescent with magical powers who saves the world from the dark forces.

The result was *Billy Clinter and the Philosophers Stoned*, in which young Billy attends a party at Oxford and discovers his amazing ability to smoke but not inhale. With that first fantastic adventure of the shy misunderstood boy blessed—and burdened—with the awesome power to feel your pain with just one touch, young Billy Clinter became the world's most popular schoolboy.

Then came *Billy Clinter and the Gusset of Fire*, in which the vast right-wing conspiracy led by the sinister Lord Newt and Doleful Bob plant a hogtail disguised as a house elf in his hotel room in Little Hangleton. The elf tricks Billy into revealing his pocket sneakoscope and she glimpses its remarkable distinguishing characteristics, the strange lightning bolt along the side that signals the tremendous potency of his Slytherin Beaubaton. After this narrow escape, the young wizard gets into yet more scrapes in *Billy Clinter and the Prisoner of Azkansas*, in which Rodham tells the story of how young Billy and his much brainier friend, Hillary Granger, finally escape the hideous swamp of Azkansas after being trapped there for far longer than Hillary had expected to be.

But in the fourth volume events take a grim turn, as the careless schoolboy becomes aware that Professor Starr has in his laboratory a magic dress that could destroy all his and Hillary's plans. In *Billy Clinter and the Chamber of Semen*, Billy realizes that he splinched while he was apparating, which had never happened before. This is all the fault of Moaning Monica, the intern who haunts the anteroom at Housewhites and has the rare power of Parcel-mouth, the ability to look into the eye of the Basilisk, the world's smallest snake, without being petrified. Is she a Niffler or a Death Eater? Billy cannot be sure. He looks to Housewhites' giant shambling groundskeeper Reno to protect him, but she's busy raining down fire on strange cults. As the book ends, their old friend Albus Bumblegore fails to become Headmaster of Housewhites after insufficient chads are found in his sorting hat.

With each new adventure, critics have predicted that the eternal school-boy has run his course. But he keeps coming back. Nonetheless, there were strange rumors this time that J. K. Rodham was preparing to kill off the most popular character. It's been known for a while that she sees the series' future depending more on the much brainier though somewhat unlikeable Hillary Granger and the four female ghosts who write all her words.

According to the pre-publicity, the latest book—*Living History: The Heavily Discounted Bulk Order of the Phoenix*—would see Hillary rise from the ashes yet again, step out of Billy's shadow, and prepare to take Housewhites back from the evil usurper Lord W. Bush (as fans know, the W stands for Woldemort, but by tradition the name is never said). But instead it's mostly hundreds of pages about who Hillary sat next to at the many school dinners she's attended, with a brief passage about when Billy told her about Moaning Monica. According to the book, after spending the summer golfing with Uncle Vernon Jordan, he admits to Hillary that, although he did play quidditch, he never put his bludger in the golden snitch. Hillary thinks this is a lot of hufflepuff, and, although he doesn't die, Billy finds himself under an impediment curse which means that for the rest of the book he hardly gets to take his wand out at all and Uncle Vernon starts calling him Nearly Headless Bill.

But has the series lost touch with its original fans? Many of those impressionable young readers from a decade ago are now in their mid-fifties and may have difficulty still believing in fantastical tales about boys who don't inhale and girls who can't remember where they placed their billing records. "Oh, you say that every time," chuckles J. K. Rodham. "Believe me, they'll still be swallowing this stuff twenty years from now."

VII

IMPERIAL ECHOES

KEEPING IT

National Review, August 19, 2013

MONARCHY IS THE natural order of things, which is why, as Ben Franklin grasped, the tricky bit about a republic is keeping it. Franklin didn't live to see how that panned out. He died in 1790, a year after the first inauguration, back when John Adams was proposing that George Washington be addressed as "Your Most Benign Highness." Instead, America gave a word to the world—the now-standard designation for a non-monarchical head of state: "President."

Many presidencies are monarchical in all but name—Putin is known to his subjects as "Tsar," and Mubarak was "Pharaoh"—and some are even hereditary—the Kims in North Korea, the Assads in Syria. For those citizens looking for a lighter touch from their rulers, there are Europe's non-executive presidents—the heads of state of Austria, Germany, Portugal, and Italy that nobody beyond the borders can name but that seem to suit post-imperial powers in search of a quiet life: A republic is the phase that comes after dreams of national greatness have flown and the world stage has been abandoned to others.

And then there's His Royal Highness Prince George Alexander Louis of Cambridge, third in line to the thrones of the United Kingdom, Canada, New Zealand, Belize, Tuvalu, and most of the other prime monarchical real estate. I kept my royal-baby fever in check—name-wise, I was hoping for Prince Trayvon Carlos Danger Windsor—but I confess that, passing a TV set tuned to BBC World, I did stop to enjoy an in-depth report on how in far-flung parts of the Commonwealth many people were reacting with total indifference to the regal newborn. You'd be surprised how long the man in the street is prepared to stop and chat about how he couldn't be less interested in the new princeling.

Such are the joys monarchy affords in a democratic age: For every loyal subject enjoying a frisson of pleasure at the blessed event, there's another getting just as much pleasure bitching to his mates down the pub about what a bunch of useless parasites they are. And, unlike the President of the United States, divisive royals are a bargain. Obama's last Christmas vacation in Hawaii cost some seven million dollars—or almost exactly the same as a year's air travel around the planet for the entire Royal Family (£4.7 million). According to the USAF, in 2010 Air Force One cost American taxpayers $181,757 per flight hour. According to the Royal Canadian Air Force, in 2011 the CC-150 Polaris military transport that flew William and Kate from Vancouver to Los Angeles cost Her Majesty's Canadian subjects $15,505 per hour—or about 8/100ths of the cost.

Unlike a republic, monarchy in a democratic age means you can't go around queening it. That RCAF boneshaker has a shower the size of a phone booth, yet the Duchess of Cambridge looked almost as glamorous as Mrs. Obama when she emerged onto the steps at LAX. That's probably because Canada's 437 Squadron decided to splash out on new bedding for the royal tour. Amanda Heron was dispatched to the local mall in Trenton, Ontario, and returned with a pale blue and white comforter and matching pillows.

Is there no end to the grotesque indulgence of these over-pampered royal deadbeats? "I found a beautiful set," said Master-Corporal Heron. "It was such a great price I bought one for myself."

Nevertheless, Canadian journalists and politicians bitched and whined about the cost of this disgusting jet-set lifestyle nonstop throughout the tour. At the conclusion of their official visit to California, Their Royal Highnesses flew on to Heathrow with their vast entourage of, er, seven people—and the ingrate whining Canadians passed the baton to their fellow ingrate whiners across the Atlantic. As *The Daily Mail* in London reported, "High Fliers: Prince William and his wife Kate spend an incredible £52,000 on the one-way flight from LA to London for themselves and their seven-strong entourage." Incredible! For £52,000, you couldn't take the President from Washington to a state visit to an ice cream parlor in a Maryland suburb. Obama flew Air Force

One from Washington to Williamsburg, Virginia, requiring a wide-bodied transatlantic jet that holds five hundred people to ferry him a distance of a little over a hundred miles. And, unlike their British and Canadian counterparts, the American media are entirely at ease with it.

Just for the record, William and Kate actually spent an "incredible" £51,410—or about eighty thousand dollars—for nine business-class tickets on British Airways to Heathrow. At the check-in desk at Los Angeles, BA graciously offered the Duke and Duchess an upgrade to first class. By now you're probably revolted by this glimpse of disgusting monarchical excess, so, if it's any consolation, halfway through the flight the cabin's entertainment consoles failed and, along with other first-class passengers, Their Highnesses were offered a two-hundred-pound voucher toward the cost of their next flight, which they declined.

My daughter and I chanced to be in Scotland at the same time as the Queen last summer, and went along to see her in Glasgow: Her limo had a car in front and a car behind. The royal couple got out and walked around the square greeting jubilee well-wishers. My thrilled teenybopper came within a foot of Her Majesty without having to go through a body search or a background check. Try doing that as the forty-car motorcade conveys President Obama to an ice-cream parlor and the surrounding streets are closed and vacuumed of all non-credentialed persons.[1] The citizen-executive has become His Mostly Benign Highness: a distant, all-powerful sovereign—but kindly, and generous with his food stamps, if merciless with his IRS audits.

In Fleet Street, the (small-"r") republicans of the columnar crowd advanced an argument that would have sounded bizarre a generation or three

---

[1]   It's not an exact comparison, because the Queen doesn't play "fundraisers," but in July 2014 a woman who'd gone into labor was prevented from getting to Cedars-Sinai Medical Center in Los Angeles and forced to wait at a bench across from the hospital on Third Street because the roads had been closed for an Obama/Democrat campaign event. "As soon as we can," said Sgt. Kurt Smith of the LAPD, "we'll be able to open it up for traffic and first thing we'll try to get to will be an ambulance. But I can't guarantee the time on that." It is not known if King Barack's grateful subject named her newborn "Motorcade" in his honor.

back: They attacked not so much the Royal Family as a citizenry stupid enough to dote on them. "The Royal Baby shows how far we've fallen back into our forelock-tugging habits," scoffed Viv Groskop in *The Independent*. Tugging his forelock was what the hatless working man once did to the local squire, but chippy republicans revived the archaism sufficiently to earn it a busy Twitter hashtag in the days around the royal birth. Surveying the "Hadrian's Wall of Kate Baby Special Editions" on every newsstand, another columnar naysayer, Grace Dent, unconsciously channeled Pauline Kael re Nixon: Nobody she knew was interested in the royal bairn. *The Guardian's* Catherine Bennett peered out of her drawing-room window to watch in horror the masses below "drool over royal and demi-royal hotness."

This is republicanism as class marker: Apparently, the only argument against an anachronistic, out-of-touch hereditary family ruling by divine right is that they're way too popular with the masses. I remember, years ago, being told by a Hampstead intellectual that the problem with the Queen was that she was too middle class. Today, for Britain's elites, monarchy is simply too, too common.

America's elites, on the other hand, are happy to drool over Barack and Michelle's neo-royal hotness. Shortly before his death, the sociologist Michael Young, the man who coined the term "meritocracy" for a satirical fantasy he wrote in 1958, observed that Britain's Blairite meritocrats "can be insufferably smug, much more so than the people who knew they had achieved advancement not on their own merit but because they were, as somebody's son or daughter, the beneficiaries of nepotism." As Young had foreseen a half-century ago, a cult of (pseudo-)meritocracy absolves a ruling class of guilt. They assume not, as princes of old did, that they were destined to rule, but that they *deserve* to. Which is wonderfully liberating—as one sees all around, from Barack Obama's neo-monarchical selectivity on which laws he'll enforce to the spambot penis of Anthony Weiner and his industrial-scale exercising of his *Tweet du seigneur*. Both men have bet that the public crave Their Most Benign Hotness.

If it's any consolation to Ben Franklin, they kept it longer than you might expect. Every so often, I take my children across the Connecticut River and down to Plymouth Notch, Vermont, where a citizen-president lies buried on a hardscrabble hillside under a headstone no different from the seven generations before him. But Coolidge is more alien to today's presidency than George III is.

Oh, well. Maybe republican virtue will be restored in the 2016 election. Jeb vs. Hillary?

QUEER THEORY

The Daily Telegraph, January 11 2005

PERSONALLY, I THOUGHT the Queen's Christmas message this year was rather old hat, or old crown. She's been peddling the let-us-celebrate-the-strength-of-our-diversity guff for a good three decades in her Canadian speeches.

Of course, they're written for her by her Canadian ministers, and one had hoped that she might be reading the multiculti boilerplate through at least partially clenched teeth. But the Christmas message is the one speech she writes without the advice of her governments, so one must assume she means it.

In which case, it seems an odd theme at a time when the internal contradictions of the multicultural society are ever more evident.

For example, last week *The Guardian* forced itself to consider the awkward fact that many young black males are "homophobic." This would be a disadvantage if one were hoping to make a career in the modern Tory party, but, on the other hand, if one's ambitions incline more to becoming a big-time gangsta rapper, it's a goldmine. Don't blame Jamaican men, though. After all, who made them homophobic? The "vilification of Jamaican homophobia," says Decca Aitkenhead, is just an attempt to distract from the real culprit: "It's a failure to recognize 400 years of Jamaican history, starting with the sodomy of male slaves by their white owners as a means of humiliation.

"Slavery laid the foundations of homophobia," writes Miss Aitkenhead. "For us to vilify Jamaicans for an attitude of which we were the architects is shameful. Jamaicans weren't the architects of their ideas about homosexuality; we were."

I should have known. It's our fault: yours, mine, the great white Queen's, for all her shameless attempts to climb aboard the diversity bandwagon.

If we hadn't enslaved these fellows and taken them to the West Indies to be our playthings under the Caribbean moon, they'd have stayed in Africa and grown up as relaxed live-and-let-live types like Zimbabwe's Robert Mugabe, who's accused Tony Blair of a plan to impose homosexuality throughout the Commonwealth;

... or Kenya's Daniel arap Moi, who attacked the "gay scourge" sweeping Africa;

... or Zambia's Frederick Chiluba, who has said gays do not have "a right to be abnormal";

... or Namibia's Sam Nujoma, who accused African homosexuals of being closet "Europeans" trying to destroy his country through the spread of "gayism";

... or Uganda's Yoweri Museveni, who proposed the arrest of all homosexuals, though he subsequently moderated his position and called for a return to the good old days when "these few individuals were either ignored or speared and killed by their parents."

But no doubt Decca Aitkenhead would respond that African homophobia is also the malign legacy of British colonialism. Who taught them to spear gays, eh?

By refusing to enslave them and take them to our Caribbean plantations and sodomize them every night, we left them with feelings of rejection and humiliation that laid the foundations of their homophobic architecture. The point to remember is, as the *Guardian* headline writer put it, cutting to the chase, "Their homophobia is our fault."

And it always will be. It's forty years since Jamaican independence, but in four hundred years, if there are any Englishmen left (which is demographically doubtful), *Guardian* columnists will still be sticking it to them for the psychological damage of colonialism.

How heartening to know that, at a time when so many quaint old British traditions are being abolished—foxhunting, free speech, national sovereignty—the traditional British leftist colonial guilt complex is alive and well. Even with hardly any colonies left.

When, say, Mahmoud Bakri of the Egyptian weekly *al-Usbu*, writes that the tsunamis were caused by Zionist nuclear testing, we roll our eyes. But, in the mass derangement stakes, blaming everything on the Jews is, if anything, marginally less loopy than blaming everything on yourself. One thing you notice, for example, in the Indian Ocean is that the countries making up the core group co-ordinating relief efforts—America, Australia, India, Japan—are three-quarters British-derived. The same can be said of the most effective second-tier nations involved, such as Singapore and Malaysia. A healthy culture should be able to weigh the pros and cons of the Britannic inheritance in a balanced way. But the wilful perverseness of Miss Aitkenhead's argument suggests that, if anything, it's the mother country that's been psychologically damaged by imperialism.

As for the notion that even the randiest plantation owner could sodomize so many male slaves that he could inculcate an ingrained homophobia enduring for centuries, that's a bit of a stretch even for advanced western self-loathers. Colin Powell, the son of Jamaicans, recalls it rather differently: "The British were mostly absentee landlords, and West Indians were mostly left on their own."

Can absentee landlords be absentee sodomites? I'll leave that one for Guardian columnists. But, before her next intervention in this area, the Queen might like to ponder the motives underlying all the sappy diversity blather. The British have always been open to other cultures: that's one reason they made much better imperialists than the French or the Belgians. But "multiculturalism" is really a suicide cult conceived by the western elites not to celebrate all cultures, but to deny their own. And that's particularly unworthy of the British, whose language, culture, and law have been the single greatest force for good in this world.

This isn't merely a question for the history books, but the issue that underpins all the others facing the country today, not least the European Constitution: at a time when the benefits of the Britannic inheritance are more and more apparent everywhere else, how come Britain has no use for them?

❋   ❋   ❋

Robert Mugabe subsequently warmed to his theme, and called Tony Blair a "gay gangster" leading "the gay government of the gay United gay Kingdom." A Downing Street spokesgay denied the charge: "The Prime Minister is not a gay gangster."

SON OF EMPIRE

In a basic sense, the essay below is wrong: Colin Powell chose not to run for the presidency. But I reread the piece in light of the man who, twelve years later, did become "the first black president." Like Colin Powell, Barack Obama is the son of a British subject—in his case from Kenya rather than Jamaica—and so America's first black president is, as Powell would have been, a man whose family history lies wholly outside the African-American experience. Of course, the big difference between them with regard to their British roots is that one loves them while the other loathes them:

The Spectator, September 29, 1995

IF YOU'RE NOT excited by the prospect of a black president of the United States look at it this way: if Colin Powell runs and wins, he'll be the first president since the Civil War to be the son of British subjects.

True, most American leaders, from Washington to Clinton, have been of Anglo-Celtic stock, but you have to go back to the first generation of Americans, to the children of George III's rebellious colonists, to find, so to speak, as British a president.

Pick up General Powell's freshly minted bestseller, *My American Journey*, and the first thing you see, even before the preface, are the original British passport photographs of Luther Theophilus Powell and Maud Ariel McKoy, taken just before they left Jamaica for America in the 1920s. They're the earliest pictures General Powell has of his parents. The English, having psychologically written off the Empire, no longer think of Jamaicans as British, but the General does: again and again, in emphasizing his Jamaicanness he also emphasizes Jamaica's Britishness.

Turn the page and the second thing you see is his grandparents' tiny cottage in St. Elizabeth parish. The text—his "American journey"—begins, in fact, with a British journey—to a small Caribbean outpost of Her Majesty's Dominions and an inspection of the Jamaican Defence Force: "All very British and very professional," he writes, approvingly. To the end, Mom and Pop referred to Jamaica as "home," and that's the culture in which young Colin was raised.

In many American memoirs, there's a moment, usually cringe-making for British readers, when the celebrity Yank visits "the old country" and talks about how he feels that he's "coming home." In General Powell's book, the equivalent passages are unusually persuasive and intense. He recalls addressing the British-American Parliamentary Group at Westminster: "The image of my mother and father, born as humble British subjects in a tiny tropical colony, flashed before me, and I wished they could see where fate had taken their son."

He didn't come across their faded British passports until December 1993, just before another trip to London: "The son of those two solemn-faced black immigrants from a tiny British colony was off to be knighted by the Queen of England."

Yet, even as he savors the scene, he's grateful he's only an honorary KCB:

> Had my parents remained British subjects, I would now be "Sir Colin" and Alma "Lady Powell." On the other hand, if my parents had stayed in Jamaica, I can't imagine I would ever have been knighted. If Luther and Ariel had shipped out for Southampton instead of New York City, I might have made sergeant major in a modest British regiment, but not likely British Chief of Defence Staff. I treasure my family's British roots, but I love our America, land of opportunity.

He's right: How many black generals does the British Army have? Powell would probably have left as a disenchanted squaddie and wound up in Brixton competing with John Major for a job on the buses. As National Security Advisor, General Powell meets Sir Charles Powell[1] and is amused to discover that he's actually Sir Charles "Pole": there's quite a lot on pronunciation in the book—the General's family still call him "Collin," in the British style, rather than "Coe-lin," as the American public does, and at the height of the Gulf War he still found time to write to the London *Times* on the matter. But it was easier to Americanize his Christian name than it would have been to Anglicize his surname, easier to be General Coelin Powell than to become General Sir Colin Pole.

Nonetheless, in searching for reasons as to why white America seems prepared to abandon its oldest and most enduring prejudice, you come back, always, to the Britishness of Colin Powell. In rare moments of honesty, whites will tell you that the black leaders blacks like scare the pants off 'em. Watching "The Reverends" Jesse Jackson and Al Sharpton, or Marion Barry, Washington's born-again crackhead mayor, on television, roaring their grievance jingles, whipping up the crowd with hallelujahs and hollerin' and other pseudo-religiosity has most middle-class whites making a mental note to order a new security system: all that shouting, all that noise, all that anger. Colin Powell doesn't shout. He's not a southern Baptist, but an Anglican, a man who likes the King James Bible and the Book of Common Prayer and the quiet dignity of the old liturgy.

When he recalls the way his Gran'ma's English "wedded African cadence to British inflection, the sound of which is still music to my soul," you're reminded that, though he's less musical, less sing-songy, his vocal timbre is closer to the soft-spoken authority of Caribbeans like Michael Manley and Lynden Pindling. Whitey likes Colin Powell because he's the antithesis of the angry, resentful black man full of "black rage"—the deeply ingrained fury at centuries of oppression which ingenious lawyers have managed to get accepted as mitigating circumstances even unto murder.

---

1   Charles Powell was Private Secretary both to Mrs. Thatcher and her successor, John Major.

So why isn't this particular black man full of hate? "For one thing, the British ended slavery in the Caribbean in 1833, well over a generation before America did. And after abolition, the lingering weight of servitude did not persist as long," he writes.

> After the British ended slavery, they told my ancestors that they were now British citizens with all the rights of any subject of the Crown. That was an exaggeration; still, the British did establish good schools and made attendance mandatory. They filled the lower ranks of the civil service with blacks. Consequently, West Indians had an opportunity to develop attitudes of independence, self-responsibility and self-worth. They did not have their individual dignity beaten down for three hundred years.

Most of General Powell's television interviewers haven't read his book, but, if they did, they'd realize their preferred label isn't quite the story: General Powell is certainly black, but is he "African-American"? Even the mandatory sense of rhythm, calypso excepted, has gone missing: "Jamaican miscegenation," he pleads, "had blocked passage of both the basketball and the dance genes in me." It gets worse: his favorite composer is Andrew Lloyd Webber. ("Is this guy even black?" wondered Jesse Jackson.) Commentators have puzzled over why the General commands less support among blacks than whites. For what it's worth, most of those to whom I've spoken seem to regard him as a honkies' patsy. Not to mention that there has never, ever, been a genuine black American called "Colin."

There is in any case a long-standing distrust by African-Americans of West Indians. They call them "black Jews." Caribbean blacks have a tradition of higher achievement in America: in the Fifties, Harry Belafonte became one of the first big-selling album artists; in the Sixties, Sidney Poitier became the first black movie star to bed a white actress in *Guess Who's Coming to Dinner?* The film seems tame stuff now: Hepburn and Tracy are supposedly shocked by their daughter's colored boyfriend, but who wouldn't want Sidney Poitier for a son-in-law? Well, Powell's in the Poitier role, with America happy to be romanced like Katharine Houghton. You can't blame the likes of Reverend Jackson for feeling miffed that, after decades of marches and bussing protests and lunch-counter demos, black America should have foisted on it a man who skipped all that, whose father got off the banana boat and followed the Jews uptown.

"Get over it," Mayor Barry told Washington's stunned white voters on the eve of his re-election, in between thanking the Lord for his deliverance from cocaine. But it's black America that can't get over it, that can't seem to flush the poison of racism from its system. General Powell's trump card is that he never had to get over it—because he grew up within a British West Indian sensibility. That reference to "miscegenation" would, in American terms, usually mean a plantation owner with a penchant for pleasuring himself with his slaves; in Colin Powell's case, it refers to his maternal grandfather, a Scots overseer on a sugar plantation, who took the General's gran'ma as his wife and fathered nine children by her. That would have been illegal in most American states.

As blacks put it, they were specifically excluded from the American Dream: where most immigrants arrived in America to escape oppression, blacks were brought here in order to endure it. There again General Powell is at odds with the broader narrative: "Mom and Pop chose to emigrate to this country for the same reason that Italians, Irish and Hungarians did, to seek better lives for themselves and their children."

Where most blacks have been contemptuous of the myths of Ellis Island, the General is now claiming to be their most potent exemplar: Irving Berlin, Sam Goldwyn, sure, all very impressive, but not till now has a son of that great immigrant tide of the early twentieth century presumed to claim the top prize of all. How odd that it takes a Powell not a Pole, a Scots-Jamaican rather than an Italian or Greek or Russian Jew, to complete that long journey from the Lower East Side to the White House.

So, even as they prepare to break with that long line of Anglo-Celts, Americans re-affirm their nation's cultural and constitutional origins. General

Powell belongs (as I do) to that wider British family beyond its shores, which the United Kingdom, in its morbid Euro-resigned defeatism, has managed to shrug off within the space of a generation. He rightly cites the evenhandedness of British nationality—the first supranational nationality, the first citizenship of the modern era not to be defined by race or ethnicity. But when did you last hear an Englishman sing its praises?

He's wrong on one point, though: had his folks stayed in Jamaica, he might well have been knighted. I think of all those group shots at all those Commonwealth Conferences, of the Queen surrounded by her black and brown prime ministers, a sight the British love to mock. But it shows a grace in transition few other societies have managed, the same grace which distinguishes General Powell and commends him to his fellow Americans, and seems set to make him the unlikeliest imperial bequest to the young republic; the first black president.

If Colin Powell does win, it will be hailed as a victory for black America or a victory for immigrant America, according to taste. But it will also be an unspoken vindication of the virtues of British Imperialism.

THE PEOPLE'S QUEEN

The National Post, November 11, 1999

AS READERS OF Monday's Comment page may have noted, I passed a jolly evening last week at the Elks Lodge in Littleton, New Hampshire, in the company of George W. Bush. Immediately afterwards, I flew to London for dinner at Buckingham Palace.

"Wow! That's quite a week," said my assistant. "One minute, you're with America's next head of state. The next, you're with Britain's and Canada's head of state."

"Or look at it another way," I said. "One minute, I'm at the Elks Lodge in Littleton. The next, I'm at Buckingham Palace."

It would be invidious for me to disclose the reasons for the Palace's call, if only because *The Financial Post*'s Linda McQuaig has already complained that I sound more like something from *Monarchy* than a Canadian newspaper column. But, at the risk of breaching the confidence of a private occasion, here's an exchange that deserves to make it into the public prints:

One of my fellow guests at the Palace, remarking on the lack of agricultural workers in Britain, said that he now brought in young Australians and South Africans, who were able to make ninety to a hundred pounds a day (about sixty thousand dollars a year) picking onions.

"Crying all the way to the bank?" said the Duke of Edinburgh.

The next day, Australians went to the polls for their referendum on whether to dump the monarchy. The Queen won. Australia, we'd been told, wanted an elected head of state, and now it's got one. Yet, rather than respect the people's verdict, the proponents of a republic flew into a rage. Aussies often refer to the English as "whinging Poms," but you've never seen anyone whinge like the sore losers on the republican side when the electorate declined to agree with them.

The overwhelmingly republican press took defeat particularly hard: It seems Australians do resent a remote autocratic foreigner from thousands of miles away running the place and lording it over them. Unfortunately, it turned out to be Rupert Murdoch rather than Elizabeth Windsor. The media mogul overplayed his hand by declaring on his front page that he'd lived under three different systems (Aussie, British, American) and republics were best. John Howard, the Prime Minister, reminded Mr. Murdoch that he was now a U.S. citizen and, in an unguarded moment, apparently suggested that he "f**k off." Even after the republican side had conceded, the Murdoch press seemed reluctant to accept the actual result: "Queen Hurt by No Vote Despite Win" was the headline on *The Sunday Times* of London. Mr. Murdoch's poodle, anxious to please, began his report as follows: "The Queen was hurt and disappointed by the strength of republican feeling in Australia...."

Come again? Her Majesty was "hurt and disappointed"? How does the *Times* hack know? He was down the pub with her? She'd called him at home, choked up with tears, to confide her innermost feelings? As the only journalist on the planet present at Buckingham Palace on the eve of the big vote, I think I can speak with complete authority on this matter when I say I haven't a clue as to the Royal Family's state of mind and private thoughts. I kept trying to slip Australia into the conversation, right up to the end when, as the Duke of Edinburgh was showing me the door and my carriage was about to turn back into a pumpkin, I opined that I thought the 1901 Australian constitution was rather better than the 1867 Canadian one. "Hmm," he said, and made some sharp observations about the differences between the two forms of federalism. But, as to how they feel about losing their antipodean throne, who knows?

Still, if I had to guess, "crying all the way to the bank" isn't a bad way to put it. Like Liberace, the Queen may have been "hurt" by some of the beastly things that have been said about her; but, on the big day, she came through: Her electoral validation may be a long way from the divine right of kings, but it's also useful ammunition against careless post-monarchists in her realms. The snubbed Australian media keep harping on about the electoral divide—between young upscale educated urban republicans and old poor rube hick monarchists—but the interesting aspect of the royalist victory is how widespread it was: On Tuesday, it emerged that, as votes continued to be counted, the sole pro-republican state—Victoria—had tipped back to the Queen's side. The only two large polling centers to plump for the republican cause were the national capital, Canberra—like Ottawa, a company town where the company happens to be big government—and London, England, where 60 percent of expats are supposed to have voted to dump the Crown. If the Republic of Oz needs the votes of Earl's Court bedsits, it's in bigger trouble than it knows.

For Canadian republicans, the Australian referendum has several lessons. First, it's a rebuke to the "inevitabilist" theory of history. Secondly, it's a telling defeat for the "minimalist" republic—the idea that you simply change the Governor-General's title to President, and life goes on as before. The defeated republican forces now say that next time the question should simply ask whether Australians want a republic per se and leave it until later to work out whether it's going to be the Václav Havel model or the Saddam Hussein model. The devil is in the details—and to demand that the electorate reject an actual specific monarchy in favor of a vague, unspecified republic is as absurd as asking them to vote for a monarchy and assuring them you'll let 'em know afterwards whether they'll be getting Elizabeth II, Emperor Bokassa, or Mad King Ludwig of Bavaria.

Some republicans who support a directly elected president recognized this and joined forces with monarchists to defeat the system on offer: a republic whose head of state would be decided by the politicians. The official republican movement mocked their more principled colleagues for forming an "incoherent" and "contradictory" alliance with Good Queen Bess's diehard forelock-tuggers. In fact, there's nothing incoherent and contradictory about it. This was an important victory for western society's real silent majority: those people who dissent from the notion that career politicians should carve up all the most visible offices of state for themselves. Some of this silent majority are monarchists; some believe in a directly elected president; a large proportion are just average contented folks who aren't obsessed about politics. But they have far more to bind them to each other than they do to the establishment republicans who believe that the presidency should be just one more gift in the ruling party's box of baubles. If Australian voters tell us anything, it's that a political state isn't enough. At heart, most of us are romantic enough to demand more—either the mystique of monarchy or the rawer form of democratic politics in which a man must embark on his campaign to win the highest prize by pressing the flesh in the Elks Lodge. Constitutional monarchy and a U.S.-style presidency don't have much in common—except insofar as, either way, you find yourself sitting next to me come early November—but both speak to something larger in a nation's sense of itself.

For my own part, I'd argue that the Royal Family comes into contact with a far wider range of ordinary Canadians than the Liberal cabinet does. By "wide range of ordinary Canadians," I mean, of course, me: I've been to dinner at the Palace, whereas that deadbeat PM at Sussex Drive[1] has never once invited me over. His grudging defense of the Crown was typical. What's extraordinary about the Australian vote was that Her Majesty won not just against the avowed republicans but also against her supposed defenders, a far more slippery crowd. For decades, Jean Chrétien and his Commonwealth confrères have been republicanizing their countries by stealth—here, a Royal crest off a mailbox; there, a forgotten politician to replace her on a banknote— until the visible symbols of the monarchy are removed from daily life. Her Majesty should take courage from her victory in Australia and decline to let herself be inched off the throne by the governing elite: There would be no better time for the Queen to embark on a campaign to bypass the Trojan horses in her various viceregal branch offices and connect directly with ordinary people throughout her realms. She won down under, she could win here, and she should let M. Chrétien know that she knows. To paraphrase Tony Blair, she is the People's Queen now.

---

1   24 Sussex Drive is the official residence of Her Majesty's Canadian Prime Minister, at that time Jean Chrétien.

CELEBRITY CAESAR

Syndicated column, June 9, 2012

QUEEN ELIZABETH II celebrated her Diamond Jubilee a few days ago—that's sixty years on the throne. Just to put it in perspective, she's been queen since Harry S. Truman was president. For the most part, her jubilee has been a huge success, save for a few churlish republicans in various corners of Her Majesty's realms from London to Toronto to Sydney pointing out how absurd it is for grown citizens to be fawning over a distant head of state who lives in a fabulous, glittering cocoon entirely disconnected from ordinary life.

Which brings us to President Obama.

Last week, the republic's citizen-president passed among his fellow Americans. Where? Cleveland? Dubuque? Presque Isle, Maine? No, Beverly Hills. These days, it's pretty much always Beverly Hills or Manhattan, because that's where the money is. That's the Green Zone, and you losers are outside it. Appearing at an Obama fundraiser at the home of *Glee* creator Ryan Murphy and his "fiancé" David Miller, the President, reasonably enough, had difficulty distinguishing one A-list Hollywood summit from another. "I just came from a wonderful event over at the Wilshire or the Hilton—I'm not sure which," said Obama, "because you go through the kitchens of all these places and so you never are quite sure where you are."

Ah, the burdens of stardom. The old celebrities-have-to-enter-through-the-kitchen line. The last time I heard that was a couple of decades back in London when someone was commiserating with Sinatra on having to be ushered in through the back. Frank brushed it aside. We were at the Savoy, or maybe the Waldorf. I can't remember, and I came in through the front door. Oddly enough, the Queen enters hotels through the lobby. So do Prince William and his lovely bride. A month ago, they stayed at a pub in Suffolk for a friend's wedding, and came in through the same door as mere mortals. Imagine that!

So far this year, President Obama has been to three times as many fundraisers as President Bush had attended by this point in the 2004 campaign. This is what *The New York Post* calls his "torrid pace," although judging from those remarks in California he's about as torrid as an overworked gigolo staggering punchily through the last mambo of the evening. According to Brendan J. Doherty's forthcoming book, *The Rise of the President's Permanent Campaign*, Obama has held more fundraisers than the previous five presidents' reelection campaigns combined.

This is all he does now. But hey, unlike those inbred monarchies with their dukes and marquesses and whatnot, at least he gets out among the masses. Why, in a typical week, you'll find him at a fundraiser at George Clooney's home in Los Angeles with Barbra Streisand and Salma Hayek. These are people who are in touch with the needs of ordinary Americans because they have played ordinary Americans in several of their movies. And then only four days later the President was in New York for a fundraiser hosted by Ricky Martin, the only man on the planet whose evolution on gayness took longer than Obama's. It's true that moneyed celebrities in, say, Pocatello or Tuscaloosa have not been able to tempt the president to hold a lavish fundraiser in Idaho or Alabama, but he does fly over them once in a while. Why, only a week ago, he was on Air Force One accompanied by Jon Bon Jovi en route to a fundraiser called *Barack on Broadway*.

Any American can attend an Obama event for a donation of a mere $35,800—the cost of the fundraiser hosted by DreamWorks honcho Jeffrey Katzenberg, and the one hosted by Facebook's Sheryl Sandberg, and the one hosted by Will Smith and Jada Pinkett, and the one hosted by Melanie Griffith and Antonio Banderas, and the one hosted by Crosby, Stills, and Nash. Thirty-five thousand eight hundred dollars is a curiously non-round figure. Perhaps the ticket cost is thirty-six thousand, but under Obamacare there's a two-hundred-dollar co-pay. Those of us who grew up in hidebound, class-ridden monarchies are familiar with the old proverb that a cat can look at a king. But in America only a cool cat can look at the king.

However, there are some cheap seats available. A year and a half ago, big-money Democrats in Rhode Island paid $7,500 per person for the privilege of having dinner with President Obama at a private home in Providence. He showed up for twenty minutes and then said he couldn't stay for dinner. "I've got to go home to walk the dog and scoop the poop," he told them, because when you've paid seven-and-a-half grand for dinner nothing puts you in the mood to eat like a guy talking about canine fecal matter. And, having done the poop gag, the President upped and exited, and left bigshot Dems to pass the evening talking to the guy from across the street. But you've got to admit that's a memorable night out: $7,500 for Dinner with Obama* (*dinner with Obama not included).

And here's an even better deal, for those who, despite the roaring economy, can't afford even $7,500 for non-dinner with Obama: The President of the United States is raffling himself off! For the cost of a three-dollar non-refundable online application processing fee, you and your loved one can have your names put in a large presidential hat from which the FBI background-check team will pluck two to be ushered into the presence of their humble citizen-executive. How great is that? Somewhere across the fruited plain, a common-or-garden non-celebrity will win the opportunity to attend an Obama fundraiser at the home of *Sex and the City* star Sarah Jessica Parker, co-hosted by *Vogue* editor Anna Wintour, the British-born inspiration for the movie *The Devil Wears Prada*. I wish this were a parody, but I'm not that good. But I'm sure Sarah Jessica and Anna will treat you just like any other minor celebrity they've accidentally been seated next to due to a hideous *faux pas* in placement, even if you do dip the wrong end of the arugula in the *amuse-bouche*.

If you're wondering who Anna Wintour is, boy, what a schlub you are: She's renowned throughout the fashion world for her scary bangs. I'm referring to her hair, not to the last sound Osama bin Laden heard as the bullet headed toward his eye socket on the personal orders of the President, in case you've forgotten. But that's the kind of inside tidbit you'll be getting, as the commander-in-chief leaks highly classified national security details to you over the zebra mussel in a Eurasian-milfoil coulis. For a donation of $35,800, he'll pose with you in a Seal Team Six uniform with one foot on Osama's corpse (played by Harry Reid). For a donation of $46,800, he'll send an unmanned drone to hover amusingly over your sister-in-law's house. For a donation of $77,800, he'll install you as the next president-for-life of Syria (liability waiver required). For a donation of $159,800, he'll take you into Sarah Jessica's guest bedroom and give you the full 007 while Carly Simon sings "Nobody Does It Better."

There are monarchies and republics aplenty, but there's only one 24/7 celebrity fundraising presidency. If it's Tuesday, it must be Kim Cattrall, or Hootie and the Blowfish, or Laverne and Shirley, or the ShamWow guy.... I wonder if the Queen ever marvels at the transformation of the American presidency since her time with Truman. As he might have advised her, if you can't stand the klieg-light heat of Obama's celebrity, stay out of the Beverly Wilshire kitchen.

THE FOOTSTOOLS OF CAMELOT

National Review, October 5, 2009

I WAS OVERSEAS when Senator Edward Kennedy died, and a European reporter asked me what my "most vivid memory" of the great man was. I didn't like to say, because it didn't seem quite the appropriate occasion. But my only close encounter with the Lion of the Senate was many years ago at Logan Airport late one night. A handful of us, tired and bedraggled, were standing on the water shuttle waiting to be ferried across the harbor to downtown Boston. A sixth gentleman hopped aboard, wearing the dark-suited garb of the advance man, and had a word in a crew-member's ear, and so we waited, and waited, in the chilly Atlantic air, wondering which eminence was the cause of our delay. And suddenly there he was on the quay, looming out of the fog. He stepped aboard. The small launch lurched and rocked, waves splashed the deck, luggage danced in the air, and the five of us all grabbed for whatever rail was to hand as the realization dawned that we'd been signed up for a watery excursion with Senator Kennedy.

This was Ted at his most ravaged, big and bloated, before his new wife (also in attendance) had had a chance to get his excesses under control. One of the recurring refrains of the weeks of eulogies was his apparently amazing affinity for "ordinary people," as if this is now in itself an impressive achievement for a United States senator, who after all can't be expected to have the same careless ease with the common run of humanity as, say, one of the more inbred late Ottoman sultans. But Ted, we were assured, was great with "ordinary people." Not that night, he wasn't. He stood in the center and glanced at us, awkwardly, in the way of celebrities who find themselves outside their comfort zone, and aren't sure the "ordinary people" know quite what the rules are. I assumed he'd offer a casual, "Hey, sorry for keeping you waiting," and then the roar of the motor would have prevented further conversation. But he said nothing, which, given that the other passengers were his constituents, struck me as a little odd.

Years later, I saw him again, in action at the Senate. Well, not in "action." It was the impeachment trial of President Clinton, and for some reason the Emirs of Incumbistan had been prevailed upon to come in on a Saturday for the proceedings. Under the convoluted trial procedures, members of the Senate had to submit questions to their respective party leaders, who then passed them to the Chief Justice, who then read them out. So the pages were run off their feet ferrying lethal interjections from lead Democrat saboteurs Tom Harkin and Patrick Leahy up to the Minority Leader Tom Daschle. The page had barely dropped off Senator Harkin's question when the wheezing, heaving senator from Massachusetts called him over. From up in the gallery, I thought, "Ah-ha!" I was there to cover the trial for various British and Commonwealth newspapers, and, as Ted Kennedy's the only senator any foreigners have heard of, his contribution to date had been disappointing: He had spluttered to life in the preceding weeks only to cough Mount St. Helens–scale eruptions across the chamber. He declined to cover his coughs. Indeed, he gave the vague sense of assuming that's what the rest of the Democrat caucus was there for. I remember Blanche Lincoln shooting him a disapproving look after one Niagara of saliva came her way.

So, on this Saturday afternoon, his unexpected contribution to the trial would clearly be a major part of my coverage. What devastating interjection, I wondered, would he be springing on the prosecutors? The page padded silently over to the senator's seat in the back. Ted whispered to him, and the page made his way to the end of the row, then worked his way along the row in front, squeezing past senators until he was directly facing Ted's desk. He then dropped to his knees—which, as it turned out, was the nearest the Clinton trial would ever get to a re-staging of the acts at issue. But instead he leaned under the desk and adjusted Ted's footrest by an inch and a half. The senior senator from Massachusetts seemed satisfied, and the page was squeezing his way back past the other senators when Ted motioned him to return. Ignoring a frantic Pat Leahy waving some critical note for Tom Daschle, the page reversed course, squeezed past Senator Graham of Florida yet again and dropped to his knees to move Ted's footrest another smidgeonette. He then rushed off to pick up Senator Leahy's note. Senator Kennedy didn't thank him.

I have been received at Buckingham Palace, and over the years I've also met the Queen of Spain, the Queen of the Netherlands, and various other Royal personages. And I can't imagine any of them demanding of their footmen what Ted Kennedy did. But then they're only Euro royalty, not Massachusetts royalty. "At the end of the day," said Evan Bayh of his colleague, "he cared most about the things that matter to ordinary people." This was, observed many a eulogist, his penance for Chappaquiddick and Mary Jo Kopechne—or, as the Aussie *Daily Telegraph*'s Tim Blair put it, "She died so that the Food Allergen Labeling and Consumer Protection Act might live." This, of course, is the classic trade-off of monarchical societies throughout the ages: The sovereign's industrial-scale exercise of his droit du seigneur with whatever comely serving wench crosses his path is mitigated by his paternalistic compassion toward the humblest of his subjects.

Strange how the monarchical urge persists even in a republic two-and-a-third centuries old.

Time to mothball the Camelot footstools? I hope so.

VIII

SEPTEMBER 12

HISTORY'S CALLING
CARD

The Daily Telegraph, September 22, 2001

ON WEDNESDAY I FINALLY SAW "Ground Zero." For those of us who've watched the endless TV replays of that second plane slamming into the tower again and again and again, what's most chilling about the scene in real life is how settled, how established it seems. I was in Oklahoma City six years ago, and in the days afterwards the Murrah Building looked like what it was: a big office block with a huge hole in it, something familiar that's been ruptured. But here you can no longer discern what the normality was before it got disrupted. It looks, in our terms, like a huge version of a New Jersey landfill that's gotten a little out of hand. Or, in a broader historical context, like the latter stages of the Germans' long siege of Stalingrad. Not the opening rounds of a first attack, but the vast accumulated detritus of a long, ongoing war—which, in a sense, is what it is. People are busy at the site, but the urgency has gone. The thousands of flyers posted by wives, husbands, parents, and children are still up, but the word "MISSING" has slid from a long shot to a euphemism.

It impressed the celebrated German composer Karlheinz Stockhausen, who told a radio interviewer the other day that the destruction of the World Trade Center was "the greatest work of art ever." I'm reminded of the late Sir Thomas Beecham when asked if he'd ever played any Stockhausen: "No," he said. "But I once stepped in some." Last week, Stockhausen stepped in his own.

With Oklahoma City I remember the smell of the bodies. At Ground Zero's burial mound the devastation is so total that there are no bodies to smell. Thousands of people lie under there, all but atomized by their killers and all but forgotten by the appeasing left. At San Francisco's service of remembrance for its dead this week, Amos Brown, representing the city's Board of Supervisors, used the occasion to launch into an examination of the "root causes" of the regrettable incident. "America, what did you do," he wailed, "in Africa, where bombs are still blasting? America, what did you do in the global warming conference when you did not embrace the smaller nations? America, what did you do two weeks ago when I stood at the world conference on racism, when you wouldn't show up?" The Bay Area lefties roared their approval.

Paul Holm, the partner of Mark Bingham, a gay six-foot, five-inch rugby jock who died on Flight 93, felt differently. He walked up to Senator Dianne Feinstein and said sadly, "This was supposed to be a memorial service." Then he quit the stage. Mark Bingham died heroically, and all the City of San Francisco can do is denigrate the cause and the nation for which he gave his life.

The totalitarian left has finally found its perfect soul mate. With Communism, the excuse was always that, whatever the practical difficulties on the ground, it retained its theoretical idealism. But the Taliban and Osama bin Laden are perfectly upfront: they're openly racist; they'd strip Dianne Feinstein of her senatorship and make her a mere chattel; they'd execute Paul Holm for being gay, by building a wall and then crushing him under it. True, I don't know their position on global warming, but it doesn't seem to be a priority.

A few blocks north of Ground Zero, I dined with some friends. "This is the biggest event in my life," said one. "Bigger than the death of Kennedy." Even the Pearl Harbor comparison doesn't seem quite right. I wonder if we aren't revisiting August 1914, when the Archduke Franz Ferdinand was assassinated in Sarajevo. It seemed a simple war: the British Tommies marching off were told it would all be over by Christmas, as today *Slate*'s Mickey Kaus is confident the World Trade Center will be off the front pages by Thanksgiving. By the time the Great War was really over, four of the world's great powers lay shattered—the German, Austrian, Russian, and Turkish Empires, all gone and so easily, though who would have predicted it in that last Edwardian summer? We don't know what this latest thread of history will unravel. But we should at least understand the stakes.

THE BRUTAL AFGHAN WINTER

The National Post, January 7, 2002

WHATEVER HAPPENED TO the "brutal Afghan winter"? It was "fast approaching" back in late September, and apparently it's still "fast approaching" today. "Winter is fast, fast approaching," reported ABC's *Nightline* on September 26.

Two weeks on, New York's *Daily News* announced that, "realistically, U.S. forces have a window of two or three weeks before the brutal Afghan winter begins to foreclose options."

Two or three weeks passed and the brutal Afghan winter's relentless approach showed no sign of letting up. "A clock is ticking," declared *The Oregonian* on October 24. "The harsh Afghan winter is approaching."

The clock ticked on. On November 8 NBC's Tom Brokaw alerted viewers to the perils posed by "a rapidly approaching winter." "They expect the conditions to deteriorate rapidly as the brutal winter soon sets in," wrote *Newsday*'s Deborah Barfield on November 11, updating her earlier sighting of "the typically brutal winter approaching" a month earlier on October 9.

Another month ticked on, and the brutal winter carried on brutally approaching. "Winter is approaching fast," said Thomas McDermott, Unicef's Regional Director, on December 9. "With winter fast approaching, women wait in line for blankets," *The Los Angeles Times* confirmed, after the clock had ticked leisurely on a couple more days.

And not just any old approaching winter, but the "brutal Afghan winter," according to ABC, NBC, National Public Radio, *The Boston Globe*, Associated Press, Agence France-Presse, etc. "Former Canadian Foreign Minister Lloyd Axworthy is in Pakistan"—in case you were wondering—"to find out how to speed up aid deliveries before the brutal Afghan winter sets in," reported the

BBC in November. "The temperature can drop to 50 below, so cold that eyelids crust and saliva turns to sludge in the mouth," said Tom Ifield of Knight-Ridder Newspapers.

Yesterday, it was 55 and clear in Kandahar and Herat. Ghurian checked in at 55, with 62 predicted for tomorrow. Fifty-seven and sunny in Bost and Laskar, with 64 expected on Thursday. In Kabul, it was 55, though with the windchill factored in it was only—let me see now—54.

Meanwhile, in Toronto it's 28, New York 38. Overseas? Belfast and Glasgow report 46, London 44, Birmingham and Manchester 42. If those Afghan refugees clogging up the French end of the Channel Tunnel ever make it through to Dover, they face a gruelling battle for survival against the horrors of the brutal British winter.

Just under four months ago, when the doom-mongers first started alerting us to the "fast approaching" "brutal Afghan winter," it was 70 degrees and I was sitting here in shorts and T-shirt. Today, in my corner of Quebec, the daytime high is 21, the predicted overnight low is 5 degrees, and tomorrow we'll be lucky to hit 14. For Saturday, they're predicting 3 degrees. Three Fahrenheit is, as the metrically inclined would say, minus 16 Celsius. So you'll understand my amusement at the *Sunday Telegraph* headline of October 21: "British Unit Prepares to Defy Extremes of the Afghan Winter / Crack Troops Will Have to Work in Temperatures as Low as -20C."

Big deal. Crack columnist has to work in temperatures as low as -16C. And for my neck of the woods, this is a very mild winter.

Now pedants will point out that there are one or two brisk parts of the Hindu Kush. On top of Mount Sikaram, at 15,620 feet the highest elevation in Afghanistan's White Mountains, it would no doubt freeze the proverbial knackers off a brass monkey. Similarly, on top of Mount Washington, highest elevation in New Hampshire's White Mountains, it's -15 with the wind chill, while down in the state capital of Concord it's a balmy 36. That's why no one except a couple of meteorologist types lives on top of Mount Washington, but thousands do down in Concord. Amazingly, despite the vast cultural differences, the same patterns of population dispersal prevail in Afghanistan. Up on Mount Sikaram, a convenient eight-day donkey-ride to the nearest 7-Eleven, the only guys interested in buying a ski condo are Osama and Mullah Omar. Al-Qaeda operatives aside, the overwhelming majority of the Afghan population live in towns currently enjoying temperatures most Canadians won't see for another three or four months.

So where did this "brutal Afghan winter" business come from? It came, pre-eminently, from spokespersons for the relief agencies. There are some special-interest groups—the National Rifle Association, Right to Life—whose press releases get dismissed by the media as propaganda, and others—environmental groups, for example—whose every claim is taken at face value. Into this last happy category fall the "humanitarian lobby." Throughout the rhetorically brutal autumn, they bombarded us:

> Predicting even more desperate times for millions of Afghans, international relief groups and federal humanitarian aid officials are scrambling to get food and medical supplies into a country they say is on the verge of famine.... They expect the conditions to deteriorate rapidly as the brutal winter sets in.

Gosh.

> The UN Children's Fund estimated that as many as 100,000 Afghan children could die of cold, disease and hunger within weeks if vital aid did not reach them.

Oh, my.

> The situation in Afghanistan is deteriorating rapidly, international aid agencies say, and they are predicting the worst humanitarian crisis ever.

The aid agencies, you'll recall, campaigned aggressively for a "bombing pause" during Ramadan. This would have enabled them to truck some food convoys through the mountains from Pakistan. These routes get snowbound and become impassable, and that's really the only salient fact about the "brutal Afghan winter."

Why are the roads to Pakistan more important than the roads to Iran, Turkmenistan, Uzbekistan, and Tajikistan? Because Pakistan, being Afghanistan's most westernized neighbor, is where the western aid agencies are based. These are the fellows like my old chum from *The Independent* in London, Alex Renton. Alex, the son of former Tory minister Lord Renton, is now an Oxfam big shot in the region. A lot of the other humanitarian coves running around out there are also English boarding-school boys, chaps with names like Rupert and Sebastian on a benign version of the journey of self-discovery that that Taliban guy from Marin County went on. I'm sure they're all very well-intentioned, but when they start shrieking about the fast approaching brutal Afghan winter and the imminent deaths of millions, what they're mainly doing is protesting that the American military action is disrupting their act.

Here's how you feed Afghanistan: You can get Rupert and Sebastian to load up the trucks in Peshawar and drive through to Kabul, where what isn't stolen by the Taliban can be distributed to the people. Or you can bomb the Taliban, drive them from office, put a non-deranged administration in place, re-open the year-round road-and-rail bridge to Uzbekistan, speed up construction on a second Uzbek bridge, and get air convoys to cover the places roads can't reach. In the seven weeks since the fall of Kabul, all this has happened. The millions who are supposed to be dying aren't. The hundred thousand child corpses are alive and kicking. The UN says all the supplies it needs to feed Afghanistan are now getting through.

Here's what would have happened had the aid agencies got their way and pressured the U.S. into a bombing pause: many more Afghans would have starved to death, the Taliban would have been secured in power at least for another few months and perhaps indefinitely, but Rupert and Sebastian would have enjoyed the stage-heroic frisson of bouncing along in the truck to Jalala-bad. That seems a high price for the Afghan people to pay. One expects a certain amount of reflexive anti-Americanism from these "humanitarian" types, but in the brutal Afghan fall they went too far: they ought at least to be big enough to admit they were wrong and be grateful the Pentagon ignored their bleatings.

Instead, they seem a little touchy about the fact that among the first food supplies to get through was a fresh supply of egg on their faces. When Axworthy and other self-proclaimed "humanitarians" start droning on next month about starving children in Iraq, always remember the lesson of Afghanistan: a bombing pause is not as "humanitarian" as a bomb. I would urge readers to be highly selective about supporting aid agencies who operate under tyrannies. Better yet, go see for yourself: after all, for Canadians, there's no better time than now to spend a sultry two weeks in Kabul enjoying the charms of the brutal Afghan winter.

✳   ✳   ✳

By the spring of 2014, U.S. troops had been in Afghanistan for thirteen "brutal Afghan winters." Yet after the first, we never heard the phrase ever again. The problem in Afghanistan was never the weather.

THE BRUTAL CUBAN WINTER

The Spectator, January 26, 2002

NOT FAR FROM ME, in the small Coos County, New Hampshire, town of Stark, is an old German POW camp. Camp Stark was basically a logging camp with barbed wire. With so many of its men in uniform overseas, the Brown Paper Company agreed to take German prisoners in order to keep its forestry operations going. The detainees arrived in the depths of a White Mountains winter and were not impressed by the huts. There were wire mesh screens on the insides of the windows, so that even when you opened them up you couldn't stick your hand out. The Germans pointed out that this was in contravention of the internationally agreed rules on prisoner accommodation, and insisted that the screens be removed immediately.

The camp guards looked at each other, shrugged, and said, "Sure, if that's what you want." The deep winter snows melted, and eventually it was safe to open the windows. A week later, Black Fly Season arrived—the black fly isn't New Hampshire's state animal but it ought to be—and thousands of the little fellers swarmed in through those big inviting apertures to chow down on all that good Aryan blood. There was a reason for the screens.

I mention this to make two points: (1) there are things that are unforeseen by international conventions, and (2) let's talk about the weather. The British, if you'll forgive a gratuitous racist generalization, seem to be remarkably obtuse about matters meteorological. Perhaps this is a natural consequence of living in a country where it's 54 and overcast all summer and 53 and overcast all winter, and the only divergence from that temperate constancy was missed entirely by your famous Mr. Fish.[1] But at least in the old days Britons were ignorant but fearless: you were the mad dogs and Englishmen out in the midday sun. Now, after four months of cowering in fear at the impending arrival of the entirely mythical "brutal Afghan winter"—currently 55 and sunny in Kandahar—Fleet Street's media doom-mongers have moved seamlessly on to the horrors of the brutal Cuban winter: oh my God, how will these poor al-Qaeda boys—you know, the ones who could supposedly hole up in the Khyber Pass eating scorpions all winter making a fool of those Yank ignoramuses—how will these fearsome warriors survive the Caribbean nights and the hordes of malaria-infested mosquitoes?

And this time it's not just the usual America haters at *The Guardian* and the BBC but the likes of Alice Thomson, Stephen Glover, Alasdair Palmer, Matthew Parris, my most esteemed *Telegraph* and *Speccie* colleagues: "They are kept in cramped outdoor cages, open to the elements and the attentions of possibly malarial mosquitoes," notes Mr. Glover. "I mind the shark cages, with their concrete floors open to the elements and the 24-hour halogen flood lights, left near mosquito-infested swamps, so the prisoners can catch malaria when some already have tuberculosis," frets Miss Thomson.

I don't know whether Alice or Stephen has ever been to Disney World. Doesn't sound quite their bag, but you never know. Disney World is in the middle of a swamp, and, if you use the employees' exit and turn right rather than left and then on to the dirt track and into the swampy groves you'll find within minutes the windscreen's full of squished, bloody bugs. Yet when you're on the other side of the fence waiting in the hot sun for two hours to go on a sixty-second ride, there are, amazingly, no bugs. Find me a mosquito in Disney World and I'll guarantee you it's an animatronic attraction. A local girl up here

---

1 Michael Fish is a longtime British telly weatherman, famous for his forecast of October 15, 1987: "A woman rang the BBC and said she heard there was a hurricane on the way," he chortled. "Don't worry, there isn't!" A couple of hours later, the worst storm in three centuries hit southern England and killed nineteen people.

ran off to Florida and hooked up with some guy who worked for the Mouse. At their Disney wedding, he told me that, among his responsibilities, he was part of the crew who bombed the perimeter at the crack of dawn each day with industrial-strength bug spray. The same procedure is being carried out at Guantanamo: the camp is sprayed with mosquito repellent.

As for malaria, that seems to have been conjured entirely out of Miss Thomson's head. There is no malaria in Cuba. None. Risk of contracting malaria: Zero percent. And before you Fidel groupies start putting that down to the wonders of the Cuban health system, do you know who eliminated malaria from the island? The United States Army, after the Spanish-American War and by draining swamps and introducing bed netting and (here they come again) window screens.

So there's no malaria, and a tiny risk of mosquitoes. As for the "cramped outdoor cages," they are, in fact, the factory version of Bloody Mary's exotic hut on the tropic isle of Bali Hai in the current West End production of *South Pacific*. They've got roofs, with eight-foot ceilings—not exactly a Kensington drawing room, but hardly "cramped." As for those concrete floors Alice disdains, all I can say is that a few years back I jacked up my old barn and poured a concrete foundation, and there are truly few more pleasurable sensations on a hot summer's day than putting one's bare feet on cold, shaded concrete. So these "shark cages" have sloped roofs and cool floors. Granted, they have no walls. If they did, they'd be sweatboxes that would likely kill you—unless, of course, you installed air-conditioning, which, as we know, you British types find frightfully vulgar.

Nonetheless, according to an ITN report carried on PBS over here, these poor prisoners will have to "endure the searing heat." Actually, these beach huts are perfectly designed for one of the most agreeable climates on earth— a daytime high in the mid-eighties and an overnight low in the low seventies, with a wafting breeze caressing one's cheek. My advice to Fleet Street is to steer clear of weather for the rest of the war. The merest nudge of the thermostat is enough to send excitable reporters rocketing from one extreme to the other, like the old cartoon of the shower faucet with only the tiniest calibration between "Scalding" and "Freezing." Kabul in the sixties is the "brutal winter," Cuba in the low seventies is the "searing heat."

So take it from me, Don Rumsfeld's Club Fed huts are cool in the day and balmy at night. They're a lot more comfortable than the windowless "concrete coffins" of Belmarsh in which your terrorist suspects are banged up twenty-two hours a day. True, it's a shame they have to have wraparound wire mesh to spoil the view, and there's no banana daiquiris from room service, but the idea is (in case you've forgotten) that they're meant to be prisoners. And, unlike the three-to-a-cell arrangements in, say, Barlinnie, the Talibannies have a room of their own, so they won't be taking it up the keister from Butch every night. They get three square meals a day, thrice-daily opportunities for showers, calls to prayer, copies of the Koran, a prayer mat—all part of a regime *The Mirror* calls "a sick attempt to appeal to the worst redneck prejudices."

It's correct that, for hygiene purposes, they were shaved, which was "culturally inappropriate." But then, if the U.S. wanted to be culturally appropriate, they'd herd 'em onto a soccer pitch and stone 'em to death as half-time entertainment. As to whether or not they are prisoners of war, there is a legitimate difference of opinion on their status: you can't ask them for name, rank, and serial number, because the last two they lack and, if Richard Reid is anything to go by, they keep a handy stack of spare monikers. This is new territory. But surely the Fleet Street whingers must know, if only from the testimony of their fellow Britons among the inmates, that there is no "torture" (*The Mail on Sunday*), not even by the weather.

In fairness, instead of coasting on non-existent diseases and wild guesses at the weather, the always elegant Matthew Parris at least attempted to expand Guantanamo into a general thesis. "We seek to project the message that there are rules to which all nations are subject," he wrote in *The Times*. "America has a simpler message: kill Americans, and you're dead meat."

This caused endless amusement over here. As the Internet wag Steven den Beste commented, "By George, I think he's got it!"

"America has simple gods and likes to keep her satan simple, too," Mr. Parris continued. "In Salem it was once witches. In Senator Joe McCarthy's heyday it was Commies. Now it is al-Qa'eda."

Just for the record, the Salem witch trials were conducted not by citizens of the United States but by British subjects. As for Senator McCarthy's heyday, well, there were a lot of Commies around: in short order, they'd seized half of Europe, neutered much of what was left, and had become the dominant influence on the Third World's political class. Suppose America had followed the rest of the west and elected a détente sophisticate like Helmut Schmidt or Pierre Trudeau, whose first act upon retirement from office was to take his young sons to see Siberia because "that was where the future was being made"—in 1984! The world would be very different today, and not to my liking. The west won't work if every country's Canada and every leader's Trudeau. The only thing that enables Belgium to be Belgium and Norway to be Norway and Britain to be Britain is the fact that America's America—for all the reasons my *Spectator* colleagues deplore.

THE LIMITS

National Review, December 30, 2008

MY PERSONAL CHRONOLOGY of the Bush years is simple enough:

For the first eight months, I did shtick. We all did. In April of 2001, he went to Quebec for the Summit of the Americas and was greeted by the then Canadian Prime Minister, whose name escapes me, as I trust it does you. "Bienvenue," he said to Dubya. "That means 'Welcome.'" Ha-ha. What fun we had. There were the usual riots, of course, led by that French farmer famous for destroying his local McDonald's on the grounds that "the free market is violence." He was accompanied by various weekending trustafarians who'd motored up from the Ivy League, plus large numbers of Canadian students who'd had their exams postponed and were given three hundred thousand dollars of taxpayers' money in order to enable them to get to Quebec City and smash the place up. I forget what the Summit was about, although I had plenty of one-on-one face-time with lonely Latin American foreign ministers who couldn't find anyone else to talk to, and I may even have filed a couple of widely unread thumbsuckers on the lines of: "The Guatemalan Deputy Trade Minister gets it. Why don't we?" In the end, the Summit wasn't really "about" anything. Not a lot was in those days.

Then came a Tuesday morning in September. And "Steyn butched up," as a Canadian columnist recently put it. There was a lot of that about. Even mild-mannered coves like the State Department's Richard Armitage were getting General Musharraf on the phone and threatening to bomb his country back to the Stone Age. The Taliban fell, and Mullah Omar scuttled out of town, hitching up his skirts and pausing only to put a false beard over his real beard, with no time to pack even the Rod Stewart cassettes subsequently found in the compound of the man who famously banned music throughout the land. (The old "Do Ya Think I'm Sexy?" Rod, not the namby-pamby *Rod*

Stewart Slays the Great American Songbook stuff.) When the troops got to Tora Bora, they discovered our enemies really did live in caves. And not the Bond-villain underground lairs the CNN graphics department mocked up—vast inverted Trump Towers burrowing deep into the earth with Osama stroking a Persian as he plotted world domination from the upside-down penthouse in Sub-Basement Level 43—but just regular caves. As in a smelly hole in the ground with a carelessly demarcated communal latrine at the back.

And then, with the Taliban gone and the world's slowest "rush to war" with Iraq just getting underway, I made the mistake of going to Europe to visit the famous banlieues of Paris and other Continental Muslim neighborhoods. And at that point I started to get the queasy feeling the bewildered investigator does when he's standing in the strange indentation at the edge of town and, just as he works out it's a giant left-foot print, he glances up to see Godzilla's right foot totaling his Honda Civic. I began to see that it's not really about angry young men in caves in the Hindu Kush; it's not even about angry young men in the fast growing Muslim populations of the west—although that's certainly part of the seven-eighths of the iceberg bobbing just below the surface of 9/11. But the bulk of that iceberg is the profound and perhaps fatal weakness of the civilization that built the modern world. We're witnessing the early stages of what the United Nations Population Division calls a "global upheaval" that's "without parallel in human history." Demographically and psychologi-cally, Europeans have chosen to commit societal suicide, and their principal heir and beneficiary will be Islam.

And once I'd stumbled on that even the thought of Mullah Omar pranc-ing round the room to Rod Stewart's "Hot Legs" couldn't cheer me up.

When I go hither and yon doing my apocalyptic vaudeville, I'm often asked a variant of the following: If what you say is true—that Islam is likely, if only by default, to take over much of the west in a generation or two—why would it be so dumb as to jump the gun on 9/11? After all, before that Tuesday morning, few of us gave any thought to the subject.

The short answer is that Islam is not monolithic, and that it's perfectly understandable for Osama bin Laden to play bad cop to the western Muslim lobby groups' good cop, granted that they share the same aim: the wish to annex the crusader lands to the House of Islam.

The longer answer is that, even if 9/11 was a strictly unnecessary provocation, it was still a useful revelation of the limits of the Great Satan's resolve. Or to look at it another way: A couple of years back, over in *The Corner* at National Review Online, some of the more bloodthirsty lads were demanding to know why Bush didn't do this and why Bush didn't do that. I forget what it was now—knock off Assad, freeze Saudi bank accounts, whatever. John Podhoretz responded that we were missing the point, which was this: Bush was as good as it was going to get.

On some or other "Whither conservatism?" panel a few years back, I remarked of George W. Bush that it requires a perverse genius to get damned day in day out as the new Hitler when 90 percent of the time you're Tony Blair with a ranch. I'll stand by that. Yet nevertheless: Bush was as good as it was going to get.

The electors have made a bet that we can return to that happy capering playground at the Summit of the Americas, where all the great questions have been settled and indulgent governments can subsidize their own anarchists. If 9/11 ultimately revealed America's self-imposed constraints, November 4 is already understood as a comprehensive repudiation even of that qualified resolve. Like I said: for America's enemies, that's useful to know.

TOO BIG TO WIN

National Review, June 6, 2011

WHY CAN'T AMERICA win wars? It's been two-thirds of a century since we saw (as President Obama vividly put it) "Emperor Hirohito coming down and signing a surrender to MacArthur." And, if that's not quite how you remember it, forget the formal guest list, forget the long-form surrender certificate, and try to think of "winning" in a more basic sense.

The United States is currently fighting, to one degree or another, three wars. Iraq—the quagmire, the "bad" war, the invasion that launched a thousand western anti-war demonstrations and official inquiries and anti Bush plays and movies—is going least badly. For now. And making allowances for the fact that the principal geostrategic legacy of our genteel protectorate is that an avowed American enemy, Iran, was able vastly to increase its influence over the country on our dime.

Afghanistan? The "good war" is now "America's longest war." Our forces have been there longer than the Red Army was. The "hearts and minds" strategy is going so well that American troops are now being killed by the Afghans who know us best. Does being murdered by the soldiers and policemen you've spent years training even count as a "combat" death?

Perhaps that's why the U.S. media disdain to cover these killings: In April, at a meeting between Afghan border police and their U.S. trainers, an Afghan cop killed two American soldiers. Oh, well, wild country, once you get up near that Turkmen border. A few weeks later, back in Kabul, an Afghan military pilot killed eight American soldiers and a civilian contractor. On May 13 a NATO "mentoring team" sat down to lunch with Afghan police in Helmand when one of their protégés opened fire and killed two of them. "The actions of this individual do not reflect the overall actions of our Afghan partners," said Major General James B. Laster of the U.S. Marine Corps. "We remain committed to our partners and to our mission here."

Libya? The good news is that we've vastly reduced the time it takes us to get quagmired. I believe the Libyan campaign is already in *The Guinness Book of World Records* as the fastest quagmire on record. In an inspired move, we've chosen to back the one Arab liberation movement incapable of knocking off the local strongman even when you lend them every NATO air force. But not to worry: President Obama, cooed an administration official to *The New Yorker*, is "leading from behind." Indeed. What could be more impeccably multilateral than a coalition pantomime horse composed entirely of rear ends? Apparently it would be "illegal" to target Colonel Qaddafi, so our strategic objective is to kill him by accident. So far we've killed a son and a couple of grandkids. Maybe by the time you read this we'll have added a maiden aunt or two to the trophy room. It's not precisely clear why offing the old pock-skinned transvestite should be a priority of the U.S. right now, but let's hope it happens soon, because otherwise there'll be no way of telling when this "war" is "ended."

According to partisan taste, one can blame the trio of current morasses on Bush or Obama, but in the bigger picture they're part of a pattern of behavior that predates either man, stretching back through non-victories great and small—Somalia, Gulf War I, Vietnam, Korea. On the more conclusive side of the ledger, we have...well, lemme see: Grenada, 1983. And, given that that was a bit of post-colonial housekeeping Britain should have taken care of but declined to, one could argue that even that lone bright spot supports a broader narrative of western enfeeblement. At any rate, America's only unambiguous military triumph since 1945 is a small Caribbean island with Queen Elizabeth II as head of state. For 43 percent of global military expenditure, that's not much bang for the buck.

Inconclusive interventionism has consequences. Korea led to Norks with nukes. The downed helicopters in the Iranian desert led to mullahs with nukes. Gulf War I led to Gulf War II. Somalia led to 9/11. Vietnam led to everything, in the sense that its trauma penetrated so deep into the American psyche that it corroded the ability to think clearly about war as a tool of national purpose.

For half a century, the Cold War provided a kind of cover. At the dawn of the so-called American era, Washington chose to downplay U.S. hegemony and instead created and funded transnational institutions in which the non-imperial superpower was so self-deprecating it artificially inflated everybody else's status in a kind of geopolitical affirmative-action program. In the military sphere, this meant NATO. If the rap against the UN Security Council is that it's the World War II victory parade preserved in aspic, NATO is the rubble of post-war Europe preserved as a situation room. In 1950, America had a unique dominance of the "free world" and it could afford to be generous, so it was: We had more money than we knew what to do with, so we absolved our allies of paying for their own security. Thanks to American defense welfare, NATO is a military alliance made up of allies that no longer have militaries.

In the Cold War, that had a kind of logic: Europe was the designated battlefield, so, whether or not they had any tanks, they had, very literally, skin in the game. But the Cold War ended and NATO lingered on, evolving into a global Super Friends made up of folks who aren't Super and don't like each other terribly much. At the beginning of the Afghan campaign, Washington invested huge amounts of diplomatic effort trying to rouse its allies into the merest gestures of war-making: The 2004 NATO summit was hailed as a landmark success after the alliance's twenty-six members agreed to commit an extra six hundred troops and three helicopters. That averages out at 23.08 troops per country, plus almost a ninth of a helicopter apiece. Half a decade of quagmire later, Washington was investing even larger amounts of diplomatic effort failing to rouse its allies into the most perfunctory gestures of non-combat pantywaist transnationalism: We know that, under ever more refined rules of engagement, certain allies won't go out at night, or in snow, or in provinces where there's fighting going on, so by the 2010 NATO confab, Robert Gates was reduced to complaining that the allies' promised 450 "trainers" for the Afghan National Army had failed to materialize. Supposedly forty-six nations are contributing to the allied effort in Afghanistan, so that would work out at ten "trainers" per country. Imagine if the energy expended in these ridiculous (and in some cases profoundly damaging) transnational fig leaves had been directed into more quaintly conventional channels—like, say, identifying America's national interest and pursuing it.

The Cold War casts other shadows. In Korea, the U.S. forbore even to cut its enemy's Chinese supply lines. You can't win that way. But in the nuclear age, all-out war—war with real nations, with serious militaries—was too terrible to contemplate, so even in proxy squabbles in Third World backwaters the overriding concern was to tamp things down, even at the price of victory. And, by the time the Cold War ended, such thinking had become ingrained. A U.S.-Soviet nuclear standoff of mutual deterrence decayed into a unipolar world of U.S. auto-deterrence. Were it not for the brave passengers of Flight 93 and the vagaries of the Oval Office social calendar, the fourth plane on 9/11 might have succeeded in hitting the White House, decapitating the regime, leaving a smoking ruin in the heart of the capital, and delivering the republic unto a Robert C. Byrd Administration or some other whimsy of presidential succession. Yet, in allowing his toxic backwater to be used as the launch pad for the deadliest foreign assault on the U.S. mainland in two centuries, Mullah Omar either discounted the possibility of total devastating destruction against his country, or didn't care.

If it was the former, he was surely right. After the Battle of Omdurman, Hilaire Belloc offered a pithy summation of technological advantage:

> *Whatever happens*
> *We have got*
> *The Maxim gun*
> *And they have not.*

But suppose they know you'll never use the Maxim gun? At a certain level, credible deterrence depends on a credible enemy. The Soviet Union disintegrated, but the surviving superpower's instinct to de-escalate intensified: In Kirkuk as in Kandahar, every Lilliputian warlord quickly grasped that you could provoke the infidel Gulliver with relative impunity. Mutually Assured Destruction had curdled into Massively Applied Desultoriness.

Clearly, if one nation is responsible for near half the world's military budget, a lot of others aren't pulling their weight. The Pentagon outspends the Chinese, British, French, Russian, Japanese, German, Saudi, Indian, Italian, South Korean, Brazilian, Canadian, Australian, Spanish, Turkish, and Israeli militaries combined. So why doesn't it feel like that?

Well, for exactly that reason: If you outspend every serious rival combined, you're obviously something other than the soldiery of a conventional nation state. But what exactly? The geopolitical sugar daddy is so busy picking up the tab for the global order he's lost all sense of national interest. Readers will be wearily familiar with the tendency of long-established pop-culture icons to go all transnational on us: Only the other week Superman took to the podium of the United Nations to renounce his U.S. citizenship on the grounds that "truth, justice, and the American way" no longer does it for him. Good ol' GI Joe is now a Brussels-based multilateral acronym—the Global Integrated Joint Operating Entity.[1] I believe they're running the Libyan operation.

An army has to wage war on behalf of something real. For better or worse, "king and country" is real, and so, mostly for worse, are the tribal loyalties of Africa's blood-drenched civil wars. But it's hardly surprising that it's difficult to win wars waged on behalf of something so chimerical as "the international community." If you're making war on behalf of an illusory concept, is it even possible to have war aims?

What's ours? "We are in Afghanistan to help the Afghan people," General Petraeus said in April. Somewhere generations of old-school imperialists are roaring their heads off, not least at the concept of "the Afghan people." But when you're the expeditionary force of the parliament of man, what else is there?

War is hell, but global "mentoring" is purgatory. In that respect, the belated dispatch of Osama bin Laden may be less strategically relevant than the near-simultaneous exposé by *60 Minutes* of Greg Mortenson's *Three Cups of Tea*. This is the bestselling book the Pentagon gives to Afghan-bound officers, and whose celebrity author has met with our most senior commanders

---

1   See "Say, It Ain't So Joe."

on multiple occasions. And it's a crock. Nevertheless, it's effected a profound cultural transformation—if only on us. "It's remarkable," an Indian diplomat chuckled to me a while back. "In Afghanistan, the Americans now drink more tea than the British. And they don't even like it." In 2009, remember, the Pentagon accounted for 43 percent of the planet's military expenditures. At this rate, by 2012 they'll account for 43 percent of the planet's tea consumption.

Nation building in Afghanistan is the ne plus ultra of a fool's errand. But even if one were so disposed, effective "nation building" is done in the national interest of the builder. The British rebuilt India in their own image, with a Westminster parliament, common law, and an English education system. In whose image are we building Afghanistan? Eight months after Petraeus announced his latest folly, the Afghan Local Police initiative, Oxfam reported that the newly formed ALP was a hotbed of torture and pederasty. Almost every Afghan institution is, of course. But for most of human history they've managed to practice both enthusiasms without international subvention. The U.S. taxpayer accepts wearily the burden of subsidy for Nevada's cowboy poets and San Francisco's mime companies, but, even by those generous standards of cultural preservation, it's hard to see why he should be facilitating the traditional predilections of Pashtun men with an eye for the "dancing boys of Kandahar."

Which brings us back to those Three Cups of Tea. So the Global Integrated Joint Operating Entity is building schoolhouses in Afghanistan. Big deal. The problem, in Kandahar as in Kansas, is not the buildings but what's being taught inside them—and we've no stomach for getting into that. So what's the point of building better infrastructure for Afghanistan's wretched tribal culture? What's our interest in state-of-the-art backwardness?

Transnational do-gooding is political correctness on tour. It takes the relativist assumptions of the multiculti varsity and applies them geopolitically: The white man's burden meets liberal guilt. No wealthy developed nation should have a national interest, because a national interest is a selfish interest. Afghanistan started out selfishly—a daringly original military campaign, brilliantly executed, to remove your enemies from power and kill as many of the bad guys as possible. Then America sobered up and gradually brought a freakish exception into compliance with the rule. In Libya as in Kosovo, war is legitimate only if you have no conceivable national interest in whatever conflict you're fighting. The fact that you have no stake in it justifies your getting into it. The principal rationale is that there's no rationale, and who could object to that? Applied globally, political correctness obliges us to forswear sovereignty. And, once you do that, then, as Country Joe and the Fish famously enquired, it's one-two-three, what are we fighting for?

When you're responsible for half the planet's military spending, and 80 percent of its military R&D, certain things can be said with confidence: No one is going to get into a nuclear war with the United States, or a large-scale tank battle, or even a dogfight. You're the Microsoft, the Standard Oil of conventional warfare: Were they interested in competing in this field, second-tier military powers would probably have filed an antitrust suit with the Department of Justice by now. When you're the only guy in town with a tennis racket, don't be surprised if no one wants to join you on center court—or that provocateurs look for other fields on which to play. If you've got uniformed infantrymen and tanks and battleships and jet fighters, you're too weak to take on the hyperpower. But, if you've got illiterate goatherds with string and hacksaws and fertilizer, you can tie him down for a decade. An IED is an "improvised" explosive device. Can we still improvise? Or does the planet's most lavishly funded military assume it has the luxury of declining to adapt to the world it's living in?

In the spring of 2003, on the deserted highway between the Jordanian border and the town of Rutba, I came across my first burnt-out Iraqi tank—a charred wreck shoved over to the shoulder. I parked, walked around it, and pondered the fate of the men inside. It seemed somehow pathetic that, facing invasion by the United States, these Iraqi conscripts had even bothered to climb in and point the thing to wherever they were heading when death rained down from the stars, or Diego Garcia, or Missouri. Yet even then I remembered the words of the great strategist of armored warfare, Basil Liddell Hart: "The destruction of the enemy's armed forces is but a means—and not necessarily an inevitable or infallible one—to the attainment of the real objective."

The object of war, wrote Liddell Hart, is not to destroy the enemy's tanks but to destroy his will.

Instead, America has fallen for the Thomas Friedman thesis, promulgated by *The New York Times'* great thinker in January 2002: "For all the talk about the vaunted Afghan fighters, this was a war between the Jetsons and the Flintstones—and the Jetsons won and the Flintstones know it."

But they didn't. They didn't know they were beaten. Because they weren't.

Because we hadn't destroyed their will—as we did to the Germans and Japanese two-thirds of a century ago, and as we surely would not do if we were fighting World War II today. That's not an argument for nuking or carpet bombing, so much as for cool clear-sightedness. Asked how he would react if the British Army invaded Germany, Bismarck said he would dispatch the local police force to arrest them: a clever Teuton sneer at the modest size of Her Britannic Majesty's forces. But that's the point: The British accomplished much with little; at the height of empire, an insignificant number of Anglo-Celts controlled the entire Indian subcontinent. A confident culture can dominate far larger numbers of people, as England did for much of modern history. By contrast, in an era of Massively Applied Desultoriness, we spend a fortune going to war with one hand tied behind our back. The Forty-Three Percent Global Operating Industrial Military Complex isn't too big to fail, but it is perhaps too big to win—as our enemies understand.

So on we stagger, with Cold War institutions, transnational sensibilities, politically correct solicitousness, fraudulent preening pseudo–nation building, expensive gizmos, little will, and no war aims... but real American lives. "These Colors Don't Run," says the T-shirt. But, bereft of national purpose, they bleed away to a grey blur on a distant horizon.

Sixty-six years after V-J Day, the American way of war needs top-to-toe reinvention.

DRONE ALONE

Syndicated column, March 8, 2013

I SHALL LEAVE it to others to argue the legal and constitutional questions surrounding drones, but they are not without practical application. For the last couple of years, Janet Napolitano/Incompetano, the Secretary of Homeland Security, has had Predator drones patrolling the U.S. border. No, silly, not the southern border. The northern one. You gotta be able to prioritize, right? At Derby Line, Vermont, the international frontier runs through the middle of the town library and its second-floor opera house. If memory serves, the stage and the best seats are in Canada, but the concession stand and the cheap seats are in America. Despite the zealots of Homeland Security's best efforts at afflicting residents of this cross-border community with ever more obstacles to daily life, I don't recall seeing any Predator drones hovering over Non-Fiction E–L. But, if there are, I'm sure they're entirely capable of identifying which delinquent borrower is a Quebecer and which a Vermonter before dispatching a Hellfire missile to vaporize him in front of the Large Print Romance shelves.

I'm a long, long way from Rand Paul's view of the world (I'm basically a nineteenth-century imperialist a hundred years past sell-by date), but I'm far from sanguine about America's drone fever.

Anwar al-Awlaki, an American citizen born in New Mexico, was whacked by a Predator not on a battlefield but after an apparently convivial lunch at a favorite Yemeni restaurant. Two weeks later, al-Awlaki's son Abdulrahman was dining on the terrace of another local eatery when the CIA served him the old Hellfire Special and he wound up splattered all over the patio. Abdulrahman was sixteen, and born in Denver. As I understand it, the Supreme Court has ruled that American minors, convicted of the most heinous crimes, cannot be executed. But you can gaily atomize them halfway round the planet. My brief experience of Yemeni restaurants was not a happy one but, granted that, I couldn't honestly say they met any recognized definition of a "battlefield."

Al-Awlaki Junior seems to have been your average anti-American teen. Al-Awlaki Senior was an al-Qaeda ideologue, and a supposed "spiritual mentor" to everyone from the 9/11 murderers to the Fort Hood killer and the thwarted Pantybomber. On the other hand, after September 11, he was invited to lunch at the Pentagon, became the first imam to conduct a prayer service at the U.S. Congress, and was hailed by NPR as an exemplar of an American "Muslim leader who could help build bridges between Islam and the West." The precise point at which he changed from American bridge-builder to Yemeni restaurant take-out is hard to determine. His public utterances when he was being feted by *The New York Times* are far more benign than those of, say, Samira Ibrahim, who was scheduled to receive a "Woman of Courage" award from Michelle Obama and John Kerry on Friday until an unfortunate flap erupted over some ill-phrased tweets from the courageous lass rejoicing on the anniversary of 9/11 that she loved to see "America burning." The same bureaucracy that booked Samira Ibrahim for an audience with the First Lady and Anwar al-Awlaki to host prayers at the Capitol now assures you that it's entirely capable of determining who needs to be zapped by a drone between the sea bass and the tiramisu at Ahmed's Bar and Grill. But it's precisely because the government is too craven to stray beyond technological warfare and take on its enemies ideologically that it winds up booking the First Lady to hand out awards to a Jew-loathing, Hitler-quoting, terrorist-supporting America-hater.

Insofar as it relieves Washington of the need to think strategically about the nature of the enemy, the drone is part of the problem. For all its advantages to this administration—no awkward prisoners to be housed at Gitmo, no military casualties for the evening news—the unheard, unseen, unmanned drone raining down death from the skies confirms for those on the receiving end al-Qaeda's critique of its enemies: As they see it, we have the best technology and the worst will; we choose aerial assassination and its attendant collateral damage because we are risk-averse—and so remote, antiseptic, long-distance, computer-programmed warfare is all that we can bear. Our technological strength betrays our psychological weakness.

And in a certain sense they're right: Afghanistan is winding down, at best, to join the long list of America's unwon wars, in which, forty-eight hours after departure, there will be no trace that we were ever there. The guys with drones are losing to the guys with fertilizer—because they mean it, and we don't. The drone thus has come to symbolize the central defect of America's "war on terror," which is that it's all means and no end: We're fighting the symptoms rather than the cause.

For a war without strategic purpose, a drone'll do.

A NATIONAL
DISGRACE

Syndicated column, September 15, 2012

SO, ON A HIGHLY symbolic date, mobs storm American diplomatic facilities and drag the corpse of a U.S. ambassador through the streets. Then the President flies to Vegas for a fundraiser.

No, no, a novelist would say; that's too pat, too neat in its symbolic contrast. Make it Cleveland, or Des Moines.

The President is surrounded by delirious fanbois and fangurls screaming "We love you," too drunk on his celebrity to understand this is the first photo-op in the aftermath of a national humiliation.

No, no, a filmmaker would say; too crass, too blunt. Make them sober, middle-aged midwesterners, shocked at first, but then quiet and respectful.

The President is too lazy and cocksure to have learned any prepared remarks or mastered the appropriate tone, notwithstanding that a government that spends more money than any government in the history of the planet has ever spent can surely provide him with both a speechwriting team and a quiet corner on his private wide-bodied jet to consider what might be fitting for the occasion. So instead he sloughs off the words, bloodless and unfelt: "And obviously our hearts are broken...."

Yeah, it's totally obvious.

And he's even more drunk on his celebrity than the fanbois are, so in his slapdashery he winds up comparing the sacrifice of a diplomat lynched by a pack of savages with the enthusiasm of his own campaign bobbysoxers.

No, no, says the Broadway director; that's too crude, too ham-fisted. How about the crowd is cheering and distracted, but he's the President, he understands the gravity of the hour, and he's the greatest orator of his generation, so he's

205

thought about what he's going to say, and it takes a few moments but his words are so moving that they still the cheers of the fanbois, and at the end there's complete silence and a few muffled sobs, and even in party-town they understand the sacrifice and loss of their compatriots on the other side of the world.

But no, that would be an utterly fantastical America. In the real America, the President is too busy to attend the security briefing on the morning after a national debacle, but he does have time to do Letterman and appear on a hip-hop radio show hosted by "The Pimp with a Limp." In the real State Department, the U.S. embassy in Cairo is guarded by Marines with no ammunition, but they do enjoy the soft-power muscle of a Foreign Service officer, one Lloyd Schwartz, tweeting frenziedly into cyberspace (including a whole chain directed at my own Twitter handle, for some reason) about how America deplores insensitive people who are so insensitively insensitive that they don't respectfully respect all religions equally respectfully and sensitively, even as the raging mob is pouring through the gates.

When it comes to a flailing, blundering superpower, I am generally wary of ascribing to malevolence what is more often sheer stupidity and incompetence. For example, we're told that, because the consulate in Benghazi was designated as an "interim facility," it did not warrant the level of security and protection that, say, an embassy in Scandinavia would have. This seems all too plausible—that security decisions are made not by individual human judgment but according to whichever rule book sub-clause at the Federal Agency of Bureaucratic Facilities Regulation it happens to fall under. However, the very next day the embassy in Yemen, which *is* a permanent facility, was also overrun, as was the embassy in Tunisia the day after. Look, these are tough crowds, as the President might say at Caesars Palace. But we spend more money on these joints than anybody else, and they're as easy to overrun as the Belgian consulate.

As I say, I'm inclined to be generous, and put some of this down to the natural torpor and ineptitude of government. But Hillary Clinton and General Martin Dempsey are guilty of something worse, in the Secretary of State's weirdly obsessive remarks about an obscure film supposedly disrespectful of

Mohammed and the Chairman of the Joint Chiefs' telephone call to a private citizen asking him if he could please ease up on the old Islamophobia.

Forget the free-speech arguments. In this case, as Secretary Clinton and General Dempsey well know, the film has even less to do with anything than did the Danish cartoons or the schoolteacher's teddy bear or any of the other innumerable grievances of Islam. The four-hundred-strong assault force in Benghazi showed up with RPGs and mortars: That's not a spontaneous movie review; that's an act of war, and better planned and executed than the dying superpower's response to it. Secretary Clinton and General Dempsey are, to put it mildly, misleading the American people when they suggest otherwise.

One can understand why they might do this, given the fiasco in Libya. The men who organized this attack knew the ambassador would be at the consulate in Benghazi rather than at the embassy in Tripoli. How did that happen? They knew when he had been moved from the consulate to a "safe house," and switched their attentions accordingly. How did that happen? The United States Government lost track of its ambassador for ten hours. How did that happen? Perhaps, when they've investigated Mitt Romney's press release for another three or four weeks, the court eunuchs of the American media might like to look into some of these fascinating questions, instead of leaving the only interesting reporting on an American story to the foreign press.

For whatever reason, Secretary Clinton chose to double down on misleading the American people. "Libyans carried Chris's body to the hospital," said Mrs. Clinton. That's one way of putting it. The photographs at the Arab TV network al-Mayadeen show Chris Stevens's body being dragged through the streets, while the locals take souvenir photographs on their cell phones. A man in a red striped shirt photographs the dead-eyed ambassador from above; another immediately behind his head moves the splayed arm and holds his cell-phone camera an inch from the ambassador's nose. Some years ago, I had occasion to assist in moving the body of a dead man: We did not stop to take photographs en route. Even allowing for cultural differences, this looks less like "carrying Chris's body to the hospital" and more like barbarians gleefully feasting on the spoils of savagery.

In a rare appearance on a non-showbiz outlet, President Obama, winging it on Telemundo, told his host that Egypt was neither an ally nor an enemy. I can understand why it can be difficult to figure out, but here's an easy way to tell: Bernard Lewis, the great scholar of Islam, said some years ago that America risked being seen as "harmless as an enemy and treacherous as a friend." So, at the Benghazi consulate, the looters stole "sensitive" papers revealing the names of Libyans who've cooperated with the United States.

Oh, well. As the President would say, obviously our hearts are with you.

Meanwhile, in Pakistan, the local doctor who fingered bin Laden to the Americans sits in jail. So, while America's clod vice president staggers around pimping limply that only Obama had the guts to take the toughest decision anyone's ever had to take, the poor schlub who actually did have the guts, who actually took the tough decision in a part of the world where taking tough decisions can get you killed, languishes in a cell because Washington would not lift a finger to help him.

Like I said, no novelist would contrast Chris Stevens on the streets of Benghazi and Barack Obama on stage in Vegas. Too crude, too telling, too devastating.

THE MAN AT THE
BORDER

SteynOnline, June 23, 2014

ELEVEN YEARS AGO, a few weeks after the fall of Saddam, on little more than a whim, I rented a beat-up Nissan and, without telling the car-hire bloke, drove from Amman through the eastern Jordanian desert, across the Iraqi border, and into the Sunni Triangle. I could not easily make the same journey today, but for a brief period in the spring of 2003 we were the "strong horse" and even a dainty little media gelding such as myself was accorded a measure of respect by the natives. The frontier is a line in the sand drawn by a British colonial civil servant, and on either side it's empty country. From the Trebil border post, you have to drive through ninety miles of nothing to get to Iraq's westernmost town, Rutba—in saner times an old refueling stop for Imperial Airways flights from Britain to India. Fewer of Her Majesty's subjects swing by these days. I had a bite to eat at a café whose patron had a trilby pushed back on his head Sinatra-style and was very pleased to see me. (Rutba was the first stop on a motoring tour that took me through Ramadi and Fallujah and up to Tikrit and various other towns.)

In those days, the Iraqi side of the Trebil border was manned by U.S. troops. So an "immigration official" from the Third Armored Cavalry glanced at my Canadian passport, and said, "Welcome to Free Iraq." We exchanged a few pleasantries, and he waved me through. A lot less cumbersome than landing at JFK. I remember there was a banner with a big oval hole in it, where I assumed Saddam's face had once been. And as I drove away I remember wondering what that hole would be filled with.

Well, now we know. That same border post today is manned by head-hacking jihadists from the "Islamic State of Iraq and Syria." Bloomberg News reports:

> Fighters from the Islamic State in Iraq and the Levant, an al-Qaeda breakaway group, took all the border crossings with Jordan and Syria, Hameed Ahmed Hashim, a member of the Anbar provincial council, said by telephone yesterday. Militants took Rutba, about 145 kilometers (90 miles) east of the Jordanian border, Faleh al-Issawi, the deputy chief of the council, said by phone. Anbar province in western Iraq borders both countries. The Jordanian army didn't immediately respond to a request for information about the situation on the border.

I should think not. The Jordanian official I met was charming if somewhat bureaucratically obstructive, and wound up asking me about how difficult it was to emigrate to Canada. More difficult than emigrating from Syria to Iraq. From the German news service Deutsche Welle:

> Rutba gives ISIS control over a stretch of highway to Jordan that has fallen into infrequent use over the past several months because of the deteriorating security situation. The town has a population of 40,000, but it has recently absorbed 20,000 people displaced from Fallujah and Ramadi.
>
> ISIS now controls much of the Iraq-Syria border. Taking crossings such as the one in Qaim allows them to more easily move weapons and heavy equipment. Rebels also control the Syrian side of the crossing.

The Iraq/Syria border no longer exists: ISIS has simply erased the Anglo-French settlement of 1922. Jordan has just one frontier post with Iraq—the one I crossed all those years ago—and it's asking an awful lot of these lads to be more respectful of Jordan's sovereignty than they've been of Iraq's or Syria's. This thought has apparently just occurred to Barack Obama, who thinks that sounding presidential is largely a matter of stating the obvious: "Obama told CBS in an interview that will be aired in full today that the fighting could spread to 'allies like Jordan.'"

Gee, thanks for that insight.

In her interrogation of Dick Cheney, Fox's Megyn Kelly mocked that line from eleven years ago about how we'd be "greeted as liberators." In May 2003, I wasn't a liberator, but I was pretty much greeted as one by the majority of the fellows I encountered in the Sunni Triangle. The towns were dusty and run-down but intact, with only two signs that anything dramatic had happened: As at the Trebil border post, the giant portraits of Saddam mounted on plinths at every rinky-dink roundabout had been removed—but very neatly, almost surgically: it was an act not of vandalism, but of political hygiene. A few weeks earlier, the dictator would have been omnipresent; now his absence was omni-present. That's what you were supposed to notice. In Rutba and Ramadi and the other western towns, you'd also see the occasional fancy house with deco-rative stonework, and gates and doors hanging off the hinges with the odd goat or donkey wandering through the compound defecating hither and yon. These were the pads of the local Baathist big shots, who'd taken off in a hurry, and, other than the drained gas stations, they were the only scenes of looting I saw.

If you had asked me, in that café in Rutba eleven years ago, as I was enjoy-ing what passed for the "mixed grill" with mein host, what utter defeat would look like in a single image, it would be hard to beat the scene that now greets you in the western desert: An Iraqi border post staffed by hardcore jihadists from an al-Qaeda spin-off. The details are choice—the black flag of al-Qaeda flies from buildings built by American taxpayers, they drive vehicles paid for by American taxpayers, they shoot aircraft out of the sky with Stinger missiles donated by American taxpayers—and thousands of their foot soldiers are nominally Britons, Frenchmen, Aussies, Canucks, Americans, and other western citizens for whom the open road in Iraq, decapitating as they go, is the greatest adventure of their lives. Until they return "home."

But, as I said, these are details. The central image—the al-Qaeda man at the border post—is in itself an image of complete and total defeat.

Where next? With Syrian refugees expanding the population of his country by 25 percent, I wonder how Jordan's King Abdullah feels about being an "ally" of Obama's. Perhaps he nodded his head at the reported comments of the Polish Foreign Minister—that being a U.S. ally "isn't worth anything" and is "even harmful because it creates a false sense of security." No matter how secure that false sense is, waking up to find yourself sharing a border crossing with ISIS is apt to shatter it.

I had a grand time in liberated Iraq in 2003, but one exchange stuck with me, and nagged at me over the years. At a rest area on the highway between Rutba and Ramadi, I fell into conversation with one of the locals. Having had to veer onto the median every few miles to dodge bomb craters, I asked him whether he was irked by his liberators. "Americans only in the sky," he told me, grinning a big toothless grin as, bang on cue, a U.S. chopper rumbled up from over the horizon and passed high above our heads. "No problem."

"Americans only in the sky" is an even better slogan in the Obama era of drone-alone warfare. In Iraq, there were a lot of boots on the ground, but when it came to non-military leverage (cultural, economic), the non-imperial hyperpower was content to remain "only in the sky." And down on the ground other players filled the vacuum, some reasonably benign (the Chinese in the oil fields), others less so (the Iranians in everything else).

Still, the roots of ISIS do not lie in the actions America took in 2003. Bush made mistakes in Iraq, and left a ramshackle state that functioned less badly than any of its neighbors. Obama walked away, pulled out a cigarette, tossed the match over his shoulder, and ignited a fuse that, from Damascus to Baghdad to Amman and beyond, will blow up the entire Middle East.

Back in America, the coastal sophisticates joke at those knuckle-dragging rubes who believe Obama is some kind of "secret Muslim." But really Occam's razor would favor such an explanation, wouldn't it? That a post-American Middle East divided between bad-cop nuclear Shia and worse-cop head-hacking Sunni was the plan all along. Because there are only two alternatives to that simplest of simple explanations:

The first is that Obama and the Z-graders who fill out his administration are just blundering buffoons. And we all know from Michael Beschloss that he's the smartest president ever, so it couldn't possibly be colossal stupidity on a scale unknown to American history, could it?

The second is that his contempt for American power—a basic class signifier in the circles in which he's moved all his life—is so deeply ingrained that he doesn't care what replaces it.

And so the border post of "Free Iraq" is now the western frontier of the new Caliphate.

IX

THE WAR ON WOMEN

MY SHARIA AMOUR

In 2002, hundreds of people died in rioting over...well, take a wild guess.
Here's how The Daily Telegraph *reported the news:*

"After escaping the riots in Nigeria, which claimed more than 200 lives,
Miss World contestants were safely installed in their ever-decreasing
numbers inside a Heathrow hotel yesterday.... Last week, a reporter for
This Day, *a Nigerian newspaper, wrote an article suggesting that Prophet*
Mohammed would 'probably' have chosen a wife from one of the
contestants, a comment which sparked the unrest....

"A number of alternative venues, such as Alexandra Palace, Wembley
Arena and the Grosvenor House hotel on Park Lane, are being considered.

"Glenda Jackson, the Labour MP for Hampstead, said:
'They should call the whole thing off....'"

Which set me thinking....

The Daily Telegraph, *November 30, 2002*

"RUN THIS BY ME AGAIN," I said as we circled Lagos Airport. "We're doing a new 'culturally sensitive' Miss World?"

"That's right," said Julia Morley. "I got the idea from all those stringy London feminists droning on about how we're only promoting a narrow exploitative western image of women. And to be honest, after a week in England listening to their bitching and whining, I'm glad to be back in Nigeria. The locals'll go crazy for this."

"I hope not," I said. But I was pleasantly surprised as we landed smoothly and taxied down the runway. "Look, Julia, a gun salute!"

"Duck, girls!" she yelled, as a SAM missile pierced the window, shot through the first class curtain, and took out the economy toilet.

"Now don't you worry, Mark," she said once we were safely in the limo. "Your material's hardly been changed at all. Just remember, when you and Tony Orlando do 'Thank Heaven for Little Girls,' there's a Sudanese warlord in a third-row aisle seat who's got a new twelve-year-old bride you don't want to be caught looking at."

"Got it," I said. The house band, made up entirely of Hausa band members, played the opening strains of Stevie Wonder's classic love song, and Julia pushed the revised culturally-sensitive lyrics into my hand. It was then that the first nagging doubts began to gnaw at the back of my mind. But what the hell, I was in my tux and they were playing my song.

I bounced out on stage, grabbed the mike, and punched the air:

> My Sharia Amour
> Hot enough for Gulf emirs
> My Sharia Amour
> But I'm the guy she really fears....

The audience seemed wary, and an alarming number appeared to be reaching into their robes. But I ploughed on:

> My Sharia Amour
> Pretty little thing in her chador
> One of only four that I beat raw
> How I wish that I had five.

There was a momentary silence, just long enough for me to start backing upstage nervously.

And then the crowd went wild! The guys in the balcony cheered deliriously and hurled their machetes across the orchestra pit, shredding my pants. An Afghan wedding party grabbed their semi-automatics and blew out the chandeliers, sending them hurtling to the aisle, where they killed a Japanese camera crew. Tough luck, fellers, but that's what happens when you get between me and my audience.

I took my usual seat with the celebrity judges, in between *Baywatch* hunk David Hasselhoff and Princess Michael of Kent. Lorraine Kelly said: "And now, ladies and gentlemen, let's give our panel a really big hand!" A really big hand landed on the table with a dull thud, courtesy of a Saudi prince in the royal box.

"How'd they like you?" I asked Princess Michael.

"Well, by the end of 'Man, I Feel Like a Woman,' I had the crowd with me all the way. But I shook 'em off at Kaduna."

"Who's the bloke next to you?"

"Oh, he's a judge."

I rolled my eyes. "Well, *duh!*"

"No, I mean, he's a real judge. He's some Fulani big shot who's here to decide who gets stoned."

"And which mother of a Mick Jagger love-child is on the panel this year?"

"That's Marsha Hunt. Had an affair with him in the late Sixties."

The small talk was somewhat stilted. "Have you ever been stoned?" asked the judge. Marsha tittered.

Princess Michael explained that the fellow on Marsha's left was Alhaji Abdutayo Ogunbati, the country's leading female genital mutilator, there to ensure every contestant was in full compliance, and next to him was Hans Blix, there to ensure every involuntary clitorectomy was in accordance with UN clitorectomy inspections-team regulations.

I glanced at my watch. "For crying out loud, when are they going to raise the curtain?"

"They *have* raised the curtain," said David. "Those are the girls."

I peered closer at the shapeless line of black cloth, and he was right: there they all were, from Miss Afghanistan to Miss Zionist Entity.

I sighed. "How long till the swimsuit round?"

"This *is* the swimsuit round," said David.

＊   ＊   ＊

Years after writing that column, I'd be on stage somewhere or other talking about honor killings or some other cheery aspect of women's "rights" in the Muslim world, and afterwards somebody would always come up and say, "Oh, I thought you were going to break into 'My Sharia Amour.'" So, eventually, I thought, hey, why not? And so I did. The arrangement's varied over the years, and I'm usually kept company these days by a largely silent burqa-sheathed female purporting to be my third wife. The lyrics have evolved from show to show, too. But this is the version performed at Steynamite! in Toronto on April 24, 2012, as the instrumental intro begins:

Yeah, like to get a little mellow romance going here at the Metro Centre.

This one goes out to all the lovers here tonight. C'mon, Toronto, smooch along with me …

My Sharia Amour
She's hot enough for Gulf emirs (yeah!)
My Sharia Amour
But I'm the cat she really fears

My Sharia Amour
Got her from an imam in Lahore
One of only four wives I beat raw
How I wish that I had five

Dig that burqa
This chick'll take away your breath
But don't even glance
Or I'll have to have her stoned to death
My Sharia Amour
I won her like the Jews won the Six-Day War
Back when I was only thirty-four
And she was entering Grade Five

A-la-la-la-la-la
A-la-la-la-la-la-la
Take it, baby …

CHILD BRIDE [*muffled, from within burqa*]:
A-la-la-la-la-la
A-la-la-la-la-la-la

Beautiful!

And tomorrow
For our wedding anniversary
We'll renew our vows
With a second clitorectomy
(Hey, what can I tell you? She wanted somethin' special.)
My Sharia Amour
She's not a bit like you, you filthy infidel whore
We honor-killed her cousin on the second floor
I hope this one can stay alive

A-la-la-la-la-la
A-la-la-la-la-la-la

A-la-la-la-la-la
A-la-la-la-la-la-la
She's my cutie, for sure
My Sharia Amour!
Who loves you, baby?

[Child bride throws up her hands, shrieks, and runs off stage left]

BARBIE IN A BURQA

Maclean's, December 14, 2009

THE OTHER DAY, George Jonas passed on to his readers a characteristically shrewd observation gleaned from the late poet George Faludy: "No one likes to think of himself as a coward," wrote Jonas. "People prefer to think they end up yielding to what the terrorists demand, not because it's safer or more convenient, but because it's the right thing.... Successful terrorism persuades the terrorized that if they do terror's bidding, it's not because they're terrified but because they're socially concerned."

This is true. Resisting terror is exhausting. It's easier to appease it, but, for the sake of your self-esteem, you have to tell yourself you're appeasing it in the cause of some or other variant of "social justice." Obviously, it's unfortunate if "Canadians" and "Americans" and "Irishmen" get arrested for plotting to murder the artists and publishers of the Danish Mohammed cartoons, but that's all the more reason to be even more accommodating of the various "sensitivities" arising from the pervasive Islamophobia throughout western society. Etc.

Yet this psychology also applies to broader challenges. By way of example, take a fluffy feature from a recent edition of Britain's *Daily Mail*: "It's Barbie in a Burqa," read the headline. Yes, as part of her fiftieth-anniversary celebrations, "one of the world's most famous children's toys, Barbie, has been given a makeover." And, in an attractive photo shoot, there was Barbie in "traditional Islamic dress," wearing full head-to-toe lime-green and red burqas. At least, I'm assuming it was Barbie. It could have been GI Joe back there for all one can tell from the letterbox slot of eyeball meshing.

But Britain's biggest Barbie fan, Angela Ellis, was thrilled. "Bring it on, Burqa Barbie," she said. "I think this is a great idea. I think this is really important for girls, wherever they are from, they should have the opportunity to play with a Barbie that they feel represents them."

Well, Barbie is fifty. And at an age when Katie Cougar—er, Couric—America's all-time champion network news-ratings limbo-dancer, is being photographed ill-advisedly doing the lambada at the Christmas office party, there is perhaps something to be said for belatedly mothballing your seventy-six-inch plastic bust. Or as the blogger Laura Rosen Cohen put it: "Great news: that bitch Barbie has finally reverted." "And there's no need for expensive accessories like books or cars or a life," added Tim Blair of Sydney's *Daily Telegraph*, "because Barbie in a Bag isn't allowed to leave her home unless accompanied by a male relative (Mullah Ken, sold separately)."

Mullah Ken? I'm not so sure about that. Given the longtime rumors, Ken'll be lucky not to find himself crushed under one of those walls the Taliban put up for their sodomite-rehabilitation program. You'll be glad to know the dolls are anatomically accurate: Burqa Barbie has no clitoris, and, just like Mohamed Atta on the morning of September 11, Ken's genital area is fully depilated.

But we mean-spirited types are in the minority. The other day, I was watching, as one does, a German lingerie ad, for Liaison Dangereuse. It began with a naked woman—bit blurry and soft-focus, but you could see she had her hair in a towel and everything else in nothing at all, and there were definite glimpses of shapely bottom, the swell of her bosom, and whatnot. All very Continental.

She applies her lipstick, sashays into her dressing room wiggling aforementioned posterior, hooks her brassiere, rolls up her seamed stockings, slips into her stilettos, and then—with one final toss of her glossy luxuriant hair—pulls on her burqa and steps out the door. Tag line: "Sexiness for Everyone. Everywhere."

Very clever. The agency is Glow of Berlin. Might win them an award. Yet the superficial cool and the O. Henry switcheroo at the tail seem less cutting-edge state-of-the-art than sad and desperate wishful thinking. For one thing, if the comely young lady were truly a believing Muslim as opposed to a jobbing infidel thespian, her underdressed acting gig would earn her death threats, if she were lucky, and, if she weren't, actual death.

Still, Burqa Barbie and Fatima's Secret are minor and peripheral. What about the so-called most powerful man in the world? "The U.S. Government has gone to court to protect the right of women and girls to wear the hijab, and to punish those who would deny it," President Obama told his audience in Cairo earlier this year. "I reject the view of some in the west that a woman who chooses to cover her hair is somehow less equal."

My oh my, he's a profile in courage, isn't he? It's true that there have been occasional frictions over, say, the refusal of Muslim women to reveal their faces for their driver's licenses—Sultaana Freeman, for example, sued the state of Florida over that "right." But the real issue in the western world is "the right of women and girls" *not* "to wear the hijab." A couple of weeks ago in Arizona, a young woman called Noor Almaleki was fatally run over by her father in his Jeep Cherokee for becoming "too westernized." If there were a Matthew Shepard–style gay crucifixion every few months, liberal columnists would be going bananas about the "climate of hate" in America. But you can run over your daughter, decapitate your wife, drown three teenage girls and a polygamous spouse (to cite merely the most lurid recent examples of North American "honor killings"), and nobody cares. Certainly, there's no danger of Barack Obama ever standing up for the likes of poor Miss Almaleki to a roomful of A-list imams. When it comes to real hate crimes, as opposed to his entirely imaginary epidemic, the President of the United States has smaller *cojones* than Ken.

If you eschew the Grand Cherokee in favor of the Toronto subway, you might have noticed that the poster girl for the latest "social justice" campaign is a Muslim woman. "Drop Fees for a Poverty-Free Ontario" is the ringing cry, and next to it is a hijab-clad lady speaking up and speaking out. It's something to do with the cost of post-secondary education, which, like everything else in Canada, is supposed to be "free." The image is a curious choice as an emblem for educational access: after all, one of the most easily discernible features of societies that adopt Islamic dress is how ignorant they are. In

Afghanistan under the Taliban, girls were forbidden by law to attend school—not just fritter-away-half-a-decade-on-Ontario-taxpayers "post-secondary" education, but kindergarten and grade one. In Pakistan, 60 percent of women are illiterate. According to the UN's 2002 Arab Development Report, half of all women in the Arab world cannot read. And even in Canada, the ability of the woman on the subway poster to access that post-secondary education depends not on the "fees" but on her father, or, if she's already been married off to her sixteen-year-old cousin back in Mirpur, her husband. The Saskatch-ewan Internet maestro Kate McMillan summed up the poster thus: "Subjuga-tion of women—it's the new normal."

"Traditional Islamic dress" is not so "traditional." Talk to any educated Muslim woman who attended university in the Fifties, Sixties, or Seventies—back when they assumed history was moving their way and a covered woman was merely a local variant of the Russian babushka, something old and wiz-ened you saw in upcountry villages. Now you see them in the heart of the metropolis—and I don't mean Beirut or Abu Dhabi so much as Paris and Brussels. It's very strange to be able to walk around, say, Zarqa, hometown of the late "insurgent" Abu Musab al-Zarqawi, and look 90 percent of the women in the eye, and even be rewarded with a friendly smile every so often, and then to fly on to London and be confronted by one masked face after another while strolling down Whitechapel Road in the East End. The burqa, the niqab, and the hijab are not fashion statements but explicitly political ones, and what they symbolize in a western context is self-segregation.

That "Drop Fees" campaign would never dream of dressing up its poster gal as June Cleaver, Donna Reed, or any other outmoded sitcom mom in twin-set and pearls. Golly, that would send all sorts of disturbing signals to today's liberated females, wouldn't it? What signal is Barbie's burqa sending? That, in Taliban-controlled Afghanistan, women were forbidden by law from ever feel-ing sunlight on their faces? Hey, there's a positive message for young girls.

Perhaps white liberal progressives figure the new patriarchy can be con-tained to the likes of Noor Almaleki, but I doubt it. I've mentioned previously a Euro-pal of mine, non-Muslim, who's taken to covering herself in certain *quartiers* of an evening in order to avoid harassment by "youths." She does exactly what that German lingerie lass does—and with the merest correction to the sign-off:

"Subjugation for Every Woman. Everywhere."

HOW UNCLEAN WAS
MY VALLEY

SteynOnline, July 13, 2011

ON SATURDAY, *The Toronto Star*'s education section carried a photograph showing a typical Friday at the cafeteria of Valley Park Middle School. That's not a private academy, it's a public school funded by Toronto taxpayers. And yet, oddly enough, what's going on is a prayer service.

Oh, relax, it's not Anglican or anything improper like that; it's Muslim Friday prayers, and the Toronto District School Board says don't worry, it's just for convenience: They put the cafeteria at the local imams' disposal because otherwise the kids would have to troop off to the local mosque, and then they'd be late for Lesbian History class or whatever subject is scheduled for Friday afternoon.

The picture is taken from the back of the cafeteria, and shows two sets of bottoms in the air from those kneeling at prayer, and a third group of backs, sitting on the floor. In the distance, way up in the expensive seats, are the boys. They're male, so they get to sit up front at prayers. Behind them are the girls. They're female, so they have to sit behind the boys because they're second-class citizens—not in the whole of Canada, not formally, not yet, but in the cafeteria of a middle school run by the Toronto District School Board they most certainly are.

And the third row? The ones with their backs to us in the foreground of the picture? Well, let the *Star*'s caption writer explain: "At Valley Park Middle School, Muslim students participate in the Friday prayer service. Menstruating girls, at the very back, do not take part."

Oh. As the blogger Kathy Shaidle says, "Yep, that's part of the caption of the *Toronto Star* photo. Yes, the country is Canada and the year is 2011."

Just so. Not some exotic photojournalism essay from an upcountry village in Krappistan. But a typical Friday at a middle school in the largest city in Canada. I forget which brand of tampon used to advertise itself with the pitch "Now with new [whatever] you can go horse-riding, water-skiing, ballet dancing, whatever you want to do," but perhaps they can just add the tag: "But not participate in Friday prayers at an Ontario public school."

Some Canadians will look at this picture and react as Miss Shaidle did, or Tasha Kheiriddin in *The National Post*:

> Is this the Middle Ages? Have I stumbled into a time warp, where "unclean" women must be prevented from "defiling" other persons? It's bad enough that the girls at Valley Park have to enter the cafeteria from the back, while the boys enter from the front, but does the entire school have the right to know they are menstruating?

But a lot of Canadians will glance at the picture and think, "Aw, diversity, ain't it a beautiful thing?"—no different from the Sikh Mountie in Prince William's escort. And even if they read the caption and get to the bit about a Toronto public school separating menstruating girls from the rest of the student body and feel their multiculti pieties wobbling just a bit, they can no longer quite articulate on what basis they're supposed to object to it. Indeed, thanks to the likes of Ontario "Human Rights" Commission chief commissar Barbara Hall, the very words in which they might object to it have been all but criminalized.

Islam understands the reality of Commissar Hall's "social justice": You give 'em an inch, and they'll take the rest. Following a 1988 cease-and-desist court judgment against the Lord's Prayer in public school, the Ontario Education Act forbids "any person to conduct religious exercises or to provide instruction that includes religious indoctrination in a particular religion or religious belief in a school." That seems clear enough. If somebody at Valley Park stood up in the cafeteria and started in with "Our Father, which art in Heaven," the full weight of the school board would come crashing down on them. Fortunately,

Valley Park is 80 to 90 percent Muslim, so there are no takers for the Lord's Prayer. And, when it comes to the prayers they do want to say, the local Islamic enforcers go ahead secure in the knowledge that the diversity pansies aren't going to do a thing about it.

Nobody would know a thing about the "mosqueteria" story were it not for the blogger Blazing Cat Fur, whom I was honored to say a word for in Ottawa a few months back. He broke this story and then saw it get picked up without credit by the Toronto media. He does that a lot. Currently, he's featuring the thoughts of Jawed Anwar, editor of *The Muslim*, a publication for Greater Toronto Area Muslims, and of Dr. Bilal Philips, a "Canadian religious scholar" who was born in Jamaica but grew up in Toronto and has many prestigious degrees not only from Saudi Arabia but also from the University of Wales, where he completed a Ph.D. in "Islamic Theology." Dr. Philips is in favor of death for homosexuals, and, as one Canadian to another, Mr. Anwar was anxious to explain to his readers that that's nothing to get alarmed about:

> Although, there is no clear-cut verse in Qur'an that categorically suggests killing of homosexuals, sayings of Prophet Muhammad suggests three types of sentences, and among that one is death. Bilal Philips is suggesting, based on his opinion on the Qur'anic/ Prophetic principles of society. He is not advising the Islamic judiciary to kill any gay person they found, but what he is "suggesting" is judicial punishment of death sentence for those who confess or are seen "performing homosexual acts" by "four reliable witnesses without any doubt."
>
> The essence of Islamic laws is to protect the life of human beings. And it happens that sometimes killing of a person can save thousands and sometimes millions of lives. The Islamic judiciary can punish a person with death sentence to save others' lives.

Okay, great, thanks. Glad you cleared that up. Two eminent "Canadian" Muslims are openly discussing the conditions under which homosexuals should be executed—and doing so in the cheerful knowledge that Commissar Hall, so determined to slap down my "Islamophobia," isn't going to do a thing about their "homophobia."

Imagine if you're a *soi-disant* moderate Muslim, genuinely so. You came to Canada because Yemen's a dump, and you don't want to waste your life there. And your daughter loves it, and wants to be Canadian, and be just like the other girls in her street. And then she goes to Valley Park Middle School: What if she doesn't feel it's a religious obligation to attend Friday prayers (as some Muslims argue)? Think there's much chance of being able to opt out easily at Valley Park? What if she wants to dress as she wishes to rather than as the Wahhabi/Salafist imam orders? What if she doesn't want to tell the creepy perve mullah whether she's menstruating or not? What, in other words, is her chance of being able to attend Valley Park as a regular Canadian schoolgirl?

I've had cause to mention before Phyllis Chesler's photographs of Cairo University's evolving dress code over the last half-century. In 1978, the female students in Cairo looked little different from the female students at the University of Toronto, or Kingston. Now the schoolgirls of Toronto look no different from Cairo, where today the female students are all covered. Ms. Chesler's pictures are a story of transformation, but that transformation is not confined to the Middle East.

"Diversity" is where nations go to die. If local Mennonites or Amish were segregating the sexes and making them enter by different doors for religious services in a Toronto grade-school cafeteria, Canadian feminists would howl them down in outrage. But when Muslims do it they fall as silent as their body-bagged sisters in Kandahar. If you're wondering how Valley Park's catchment district got to be 80 to 90 percent Muslim in nothing flat, well, Islam is currently the biggest supplier of new Canadians, as it is of new Britons and new Europeans. Not many western statistics agencies keep tabs on religion, but the Vienna Institute of Demography, for example, calculates that by 2050 a majority of Austrians under fifteen will be Muslim. 2050 isn't that far away. It's as far from today as 2011 is from 1972: The future shows up faster than you think.

A world that becomes more Muslim becomes less everything else: First it's Jews, already abandoning France. Then it's homosexuals, already under siege from gay-bashing in Amsterdam, "the most tolerant city in Europe." Then it's uncovered women, already targeted for rape in Oslo and other Continental cities. And, if you don't any longer have any Jews or (officially) any gays or (increasingly) uncovered women, there are always just Christians in general, from Nigeria to Egypt to Pakistan.

More space for Islam means less space for everything else, and in the end less space for you.

Jawed Anwar is not Canadian. Dr. Bilal Philips is not Canadian. The men who separate boys from girls and menstruating girls from non-menstruating girls every Friday at Valley Park Middle School are not Canadian. Perhaps, were we a different kind of society, they would over time become Canadian. But, because they don't have to, they won't. Because they look at the witless "Pride" parade and the multiculti blather and the diversity commissars handing each other Mutual Backslap Awards all year long, and Jawed and Bilal understand that they're what comes after Canada. This year it's maybe just one mosqueteria. Next year, two or three more. Half a decade on, who knows? South of the border? The Los Angeles Sheriff's Department, for reasons that are unclear, already has a taxpayer-funded "Muslim Community Affairs Unit." But don't worry, your small town in Minnesota will be getting one soon enough. As one Salafist lady told the woman from *The New York Times*, demonstrating how she gradually adopted full-face covering: "It just takes time.... You get used to it."

Look at that picture from Valley Park: Toronto's already used to it.

X

MYSTIC CHORDS

SOUNDS OF THE RUDE WORLD

Steyn's Song of the Week, January 19, 2014

ONE HUNDRED AND FIFTY YEARS AGO, living in a cheap hotel on the Bowery in New York's Lower East Side, a young man laid low by a fever tried to rise from his sick bed. He slipped and fell against the wash basin, shattering it and thereby gashing his throat and gouging his head. It was some time before he was found and taken to the Welfare Island hospital, the same hospital to which Jerome Kern (composer of "The Way You Look Tonight," "Ol' Man River," and many more) would be taken when he collapsed on a New York street in 1945 with no identification on him. And like Kern all those decades later, Stephen Foster died there—on January 13, 1864, three days after his fall. He was only thirty-seven and had in his pocket just a little more than his years in pennies: thirty-eight cents.

Foster's name isn't as famous today as it was in, say, the mid-twentieth century, but his songs are still known: "Camptown Races," "Oh! Susanna," "I Dream of Jeanie with the Light Brown Hair"—or as Bugs Bunny liked to sing, "I dream of Jeanie—she's a light brown hare." Two Stephen Foster compositions are official state songs—"My Old Kentucky Home," and, in Florida, "The Old Folks at Home (Swanee River)." Twenty-first-century Americans know far more songs by Stephen Foster than they do by any American songwriter before Irving Berlin. As for Berlin, Ann Ronell (composer of "Willow, Weep for Me" and "Who's Afraid of the Big Bad Wolf?") worked for his publishing house as a young woman and told me years later of being in Berlin's private office and seeing all his Foster books and memorabilia. "Mr. Berlin," his copyist informed Ann, "considers himself the reincarnation of Stephen Foster." But

Berlin died at 101 owning and enforcing all his copyrights (from "White Christmas" down) and with a lot more than thirty-eight cents in his pocket.

Before his career went south, his songs did. Stephen Foster wrote "Ethiopian songs" for the minstrel shows and plantation ballads ("Massa's in de Cold, Cold Ground") for parlor pianos. For all the copious deployments of the D-word ("darkies") that have to be airbrushed out in contemporary renditions, he brought the sensibility of the South vividly to life for Northern audiences in a way that no one else did. During the Civil War, his songs remained popular on both sides. But he was not a Southerner. He was born in a Pennsylvania town called Lawrenceville, just outside Pittsburgh, on the perfect day for a man whose songs would weave themselves into the fabric of the nation: the Fourth of July—and not just any Glorious Fourth but July 4, 1826, America's fiftieth birthday and the day on which its second and third presidents, John Adams and Thomas Jefferson, both chanced to die.

After Tin Pan Alley got going in the 1890s, and even more so after ASCAP (the composers' enforcement arm) came along, songwriting was a potentially very lucrative activity. But in the mid-nineteenth century it was a much more perilous way to make a living. You could pitch a song to a music publisher, but they generally offered only a one-time fee to purchase the composition outright. In 1848 Foster sold a number he'd written to the Peters firm in Cincinnati for one hundred dollars. It was an insistent polka-like melody with nonsense lyrics ("De sun so hot I froze to death") called "Oh! Susanna." Christy's Minstrels, the biggest stars of the day, liked it enough to make it their theme song, and it became, without any help from radio or records or iTunes, a national hit. In theory, that should have been great news for its author. In practice, it meant that other minstrel troupes took up the song and published it under their own names in cities far away from Mr. Peters in Cincinnati. In the three years after its original publication, it was re-published and re-copyrighted—i.e., stolen—by at least twenty other publishers. Before "Oh! Susanna," no American song had sold more than five thousand copies of sheet music. In nothing flat, "Oh! Susanna" sold over a hundred thousand copies—and all Stephen Foster had to show for it was that original hundred bucks.

Today, most Americans think of "Camptown Races," "Old Black Joe," "Nelly Was a Lady," and the rest of the Foster catalogue as "folk songs"—numbers that just sprang up somewhere out of some vernacular musical tradition, rather than the fruits of one particular individual's labor. But even at the time many Americans thought of Foster's songs as "folk music"—the '49ers who sang "Oh! Susanna" all the way to California assumed it was a folk tune; wasn't everything? I mean, who expected to be paid for writing songs?

Stephen Foster did. Firth, Pond & Co. of New York noticed "Oh! Susanna" and its spectacular sales, and the following year—1849—offered Foster a contract to write songs for them for a royalty rate of two cents per copy of sheet music. And thus Stephen Foster became America's first professional songwriter—that's to say, the first man in America paid to write songs, rather than a blackface minstrel who happened to cook up his own material, like Dan Emmett ("Dixie") or Thomas Rice ("Jump Jim Crow"). Writing songs was what he did: He composed music and lyrics, and then found someone else to sing them. On the strength of his Firth, Pond contract, Foster felt he was financially secure enough to marry his sweetheart Jane— the real-life Jeanie with the light brown hair—and in 1851 they had a daughter, Marion.

It never quite worked, not really. His parents died, his writing sputtered, Jane left him for a while and took Marion with her, his output dwindled further, to four songs a year—and his debts mounted. He persuaded Firth, Pond to advance him cash against future songs—and then found he had no future songs. The contract expired, and he sold his rights to pay his debts. Then came the Civil War. He moved with Jane and Marion to New York, but in 1861 they left—this time for good. Broke and abandoned, Stephen Foster was living the lyric he'd written the best part of a decade earlier:

> *'Tis the song, the sigh of the weary*
> *Hard Times, Hard Times, come again no more*
> *Many days you have lingered around my cabin door*
> *Oh, Hard Times, come again no more....*

But they did, and they got harder, and on that bleak January day in 1864 they finally penetrated his cabin door. Two months later, in March 1864, Wm. A. Pond of New York (Mr. Pond having separated from Mr. Firth) published what he billed as "the last song ever written by Stephen C. Foster. Composed but a few days prior to his death." On my own copy of the sheet music, printed shortly thereafter, Mr. Pond was more circumspect, calling it "one of the latest songs of Stephen C. Foster"—and, lest that confuse anyone who'd been reading the obituaries column, a parenthesis appears under his name: "Composed a short time before his death." Presumably, all of his "latest songs" would have had to be "composed a short time before his death." In those last grim years in New York, there were supposedly over a hundred of them, but, in one of his many moves from seedy rooming house to seedier rooming house, Foster's trunk of manuscripts was lost and never found. And so there was only really one "latest song"—if not, as it's often claimed to be, the very last song he ever wrote, then certainly the last Stephen Foster song to implant itself in the popular consciousness:

> Beautiful Dreamer
> Wake unto me
> Starlight and dewdrops are waiting for thee
> Sounds of the rude world
> Heard in the day
> Lull'd by the moonlight have all pass'd away!

Who is he writing about? If, as some musicologists think, the song was composed in 1862—two years before his death—was it a lament for his wife Jane, recently decamped to Pennsylvania? Or is it merely a sentimental ballad by a professional songwriter, the first American paid to write such things? It's a haunting tune in a 9/8 time signature and chock full of triplets—"beau-ti-ful"…"wake un-to"—that in the wrong hands would be awfully boring. But the melody is so pure and translucent it seems the very essence of song, a song that sounds as if it's always been here, just waiting to be plucked from the air.

And for Stephen Foster's last hurrah it is appropriately a pledge of faith in the beguiling, transformative powers of music:

> *Beautiful Dreamer*
> *Queen of my song*
> *List while I woo thee with soft melody*
> *Gone are the cares*
> *Of life's busy throng*
> *Beautiful Dreamer*
> *Awake unto me!*

But the queen of his song is far away in another state, and the cares of life's busy throng, the sounds of the rude world, are not gone but pressing in all around. Al Jolson, Bing Crosby, Nelson Eddy, the Ink Spots, Jerry Lee Lewis, Roy Orbison, Suzy Bogguss, Sheryl Crow, and thousands more sang "Beautiful Dreamer" in the course of the twentieth century. Not a soul sang it in Stephen Foster's lifetime. The total musical earnings of his short time on earth came to $15,091.08. In the years after his death, his widow and daughter earned from "Beautiful Dreamer" and the rest of his catalogue a mere $4,199 between them. In the last hundred years, those songs would have been worth millions. But by then they were out of the copyright they'd never quite been in.

Along with the thirty-eight cents, they also found a scrap of paper with the penciled words "Dear friends and gentle hearts." A title for a new song? Eighty-five years later, Sammy Fain, composer of "I'll Be Seeing You," and Bob Hilliard, writer of "Our Day Will Come," were sufficiently inspired by the tale of Stephen Foster's last words to turn them around and write a song called "Dear Hearts and Gentle People"—a big hit for Bing Crosby and Dinah Shore but not the kind of tune Foster would have written on the theme.

Dear friends and gentle hearts: A century and a half ago, Stephen Foster could have used more of each. But he wrote "Beautiful Dreamer" in a flophouse, and it will live forever.

DECORATION DAY

The Chicago Sun-Times, May 30, 2004

MEMORIAL DAY IN my corner of New Hampshire is always the same. A clutch of veterans from the Second World War to the Gulf march round the common, followed by the town band, and the scouts, and the fifth-graders. The band plays "Anchors Aweigh," "My Country, 'Tis of Thee," "God Bless America," and, in an alarming nod to modernity, Ray Stevens's "Everything Is Beautiful (In Its Own Way)" (*Billboard* Number One, May 1970). One of the town's selectmen gives a short speech, so do a couple of representatives from state organizations, and then the fifth-graders recite the Gettysburg Address and the Great War's great poetry. There's a brief prayer and a three-gun salute, exciting the dogs and babies. Wreaths are laid. And then the crowd wends slowly up the hill to the Legion hut for ice cream, and a few veterans wonder, as they always do, if anybody understands what they did, and why they did it.

Before the First World War, it was called Decoration Day—a day for going to the cemetery and "strewing with flowers or otherwise decorating the graves of comrades who died in defense of their country during the late rebellion." Some decorated the resting places of fallen family members; others adopted for a day the graves of those who died too young to leave any descendants.

I wish we still did that. Lincoln's "mystic chords of memory" are difficult to hear in the din of the modern world, and one of the best ways to do it is to stand before an old headstone, read the name, and wonder at the young life compressed into those brute dates: 1840–1862. 1843–1864.

In my local cemetery, there's a monument over three graves, forebears of my hardworking assistant, although I didn't know that at the time I first came across them. Turner Grant, his cousin John Gilbert, and his sister's fiancé, Charles Lovejoy, had been friends since boyhood and all three enlisted on the same day. Charles died on March 5, 1863, Turner on March 6, and John on

240

March 11. Nothing splendid or heroic. They were tentmates in Virginia, and there was an outbreak of measles in the camp.

For some reason, there was a bureaucratic mix-up, as there often is, and the army neglected to inform the families. Then, on their final journey home, the bodies were taken off the train at the wrong town. It was a Saturday afternoon and the station master didn't want the caskets sitting there all weekend. So a man who knew where the Grants lived offered to take them up to the next town and drop them off on Sunday morning.

When he arrived, the family was at church, so he unloaded the coffins from his buggy and left without a word or a note to anyone. Imagine coming home from Sunday worship and finding three caskets waiting on the porch. Imagine being young Caroline Grant, and those caskets contain the bodies of your brother, your cousin, and the man to whom you're betrothed.

That's a hell of a story behind the bald dates on three plain tombstones. If it happened today, maybe Caroline would be on Diane Sawyer and Katie Couric demanding proper compensation, and the truth about what happened, and why the politicians were covering it up. Maybe she'd form a group of victims' families. Maybe she'd call for a special commission to establish whether the government did everything it could to prevent disease outbreaks at army camps. Maybe, when they got around to forming the commission, she'd be booing and chanting during the officials' testimony, as several of the 9/11 families did during Mayor Rudy Giuliani's statement.

All wars are messy, and many of them seem small and unworthy even at the moment of triumph. The sight of unkempt lice-infested Saddam Hussein yanked from his spider hole last December is not so very different from the published reports of Jefferson Davis's capture in May 1865, when he was said to be trying to skulk away in women's clothing, and spent the next several months being depicted by gleeful Northern cartoonists in hoop skirts, petticoats, and crinolines (none of which he was actually wearing).

But, conquered and captured, an enemy shrivels, and you question what he ever had that necessitated such a sacrifice. The piercing clarity of war shades into the murky greys of post-war reconstruction. You think Iraq's a quagmire?

Lincoln's "new birth of freedom" bogged down into a century-long quagmire of segregation, Jim Crow, and the Ku Klux Klan. Does that mean that, as Al Gore and other excitable types would say, Abe W. Lincoln *lied* to us?

Like the French Resistance, tiny in its day but of apparently unlimited manpower since the war ended, for some people it's not obvious which side to be on until the dust's settled. New York, for example, resisted the Civil War my small town's menfolk were so eager to enlist in. The big city was racked by bloody riots against the draft. And you can sort of see the rioters' point. More than six hundred thousand Americans died in the Civil War—or about 1.8 percent of the population. Today, if 1.8 percent of the population were killed in the Afghan-Iraq wars, there would be 5.4 million graves to decorate on Decoration Day.

But that's the difference between then and now: the loss of proportion. They had victims galore back in 1863, but they weren't a victim culture. They had a lot of crummy decisions and bureaucratic screw-ups worth re-examining, but they weren't a nation that prioritized retroactive pseudo-legalistic self-flagellating vaudeville over all else. They had hellish setbacks but they didn't lose sight of the forest in order to obsess week after week on one tiny twig of one weedy little tree, as the Democrats do over Abu Ghraib. They were not a people willing to pay any price, bear any burden, as long as it's pain-free, squeaky-clean, and over in a week. The sheer silliness dishonors the memory of all those we're supposed to be remembering this Memorial Day.

*   *   *

Time passes, and moss and lichen creep across ancient grave stones. But the men beneath them are forever young. As I mentioned above, at Memorial Day observances in my neck of the woods the veterans are honored by the fifth-graders, who read verses for the occasion—both the classics and their own poems. The latter can be a bit hit and miss, and one has to be alert, given the dispositions of some of my neighbors, for give-peace-a-chance war-is-never-the-answer not-so-subtle subtexts. But a few years after the above column my then fifth-grade daughter was asked to write something, and so she did. Nothing to do with me—I was away in Chicago all that week—but I was pleased to see that all the rhymes are true. She is older now and has gotten a little teenagey, as they do, and today she would try to write it more sophisticatedly. But I have always liked its heartfelt directness. So this is my daughter Ceci's fifth-grade poem, as a ten-year-old girl delivered it on a small town common in New Hampshire for Memorial Day:

> *The stars and stripes, red, white, and blue*
> *Wave above our heroes true*
> *It makes us cry, it makes us weep*
> *But in our hearts we will keep*
> *The sacrifice our soldiers gave, they shall not die in vain*
> *For they have given us the freedom they have fought to gain.*

SAY, IT AIN'T SO JOE

Maclean's, September 24, 2007

IT'S BEEN A WHILE since I played with GI Joe. At my age, it tends to attract stares from the playground security guard. Nevertheless, I vaguely recall two details about the prototype "action figure": (1) he was something to do with—if you'll pardon the expression—the U.S. military; and (2) he had no private parts.

Flash forward to 2007 and this news item in *Variety* about the forthcoming live-action GI Joe movie:

> While some remember the character from its gung-ho fighting man '60s incarnation, he's evolved. GI Joe is now a Brussels-based outfit that stands for Global Integrated Joint Operating Entity, an international coed force of operatives who use hi-tech equipment to battle Cobra, an evil organization headed by a double-crossing Scottish arms dealer. The property is closer in tone to X-Men and James Bond than a war film.

Golly. So much for my two childhood memories: (1) he's no longer anything to do with the U.S. military; and (2) the guys with no private parts are the execs at Paramount and Hasbro who concluded that an American serviceman would be too tough a sell in the global marketplace. "GI Joe is not just a brand that represents the military," says Brian Goldner, Hasbro's chief operating officer. "It also represents great characters." And nothing says great characters like a Belgian bureaucracy.

The "evolution" of GI Joe is an instructive one. The term "GI" stands for "Galvanized Iron" (which so much army stuff was made of that the initials became a routine speed bump in military bookkeeping) and not, as many assume, for "General Infantry." But it was certainly the poor bloody infantry who embraced the abbreviation, initially for the stuff they were on the receiving end of: In the Great War, U.S. troops used to refer to incoming German artillery shells as "GI cans." By the next global conflict, it was firmly established as an instantly recognizable shorthand for the regular enlisted man, as in Johnny Mercer's hit song:

> *This is the GI Jive*
> *Man alive!*
> *It starts with the bugler blowin' reveille over your head when you*
> *arrive*
> *Jack, that's the GI Jive*
> *Root-tee-tee-toot*
> *Jump in your suit*
> *Make a salute*
> *Voot!*

Who wouldn't love the American GI? He was the citizen soldier—the hapless farmer, the befuddled accountant, the amiable grease monkey, pressed into service to save places like Belgium from the depredations of darker forces. It was the cartoonist David Breger who made him the formal embodiment of the men in uniform. "GI Joe" debuted in *Yank, The Army Weekly*, in 1942 and planted a phrase in the language:

> *When the war was over*
> *There were jobs galore*
> *For the GI Josephs*
> *Who were in the war …*

That's Bing singing Irving Berlin in *White Christmas*, a big Hollywood smash in 1954, with a score that also included the slyly titled "Gee, I Wish I Was Back in the Army." But here's another movie—from 2006, Oliver Stone's *World*

Trade Center—as reviewed by my colleague Brian D. Johnson: "Karnes comes across as a vigilante GI Joe action figure—a born-again Christian soldier who says things like 'We're going to need some good men out there to avenge this.'"

Whoa! That's quite the etymological trip, from shorthand for the little guy to psychotic Christofascist mercenary in a mere half-century. What happened? Well, there was Vietnam, after which Hasbro decided the army was a bummer and relaunched Joe as the head of the "Super Joe Adventure Team." But, when that sputtered and died, he returned as "GI Joe, A Real American Hero."

Question: Can "A Real American Hero" be based in Belgium?

It's often said that what Americans call "globalization" the rest of the world calls "Americanization," and you can see what they mean: if you're French, there doesn't seem anything terribly "globalized" about every airport on the planet offering the same half-dozen American fast-food franchises. The rest of the world knows the routine by now: you're in Hollywood pitching Helen Mirren as the Queen, but the studio exec sees it as a great vehicle for Angelina Jolie, maybe with Ben Affleck as the Duke of Edinburgh. That fellow who wrote *The Horse Whisperer* was a bloke from Yorkshire or some such but he knew enough to set it in Montana. And, sitting through *Saving Private Ryan* or *Pearl Harbor*, I long ago stopped wondering when we'd get an epic tale of derring-do by the Princess Patricia's Canadian Light Infantry or Lord Strathcona's Horse or any of Canada's storied regiments: you can live to 130 and you won't see *Lord Strathcona's Horse Whisperer* at the multiplex.

But cultural globalization cuts both ways. If Hollywood is making product for the planet, in what sense is it any longer "American"? When conservatives complain that the movies' dreary biases are not even in the studios' commercial interest, they correctly point out that the U.S. is pretty much a 50-50 red state–blue state split, and there's a huge underserved market waiting for a picture in which Brian D. Johnson's vigilante GI Joe born-again Christian crazy kicks Islamobutt from Ramadi to Jalalabad and back. But, back at corporate HQ, the vice presidents look at the real market, and throw in all the bonus blue states—Canada, Europe, Asia—and commission yet another lame-o conspiracy thriller in which the stereotypical young Saudi male everyone thinks is going to blow up the plane turns out to have been framed by one of Dick Cheney's Halliburton subsidiaries to distract attention from global warming.

That's not to say there aren't any movies about regular GI Joes. Brian De Palma's just made one. It's called *Redacted*, and it's already won a couple of prestigious prizes in Venice. To be honest, I've never been able to take De Palma seriously since he used that ridiculous body double for Angie Dickinson in the nude shower scenes of *Dressed to Kill*. But he's certainly come a long way since then. *Redacted* is based on real events: the brutal rape and murder of an Iraqi girl at the hands of four good ol' GIs. Sergeant Paul Cortez was sentenced earlier this year to one hundred years in jail for the killing, which suggests that the U.S. military takes these things seriously. Statistically speaking, American soldiers rape and murder at a significantly lower rate than the citizens of America's "liberal" cities. Nonetheless, for De Palma these events represent the larger U.S. adventure in Iraq, and only he has the courage to speak out! "I have done something that just cannot be done," he crowed on the BBC the other day. "You can never say anything critical of the troops."

Oh, come on. You can say what you like about American troops: among U.S. senators alone, Ted Kennedy's compared them to Baathists, and Dick Durbin to Nazis. What you can't do is make a movie showing them as a force for good in the world. So the great iconic shorthand for the American fighting man has to be appropriated and "evolved" into an acronym for some multilateral Belgian action team. Talk about suspension of disbelief. Do you know what the chances of basing any kick-ass "joint operating entity" in Brussels are? This is a country that in the spring of 2003 announced it was considering war crimes prosecutions against Rumsfeld, Powell, and America's commanders—at least until Rumsfeld quietly remarked that maybe the new American-funded NATO headquarters didn't need to be in Brussels after all. Any Belgian action team would be constrained by rules of engagement drawn so tight (see the Norwegians et al. in Afghanistan) that they'd be spending most of the movie sending memos to each other. So instead the planet's moviegoers will be subjected to a fiction more absurd than any comic book: American-style action, yes please! But no American values.

Maybe Hollywood directors should get themselves a new bumper sticker: "We Support Our Troops. But Our Troops Can't Support Our Business Model."

HAPPY BIRTHDAY, MISTER BOB

The National Post, May 24, 2001

I FIRST NOTICED a sudden uptick in Bob Dylan articles maybe a couple of months ago, when instead of Pamela Anderson's breasts or J-Lo's bottom bursting through the *National Post* masthead there appeared to be a shriveled penis that had spent way too long in the bath. On closer inspection, this turned out to be Bob Dylan's head. He was, it seems, getting ready to celebrate his birthday. For today he turns sixty.

Sixty? I think the last time I saw him on TV was the eightieth-birthday tribute to Sinatra six years ago, and, to judge from their respective states, if Frank was eighty, Bob had to be at least 130. He mumbled his way through "Restless Farewell," though neither words nor tune were discernible, and then shyly offered, "Happy Birthday, Mister Frank." Frank sat through the number with a stunned look, no doubt thinking, "Geez, that's what I could look like in another twenty, twenty-five years if I don't ease up on the late nights."

Still, Bob's made it to sixty, and for that we should be grateful. After all, for the grizzled old hippies, folkies, and peaceniks who spent the Sixties bellowing along with "How does it *feeeeeel?*" these have been worrying times. A couple of years ago, Bob's management were canceling his tours, and the only people demanding to know "How does it *feeeeeel?*" were Dylan's doctors, treating him in New York for histoplasmosis, a fungal infection that in rare cases can lead to potentially fatal swelling in the pericardial sac. If the first question on your lips is "How is histoplasmosis spread?" well, it's caused by fungal spores which invade the lungs through airborne bat droppings. In other words, the answer, my friend, is blowin' in the wind.

He has, of course, looked famously unhealthy for years, even by the impressive standards of Sixties survivors. He was at the Vatican not so long ago, and, although we do not know for certain what the Pope said as the leathery, wizened, stooped figure with gnarled hands and worn garb was ushered into the holy presence, it was probably something along the lines of, "Mother Teresa! But they told me you were dead!" "No, no, your Holiness," an aide would have hastily explained. "This is Bob Dylan, the voice of a disaffected generation."

It is not for me to join the vast army of Dylanologists who've been poring over his songs for thirty years. As Bob himself once said, "They are whatever they are to whoever's listening to them." End of story. But it does seem to me that, while most rock stars pursue eternal youth, Dylan has always sought premature geezerdom. The traditional elderly rocker look is best exemplified by Gram'pa Rod Stewart: peroxide hair with that toss-a-space-heater-in-the-bathtub look, tight gold lamé pants with extravagant codpiece, pneumatic supermodel on your arm. By contrast, Bob, barely out of his teens, consciously adopted an aged singing voice and the experience it implied, a quintessentially Dylanesque jest on pop's Peter Pan ethos.

When he emerged in the early Sixties, he was supposedly a drifter who had spent years on the backroads of America picking up folk songs from wrinkly old-timers, and who provoked Robert Shelton of *The New York Times* to rhapsodize about "the rude beauty of a southern field hand musing in melody on his porch." Actually, he'd toiled instead at the University of Minnesota—a Jewish college boy, son of an appliance store manager. The folk songs he knew had been picked up not from any real live folk, but from the records of Ramblin' Jack Elliott. Ramblin' Jack had rambled over from Brooklyn, dropping his own Jewish name—Elliott Adnopoz—en route. "There was not another sonofabitch in the country that could sing until Bob Dylan came along," pronounced Ramblin' Jack, with a pithiness that belies his sobriquet. "Everybody else was singing like a damned faggot." It remains one of the more modest claims made on Dylan's behalf.

His first album was composed almost entirely of traditional material. But by the second he was singing his own compositions, pioneering the musical oxymoron of the era, the "original folk song": No longer did a folk song have to be something of indeterminate origin sung by generations of inbred mountain men after a couple of jiggers of moonshine and a bunk-up with their sisters. Now a "folk song" could be "A Hard Rain's A-Gonna Fall" or "The Times They Are A-Changin'." I'm reminded of that episode of, appropriately enough, *The Golden Girls*, when Estelle Getty comes rushing in shouting, "The hurricane's a-comin'! The hurricane's a-comin'!" "Ma!" Bea Arthur scolds her. "*A*-comin'?" With Dylan, the songwriting styles they were a-regressin', the slyly seductive archaisms and harmonica obbligato designed to evoke the integrity of American popular music before the Tin Pan Alley hucksters took over.

"Without Bob the Beatles wouldn't have made *Sergeant Pepper*, the Beach Boys wouldn't have made *Pet Sounds*," said Bruce Springsteen. "U2 wouldn't have done 'Pride in the Name of Love'," he continued, warming to his theme. "The Count Five would not have done 'Psychotic Reaction'. There never would have been a group named the Electric Prunes." But why hold all that against Bob? If rock lyrics wound up as clogged and bloated as Dylan's pericardial sac, that's hardly his fault. Bob, for his part, has doggedly pursued his quest to turn back the clock. He's on the new *Sopranos* soundtrack CD, singing Dean Martin's "Return to Me," complete with chorus in Italian. Just the latest reinvention: Bob Dino, suburban crooner.

Visiting America a few years ago, Dave Stewart, of the Eurythmics, said to Dylan that the next time he was in England he should drop by his recording studio in Crouch End, an undistinguished north London suburb. Dylan, at a loose end one afternoon, decided to take him up on it and asked a taxi driver to take him to Crouch End Hill. Cruising the bewildering array of near-namesake streets—Crouch End Hill, Crouch End Road, Crouch Hill End, Crouch Hill Road, and various other permutations of "Crouch," "End," and "Hill," not to mention Crouch Hall Road—the cabbie accidentally dropped him off at the right number but in an adjoining street of small row houses. Dylan knocked at the front door and asked the woman who answered if Dave was in.

"No," she said, assuming he was referring to her husband, Dave, who was out on a plumbing job. "But he should be back soon." Bob asked if she would mind if he waited. Twenty minutes later, Dave—the plumber, not the rock star—returned and asked the missus whether there were any messages. "No," she said, "but Bob Dylan's in the front room having a cup of tea."

It's a sweet image, compounded by the subsequent rumor that Dylan had been seen with local realtors looking for a house in the area. Perhaps deep inside his Southern field-hand persona is a suburban sexagenarian pining for a quiet life in a residential cul-de-sac, dispensing advice over the fence to the next-door neighbor on how to keep your lawn free of grass clippings: "The answer, my friend, is mowin' in the wind."

Happy birthday, Mister Bob.

WE AREN'T THE WORLD

The National Post, January 2, 2003

WELL, IT'S JANUARY 2 and you, the loyal reader, have a right to expect that we media types have given up sloughing off lame-o "Best of the Year" lists for another eleven-and-a-half months. But not so fast. If I were compiling a "Best Lists of the Year" list, my best list of the year would be this one: the BBC World Service poll of the Top Ten Songs of All Time.

I know a bit about these kinds of surveys from my disc-jockey days. Listeners are always surprised to find that the Beatles and Elvis get nowhere. That's because their vote gets split between a dozen hits all about equally popular. A superstar needs a mega-ultra-anthemic blockbuster big enough to counter his vote getting dispersed among the rest of his catalogue: Sinatra has "My Way," Simon and Garfunkel "Bridge over Troubled Water," Queen "Bohemian Rhapsody," Whitney Houston "I Will Always Love You-ulating," all the big hit-list reliables.

Not everyone goes for these all-time standbys. Among several minor celebrities who voted in the BBC poll, Bianca Jagger opted for Bob Dylan's "Knockin' on Heaven's Door," Kevin Spacey for Bobby Darin's "Mack the Knife," and Imelda Marcos for the Hallelujah chorus from Handel's *Messiah*—the widow of the late Filipino strongman usefully reminding us that pre-Sixties smashes were also eligible for the survey. Over 150,000 votes from 155 countries were recorded, and this is how it all came out. To add to the suspense, I'll count them down in reverse order. As the host Steve Wright put it, "Enjoy listening to the world's favorite songs!"

10. "Bohemian Rhapsody," Queen

9. "Chaiyya Chaiyya," A. R. Rahman

8. "Believe," Cher

7. "Reetu Haruma Timi," Arun Thapa

6. "Ana wa Laila," Kazem al-Saher

5. "Pooyum Nadakkuthu Pinchum Nadakkuthu," Thirumalai Chandran

4. "Rakkamma Kaiya Thattu," Ilayaraja

3. "Dil Dil Pakistan," Vital Signs

2. "Vande Mataram," various artists

1. "A Nation Once Again," The Wolfe Tones

So much for the Great Satan's suffocating cultural imperialism. I'll bet I'm the only *National Post* columnist who can even hum the Number One song. It's an Irish Republican rebel ballad from the 1840s. The reason I know is because I was once in a bar in Liverpool and a couple of lads started singing it and a couple of others objected and a fight broke out. As a loyal subject of the Crown, I was on the side of the objectors. We eventually prevailed, but, even if we hadn't, "A Nation Once Again" is a fine song to get your head kicked into, at least when compared to "Believe" by Cher, which would rank pretty high on a list of numbers I'd least like to be listening to as my eye's gouged out and I fall into a coma, although it would in a way be a merciful release.

But the point is we're not in Casey Kasem territory. My cunning plan was to wait till the BBC announced the World's Favorite Songs, record them on a CD, and make a killing at the mall. But I have a feeling it's not gonna work. We must take the Corporation's spokespersons at their word when they deny their poll was nobbled by a bunch of wily nationalist bog-trotters plotting to put one over on the hated Brit oppressor's cultural mouthpiece. And, for all the talk of vote fixing, the sample's a lot bigger than those polls that claim to measure anti-Americanism throughout Europe and the Middle East. But, whatever the problems of methodology, there's something rather appealing about the way the list disdains Anglo-American pop hegemony—no Sir Elton caterwauling "Goodbye, England's Rose," no Céline and her *Songs for Sinkin' Liners*.

Superficially, the chart has the appeal of those shows you hear late in the evening on public radio, usually called "Worldbeat" or "Rhythms of the Planet" or some such. They work less well on private stations. In the small hours of a snowy January night about a decade ago, I was driving through the Green Mountains of Vermont with Anthony Lane, *The New Yorker*'s film critic, and housewives' darling Sebastian Faulks, whose novel *Birdsong* has enriched so many airport concession stands. There was a big Latin dance thing back then that was all the rage called the Lambada, but the overnight jock on WKXE said you'd never really heard the song until you'd heard the twelve-minute Hindu version.

"Wow!" said Anthony. "This is the best record I've ever heard," said Sebastian, "except for 'I Just Called to Say I Loved You.'" But it turns out there aren't all that many Vermonters who want to hear Hindu versions of Latin dance sensations. About a month later, the station switched to soft 'n' easy favorites, and the late-night guy got fired.

In that sense, the BBC's Top Ten Songs of All Time are admirably multicultural. Certainly, a multitude of cultures is represented: the Irish rebel ballad narrowly edged out the Indian patriotic song from an 1882 novel by Bankim Chandra Chattopadhyay at Number Two and the pop national anthem of Pakistan at Number Three; just below them you'll find a love song from Nepal, a Tamil Tiger song about the oppression of the Tamils in Sri Lanka, the theme from a Bollywood version of *The Godfather*, and a perennial favorite by Iraq's biggest pop star (Kazem al-Saher).

But the list is also multicultural in its rejection of a common culture. On the face of it, it's preposterous that "A Nation Once Again," a dreary dirge no non-Irishman has the slightest interest in, can now claim to be the planet's all-time favorite song. But it's no more preposterous than some happy-sappy mumbo-jumbo like "We Are the World" followed by Quincy Jones doing his usual acceptance-speech shtick about how, whether you're a New York sideman or an Alabama gangsta rapper or an Uzbekistani bluegrass fiddler or a Saudi lounge act, there are no borders in music. Indeed, in its new role as underminer of the BBC Top Ten, "A Nation Once Again" is far more subversive than it ever was as a rallying cry against the reviled Crown: For what could be more exquisitely mischievous than a virulently parochial anthem of unregenerate nationalism winning a survey intended to demonstrate that music is the universal language?

The great Canadian media seer Marshall McLuhan was never more wrong than when he was peddling that "global village" hooey. Multiculturalism is more like a global housing project where we all do our own thing and nobody knows their neighbors. Thus, fans of individual numbers in this Top Ten have no interest in hearing any of the other nine; try going into an Irish bar and singing "Vande Mataram."

But the BBC poll goes further than mere multiculti isolationism, featuring as it does not just songs which appeal to very narrow ethnic groups but songs which are positively offensive to large numbers of other ethnic groups. Don't open with "A Nation Once Again" in an East Belfast pub, or with "Dil Dil Pakistan" in India, or with "Pooyum Nadakkuthu Pinchum Nadakkuthu" if you've got a big Sinhalese crowd in the house tonight. You'll be lucky to get out alive.

The BBC World Service, founded to bind the Empire and promote Britannic values, these days cruises mushily under the slogan "Many Voices, One World." But many of these voices cheerily reject the multicultural, multilateral, multinational pieties of one world in favor of a fierce musical jingoism: Tamils vote Tamil, Irish Catholics vote Irish Catholic. The only listeners who made any effort to live up to the virtues of the multicultural utopia were the Americans, who voted for "The Girl from Ipanema" by Brazilian bossa maestro Antonio Carlos Jobim. Typical. The only evidence in the BBC's "one world" that any of us are open to any "voices" other than our own is the much-mocked cocktail-hour staple of every suburban hi-fi in the mid-Sixties.

I can't help feeling that in this strange poll there are some profound lessons about the illusions of the age. Those of us skeptical of multiculturalism will be heartened by the dizzying variety of local prejudices on display in these unlovely songs. Today, we are not provinces of empire but of the slyer, suppler transnational elites. For that reason, in its stirring cry of nationalist pride, the

Wolfe Tones' rebel yell, now sanctified as the world's favorite song, is truly a song for the world:

> *And then I prayed I yet might see our fetters rent in twain,*
> *And Ireland, long a province, be a nation once again!*

We Are the World. Not.

THE PARLIAMENT OF
EURO-MAN

Maclean's, June 22, 2009

TO PROMOTE A greater sense of Euro-harmony, the European Parliament—actually, make that the European "Parliament"—is organized into ideological blocs, ensuring that French liberals sit with Slovene liberals, and Belgian greens sit with Latvian greens, rather than hunkering down in their ethnic ghettoes. The largest bloc is the "center-right," the second-largest are the socialists, and the third is now the "non-inscrits," the bloc for people who don't want to belong to blocs. As a result of this month's election, this Groucho Marxist grouping of "Others" tripled in size to just under a hundred seats. So, if they're not liberals, socialists, greens, "European democrats," or the "Nordic Green Left," what the hell are they?

Okay, here goes. The members of the non-bloc bloc include: one member of the "True Finns" party; one member of the Slovak National Party; two members of the British National Party; two members of the Austrian Freedom Party; two members of the Vlaams Belang, the "Flemish Interest" party; two members of the Civic Union, which sounds like a gay marriage in Vermont but is in fact an offshoot of the Latvian nationalist For Fatherland and Freedom Party; three members of France's National Front; three members of Jobbik, the Hungarian nationalist party; three members of the Greater Romania Party....

Well, you get the picture. The European Parliament isn't exactly working out as Lord Tennyson foresaw:

> ... the war-drum throbb'd no longer, and the battle-flags were
> furl'd

In the Parliament of man, the Federation of the world.
There the common sense of most shall hold a fretful realm in awe
And the kindly earth shall slumber, lapt in universal law.

A Federation of Euro-harmony filled by ultra-nationalist xenophobes is almost too droll a jest. My favorite of these new national parties is Ataka, which is a Bulgarian word meaning—oh, go on, take a wild guess. That's right: "Attack." What a splendidly butch name. The Attack party was formed from last year's merger of the Bulgarian National Patriotic Party, the Union of Patriotic Forces, and the National Movement for the Salvation of the Fatherland, and in nothing flat managed to get 13 percent of the vote.

Like Attack, many of these lively additions to the political scene favor party emblems that slyly evoke swastikas while bending the prongs in different directions just enough to maintain deniability. Other than that, they don't have a lot in common with their colleagues in the no-bloc bloc.

I don't just mean in the sense that the leader of the Slovak National Party said a couple of years back, "Let's all get in tanks and go and flatten Budapest," which presumably is not a policy position the Hungarian nationalists in Jobbik would endorse. But there are broader differences, too. The SNP is antipathetic to homosexuals, whereas Krisztina Morvai, the attractive blonde Jobbik member just elected to the Euro-parliament, is a former winner of the Freddie Mercury Prize for raising AIDS awareness. I can't be the only political analyst who wishes that, instead of a victory speech last Sunday, Doktor Morvai had stood on the table in black tights and bellowed out "We Are the Champions."

Like our chums at Canada's "human rights" commissions, Doktor Morvai is a "human rights" activist—and, indeed, a former delegate to the UN Women's Rights Committee. One thing a woman has a right to is an uncircumcised penis. In the course of her successful election campaign, the good doctor told Hungarian Jews to "go back to playing with their tiny little circumcised tails." I don't know what Krisztina has against circumcised penises, but presumably it's not her pelvis.

It's unclear whether any member of the Austrian Freedom Party has won the Freddie Mercury Prize, but its late leader, Jörg Haider, wound up pushing up edelweiss eight months ago when he flipped his Volkswagen limo after leaving a gay bar in Klagenfurt somewhat the worse for wear. "He never helped his family man image by turning up at rallies and local events with an entourage of young blond men," reported *The Daily Mail*. "Newspapers in his homeland said they were reluctant to publish 'full details' of his homosexuality fearing an outburst of hate toward the gay community would overtake hatred towards foreigners."

Er, if you say so. So hard to know who to hate first, isn't it? And you've gotta be able to prioritize.

In Austria's Euro-election, two explicitly anti-immigrant parties won 18 percent of the vote. In the United Kingdom, meanwhile, the new nationalist vote was divided between the British National Party and the UK Independence Party, which supports British withdrawal from the European Union and managed to elect thirteen members to the European Parliament, winning 17 percent of the vote and pushing Gordon Brown's Labour Party into third place. The two seats won by the BNP represent the first victory in a national election by any British Fascist party, however squishily one cares to define that term. Seventy years ago, under Sir Oswald Mosley, a far more charismatic leader than the BNP's Nick Griffin, the British Union of Fascists never managed to elect a single local councilor. So the electors of the United Kingdom crossed a dark Rubicon this month.

For forty years, London's Europhile politico-media elites have attempted to impose a "European identity" on the masses, condescendingly assuring the British people that they are, indeed, European, they're just too parochial and ill-informed to realize it. Thus the paradox: in its rejection of Europe, the British electorate has never been more European. The Brits have finally got with the program: just like the Continentals, they're voting for fascists.

Woody Guthrie used to have a label on his guitar: "This Machine Kills Fascists." Not true, of course. Just the usual self-flattery to which singing Commies are prone. But, in the room where they cook up European conventional wisdom, they could easily pin a sign on the door saying: "This Political Machine Creates Fascists." One can forgive Bulgaria its wackier demagogues: they are, after all, only two decades removed from one-party totalitarianism. But, in the western half of Continental Europe, politics evolved to the point where almost any issue worth talking about was ruled beyond the bounds of polite society. In good times, it doesn't matter so much. But in bad times, if the political culture forbids respectable politicians from raising certain issues, then the electorate will turn to unrespectable ones. Europe has taken a worse hit than North America in the first crisis of economic globalization: unemployment in Spain, for example, is over 17 percent. To the Marxist historian Eric Hobsbawm, this "crisis of capitalism" is the biggest event since the fall of the Soviet Union. But, if it's a "crisis of capitalism," why did the mainstream Euroleft take the electoral hit rather than the mainstream Euro-right? Instead of turning to socialist parties promising more state booty, voters boosted the fortunes of the neo-nationalists. Many of these groups are economically protectionist (and in some cases more "left wing" than, say, the British Labour Party), but they're also culturally protectionist in a way the polytechnic left most certainly isn't. They raise the subjects you're not meant to. You want to talk about immigration?

Whoa, racist!

Crime?

Racist!

Welfare?

Racist!

Islam?

Racistracistdoubleracist!!! Nya-nya, can't hear you with my two anti-racist thumbs in my ears!

Already, the European political class is congratulating itself at holding the tide of neo-nationalism to the low double-digits. I'd say some of these results are pretty remarkable given that these parties are all but excluded from the public discourse and that even a relatively mild dissenter from the consensus such as the Dutch parliamentarian Geert Wilders has been banned from setting foot in Britain and is undergoing prosecution for his views in the Netherlands. What makes the Labour Party "mainstream" with 15 percent of the vote and UKIP the "fringe" with 17 percent? Nothing, other than the blinkers of the politico-media class.

But if you want to drive the electorate toward the wilder shores in ever greater numbers, keep crying "Racist!" at every opportunity.

Things are not going to get any prettier in the next European electoral cycle.[1] Aside from professions of "horror" at the success of the neo-nationalists, there is now talk of shutting down these parties by using the legal system (as was done in Belgium) or by denying them the public funding to which their share of the vote entitles them. Subverting democracy to suppress neo-nationalism doesn't seem a smart move. But then if the political class were that smart it wouldn't be in this situation.

The problem in Europe is not a lunatic fringe but a lunatic mainstream ever more estranged from its voters.

---

1   In the 2014 Euro election, the anti-EU UKIP won the vote in the United Kingdom, the anti-EU Front National won the vote in France, and the Finns Party doubled its seats to two.

CHANGING HIS TUNE

*Pete Seeger lived long—long enough to play at the Obama inauguration,
long enough to enjoy extensive public celebrations of his ninetieth birthday, long enough to go down and join the Occupy Wall Street protesters:
I believe he serenaded them with "Where Have All the Flowers Gone?"
although with that crowd "Where Have All the Showers Gone?" might
have been more appropriate. The old banjo-picker lived longer than the
penniless African he fleeced in his copyright heist of "Wimoweh (The Lion
Sleeps Tonight)"; and twice or thrice as long as the average "dissenting artist" made it to under the regimes he admired over the years. He died in 2014
at the age of ninety-four. And cutting it mighty fine in that four-score-and-
ten-and-then-some he had a re-think:*

National Review, September 24, 2007

IN THE NEW YORK SUN the other day, Ron Radosh had a notable scoop: Hold
the front page! Stop the presses! Grizzled Leftie Icon Repudiates....

Who? Castro? Chávez? Al-Qaeda?

Whoa, let's not rush to judgment. No, the big story was: Grizzled Leftie
Icon Repudiates...Stalin.

A couple of months ago, there was some documentary or other "celebrating" the "spirit" of Pete Seeger, the folkie colossus, with contributions from
the usual suspects—Joan Baez, Bruce Springsteen, one or more Dixie Chicks,
two-thirds of Peter, Paul, and Mary, etc. Mr. Radosh had also been interviewed
but his remarks about Seeger's lifelong support of Stalinism had not made the
final cut. No surprise there. In such circumstances, the rule is to hail someone
for his "activism" and "commitment" and "passion" without getting hung up
on the specifics of what exactly he's actively and passionately committing to.

Giving him a Kennedy Center Honor a decade or so back, President Clinton hailed ol' Pete as "an inconvenient artist who dared to sing things as he saw them," which is one way of putting it. You can't help noticing, though, that it's all the documentaries and honors ceremonies and lifetime-achievement tributes to Mr. Seeger that seem to find certain things "inconvenient." *The Washington Post's* Style section, with its usual sly élan, hailed him as America's "best-loved Commie"—which I think translates as "Okay, so the genial old coot spent a lifetime shilling for totalitarian murderers, but only uptight Republican squares would be boorish enough to dwell on it."

Anyway, in *The Sun*, Mr. Radosh, a former banjo pupil of the great man, did dwell on it, and a few weeks later got a letter in response. "I think you're right," wrote Pete. "I should have asked to see the gulags when I was in [the] USSR." And he enclosed a new song he'd composed:

> *I'm singing about old Joe, cruel Joe*
> *He ruled with an iron hand*
> *He put an end to the dreams*
> *Of so many in every land*
> *He had a chance to make*
> *A brand new start for the human race*
> *Instead he set it back*
> *Right in the same nasty place*
> *I got the Big Joe Blues*
> *(Keep your mouth shut or you will die fast)*
> *I got the Big Joe Blues*
> *(Do this job, no questions asked)*
> *I got the Big Joe Blues …*

It's heartening to see that age (he's now eighty-eight) hasn't withered Seeger's unerring instinct for bum rhymes ("fast/asked"). Still, Ron Radosh was thrilled that, just fifty-four years after the old brute's death, a mere three-quarters of a century after the purges and show trials, the old protest singer had finally got around to protesting Stalin, albeit somewhat evasively: He put the human race "right in the same nasty place"? Sorry, not good enough. Stalin created whole new degrees of nastiness.

But, given that Seeger got the two great conflicts of the twentieth century wrong (in 1940, he was anti-war and singing "Wendell Willkie and Franklin D / Both agree on killing me"), it's a start. I can't wait for his anti-Osama LP circa 2078.

Mr. Seeger has a song called "Treblinka," because he thinks it's important that we "never forget." But wouldn't it be better if we were hip to it before it snowballed into one of those things we had to remember not to forget? Would it kill the icons of the left just for once to be on the right side at the time? America has no "best-loved Nazi" or "best-loved Fascist" or even "best-loved Republican," but its best-loved Stalinist stooge is hailed in his dotage as a secular saint who's spent his life "singing for peace."

He sang for "peace" when he opposed the fascistic arms-lobby stooge Roosevelt and imperialist Britain, and he sang for "peace" when he attacked the Cold War paranoiac Truman, and he kept on singing for "peace" no matter how many millions died and millions more had to live in bondage, and, while that may seem agreeably peaceful when you're singing "If I Had a Hammer" in Ann Arbor, it's not if you're on the sharp end of the deal thousands of miles away.

Explaining how Stalin had "put an end to the dreams" of a Communist utopia, Seeger told Ron Radosh that he'd underestimated "how the majority of the human race has faith in violence." But that isn't true, is it? Very few of us are violent. Those who order the killings are few in number, and those who carry them out aren't significantly numerous. But those willing to string along and those too fainthearted to object and those who just want to keep their heads down and wait for things to blow over are numbered in the millions. And so are those many miles away in the plump prosperous western democracies who don't see why this or that dictator is their problem. One can perhaps understand the great shrug of indifference to distant monsters. It's harder, though, to forgive the contemporary urge to celebrate it as a form of "idealism."

James Lileks, the bard of Minnesota, once offered this trenchant analysis of Pete Seeger: "'If I Had a Hammer'? Well, what's stopping you? Go to the hardware store; they're about a buck-ninety, tops."

Very true. For the cost of a restricted-view seat at a Peter, Paul, and Mary revival, you could buy half a dozen top-of-the-line hammers and have a lot more fun, even if you used them on yourself. Yet in a sense Lileks is missing the point: Yes, they're dopey nursery-school jingles, but that's why they're so insidious. The numbing simplicity allows them to be passed off as uncontentious unexceptionable all-purpose anthems of goodwill. Which is why you hear "This Land Is Your Land" in American grade schools, but not "The Battle Hymn of the Republic."

The invention of the faux-childlike faux–folk song was one of the greatest forces in the infantilization of American culture. Seeger's hymn to the "senselessness" of all war, "Where Have All the Flowers Gone?," combined passivity with condescension—"When will they ever learn?"—and established the default mode of contemporary artistic "dissent." Mr. Seeger's ongoing veneration is indestructible. But at least we now know the answer to the question "When will *he* ever learn?"

At least half a century too late.

CHANGING HIS WORDS

The National Post, January 4, 2001

UNDOUBTEDLY, THE HIGHLIGHT of New Year's Eve was the first performance of the new Russian national anthem, which is the old Soviet anthem but with new words. What impressed me most about the new lyrics was the author, Sergei Mikhalkov. The same guy who wrote the old lyrics! And the lyrics for the version before that!

Comrade Mikhalkov's first shot at the national anthem was in 1943, when he wrote it as a paean to his then mentor: "Great Stalin raised us to be loyal to the people / To labor and great exploits he inspired us."

But Stalin died, and Khrushchev had him airbrushed out of the people's iconography. So Mikhalkov was told to write some new words. Wary of hymning any more here-today-gone-tomorrow dictators, the versatile comrade confined himself to rhapsodizing about the more general virtues of Communism:

> *Sing to the Motherland, home of the free*
> *Bulwark of peoples in brotherhood strong*
> *O Party of Lenin, the strength of the people*
> *To Communism's triumph lead us on!*

But times change more often than you think. So, when Vladimir Putin said Russia needed yet another rewrite, the eighty-seven-year-old Mikhalkov did his duty. After the "My kind of guy, Joe Stalin is" version and the "Commie, fly with me" version, Mikhalkov had no problem rustling up another set of verses for the "new" Russia. Let's see: no passing strongmen, no explicit political philosophy, best to stick to the lie of the land....

> *Be glorious, our country!*
> *We are proud of you!*
> *From the southern seas to the polar north*
> *Our forests and fields spread*
> *You are unique in the world, inimitable....*

I'll tell you who's uniquely inimitable: Comrade Sergei. What a survivor! He could do an entire "And then I wrote ..." evening with just the one song: "And now Sergei Mikhalkov performs a medley of his hit." Is there no subject he can't set to that tune? Go on, give him a call. "Hey, Sergei, love that melody! But I'm opening in Vegas and I'd love a couple of topical verses about Hillary's new book deal."

The wily old thing popped up on state television last week, and I thought we might get a little insight into his songwriting methods: "You know, when people ask, 'What comes first? The words or the music?' I always say: the regime!" But, instead, the Berlin of the Bolsheviks waxed philosophical: "The country is now different," he shrugged. "Russia has moved along its own path." He insisted he didn't miss his earlier lyrics: This was one red who ain't singing the blues. "What I have written now is very close to my heart. I wrote what I believe." Really? Pinned to his lapel was one of his four Orders of Lenin.

His first set of lyrics—the Stalin one—was dismissed by a famous Russian actor as "shit."

"So what?" said Mikhalkov. "When they play it, you'll still have to stand up."

The second version—the post-Stalin one—was dismissed by the dissident poet Yevgeny Yevtushenko as "feeble."

"Go home and learn it," Mikhalkov said.

And now we have the third version, a lyric for the ages: "Loyalty to the Fatherland gives us strength...." I suppose so, if you're as boundlessly flexible as Comrade Mikhalkov.... "Loyalty to the Fatherland gives us strength! / Thus it was, it is, and always shall be!"

Well, at least for a year or two.

MOON RIVER AND ME

Maclean's, November 23, 2009

We're after the same rainbow's end
Waiting round the bend
My huckleberry friend
Moon River and me ...

WHERE IS MOON RIVER? Everywhere and nowhere. But, if you had to pin it down, you'd find it meandering at least metaphorically somewhere in the neighborhood of Savannah, Georgia. At one point, the town's most celebrated musical emissary was Hard-Hearted Hannah, the Vamp of Savannah. But then the American Songbook's huckleberry friend showed up: John Herndon Mercer, born in Savannah one hundred years ago, November 18, 1909. The family home, the Mercer House, is the setting for the most famous book written about Savannah, *Midnight in the Garden of Good and Evil*, and Clint Eastwood's film made the connection even more explicit with an all-Mercer soundtrack: Kevin Spacey singing "That Old Black Magic," k. d. lang "Skylark," Diana Krall "Midnight Sun," and Clint himself taking a respectable thwack at "Ac-Cent-Tchu-Ate the Positive."

Johnny Mercer didn't linger in Savannah—as a teenager he stowed away on a ship to New York and the bright lights—but a lot of Savannah lingered in him. To mark his centenary, Knopf has produced the latest in its series of lavish, handsome coffee-table *Complete Lyrics*. Mercer's predecessors in the set are Cole Porter, Irving Berlin, Lorenz Hart, Ira Gershwin, Oscar Hammerstein—the Broadway guys who wrote songs for characters and plots. Insofar as there are famous lyric-writers, that's who they are: Cole Porter "punishing the parquet" (in his words) as he paces his penthouse polishing the polysyllables for a sophisticated triple-rhymed sixth chorus in the second act name-dropping all his Park Avenue pals. Mercer never had a real Broadway hit, but he's the link between New York's songwriting royalty and a more rural tradition. Like Hart and Gershwin, he was a fan of W. S. Gilbert and the Savoy Operas. Unlike them, he also had an eye for the great American landscape west of the Hudson River:

> *From Natchez to Mobile*
> *From Memphis to St. Joe*
> *Wherever the four winds blow*
> *I been in some big towns*
> *An' heard me some big talk*
> *But there is one thing I know …*

"Blues in the Night" was written for some nothing film in 1941 that didn't even know what it had. Harold Arlen's tune is less a twelve-bar blues than a fifty-eight-bar blues aria, its harmony full of plaintive lonesome sevenths, and Mercer's lyric eschews the blues device of repetition for a kind of lightly worn vernacular poetry:

> *Now the rain's a-fallin'*
> *Hear the train a-callin'*
> *Whoo-ee!*
> *(My mama done tol' me)*
> *Hear that lonesome whistle*
> *Blowin' cross the trestle*
> *Whoo-ee!*
> *(My mama done tol' me….)*

He loved trains, hated planes. So he wrote great train songs: "On the Atchison, Topeka and the Santa Fe"; "(I took a trip on a train and) I Thought about You"; "And you see Laura / On a train that is passing through...." Ira Gershwin or Larry Hart would never have heard the music in that "lonesome whistle." For one thing, it doesn't even rhyme with "trestle." It just fits in some strange organic way you can't precisely define. That's how he approached the job: music suggests a sound, a sound suggests certain syllables, and eventually a word or a thought will emerge and you're in business.

In the Forties, he founded Capitol Records and became a big pop singer with a lot of Top Ten records and a handful of number ones, not just of his songs but of other folks' ("Zip-a-Dee-Doo-Dah"). It was famously said of Bing Crosby that he sang like every guy in America thought he sounded like when he sang in the shower. But, if anything, that description applies more to Mercer (he and Bing duetted together, lots, from the Thirties to the Seventies). There's something about that Savannah drawl that gave him a warm mellow tone that sounds like a regular guy jes' wandering from the living room to the backyard and maybe out onto the golf course and doing a little warbling along the way. And, in part because he sang himself, his songs have a singable ease. He liked to say that writing music took more talent, but writing lyrics took more courage. A tune can be beguiling and wistful and intoxicating and a bunch of other vagaries, but the lyricist has to sit down and get specific and put words on top of those notes. Stick an overripe adjective or an awkward image in there and a vaguely pleasant melody is suddenly precious or contrived or ridiculous. Not in "Fools Rush In" or "Jeepers Creepers." With Mercer, you rarely hear the false tinkle of an over-clever word in a love ballad or an obtrusive rhyme in a rural charm song.

That said, he gave the movie industry its theme song and summed it up in a single couplet:

Hooray for Hollywood
Where you're terrific if you're even good.

And how about this rhyme? "Spring, Spring, Spring" is a catalogue song, a laundry list of the joys of the mating season when "the barnyard is busy / In a regular tizzy." But, after getting through the various habits of the farm animals, the birds and the bees, the fish and the fowl, Mercer throws in this:

> *To itself each amoeba*
> *Softly croons "Ach, du liebe. . . .*

A biological and bilingual rhyme: that's positively Porteresque.

Mercer wrote "Spring, Spring, Spring" and "Summer Wind" and always wanted to write a Christmas standard but never managed it (though his recording of "Jingle Bells" is marvelous). But what he really liked was autumn. Lyric-wise, he got old early, and intimations of mortality hang over a lot of his work from the late Forties on. Yes, the days grow short when you reach September and dwindle down to a precious few and so on, but Mercer chose to embrace (as one of his titles has it) an "Early Autumn." Thereafter came "Autumn Leaves" and "When the World Was Young" and . . .

> *The days of wine and roses*
> *Laugh and run away*
> *Like a child at play . . .*

> *The lonely night discloses*
> *Just a passing breeze*
> *Filled with memories . . .*

Memories that, as with "Laura," "you can never quite recall." Mercer became near obsessed with the elusiveness of memory, of love and youth. Along the way, there was a lot of wine at night, and roses the morning after. He was the nicest guy, and the nastiest—once the bottle got south of two inches from the bottom. The following day, he'd feel bad about being a mean drunk to a close friend or a casual acquaintance or the cocktail waitress, and many florists benefited from his guilt. But, as Jo Stafford said to him as he staggered up to her one evening, "Please, John. I don't want any of your roses in the morning." If he'd been sober, he'd have written that down as a potential title, the way he did with "Goody Goody" and "PS I Love You." But he was sufficiently self-aware to get more than a few songs out of it:

> *Drinking again*
> *And thinking of when*
> *You loved me*
> *Having a few*
> *And wishing that you*
> *Were here*
> *Making the rounds*
> *And buying the rounds*
> *For strangers . . .*

Sinatra liked that one, and he *loved* Mercer's all-time great saloon song:

> *It's quarter to three*
> *There's no one in the place except you and me*
> *So set 'em up, Joe*
> *I got a little story you oughtta know . . .*

Supposedly he wrote that as catharsis after a doomed affair with Judy Garland, but we only found that out years later. Like he said:

> *Could tell you a lot*
> *But you've got*
> *To be true to your code*
> *Make it one for my baby*
> *And one more for the road . . .*

Thinking about Mercer songs for this column, I remembered an evening long ago when, a mere slip of a lad, I took a gal I adored to a country club dance I couldn't really afford. Johnny Mercer saved the night for me: The master of ceremonies announced a competition. To win, you had to answer a simple question:

"How wide is Moon River?"

"Wider than a mile," of course. We won a magnum of champagne, and the waiters treated us like royalty. A magical night. But the days of wine and roses laugh and run away toward a closing door, a door marked "Nevermore...." Conjuring up that evening for the first time in years, I wondered about my lost love, and whether that country club was still there. But then I remembered Mercer had got to all that, too:

> *There's a dance pavilion in the rain*
> *All shuttered down*
> *A winding country lane*
> *All russet brown ...*

Not long before his death in 1976, he said that in fifty years' time the best of Porter and Hart and Gershwin will be "studied and taught in schools, and collected ... and forgotten." But we're getting mighty near 2026, and we're still singing Johnny Mercer. It's quarter to three, and somewhere out there Willie Nelson's promoting his new record of "Come Rain or Come Shine" and Michael Bublé's doing his hugely successful if somewhat vulgar revival of Mercer and Mancini's "Meglio Stasera" from *The Pink Panther*.

Set 'em up, Joe ... and drop another nickel in the machine.

XI

AFTER WORK

THE ARISTOROCKRACY

National Review, April 30, 2012

MIDWAY THROUGH A Julie Burchill column in *The Guardian* bemoaning the Queen's Diamond Jubilee, I was startled to learn the following: Although fewer than 10 percent of British children attend private schools, their alumni make up over 60 percent of the acts on the UK pop charts. Twenty years ago, it was 1 percent.

There's always been a bit of this, of course: Mick Jagger went to the London School of Economics and made more money singing the songs of hardscrabble Mississippi bluesmen than the gnarled old-timers who'd lived those lyrics could ever dream of. But he was "middle class" in what your average exquisitely attuned snob would regard as a very drearily provincial sense: Mick's dad was a teacher in Kent and his mum was an Aussie hairdresser, and he went to the local grammar school. The new pop stars attended some of the most exclusive and expensive academies in the land: Chris Martin (of Coldplay and Gwyneth Paltrow) went to Sherborne, and Lily Allen to Bedales, and James Blunt to Harrow. The five lads from Radiohead got together at Abingdon, founded by Richard the Pedagogue in 1100 and where annual boarding fees are now just shy of fifty thousand dollars. So, to recreate the conditions that enabled Radiohead, you'd have to spend about one-and-three-quarter-million bucks. You could try it the Elvis way—drive a truck, blow $8.25 to make an acetate, and record your mama's favorite Ink Spots song—but it's not clear that works anymore. In the space of two generations, almost every traditional escape route out of England's slums—from pop music to journalism—has become the preserve of the expensively credentialed. I say "almost," because as far as I know no Old Abingdonian has yet won the heavyweight boxing championship.

A couple of weeks earlier, another Guardianista, Zoe Williams, filed a column deploring the fashionable professions' increasing reliance on unpaid interns. The first time I used the word "intern" on Fleet Street was fourteen years ago when the Monica story broke and my editor asked me to explain to British readers what it meant. Now they're everywhere. "Most people could weather a fortnight of unpaid work," writes Miss Williams, "but once you start talking about three or six months, you basically have to be living with your parents, they have to live in the same city—usually London for the desirable posts—and they have to be able to support you. So pretty soon the point arrives when there's a middle-class stranglehold on the jobs that people want to do—notably in politics, the media and the third sector."

The "third sector" is what the British call all those non-profits the cool kids aspire to. If memory serves, Mr. Blair introduced to Her Majesty's Government a department called the "Office of the Third Sector," which sounds so bland it ought to be one of those covers for a ruthless wet-work operation the spooks want to keep off the books, but is instead just a way of "coordinating" "resources" between the public sector and the third sector—i.e., a colossal waste of the private sector's money.

The Internet wallah Tim Worstall thought that Miss Williams had sort of missed her own point with that bit about politics, media, and the third sector: "When the desirable jobs are spending other people's money, reporting on spending other people's money and lobbying to spend other people's money then you know that the society is f***ed."

While the upper-middle-class corner the pop biz and the NGOs, what's left for the masses? Back when Mick Jagger was at the LSE, the futuristic comic books were full of computer-brained robot maids whirring from room to room dusting the table, bringing our afternoon tea, and generally liberating humanity from menial labor. How'd that work out? In America, 40 percent of the population now do minimal-skill service jobs. Meanwhile, the robot maids are thin on the ground, but computers have replaced the typing pool and the receptionist and the bookkeeping clerk—i.e., most of the entry-level jobs to the middle class. If you lack the schooling of a typical British pop star but you've mastered flipping tacos and the night shift at the KwikkiKrap, what's there to move on to?

Social mobility is already declining in the credential-crazed United States and the wider west, and will decline further. If you're already on the right side of the great divide, the world emerging isn't so different from the way it was back when Harrow was producing Winston Churchill rather than James Blunt: The less ambitious scions of great and well-to-do families amuse themselves with a leisurely varsity and then something not too onerous with a non-profit, in the way that the younger sons of Victorian toffs passed a couple of years in a minor post in a British legation in an agreeable capital.

If you're on the wrong side of the divide, it's less like *Downton Abbey* and more like one of those Latin-American *favelas* the presidential motorcade makes a point of giving a wide berth to. Even Mick Jagger's parentage—teacher and hairdresser—sounds a bit of an unlikely match in an age when the professionally credentialed prefer to marry within their caste. Perhaps we'll see a resurgence of the love-across-the-classes plot beloved by Edwardian England, back when real-life showgirls (Connie Gilchrist) married real-life earls (the seventh Lord Orkney). But I wouldn't bet on it: These days, at least on the British pop charts, the earl is his own showgirl.

THE WASTE OF
PEOPLE

The Daily Telegraph, February 24, 2004

THE OTHER DAY *The Sun* bestowed the title of "Britain's Laziest Woman" on Susan Moore of Burythorpe, North Yorkshire. Miss Moore had come to the paper's attention courtesy of its Shop-A-Sponger Hotline: as Alastair Taylor explained, "Super-sponger Susan, 34, has not done a day's work since dropping out of college in 1988."

Despite receiving "Jobseeker's Allowance" for sixteen years, she does not seek jobs, and never has. She was offered one by a supermarket, but it was five miles away so she wasn't interested. Ryedale Jobcentre put her on a "New Deal" course and, to make sure she attended, sent a taxi for her every morning. But one day the cab didn't show up, so Susan gave up the course. She lives with her divorced mum, who's also on "Jobseeker's Allowance," though she hasn't sought a job since giving birth to Susan in 1969.

Sportingly, *The Sun* offered Susan the chance to make a few quid manning the Shop-A-Sponger Hotline over the weekend, but she didn't fancy the disruption. "I shop on a Saturday," she said, "and on Sunday I sit at home and relax a bit."

But then my eye fell on the amount "scrounger Susan" had managed to scrounge: thirty thousand pounds in sixteen years—two thousand pounds per annum. Forty quid a week. She and her mum get another forty-five-pound housing benefit to live in what looks like an attractive and spacious semi-detached house, and she's trying to claim "income support" on medical grounds, because she suffers "monthly painful spells." But, if an average forty pounds a week is the best a "super-sponger" can do, it should remind us of a basic truth: the greatest crime of welfare isn't that it's a waste of money, but that it's a waste of people. Forty quid wasn't enough for a "welfare queen" to queen around on, but it was just enough to enable her to avoid making anything of her life, enough to let her sit around all week "listening to CDs and watching videos."

"I just haven't been given a chance," says Susan. But when the space on your CV for the period from adolescence to early middle-age is one big blank, no one's ever going to give you a chance. It's hard to think of anything capitalism red in tooth and claw could have done to Susan Moore that would have left her worse off than the great sapping nullity in which Her Majesty's Government has maintained her for her entire adult life.

When welfarism becomes the organizing principle of society, as it is in much of the west these days, the danger is that a Susan Moorish inertia descends on the entire state. I see that the Duke of Edinburgh has called for schoolchildren to play more team games because they learn so many "valuable lessons"—effective cooperation, self-discipline, rules, competition, etc. Good luck to His Royal Highness commending those to Britain's educational establishment.

Primary schools have given up on the egg-and-spoon and sack race because, under the great Cult of Self-Esteem, it's too much to ask a child to endure the sting of defeat. A third of London schools play no competitive sports. Teachers are uncomfortable with the notion of an "opposing side" one must strive to "beat"—just as, in the war on terror, many grown-ups are uncomfortable with the notion of "the enemy": to the progressive mind, there are no enemies, just friends whose grievances we haven't yet fully acknowledged.

If the Battle of Waterloo was won on the playing fields of Eton, it seems unlikely victory in Afghanistan owed much to the playing fields of Tipton Comp. Assuming the schools of Tipton and Luton still have any playing fields, their main contribution appears to have been to the losing side—the British Muslims captured among the Taliban and al-Qaeda forces. Even when it's not specifically teaching you about the millennia of atrocities committed in the name of British imperialism, the modern multicultural state at the very minimum absolves you of any meaningful allegiance. So it's not surprising some of us seek it elsewhere.

As an idea, the multicultural welfare state is too weak to have any purchase on us: that, indeed, is its principal virtue in the eyes of its few boosters; politically speaking, it's an allegiance for those who disdain allegiance. Most of us give a shrug of indifference and go back to watching the telly, like Susan Moore. A few look elsewhere, like those Tipton Talibannies. On the Continent, they're just beginning to wake up to the looming iceberg of unsustainable welfare systems. But, like *The Sun*'s Shop-A-Sponger Hotline, they're missing the point. It's not the cost, it's the system itself. The cradle-to-grave welfare society enfeebles the citizenry to such a degree you can never generate enough money.

Happily, not all recipients waste their time on the dole: Muhammed Metin Kaplan set up his Islamist group, Caliphate State, while on welfare in Cologne; Ahmed Ressam, arrested in Washington State en route to blow up Los Angeles International Airport, hatched his plot while on welfare in Montreal; Zacarias Moussaoui, the "twentieth hijacker" currently on trial in America, became an Islamist radical while on welfare in London; Abu Hamza became Britain's most famous fire-breathing imam while on welfare in London; Abu Qatada, a leading al-Qaeda recruiter, became an Islamist bigshot while British taxpayers were giving him ten times as much per week as Susan Moore. If only the Susan Moore-ish super-spongers were as purposeful as the neo-Moorish super-spongers.

I'm not saying every recipient of Jobseeker's Allowance is a terrorist welfare queen. I am saying that the best bet at saving the next generation of Susan Moores is if the U.S. declares European welfare systems a national security threat.

A TOWN WITH PITY

The Western Standard, October 25, 2004

ASIDE FROM THE small matter of the war for civilization, I don't have much time for Tony Blair. But, among many marvelous passages in his speech to the Labour Party Conference the other day, he had one especially striking moment: "When I hear people say, 'I want the old Tony Blair back, the one who cares,' I tell you something. I don't think as a human being, as a family man, I've changed at all. But I have changed as a leader. I have come to realize that caring in politics isn't really about 'caring.' It's about doing what you think is right and sticking to it."

Anyone can "care," for what it's worth. Anyone can say, as Tony Blair's fellow Third Wayer did, "I feel your pain." But he doesn't really feel it, does he? He doesn't have to live with it, day in, day out. Under the debased rules of politics, self-proclaimed empathy is all that's required. The question is, when you stop talking, what do you do?

A decade ago, Canadians and their government were "shocked" by TV images of the Innu community of Davis Inlet in Labrador, a shantytown whose inhabitants were snorting drugs, glue, gas, and pretty much anything else that came their way. Having claimed to be "shocked," our rulers then claimed to "care."

So they decided to build the Innu a new town a few miles inland, with new homes with new heating systems and a new schoolhouse with all the newest accessories. The new town—Natuashish—cost taxpayers $152 million.

Two years after the resettlement of the Mushuau, let us turn to our good friends at the Canadian Broadcasting Corporation for a progress report:

Alcoholism and gas sniffing continue to be a problem for people living in Natuashish, two years after the Innu community was relocated from Davis Inlet. The community of about 700 has seen four suicides in the past few months, and drug and alcohol abuse is rampant, say local officials.

Former Mushuau Chief Katie Rich says she has never seen anything like it before.... Rich says children are going to school hungry because their parents are drunk or stoned....

RCMP officers in Labrador agree with the assessment, saying alcohol-related problems in the community are worse than ever....

At this point, let's ask every reader who's surprised by this to put up his or her hand.

Well, okay. You're *Western Standard* readers. But let's ask *Toronto Star* and *Globe and Mail* readers, and *Maclean's* subscribers, and CBC viewers and listeners: how many of you impeccably liberal, "caring" Canadians stuffed to the gills with the Chrétien Liberals' "Canadian values" are truly, genuinely, honestly surprised by the results of your "caring"?

I thought as much. Now what are you going to do about it? Build another new town ten miles down the road from Natuashish but spend three hundred million dollars this time, and then another ten miles from that costing six hundred million, and another for a billion, and another and another, secure in the knowledge that by the time you run out of vacant land in Labrador, the government will have been able to refurbish the original Davis Inlet trash heap for another two or three billion?

Gas-sniffing is not a traditional Innu activity. Before the first European settlers came, the Mushuau did not roam the tundra hunting for Chevy Silverados. That's something the white man taught him. Or, to be more precise, the lazy, posturing Liberal establishment white man. And, if any of us propose trying anything different, the Liberal Party white man and his cronies in the rotten "First Nations" tribal band structure dismiss us as racist.

Remember a year or two back, when the papers were full of stories about the aggrieved alumni of residential schools? They were doing a grand job of suing Canada's Catholic and Protestant churches into oblivion, a very small number of them for the usual excesses of randy clerics, but the overwhelming majority for the far vaguer offense of "cultural genocide." On closer inspection—which not a lot of guilt-ridden liberals could be bothered giving it—"cultural genocide" turned out to involve not genocide in the Sudanese, Rwandan, or Holocaust meaning of the word but in the sense that generations of Canadian natives had been forced to learn about Queen Victoria, Shakespeare, Magna Carta, Sir Isaac Newton, etc. Or all the stuff which, back when Lord Macaulay was writing his famous memo to Her Majesty's Government on education for (east) Indians, it was felt that everyone needed to know in order to be able to function in the modern world. The (east) Indians still feel like this, which is why when you dial for tech support you wind up talking to Suresh or Rajiv.

Imagine if our own Indians had just, oh, 2 or 3 percent of that business. Instead, they fell into the hands of a vile alliance between the ostentatious "carers" of Ottawa and a corrupt artificial form of "self-government." Residential schools aren't "cultural genocide," but what's happened to the Mushuau of Davis Inlet should surely qualify. They were hunters and trappers originally, like the first Frenchmen on this continent. But the *pur laine* Quebecker doesn't do much trapping these days. He moved to Montreal's village gai, settled down with a nice young constable from the LGBT outreach unit, and has no desire to return to James Bay. The Mushuau were denied those kinds of choices. Their old culture died, but we "cared" about them so much that instead of embracing them as full, free citizens we've maintained them in an artificial government cocoon for four decades. The gas-sniffing adolescents of those "shocking" 1993 TV pictures are now gas-sniffing parents with wee little soon-to-be gas-sniffers of their own. And on it goes, the curse of Canadian compassion, unto the next generation.

Consider the sums of money involved: $152 million for seven hundred people. That's $217,142.85 for each man, woman, or child. Totting up my household, I see that, had we been in Davis Inlet, that would have been

$1,085,714.20 just for us. Imagine what you could do with that. Build a new house. Start a company. Hire some people. Invest in business opportunities. Get the kid an Ivy League education.

But the Innu don't have to do any of these things. They don't need to work, because the "caring" government pays them to lie around the house all day. And they don't need to buy a house because property rights is some racist whitey racket, so all the homes are communally owned. That $152-million new town was a one-off, but the regular payments aren't so bad. In 2002, the local band council got fourteen million dollars just in federal funds. That's twenty thousand per—or, for me and my family, a hundred grand a year to do nothing. The result is pretty much as you'd expect. Everyone cruises around in brand-new pickups on roads that go nowhere, and, although there's no liquor outlet in Natuashish, when a town's that flush with cash, there's plenty of bootleggers prepared to provide the service: a forty-ounce bottle costs three hundred dollars, and up to eight hundred dollars on popular holidays. But, in a town where the government gives you twenty thousand dollars to do zip, it's holiday season all year round.

The difference between Natuashish and other native communities is one only of degree. If you drive along the Lower North Shore of the St. Lawrence, where Quebec towns and Indian reserves nestle side by side, you'll see the "regular" schoolhouse—an older, cramped building past its best and remodeled one time too often, but still showing signs of life—and then the reserve school—new, vast, money no object, and already a dump. At Natuashish, a hundred children show up for class in a school that cost fifteen million dollars. Lop that and a couple of other public buildings off the total of $152 million, and the 130 family homes cost on paper a million bucks apiece.

Would it have been any more expensive to put everyone up in the Ritz-Carlton in Montreal with an unlimited room-service tab? That way, their vices might have been the comparatively mild ones of club sandwiches and mini-bar Toblerones. And there's a small chance that, after a year or two of watching pay-per-view movies round the clock, a handful of them might have ventured

out onto Sherbrooke Street, and taken the first steps to becoming full partici-
pating citizens of a developed society.

The buildings were never the problem in Davis Inlet, only a symptom of
it. There's a reason why certain ways of life (those taught in residential schools
a century ago, for example) spread around the world, and others (the Innu's)
didn't. When you isolate people from the system that's created the most prosperous, healthiest, and longest-living communities in human history, when
you insulate them from the impulses that drive most of us—to build a home,
raise our children, live full lives—the result is the government-funded human
landfill that is Indian Affairs. Natuashish is a plantation with the government
as absentee landlord, but the absence of work makes it, in fact, far more
destructive than the cotton fields of Virginia ever were. How many more
generations of the most lavishly endowed underclass on the planet have to be
destroyed in the name of Canadian "caring"? We need to blow up the Department of Indian Affairs and end the compassionate apartheid that segregates
natives from their fellow Canadians.

THE POST-WORK ECONOMY

Syndicated column, December 6, 2013

ONE CONSEQUENCE OF the botched launch of Obamacare is that it has, judging from his plummeting numbers with "Millennials," diminished Barack Obama's cool. It's not merely that the website isn't state-of-the-art but that the art it's failing to be state of is that of the mid-twentieth-century social program. The emperor has hipster garb, but underneath he's just another Commissar Squaresville. So, health care being an irredeemable downer for the foreseeable future, this week the president pivoted (as they say) to "economic inequality," which will be, he assures us, his principal focus for the rest of his term. And what's his big idea for this new priority? Stand well back: He wants to increase the minimum wage!

Meanwhile, Jeff Bezos of Amazon (a non-government website) is musing about delivering his products to customers across the country (and the planet) within hours by using drones.

Drones! If there's one thing Obama can do, it's drones. He's renowned across Yemen and Waziristan as the Domino's of drones. If he'd thought to have your health-insurance-cancellation notices dropped by drone, Obamacare might have been a viable business model. Yet, even in Obama's sole area of expertise and dominant market share, the private sector is already outpacing him.

Who has a greater grasp of the economic contours of the day after tomorrow—Bezos or Obama? My colleague Jonah Goldberg notes that the day before the President's speech on "inequality" Applebee's announced that it was introducing computer "menu tablets" to its restaurants. Automated supermarket checkout, 3D printing, driverless vehicles...what has the "minimum wage" to do with any of that? To get your minimum wage increased, you first have to have a minimum-wage job.

In my book (which I shall forbear to plug, but is available at Amazon, and with which Jeff Bezos will be happy to drone your aunt this holiday season), I write:

> Once upon a time, millions of Americans worked on farms. Then, as agriculture declined, they moved into the factories. When manufacturing was outsourced, they settled into low-paying service jobs or better-paying cubicle jobs—so-called "professional services" often deriving from the ever swelling accounting and legal administration that now attends almost any activity in America. What comes next?
>
> Or, more to the point, what if there is no "next"?

What do millions of people do in a world in which, in Marxian terms, "capital" no longer needs "labor"? America's liberal elite seem to enjoy having a domestic-servant class on hand, but, unlike the *Downton Abbey* crowd, are vaguely uncomfortable with having them drawn from the sturdy yokel stock of the village, and thus favor, to a degree only the Saudis can match, importing their maids and pool-boys from a permanent subordinate class of cheap foreign labor. Hence the fetishization of the "undocumented," soon to be reflected in the multi-million bipartisan amnesty for those willing to do "the jobs Americans won't do."

So what jobs will Americans get to do? We dignify the new age as "the knowledge economy," although, to the casual observer, it doesn't seem to require a lot of knowledge. One of the advantages of Obamacare, according to Nancy Pelosi, is that it will liberate the citizenry: "Think of an economy where people could be an artist or a photographer or a writer without worrying about keeping their day job in order to have health insurance." It's certainly true that employer-based health coverage distorts the job market, but what's more likely in a world without work? A new golden age of American sculpture and opera? Or millions more people who live vicariously through celebrity gossip and electronic diversions? One of the differences between government health care in America compared to, say, Sweden is the costs of obesity, heart disease, childhood diabetes, etc. In an ever more sedentary society where fewer and fewer have to get up to go to work in the morning, is it likely that those trends will diminish or increase?

Consider Vermont. Unlike my own state of New Hampshire, it has a bucolic image: Holsteins, dirt roads, the Vermont Teddy Bear Company, Ben & Jerry's, Howard Dean... And yet the Green Mountain State now has appalling levels of heroin and meth addiction, and the social chaos that follows. Geoffrey Norman began a recent essay in *The Weekly Standard* with a vignette from a town I know very well—St. Johnsbury, population 7,600, motto "Very Vermont," the capital of the remote North-East Kingdom hard by the Quebec border and as far from urban pathologies as you can get. Or so you'd think. But on a recent Saturday morning, Norman reports, there were more cars parked at the needle-exchange clinic than at the farmers' market. In Vermont, there's no inner-city underclass, because there are no cities, inner or outer; there's no disadvantaged minorities, because there's only three blacks and seven Hispanics in the entire state; there's no nothing. Which is the real problem.

Large numbers of Vermonters have adopted the dysfunctions of the urban underclass for no reason more compelling than that there's not much else to do. Once upon a time, St. Johnsbury made Fairbanks scales, but now a still handsome town is, as Norman puts it, "hollowed out by the loss of work and purpose." Their grandparents got up at four in the morning to work the farm, and their great-great-great-whatever-parents slogged up the Connecticut River, cleared the land, and built homes and towns and a civilization in the wilderness. And now? A couple of months back, I sat in the café in St. Johnsbury, and overheard a state bureaucrat and a Chamber of Commerce official discuss enthusiastically how the town could access some federal funds to convert an abandoned building into welfare housing.

"Work" and "purpose" are intimately connected: Researchers at the University of Michigan, for example, found that welfare payments make one unhappier than a modest income honestly earned and used to provide for one's family. "It drains too much of the life from life," said Charles Murray in a speech in 2009. "And that statement applies as much to the lives of janitors—even more to the lives of janitors—as it does to the lives of CEOs." Self-reliance—"work"—is intimately connected to human dignity—"purpose."

So what does every initiative of the Obama era have in common? Obamacare, Obamaphones, Social Security disability expansion, fifty million people on food stamps.... The assumption is that mass, multi-generational dependency is now a permanent feature of life. A coastal elite will devise ever smarter and slicker trinkets, and pretty much everyone else will be a member of either the dependency class or the vast bureaucracy that ministers to them. And, if you're wondering why every Big Government program assumes you're a feeble child, that's because a citizenry without "work and purpose" is ultimately incompatible with liberty. The elites think a smart society will be wealthy enough to relieve the masses from the need to work. In reality, it would be neo-feudal, but with fatter, sicker peasants. It wouldn't just be "economic inequality," but a far more profound kind, and seething with resentments.

One wouldn't expect the governing class to be as far-sighted as visionaries like Bezos. But it's hard to be visionary if you're pointing in the wrong direction. Which is why the signature achievement of Obama's "hope and change" combines 1940s British public-health theories with 1970s Soviet supermarket delivery systems.

But don't worry: Maybe one day soon, your needle-exchange clinic will be able to deliver by drone.

Look out below.

TRIBAL AMERICA

Syndicated column, November 16, 2012

TO AN IMMIGRANT such as myself (not the undocumented kind, but documented up to the hilt, alas), one of the most striking features of election night analysis was the lightly worn racial obsession. On Fox News, Democrat Kirsten Powers argued that Republicans needed to deal with the reality that America is becoming what she called a "brown country." Her fellow Democrat Bob Beckel observed on several occasions that if the share of "the white vote" was held down below 73 percent Romney would lose. In the end, it was 72 percent, and he did. Beckel's assertion—that if you knew the ethnic composition of the electorate you also knew the result—turned out to be correct.

This is what less enlightened societies call tribalism: For example, in the 1980 election leading to Zimbabwe's independence, Joshua Nkomo's ZAPU-PF got the votes of the Ndebele people, while Robert Mugabe's ZANU-PF secured those of the Shona—and, as there were more Shona than Ndebele, Mugabe won. That same year America held an election, and Ronald Reagan won a landslide victory. Nobody talked about tribal-vote shares back then, but had the percentage of what Beckel calls "the white vote" been the same in 2012 as it was in 1980 (88 percent), Mitt Romney would have won in an even bigger landslide than Reagan. The "white vote" will be even lower in 2016, and so, on the Beckel model, Republicans are set to lose all over again.

Hence the urge to get on the right side of America's fastest-growing demographic. Only 27 percent of Hispanics voted for Romney. But all that could change if the GOP were to sign on to support some means of legalizing the presence of the twelve to twenty million fine upstanding members of the Undocumented-American community who are allegedly "social conservatives" and thus natural Republican voters. Once we pass amnesty, argues Grover Norquist's Americans for Tax Reform, "future immigrants will be more open to the Republican Party because, unlike many immigrants who are already here, they won't have been harmed or insulted by Republican politicians."

So if I follow correctly, instead of getting 27 percent of the 10-percent Hispanic vote, Republicans will get, oh, 38 percent of the 25-percent Hispanic vote, and sweep to victory.

Everyone talks about this demographic transformation as if it's a natural phenomenon, like Hurricane Sandy. Indeed, I notice that many of those exulting in the inevitable eclipse of "white America" are the same people who assure me that demographic arguments about the Islamization of Europe are completely preposterous. But in neither the United States nor Europe is it a natural phenomenon. Rather, it's the fruit of conscious government policy.

According to the Census, in 1970 the "Non-Hispanic White" population of California was 78 percent. By the 2010 census, it was 40 percent. Over the same period, the 10-percent Hispanic population quadrupled and caught up with whites.

That doesn't sound terribly "natural," does it? If one were informed that, say, the population of Nigeria had gone from 80 percent black in 1970 to 40 percent black today, one would suspect something rather odd and profoundly unnatural had been going on. Twenty years ago, Rwanda was about 14 percent Tutsi. Now it's just under 10 percent. So it takes a bunch of Hutu butchers getting out their machetes and engaging in seven-figure genocide to lower the Tutsi population by a third. But when the white population of California falls by half, that's "natural," just the way it is, one of those things, could happen to anyone.

Every four years, the Republican Party pines for another Reagan. But Ronald Reagan, Governor of California for eight years, couldn't get elected in today's not-so-Golden State. Jerry Brown, Governor Moonbeam back in the Seventies, now presides as Governor Twilight, lead vampire of a malign alliance of unionized bureaucrats and a swollen dependency class that maintains them in office at the expense of a remorselessly shrinking productive class. As the nation's demographic profile trends ever more Californian, perhaps Norquist's predictions of naturally conservative Hispanics pining for a new Coolidge will come to fruition. Or perhaps Bob Beckel's more crudely determinative analysis will prove correct—that, in a multicultural society, jostling identity groups will stick with the party of ethnocultural spoils.

Once upon a time, the Democrats thought differently. It was their first progressive president, Woodrow Wilson, who imposed the concept of "self-determination" on post–Great War Europe, insisting that the multicultural empires of the Habsburgs and Romanovs be replaced by a patchwork of ethnic statelets from the Balkans to the Baltic. He would be surprised to find his own party presiding over a Habsburgian America of bilingual Balkanization as a matter of electoral strategy.

The short history of the Western Hemisphere is as follows: North America was colonized by Anglo-Celts, Central and South America by "Hispanics." Up north, two centuries of constitutional evolution and economic growth; down south, coups, corruption, generalissimos, and presidents-for-life. None of us can know the future. It may be that Charles Krauthammer is correct that Hispanics are natural Republicans merely pining for amnesty, a Hallmark Cinco de Mayo card, and a mariachi band at the inaugural ball. Or it may be that, in defiance of Dr. Krauthammer, Grover Norquist, and Little Mary Sunshine, demographics is destiny, and, absent assimilationist incentives this country no longer imposes, a Latin-American population will wind up living in a Latin-American society. Don't take it from a right-wing bigot like me, take it from *The New York Times*. In 2009, Jason DeParle filed a story about suburban Maryland, in which he helpfully explained the municipality of Langley Park to *Times* readers:

> Now nearly two-thirds Latino and foreign-born, it has the aesthetics of suburban sprawl and the aura of Central America. Laundromats double as money-transfer stores. Jobless men drink and sleep in the sun. There is no city government, few community leaders, and little community.

Golly. You'd almost get the impression that Mr. DeParle thinks that laundromats doubling as money-transfer stores, jobless men drinking and sleeping in the sun, and dysfunctional government are somehow characteristic of Central America. That sounds awfully judgmental for a *Times* man, no?

Republicans think they're importing hardworking immigrants who want a shot at the American Dream; the Democrats think they're importing clients for Big Government. The left is right: Just under 60 percent of immigrants receive some form of welfare. I see the recent Republican proposals for some form of amnesty contain all sorts of supposed safeguards against gaming the system, including a $525 application fee for each stage of the legalization process. On my own recent visit to a U.S. Immigration office, I was interested to be told that, as a matter of policy, the Obama Administration is now rubberstamping all "fee waiver" requests for "exceptional hardship" filed by members of approved identity groups. And so it will go for all those GOP safeguards. While Canada and Australia compete for high-skilled immigrants, America fast-tracks an unskilled welfare class of such economic benefit to their new homeland they can't even afford a couple of hundred bucks for the necessary paperwork.

It's hardly their fault. If you were told you could walk into a First World nation and access free education, free health care, free services in your own language, and have someone else pay your entrance fee, why wouldn't you? So, yes, Republicans should "moderate" their tone toward immigrants, and de-moderate their attitude to the Dems who suckered the GOP all too predictably. Decades of faintheartedness toward some of the most destabilizing features of any society, including bilingualism (take it from a semi-Belgian Canadian), have brought the party to its date with destiny.

Or as Peggy Lee sang long ago in a lost land, "*Mañana* is soon enough for me."

XII

BIRTH OF TOMORROW

POST-MODERN
FAMILY

Syndicated column, March 30, 2013

GAY MARRIAGE? IT came up at dinner Down Under this time last year, and the prominent Aussie politician on my right said matter-of-factly, "It's not about expanding marriage, it's about destroying marriage."

That would be the most obvious explanation as to why the same societal groups who assured us in the Seventies that marriage was either (a) a "meaningless piece of paper" or (b) institutionalized rape are now insisting it's a universal human right. They've figured out what, say, terrorist-turned-educator Bill Ayers did—that, when it comes to destroying core civilizational institutions, trying to blow them up is less effective than hollowing them out from within.

On the other hand, there are those who argue it's a victory for the powerful undertow of bourgeois values over the surface ripples of sexual transgressiveness: gays will now be as drearily suburban as the rest of us. A couple of years back, I saw a picture in the paper of two chubby old queens tying the knot at City Hall in Vancouver, and the thought occurred that western liberalism had finally succeeded in boring all the fun out of homosexuality.

Which of these alternative scenarios—the demolition of marriage or the taming of the gay—will come to pass? Most likely, both. In the upper echelons of society, our elites practice what they don't preach. Scrupulously nonjudgmental about everything except traditional Christian morality, they nevertheless lead lives in which, as Charles Murray documents in his book *Coming Apart*, marriage is still expected to be a lifelong commitment. It is easy to see moneyed gay newlyweds moving into such enclaves, and making a go of it. As the Most Reverend Justin Welby, the new Archbishop of Canterbury and head of the worldwide Anglican Communion, said just before his enthronement the other day, "You see gay relationships that are just stunning in the quality of the relationship." "Stunning": what a fabulous endorsement! But, amongst the type of gay couple that gets to dine with the Archbishop of Canterbury, he's probably right.

Lower down the socioeconomic scale, the quality gets more variable. One reason why conservative appeals to protect the sacred procreative essence of marriage have gone nowhere is because Americans are rapidly joining the Scandinavians in doing most of their procreating without benefit of clergy. Seventy percent of black babies are born out of wedlock, so are 53 percent of Hispanics (the "natural conservative constituency" *du jour*, according to every lavishly remunerated Republican consultant), and 70 percent of the offspring of poor white women. Over half the babies born to mothers under thirty are now "illegitimate" (to use a quaintly judgmental formulation). For the first three-and-a-half centuries of American settlement the bastardy rate (to be even quainter) was a flat line in the basement of the graph, stuck at 2 or 3 percent all the way to the eve of the Sixties. Today over 40 percent of American births are "nonmarital," which is significantly higher than in Canada or Germany. "Stunning" upscale gays will join what's left of the American family, holed up in a chichi Green Zone, while, beyond the perimeter, the vast mounds of human rubble pile up remorselessly. The conservative defense of marriage rings hollow because for millions of families across this land the American marriage is hollow.

If the right's case has been disfigured by delusion, the left's has been marked by a pitiful parochialism. At the Supreme Court this week, Ted Olson, the former Solicitor-General, was one of many to invoke comparisons with *Loving v. Virginia*, the 1967 case that struck down laws prohibiting interracial marriage. But such laws were never more than a localized American perversion of marriage. In almost all other common-law jurisdictions, from the British West Indies to Australia, there was no such prohibition. Indeed, under the Raj, it's estimated that one in three British men in the Indian subcontinent took a local wife. "Miscegenation" is a nineteenth-century American neologism.

When the Supreme Court struck down laws on interracial marriage, it was not embarking on a wild unprecedented experiment but merely restoring the United States to the community of civilized nations within its own legal tradition. Ted Olson is a smart guy, but he sounded like Mary-Kate and Ashley's third twin in his happy-face banalities last week.

Yet, beyond the court, liberal appeals to "fairness" are always the easiest to make. Because, for too much of its history, this country was disfigured by halfwit rules about who can sit where on public transportation and at lunch counters, the default position of most Americans today is that everyone should have the right to sit anywhere: If a man self-identifies as a woman and wants to sit on the ladies' toilet, where's the harm? If a woman wants to be a soldier and sit in a foxhole in the Hindu Kush, sure, let her. If a mediocre high school student wants to sit in a college class, well, diversity is our strength. American "rights" have taken on the same vapid character as grade-school sports: Everyone must be allowed to participate, and everyone is entitled to the same participation ribbon.

Underneath all this apparent "fairness" is a lot of unfairness. Entire new categories of crime have arisen in the wake of familial collapse, like the legions of adolescent daughters abused by mom's latest live-in boyfriend. Millions of children are now raised in transient households that make not just economic opportunity but even elementary character formation all but impossible. In the absence of an agreed moral language to address this brave new world, Americans retreat to comforting euphemisms like "blended families," notwithstanding that the familial Cuisinart seems to atomize at least as often as it blends.

Meanwhile, social mobility declines: doctors who once married their nurses now marry their fellow doctors; attorneys who once married their secretaries now contract with fellow super-lawyers, like dynastic unions in medieval Europe. Underneath the self-insulating elite, millions of Americans are downwardly mobile: The family farmers and mill workers, the pioneers who hacked their way into the wilderness and built a township, could afford marriage and children; indeed, it was an economic benefit. For their descendants doing minimum-wage service jobs about to be rendered obsolete by technology, functioning families are a tougher act, and children an economic burden. The gays looked at contemporary marriage and called the traditionalists' bluff.

Modern Family works well on TV, less so in the rusting doublewides of decrepit mill towns where, very quickly, the accumulated social capital of two centuries is drained, and too much is too wrecked. In Europe, where dependency, decadence, and demographic decline are extinguishing some of the oldest nations on earth, a successor population is already in place in the restive Muslim housing projects. With their vibrant multicultural attitudes to feminism and homosexuality, there might even be a great sitcom in it: *Pre-Modern Family*—and, ultimately, post-*Modern*.

"Fiscal conservatives" recoil from this kind of talk like homophobes at a bathhouse: The sooner some judge somewhere takes gay marriage off the table, the sooner the right can go back to talking about debt and Obamacare without being dismissed as uptight theocratic bigots. But it doesn't work like that. Most of the social liberalism comes with quite a price tag. The most reliable constituency for Big Government is single women, for whom the state is a girl's best friend, the sugar daddy whose checks never bounce. A society in which a majority of births are out of wedlock cannot be other than a Big Government welfare society. Ruining a nation's finances is one thing; debauching its human capital is far harder to fix.

ONLY THE CLONELY

The Daily Telegraph, March 1, 1997

THE DAY HAD been going downhill ever since lunch. "This lamb tastes awfully bland," I said.

"Sorry, darling," apologized the wife. "I could only afford clone this week."

We made Covent Garden with minutes to spare, just in time for the inevitable announcement: "Ladies and gentlemen, at today's matinee, the part of Cho-Cho-San will be played by Dame Kiri Te Kanawa's clone, Dame Kiri 2 Kanawa."

"Not again," I groaned. "Ninety-eight quid a ticket and all we get is the clone."

"Oh, come on," whispered Chloe, determined to look on the bright side. "She can't be worse than Dame Clone Sutherland." As she spoke, I spied the familiar figure of Sir Georg Solti making his way to the podium, though, on closer inspection, it proved to be Sir Georg Soltoo. They're almost indistinguishable, but Soltoo likes to wear a revolving bow-tie and a buttonhole that squirts. As he passed, he glanced down my wife's cleavage and said, in that distinctive Hungarian accent: "Don't get many of those to the pound, luv."

"You see?" I hissed. "Solti would never have said that. You can't tell me that's an exact clone."

"I know," said Chloe. "But it's his own fault. He had it done on the NHS. And at least this one doesn't start with 'I Will Survive' like Sir Georg Solthree does."

Well, it drove me mad sitting there thinking that the real Dame Kiri was probably cleaning up at La Scala and the real Sir Georg was getting in a little light lunchtime recital with the Chicago Symphony. Things got worse at the interval, when my ex-wife Arabella spotted me from across the bar. It had been

305

a messy divorce, resolved only when the judge came up with the ingenious solution of awarding sole custody to both of us.

"Mark!" she said. "You look great! Been cloned?"

"Certainly not," I retorted, and made a perfunctory inquiry about the kid. "How's Rupert One?"

"Oh, he's fine," said Arabella airily. "How's Rupert Two?"

"He's doing well," I said. "He's out on probation and we've got him into a good substance abuse clinic and the vicar says he's thinking about dropping the charges."

"Really?" said Arabella. "We're very concerned about Rupert One. I'm worried that being captain of the First Fifteen this year will leave him less time to concentrate on his violin—EMI did so want a second album. Calvin Klone has asked him to do one of those heroin ads, but we're not sure. Might be more suited to Rupert Two?"

By now, I was grinding my teeth so much I never heard the orchestra tuning up. As we walked back down the aisle, a young lady complimented me on my cologne/after-shave. "Why, thanks," I said. "It's Clone Cologne—For Men Who Want to Smell like Themselves. What they do is extract the DNA from your armpit, put it in an attractive bottle, and sell it back to you for forty-seven pounds."

The next day, I was up bright and early for my role as Mr. Rochester opposite Demi Moore in the new *Jane Eyre*. I hadn't seen Demi in a while, but I instantly recognized her as she stood there naked oiling her breasts in a scene I couldn't quite recall from the novel. "Hi, Demi!" I said. "I believe we're doing the next bit together."

"In your dreams," she said snootily. "Everyone knows I don't do clothed scenes. I leave that to my body double."

"Which one do you want today, Demi?" shouted the director, Oliver Clone, and on cue a veritable entourage appeared—Semi-Demi Moore, Hemi-Semi-Demi Moore, and Demi Moore-Or-Less—all entirely indistinguishable, give or take a cup size or two.

I'd only taken the role because I was still a bit short after giving a hundred thousand dollars to Bill Clinton's re-election campaign in return for a night in the Lincoln Bedroom and coffee with the president. The bed was incredibly historic, complete with a sign saying: "Abe Lincoln Slept Here. So Did Barbra Streisand And Several Dozen Indonesian Businessmen." But at coffee I began to suspect something was wrong. "Great coffee, Mr. President," I said.

"Thanks. It's Nescafé," he said, and looked soulfully into my eyes.

"You mean I paid a hundred thousand bucks for instant coffee?"

"Ah feel yo' pain," said the President, putting on his sincere expression, and stroking my hand. Which I thought was very thoughtful of him, until his other hand flew up to my chest and started unbuttoning my shirt. Instantly I leapt to my feet.

"You're not the President! Bill Clinton's ferociously heterosexual. You're a clone...."

"The clone with the gay gene," said a sinister Manchurian type in a white coat who'd slipped into the room quietly behind me. "Normally, we don't let him host fundraisers except in Fire Island, West Hollywood, and Riyadh. But we were short-staffed this morning."

"But where's the real Clinton?"

"Ha-ha-ha-ha," he cackled, in an oddly Hillary-like manner. "Ha-ha-ha-ha, you poor deluded fool. Don't you get it? There is no real Clinton. There's a left-of-center Clinton, there's a right-of-center Clinton, there's a tax-raising Clinton, there's a tax-cutting Clinton, there's a non-inhaling Clinton, there's a triangulating Clinton, there's a demagoguing Clinton.... But they're all Clonetons. There's no such thing as a genuine Clinton."

"But what about his distinguishing characteristics?"

"Oh, they've all got those." And I noticed that down on the floor the President had begun humping my leg.

On the way home, I listened to the news: Tony Blair announced that he was cloning himself so that he could stand in all 650 constituencies. "We believe," he said in unison, "that this further demonstrates New Labour's ability to fully and totally unite behind the leadership."

"What's the world coming to?" I said to my clone back home.

"Relax, have a drink," he said. "Everything's under control. I've washed the car, put the cat out, had sex with the wife. Nothing special, she won't suspect."

"Thanks," I said. "What about the *Telegraph* column?"

"Done it."

STORK REPORT

The Sunday Telegraph, October 31, 1999

A FEW YEARS BACK, I happened to be on a radio show with Gore Vidal, who, for some reason, assumed I was gay. During the off-air banter, another guest began talking about her newborn. The great man of letters gave me a conspiratorial twinkle and sighed wearily, "Breeders!"

Gore may still be a non-breeder, but he's the last of a dying non-breed. The twenty-first century is upon us, everyone's broody, and, in case Gore's wondering, it no longer involves anything as ghastly as being in the same room as a woman with no clothes on. The stork has diversified: You don't have to look for his little bundles of joy under the gooseberry bush any more—now you can order them online. And, as his traditional market—or, as *The Guardian* calls it, "the family lobby"—has shrunk, he's moved on to expand his share of key niche demographics. Now, infertile women can have babies, and so can sexagenarian women and gay men.

Take Barrie and Tony, a couple from Chelmsford, Essex. They'd been trying for a baby for some time, but nothing seemed to work. Then it occurred to them that this might be because they're both men. So they found a woman who happened to have four eggs lying around that she hadn't yet auctioned over the Internet. You'd think two boys and a girl would have been enough, but they figured they needed someone else just to even up the numbers, so they roped in another woman who happened to have a rare nine-month vacancy in her fallopian timeshare. After that, it was just a question of getting the girls in the mood: the lights down low, Johnny Mathis on the hi-fi, the FedEx package with Barrie and Tony's beaker of co-mingled sperm on the coffee table, the check for two hundred thousand dollars in the mail, and the turkey baster wandering in from the kitchen with a come-hither look in his eye.

The result of this happy union is twins: a boy for him and a girl for him, to modify "Tea for Two." Barrie Drewitt and Tony Barlow are planning to name their son and daughter (or vice-versa) Aspen and Saffron Drewitt-Barlow. In a landmark decision in a California court, the proud parents will be the first British couple to both be named as father on the birth certificate, though neither mother rates a credit.

The babies have not yet been born, but both mother and surrogate mother and co-father one and co-father two are doing well: Barrie and Tony still have a few eggs in the freezer from the same woman so, in a year or two, they intend to provide Aspen and Saffron with a sibling named after some other spice or ski resort. "This ruling," said Tony, "affirms that gay couples are entitled to the same fundamental procreative freedoms as heterosexual couples."

It's fair to say heterosexual couples of the old school did not think of "procreative freedom" as an "entitlement"—like, say, public education or a senior citizen's bus pass—but rather as, to use an archaic phrase, a "fact of life." Today, though, there are no "facts of life": de facto, it would seem biologically impossible for Messrs Drewitt and Barlow to come together to produce young Saffron or Aspen, but, de jure, it's a breeze. Neither parent supplied the egg, neither parent carried the child, neither even went to the minimal effort of personally whacking the seed up the ol' vaginal canal, but nonetheless the birth certificate will certify that they're responsible for the birth—essentially for the reason that that's the way they want it: Yes, sirs, that's your baby / No, sirs, we don't mean maybe. "The nuclear family as we know it is evolving," said Barrie. "The emphasis should not be on it being a father and a mother but on loving, nurturing parents, whether that be a single mother or a gay couple living in a committed relationship."

That's great news if you're a gay couple living in a committed relationship or a single mother living in several uncommitted relationships, but in the murky territory in between lurk all kinds of unsuitable parents. In Britain, as was reported last week, Penny and Stephen Greenwood's baby will emerge from the womb and immediately be taken away by social workers and put into foster care. The Greenwoods, of Bradford, who have already had one child confiscated by the state, are both epileptics and, although they insist their conditions are mild and controlled, the authorities aren't prepared to let them be loving, nurturing parents. Apparently, it could be very traumatizing for a child to see his parent with his head thrown back and his tongue lolling out— unless, of course, it's at the local bathhouse.

Despite the claims of the technobores, in the second half of the century hardly anything has changed—except the nature of change. Our bathrooms, kitchens, cars, planes, and high-rises have barely altered. Instead, having run out of useful things to invent, we've reinvented ourselves and embarked, with a remarkable insouciance, on redefining human identity. In the two decades since the first test-tube baby, "procreative freedoms" have become the new frontier. We began with "a woman's right to choose"—whether or not to abort. Next came an Asian's right to choose the sex of his child and get rid of any unwanted female fetus (at one point China had 153 boys for every one hundred girls). We've now moved on to a couple's right to choose their baby's genetic characteristics on the Internet, a lesbian's right to choose to be impregnated by a gay male friend, and a career woman's right to choose to have her eggs frozen in her late twenties, stored away, and fertilized in her forties or fifties or whenever she feels she's ready to raise a baby. There is a logical progression in all this: if you have the right to end life (with abortion), surely you also have the right to decide when, where, how, and with whom you wish to initiate it. And, in one sense, the culture of death and the culture of new life form a kind of balancing act: if there is a gay gene and straight parents start aborting their gay fetuses, it seems only fair to allow gay parenting as a kind of corrective. Likewise, if girl fetuses are shouldering an unfair percentage of abortions in regrettably misogynist societies, female numbers can be kept up by human cloning—which, in theory, eliminates the need for sperm. And, if you don't need sperm, do you really need men? Women could go on cloning women until Amazons ruled the earth, except for a handful of gay male enclaves in West Hollywood and Miami.

Human cloning will happen, if only because there's a market for it—as there's proved to be with eggs and surrogates. If it were simply a matter of wanting to be "loving, nurturing parents," adoption would do it. But there's a biological imperative driving these advances. Since Barrie and Tony are so proud of their "committed relationship," it must be irksome to have to let Tracie the egg-donor and Rosalind the womb-renter into the picture, since neither woman has any commitment to the relationship once the check's cleared. Lesbian parents, like the pop star Melissa Etheridge and her partner Julie Cypher, would in future have no need of third parties: the clone of one would grow in the womb of the other—and what could be more loving and nurturing than that? The first human clone will enter the world in a clinic in Mexico or Morocco or some such, but one day she will come to the United States or Britain and endeavor to get a driving license, and at that point, even if cloning remains illegal in those jurisdictions, the state will balk at turning her away because she's officially a nonhuman. They will recognize her as a legal human being on the grounds that that's what Morocco says she is—just as the British authorities are recognizing the California court's decision on Barrie and Tony.

The public will most likely go along with these innovations. Half a century ago, Ingrid Bergman gave birth out of wedlock and it almost finished her career. Now, single mom Jodie Foster is put on the cover of *People* magazine as a paragon of motherhood, and everyone thinks it's bad form to inquire who or where the dad is, never mind whether a woman who thinks the only function of a father is to get the globules of bodily fluid into the beaker and then push off is really such a great role model. As always, the dismantling of ancient social structures is more positively expressed as a tolerance for diversity. "There is no one 'perfect' model on which all family structures can be based," Barbra Streisand recently told America's leading gay newspaper, *The Advocate*. "If we surveyed human history, we would see representations of every type of possible social arrangement." Miss Streisand doesn't give any examples, but you could survey all human history and be hard put to find any precedent for Barrie and Tony's social arrangement. The reality is that, rather than returning to some pre-Judeo-Christian utopia, we've chosen as an exercise in self-expression to embark on a radical rejection of a universal societal unit.

Maybe it will work out. Maybe in fifteen years' time Aspen and Saffron will be sitting in class surrounded by offspring of lesbian couples and geriatrics plus a handful of clones, and they'll all be happy and well-adjusted. Or maybe they'll be like America's vast army of children born out of wedlock—six times more likely to develop drug addictions or commit serious crimes. Those statistics are part of the new "facts of life." If you can afford it, like Barrie and Tony and Melissa Etheridge, you get to create your own "facts." It will fall to the next generation to live with them.

THE RIGHT TO CHOOSE

Syndicated column, May 31, 2008

"SOMEONE WINS, SOMEONE doesn't win, that's life," Nancy Kopp, Maryland's treasurer, told *The Washington Post*. "But women don't want to be totally dissed." She was talking about her political candidate, Hillary Clinton. Democratic women are feeling metaphorically battered by the Obama campaign. "Healing the Wounds of Democrats' Sexism," as *The Boston Globe* headline put it, will not be easy. Geraldine Ferraro is among many prominent Democrat ladies putting up their own money for a study from the Shorenstein Center at Harvard to determine whether Senator Clinton's presidential hopes fell victim to party and media sexism. How else to explain why their gal got clobbered by a pretty boy with a résumé you could print on the back of his driver's license; a Rolodex apparently limited to neo-segregationist racebaiters, campus Marxist terrorists, and indicted fraudsters; and a rhetorical surefootedness that makes Dan Quayle look like Socrates. "On this Memorial Day," said Barack Obama last Monday, "as our nation honors its unbroken line of fallen heroes—and I see many of them in the audience here today...."

Hey, why not? In Obama's Cook County, many fallen heroes from the Spanish-American War still show up in the voting booths come November. It's not unreasonable for some of them to turn up at an Obama campaign rally, too.

But what of the fallen heroine? If it's any consolation to Senator Clinton, she's not the only female to find that social progress is strangely accommodating of old-time sexism. There was a front-page story in London last week about a British Indian couple in Birmingham—she's fifty-nine, he's seventy-two— who'd had twins through in vitro fertilization and then abandoned the babies

314

at the hospital when they turned out to be daughters, announcing their plans to fly back to India for another round of IVF in hopes of getting a boy. In the wake of the media uproar, the parents now claim something got "lost in translation" and have been back to the hospital to visit the wee bairns. But think of mom and dad as the Democratic Party and the abandoned daughters as Hillary, and it all makes sense.

There's a lot of that about. Sex-selective abortion is a fact of life in India, where the ratio has declined to one thousand boys to nine hundred girls nationally, and as low as one thousand boys to three hundred girls in some Punjabi cities. In China, the state-enforced "one child" policy has brought about the most sex-distorted demographic cohort in global history, the so-called *guang gun*—"bare branches." If you can only have one kid, parents choose to abort girls and wait for a boy, to the point where in the first generation to grow to adulthood under this policy there are 119 boys for every one hundred girls. In practice, a "woman's right to choose" turns out to mean the right to choose not to have any women.

And what of the western world? Between 2000 and 2005, Indian women in England and Wales gave birth to 114 boys for every one hundred girls. A similar pattern seems to be emerging among Chinese, Korean, and Indian communities in America. "The sex of a firstborn child in these families conformed to the natural pattern of 1.05 boys to every girl, a pattern that continued for other children when the firstborn was a boy," wrote Colleen Carroll Campbell in *The St. Louis Post-Dispatch* the other day. "But if the firstborn child was a girl, the likelihood of a boy coming next was considerably higher than normal at 1.17-to-1. After two girls, the probability of a boy's birth rose to a decidedly unnatural 1.51-to-1."

By midcentury, when today's millions of surplus boys will be entering middle age, India and China are expected to account for a combined 50 percent of global GDP. On present trends, they will be the most male-heavy societies that have ever existed. As I wrote in my book *America Alone*, unless China's planning on becoming the first gay superpower since Sparta, what's going to happen to all those excess men? As a general rule, large numbers of excitable lads who can't get any action are not a recipe for societal stability. Unless the Japanese have invented amazingly lifelike sex robots by then (think Austin Powers's "fembots"), we're likely to be in a planet-wide rape epidemic and a world of globalized industrial-scale sex slavery. And what of the western world? Canada and Europe are in steep demographic decline and dependent on immigration to sustain their populations. And—as those Anglo-Welsh statistics suggest—many of the available immigrants are already from male-dominated cultures and will eventually be male-dominated numbers-wise, too: circa 2020, the personal ads in the Shanghai classifieds seeking SWF with good sense of humor will be defining "must live locally" as any ZIP code this side of Mars.

Smaller families may mean just a boy or a girl for liberal Democrats, but in other societies it means just a boy. The Indian writer Gita Aravamudan calls this the "female feticide." Colleen Carroll Campbell writes that abortion, "touted as the key to liberating future generations of women," has become instead "the preferred means of eradicating them." And while it won't eradicate all of them, Phillip Longman, a demographer of impeccably liberal credentials, put the future in a nutshell in the title of his essay: "The Return of Patriarchy."

Enlightened progressives take it for granted that social progress is like technological progress—that women's rights are like the internal combustion engine or the jet aeroplane: once invented they can't be uninvented. But that's a careless assumption. There was a small, nothing story out of Toronto this week—the York University Federation of Students wants a campus-wide ban on any pro-life student clubs. Henceforth, students would be permitted to debate abortion only "within a pro-choice realm," as the vice-president Gilary Massa put it. Nothing unusual there. A distressing number of student groups are inimical to free speech these days. But then I saw a picture of the gung-ho abortion absolutist: Gilary Massa is a young Muslim woman covered in a hijab.

On such internal contradictions is the future being built. By "The Return of Patriarchy," Phillip Longman doesn't mean 1950s sitcom dads. No doubt western feminists will be relieved to hear that.

HOW WEIRD HOW SOON?

National Review, August 15, 2011

FROM LONDON'S *Daily Mail*:

> Scientists have created more than 150 human-animal hybrid
> embryos in British laboratories.

You don't say. Now why would they do that? Don't worry, it's all perfectly legit, the fruits of the 2008 Human Fertilisation Embryology Act. So some scientists have successfully fertilized animal eggs with human sperm, and others have created "cybrids," using a human nucleus implanted into an animal cell, or "chimeras," in which human cells are mixed with animal embryos.

Writing *After America*, I had to resist the temptation to go too far down this path. If you start off analyzing unsustainable debt-to-GDP ratios and possible downgrades of U.S. Treasury debt and suddenly lurch into disquisitions on a part-Welsh, part-meerkat chimera, the fiscal types tend to think you've flown the coop. Yet as I contemplate the prospects of the developed world I confess I do find myself wondering: How weird how soon?

Transformative innovation requires a socio-economic context: A few years back, a European cabinet minister explained to me at great length that governments had enthusiastically supported both the contraceptive pill and abortion because there was an urgent need for massive numbers of women to enter the workforce. A few years hence, developed nations will have a need for *anyone* to enter the workforce. Japan is the oldest society on earth. China, as I always say, is getting old before it gets rich. Europe is richer but lazier: Fewer than two-fifths of eurozone citizens work, and over 60 percent receive state benefits.

If you track, as prudent investors should, GDP vs. median age in the world's major economies, this story is going nowhere good.

When President Sarkozy's government mooted raising the retirement age from sixty to (stand well back) sixty-two, the French rioted. "Retirement" is a very recent invention, but it's caught on in nothing flat to the point that most western citizens now believe they're entitled to enjoy the last third of their adult lives as a twenty-year holiday weekend at government expense. And that two-decade weekend is only getting longer: Developed societies face the prospect of millions of citizens living into their nineties and beyond and spending the last twenty years in increasing stages of dementia—at state expense. That sounds pricey, whether you rely on immigrants to tend them (as in Europe) or "humanoid" "welfare robots" (as the Japanese are developing).

So the disease the west would most like to cure is Alzheimer's. How would you do that? The obvious way to experiment would be one of these human/animal hybrids the British are hot for: You'd inject human material (brain cells) into animals that are closest to man (primates). As it happens, that's the plot of this summer's new movie, *Rise of the Planet of the Apes*, which title suggests the experiment went somewhat awry. "If you start putting very large numbers of human brain cells into the brains of primates," worries Professor Thomas Baldwin, co-author of a new report for Britain's Academy of Medical Sciences, "suddenly you might transform the primate into something that has some of the capacities that we regard as distinctively human—speech, or other ways of being able to manipulate or relate to us." "The closer an animal brain is to a human brain, the harder it is to predict what might happen," warns Martin Bobrow, professor of genetics at Cambridge University.

So the Brits retain a bit of squeamishness in this area: They're aware of the pitfalls of injecting Ozzy Osbourne's brain into an orangutan. Who might be less concerned about this fine ethical line? It was recently disclosed that China has a herd of thirty-nine goats with human-style blood and internal organs created by injecting stem cells into their embryos, the work of Professor Huang Shuzheng of Jiao Tong University.

I wonder what else the Chinese are sticking human stem cells into. I'm sure they'll tell us when they're ready.

The Coming of Age changes everything. The developed world will have insufficient numbers of young people to sell new stuff to: That's an economic issue. But a distorted societal age profile doesn't stop there: Switzerland, once famous for expensive sanatoria where one went to prolong life, is now doing gangbusters business with its "dignified death" resorts. With the increase in demand for "assisted" suicide at their general hospitals, the Dutch are talking about purpose-built facilities: You have an ear, nose, and throat hospital, so why not a death hospital? After all, it's more "humane" than the alternatives— for example, the mini epidemic of missing centenarians in Japan: Tokyo's oldest man was supposedly Sogen Kato, 111 years old. Last year, police broke into his daughter's home and discovered his mummified corpse, still in his bedclothes. His relatives were arrested for bilking the government of millions of yen in fraudulent welfare payments. Tokyo's oldest woman was supposedly Fusa Furuya, 113 years old. When welfare officials called at her home, her daughter said she was now living at another address just outside the city. This second building turned out to have been razed to put a highway through. "Human bonds are weakening," a glum Prime Minister, Naoto Kan, told Parliament. "Society as a whole tends to sever human relationships."

Like I said: How weird how soon? Dutch drive-through death clinics on Main Street. Japanese welfare robots doing the jobs humans won't do. British scientists breeding a Brit-animal hybrid class purely for the purposes of experimenting on them....

And at a research facility somewhere deep in the Chinese hinterlands, an ape injected with human brain cells waits for the midnight shift change and a chance to bust through the security fence....

XIII

CURTAINS

DOUBLE ACT

Maclean's, February 18, 2008

And that's why birds do it, bees do it
Even educated fleas do it …

"LET'S DO IT" was the first of Cole Porter's great "laundry list" songs, an accumulation of examples that all go to illustrate a single point—in this case, "Let's do it." And, despite the qualifying phrase of "let's fall in love," you get the distinct impression the "it" he was urging you to do was an encounter of a more transitory nature:

The most refined ladybugs do it
When a gentleman calls
Moths in your rugs do it
What's the use of moth balls?

When I was a child and the song came on the radio, my father would sing along and my mother would coo in pleasure, until the following quatrain:

The Dutch in old Amsterdam do it
Not to mention the Finns
Folks in Siam do it
Think of Siamese twins

—at which point my mum would always grimace and say she didn't think the line was appropriate. Indeed. Why would the thought of Siamese twins be a spur to erotic intimacy? It's an unforeseen calamity, not an incentive.

Well, we're a long way from 1928, when Porter wrote the song, and Siamese twins as a pop-culture phenomenon have waned somewhat since then. Still, it was exactly one hundred years ago—February 5, 1908—that the most famous Siamese twins of the twentieth century were born. They weren't Siamese, but English, born in a room above the Queen's Head pub in Brighton to an unwed barmaid, and delivered by the landlady. Violet and Daisy Hilton went on to star in a memorable film by Tod Browning (director of the Bela Lugosi *Dracula*) and to inspire in the 1990s at least two musicals.

How'd they get from Brighton to Broadway? Well, Daisy and Violet were pygopagus twins, conjoined at the buttocks. And, having delivered the babies, the pub landlady saw her opportunity and more or less bought the kids from her employee. Shortly thereafter, they were entrusted to the management of Ike Rose, impresario of Rose's Royal Midgets, who arranged to "exhibit" them with Josefa and Rosa Blazek in a show business first: never before had two sets of Siamese twins appeared on a single bill—the Hilton babies and the grown-up Blazek sisters, who were then about thirty. They weren't Siamese, either, but rather Bohemian—although Rosa, the alleged nymphomaniac of the pair, was considerably more bohemian than Josefa, who disapproved of her sister shagging like a minx, even though, according to rumor, she experienced her sister's coital sensations simultaneously in her own erogenous zones.

The Siamese angle derives from Chang and Eng, who were born in Siam and made so famous by P. T. Barnum that ever after all "conjoined twins" were Siamese. As it happens, Chang and Eng were three-quarters Chinese and known in their native village as "the Chinese twins." But, in global media terms, it was Barnum's designation that prevailed. They were joined at the sternum and, even in the nineteenth century, could easily have been separated. But they were able to stretch the tissue and stand side by side, looking like two Thais joined at the thighs. That image came to define Siamese twins in popular culture. Chang and Eng married the daughters of a North Carolina minister, kept them in separate homes and divided their time between the two. Chang had ten kids, Eng nine, and their descendants can apparently still be found scattered throughout the Piedmont.

That's what every Siamese-twin manager in the early twentieth century was shooting for: a slice of the Chang and Eng action. The pub landlady died and "bequeathed" Violet and Daisy to her daughter, and they all wound up in a big house in San Antonio, with the sisters touring in vaudeville as singers, dancers, and musicians. By 1926 they were part of an act called the Dance-medians, with another up-and-coming British-born performer, Bob Hope. The gals' three-legged tap routines didn't leave a lot of room for him. "They're too much of a woman for me," said Hope.

The high point of their fame was Tod Browning's 1932 film *Freaks*, which is no more or less than what it says: a portrait of the "freaks" in a travelling circus. Daisy and Violet played themselves, a novelty act who appear mainly in scenes with their two fiancés: when Daisy is kissed by her betrothed, you can see the sexual charge on Violet's face. Today, such a film would use computer technology, or some Hollywood A-lister augmented by Oscar-bait prosthetics. But in 1932 *Freaks* had no option but to use 100 percent bona fide freaks—not just the Hilton twins, but Martha the Armless Wonder, Koo Koo the Bird Girl, and all kinds of visually arresting people missing various combinations of body parts. There's a bearded lady in childbirth, and a handsome fellow with no legs or lower torso walking around on long arms and feet-like hands. There's another chap dragging around the grounds who's just a head and about eighteen inches of fleshy lump. It ought to be cruel and exploitative, but, by the time Browning's wrapped it up, it doesn't seem that way.

By this stage, the twins were, well, not exactly stars, but certainly celebrities. They posed for cheesecake shots, crouched on the beach in artfully conjoined bathing suits. Violet had a run of B-list boyfriends—boxers and musicians—before announcing her engagement to the gals' bandleader Maurice Lambert. Twenty-one states denied them a marriage license. "The very idea of such a marriage is quite immoral and indecent," pronounced William C. Chanler of the Manhattan license bureau. Violet, her betrothed, and her sister crossed the Hudson to Newark, New Jersey. "Nothing doing!" said town clerk Harry S. Reichenstein. "Moral reasons." Reporting the story, *Time* magazine explained to its readers that "Daisy-&-Violet Hilton are a pygopagus, a double-monster joined at the buttocks." Violet had to wait till 1936 to wed some other fellow entirely in a quiet ceremony on the fifty-yard line of the Cotton Bowl at the Texas Centennial Exhibition.

By 1950, their exploitation movie, *Chained for Life*, had bombed and they were broke. By 1955, their hot-dog stand was run out of Miami by other vendors resentful of their unique marketing gimmick. By 1962, they were bagging groceries in Charlotte, taken in by a kindly store manager who bought them some work clothes: all they had in their wardrobe were specialty costumes from obsolescent routines for long-shuttered vaudeville circuits. One morning in the winter of 1969, they failed to show up at the store. Daisy had succumbed to Hong Kong flu, and, sharing the same circulatory system, Violet inevitably followed.

Hilton-wise, I'll take Daisy and Violet over Paris. Unlike her, they had a modicum of talent—instrument-playing, tap-dancing, even acting—and their sex lives are more original, too. I said above that Siamese twins have waned in pop culture, which is certainly true compared to the Chang and Eng era. But the phenomenon waxed quite impressively during the Nineties. We don't have films like *Freaks* and *Chained for Life* anymore, but in recent years we've had *Twin Falls Idaho* and *Stuck on You*. In 2006, Dean Jensen published a full-blown biography of Daisy and Violet, not bad for a couple who were the very acme of has-been: grocery baggers with a vaudevillian wardrobe. In 1990, I saw my first Hilton twins musical, *20 Fingers, 20 Toes*, full of lines like "When it comes to dancing, you girls got four left feet." *Side Show* in 1997 was more self-consciously arty: "Come look at the freaks / Come gaze at the geeks," sang the creepy carny boss, introducing us to his parade of attractions. The stark directness of that couplet was somewhat diluted as the song proceeds and the lyricist found himself encumbered with that "-eek" rhyme scheme: "Come explore how they fascinate you / Exasperate you / For weeks." Also, they have the "best physiques" and they "flush your cheeks." As for the music, the composer was utterly incapable of evoking the rowdiness of the era, either in its vulgar energy or its casual cruelties. In his worst strategic error, the director first showed us Violet and Daisy not as Siamese twins but as detached individuals.

Yet, if we're to understand their predicament, we have to try and imagine what it must be like never to be alone—when you're asleep, when you're taking a shower, when you and your husband want to go on your honeymoon.... Unable to separate physically, Violet and Daisy were given exercises by Harry Houdini, one of their celebrity chums, to help them separate mentally.

What they really felt about life, we can only guess. But Browning's *Freaks* remains a compelling glimpse of a lost tradition. The plot's simple. Cleopatra, a blowsy Teutonic bitch of a trapeze artist, is putting the moves on Hans the midget in order to get his money. Hans disregards the warnings, putting them down to jealousy: "Let them laugh, the swine!" In this community, the regular full-sized circus folk are corrupt and conniving and emotionally stunted, and the genuine human warmth is found among the misfits. Thus, Browning is an early pioneer of the now conventional Hollywood thesis of the self-defined "alternative family." And his direction is so skilled that, although you never quite lose your awareness of their physical deformity, he does succeed in shifting your point of view to the freaks' perspective—literally, in fact, since most of the smaller creatures spend much of their time under the circus wagons rather than up inside them—and making Cleopatra and her violent drunken lunk Hercules seem like the real deformations of the human spirit. The wedding-feast scene is one of the best examples in film history of a fully realized, self-contained world existing on its own terms. *Freaks* starts off feeling like weird, overspecialized porn but, by its closing, is both touching and moral. Violet and Daisy Hilton were born too late for the Chang and Eng big-time, but they had their moment and they made their mark.

CROC OF GOLD

The Atlantic, November 2006

I'D JUST FILED a column for *The Australian* when I got the first email from Down Under—about reports of an accident involving the Crocodile Hunter. All journalists, on hearing breaking news of a famous person's injury, assume the announcement of death will follow shortly, President Kennedy and the Princess of Wales being merely the most obvious proof of the soundness of this rule. But, in the early hours of Monday morning, Eastern time, when my editor in Sydney told me my piece was being held because Steve Irwin had been killed by the barbed tip of a stingray, I found myself re-suspending disbelief. Like a long-distance cyber version of an escapologist's audience, I felt vaguely that it was too good an ending and therefore must be part of the act—that at any minute the hyperactive overgrown schoolboy would emerge off the Queensland coast with his trademark "Crikey!" and a souvenir barb for the trophy room at the family's Australia Zoo.

The Crocodile Hunter didn't exactly laugh at death, but he was happy to play its straight man. In his FedEx commercial a few years ago, Irwin introduced us to the "Fear Snake," "the most venomous snake in the world." "One bite from him and it's all over," he began in his exuberantly emphatic semi-parodic Aussie vowels, and then let the creature sink its fangs in. "Yow! ... Luckily we have had the anti-venom sent from America by FedEx."

But, as it turned out, they'd used a less reliable courier. Fatal error. "In my line of work, if you are not absolutely sure, you are absolutely dead."

When the stingray struck off Batt Reef, Steve Irwin was absolutely sure: he immediately yanked the barb out of his chest; he knew what had happened. But he was still absolutely dead, the first Australian to be felled by a stingray in six decades. The reaction from his compatriots fell into two camps. "It was the way he would have wanted to go," said more than a few, though I doubt, with an eight-year-old girl and three-year-old boy, he would have wanted it quite so soon. From London, the grizzled Aussie feminist Germaine Greer shafted him with a toxic barb all her own: "The animal world has finally taken its revenge on Steve Irwin," she gloated in *The Guardian*. "You can just imagine Irwin yelling: 'Just look at these beauties! Crikey! With those barbs a stingray can kill a horse!' (Yes, Steve, but a stingray doesn't want to kill a horse. It eats crustaceans, for God's sake)," parenthesized Ms. Greer, deploying the novel journalistic device of correcting the dialogue she'd invented for him.

Ms. Greer represented the views of many self-advertised conservationists in her aesthetic distaste for Irwin. By the Nineties the old head-in-the-lion's-mouth shirt-sodden-by-the-incontinent-lemur wildlife showman was on the endangered species list, and the embodiment of the telly naturalist was the BBC's David Attenborough. In the presence of animals, he lowers his voice to a breathy whisper, maintaining his evenly modulated hushed reverence even during a terrible outbreak of crabs—120 million of them arriving on the beach at Christmas Island for their annual spawning season. Across the shifting sands, he whispers. The little nippers have been showing up same time every year since time immemorial. Suppose he'd raised his voice. How many of the 120 million in that wall-to-wall crustacean broadloom would have flounced off in a huff? Seven? Twenty-nine? Can crabs even hear the human speaking voice? But Sir David keeps his breathy whisper even when he's back in the BBC studio doing the voiceover.

Irwin never cared much for this approach. "We can't keep looking at wildlife on a long lens on a tripod," he said. "Then there's this voice of God telling you about the cheetah kill. After 450,000 cheetah kills, it's not entertaining anymore." In contrast to Attenborough, the boyishly eager Irwin bounded into the frame like Tigger, leaping after the crocs and bantering at full volume: "Crikey!" "Gorgeous! "What a beauty!"—lines that Sir David would be unlikely to deploy anywhere other than the later stages of the BBC office Christmas party. Asked by Jay Leno how he determined the sex of a croc, Irwin replied, "I put my finger in here and if it smiles it's a girl, and if it bites me it's a boy." There was more than a grain of truth in the *South Park* episode in which the guys are lounging on the couch watching an Aussie crocodile hunter and his missus gliding down the river. "As we steer our boat down, looking for these dangerous predators...boy, there's a king croc right here!" says the telly naturalist. "He must be four meters; twelve, thirteen feet long at least." The mighty beast raises its head out of the water. "This croc has enough power in its jaws to rip my head right off.... I've got to be careful. So what I'm gonna do is sneak up on it and jam my thumb in its butthole."

Back on the couch, the fellows are impressed. "Holy crap!" marvels Stan, as the Aussie leaps in and grabs the croc. "Go, dude, go!" cheers Kyle.

"This should really piss it off!" says the Aussie, raising his left thumb. "I've gotta be careful." The croc yelps up in surprise and then falls back into the water. "That was quite an angry croc," explains the hunter in the next scene. "But I managed to escape with only a few bruises and a shattered left testicle. Next week we'll look for more of these beautiful creatures, so we can learn more about them by pissing them off immensely. Thanks for watching."

Bob and Lyn Irwin were a plumber and a nurse in Victoria who moved up north to the Sunshine Coast, bought four acres, and started a reptile park. Given a scrub python for his sixth birthday, Steve was more or less his TV persona by the time he was a teenager, the larky lad with the winning spiel who talked the punters through his parents' more ferocious exhibits. A lot of small, broken-down, underfunded animal parks around the world have an Irwinesque figure on the lot, and, in 99.99 percent of cases, the shtick's good enough to get them that far but no farther. But Irwin was the right man at the right time, just as cable TV specialty channels were taking off and just as environmentalism had sapped wildlife education of much of its fun. Irwin was always bursting with joy, and why wouldn't he be? There are more crocs in Oz than ever before, and they're also larger than they were.

And he had the advantage of being Australian, which to American audiences puts you in the category of least foreign foreigner: Australia, as Ishmael says in a book about another famous hunter who came a cropper under water, is "that great America on the other side of the sphere." Herman Melville was overstating it a bit, but if you want to make it big in America as a media outdoorsman, being Aussie isn't a bad idea. An American croc hunter comes freighted with all kinds of baggage: is he your authentic red-state stump-toothed mountain man out of *Deliverance*? or some pantywaist NPR Bambi-boomer enviro-ninny like that bear guy up in Alaska trying to get in touch with his inner self until the grizzlies ripped it out of his chest for him? If you're from Down Under, you avoid all that. Irwin hailed Australia's (conservative) Prime Minister John Howard as "the greatest leader Australia has ever had and the greatest leader in the world." If he'd said that about Bush, he'd have been savaged more thoroughly than by any croc, but fortunately only seven Americans have heard of Mr. Howard.

There's really only room for one popular Oz character in the American imagination at any one time, and Irwin took Paul Hogan's Crocodile Dundee persona and artfully extended it to actual crocodiles. He stayed in his uniform of khaki shorts and short-sleeved shirt even when attending awards ceremonies. There were moments when he was laying on the "crikeys!" and "bonzas!" and "fair dinkums!" so thick that you vaguely suspected he might be the strine (that's Oz talk) version of Maurice Chevalier, who enquired after the run-through of "Thank Heaven for Little Girls," "Did I sound French enough?" Irwin always sounded Australian enough, happy in his role as his nation's most internationally recognized "larrikin" and "ocker" and several other words that don't translate terribly easily into American English. When the larrikin was interviewed by the near homophonic Larry King, the host attempted to pin down Steve on some of the argot but never progressed much beyond: "'Bloke' is a man?"

You can't put anything over on Larry. Some of Irwin's compatriots were a tougher sell. It must be frustrating to explain to foreigners that your modern confident multicultural nation has outgrown its corked hat/boomerang/kangaroo caricature only to discover that the only Aussie they've heard of is the umpteenth variation of it. It's true that, statistically, Australians are one of the most urbanized peoples on earth, and few have spent time in the outback, never mind wrestled crocs there. It's also the case that Sydney has a lot more Thai restaurants than it used to, and, come to that, Muslim riots. But few national stereotypes are as appealing as Australia's. By the time Steve Irwin's countrymen became aware of his global success, he had more viewers in the U.S. than there are Australians in Australia.

If it was an act, it was very well done. He was forty-four but still a boyish charmer with a puppy-fat face and long hair that flipped up and down Charlie's Angel–like through the bush. At the Australia Zoo, if his wife Terri caught him bending over to attend to an animal, she'd always give an appreciative wolf whistle. To be sure, it was something of a surprise to discover that Irwin died filming a segment for his eight-year-old daughter's forthcoming TV series, and that Bindi already has her own line of clothing. But they handled global celebrity less creepily than most.

I spent most of August in Australia, and the first question my children asked was: "Did you meet Steve Irwin?" Sadly, no, but they were impressed to hear I'd met folks who'd met him, like the Prime Minister and the Foreign Minister, whose Christmas card showed the family at the Irwins' zoo. And up in Queensland I had the odd feeling of walking through a deserted set. I passed a weird potato-shaped mountain that seemed strangely familiar and realized I knew it from a picture with the Croc Hunter posed in front of it in his trademark crouch.

Less than twenty-four hours had passed before the Discovery honchos announced that Animal Planet would continue to air the Crocodile Hunter shows. But will those millions of children who adored his life-affirming presence stick with him in posthumous reruns? Or will all those years of close encounters be retrospectively darkened by the very last one? However it turns out, anyone who raised young kids in the half-decade either side of the turn of the century will retain a distant memory of a crazy bloke in shorts hugging some leathery old croc or fleeing a komodo dragon. For him not to be doing it another decade or three seems a great injustice. Or, to modify a phrase, unfair dinkum.

EVERY DOG SHOULD
HAVE HIS DAY

SteynOnline, April 2, 2014

DORIS DAY'S FIRST public performance was in kindergarten, in the olio to a minstrel show. The olio was a sort of warm-up to the main bill, and, in the late Twenties in Cincinnati, little Doris was supposed to do a recitation which began:

> *I'se goin' down to the Cushville hop*
> *And there ain't no niggie goin' to make me stop!*

"I was in a red tutu," she told me, "and they kept us backstage so long that I wet my pants. And, when I went on, you could see it—the red satin had turned black. I burst into tears after the second line and ran off stage. Some debut. Maybe that's where it started."

"It" is her famous aversion to public appearances. In the Forties, in the half-hour before her nightclub act or live radio shows, she would spend most of her time in the toilet with, as she puts it, "one end or the other erupting." If it's hard for her fans to imagine Doris Day having bodily functions, it's been even harder these last decades to imagine they'll ever see her live on stage ever again.

From time to time, an appearance is scheduled, but somehow the fickle finger of fate conspires to keep her with her beloved dogs in Carmel, California. Oscars producer Allan Carr thought he'd nailed her for the 1988 Awards: "We got a sitter for the dogs and she said *yes!!!!*" he roared in triumph. But, come the big day, she tripped over a water sprinkler and had to cancel. Que sera, sera.

She dislikes cameras and microphones but one day back in the Nineties she was happy to talk to me on the telephone at a safe distance of three time zones and twelve state lines. To be honest, it was a bit of a relief for me, too, since I didn't have to cozy up to all those damn pooches, with whom she's shared her life since her third husband died in 1968. Nothing against dogs, I hasten to add, but a few years earlier an old acquaintance of mine from the BBC days, the eminent cultural critic Sir Christopher Frayling, had wanted to do a big telly re-evaluation of Doris Day as the proto-feminist, and my memory of the resulting show, after much negotiation between the parties, is that an inordinate amount of time was shots of him walking various of her canines.

Oddly, back in the Fifties, when she had most of her hit records, she was just about the only pop star not to have a terrible dog song inflicted on her: Patti Page spent four decades trying to crawl out from under "How Much Is That Doggie in the Window?"; Sinatra would punch you in the kisser if you so much as mentioned "Mama Will Bark," his canine love-duet with the big-breasted but small-voiced "personality" Dagmar; the Singing Dogs, who barked their way through "Oh! Susannah," are more relaxed about it, but then, of course, they're dogs. Meanwhile, Doris was having hits with songs about telephones ("Shanghai"—"I'm right around the corner in a phone booth"), trains ("Sentimental Journey"—"Counting ev'ry mile of railroad track"), stalkers ("A Guy Is a Guy"—"He followed me down the street like I knew he would"), and whips ("The Deadwood Stage"—"Whip crack away! Whip crack away! Whip crack awaaay!!!").

With Sinatra, we assume the songs tell us something about the man. So I was interested to know whether "Move Over, Darling" and "It's Magic" really sum up Doris Day. "Well, I think they're part of who I am," she began, and a cacophony that sounded like the Singing Dogs reunion tour rent the air. "Uh-oh," she explained, "that's Buster Brown. He's a cross between a German short-haired pointer and an English sheepdog...."

"About your work with André Previn...." I said, struggling over the barks to stay on track.

"He looks like a wire-haired pointer," said Doris. Which, to be honest, I couldn't quite see, until I realized she was still talking about Buster Brown. "And I have a beautiful shitsu called Wesley Winfield." Most of her dozens of dogs, it seems, are mongrel strays, and she can't understand the fuss about purebreds—although as it happens, Doris Day, née Doris Kappelhoff, is purebred Aryan (all four of her grandparents were German).

Buster Brown, Wesley Winfield... Doris Day likes any alliterative appellation apart from her own. She was renamed after "Day after Day," an old ballad from the Twenties that the Princeton Triangle Club Jazz Band recorded with freshman vocalist Jimmy Stewart:

> *Just as evening follows afternoon*
> *I follow you round*
> *Just as age can't change the sun or moon*
> *Our love stays sublime*
> *Regardless of time …*

Doris Kappelhoff sang it at her first club booking in Cincinnati, and it went over so well that the bandleader proposed she become "Doris Day." She never cared for it: it was no "Buster Brown." "Doris Day sounds phony," she told me. "I've always thought that." Many friends call her "Clara," because (she says) she looks more like a Clara; Rock Hudson called her "Eunice"; and Bob Hope favored "JB," short for "Jut Butt": As he once said to me, very appreciatively, "You could play bridge on her ass," although I don't believe he ever did.

JB was in her early seventies when we spoke, and looked pretty much the same as ever, eager and perky, like a short-haired pointer. Singing contemporaries like Rosemary Clooney and Margaret Whiting were still out there on the road day after day, night after night, but Doris had no desire to join them. "Maybe they need the money," she said. "Maybe they're not okay in that department."

Doris is famously okay in that department. The standard music-industry line on her is that she's the most unappreciated female singer in the business.

The second standard music-industry line on her is: if she's that unappreciated, how come she's so rich? After her husband Marty Melcher's sudden death in 1968, she discovered he'd blown through all the money. Half a decade later, a California judge awarded her damages of $22,835,646 from her business manager, and that buys a lot of dog chow.

"Yes, but," I said, "Sinatra's okay in the money department. But he's still touring...."

"Men have a need to go out and work," she said firmly. "Women are content to be at home. We've got our friends to talk to, and go to the supermarket with." Notwithstanding Chris Frayling and the other eminent scholars who hail Doris Day as a pioneer feminist icon (mainly for her refusal to surrender to Rock Hudson in those sex comedies), the star herself has a casual way of wreaking havoc with their theses. And, while I like *Pillow Talk* and *Lover Come Back*, if you're looking for strong-woman stuff try the earlier movies: as Ruth Etting doing "Ten Cents a Dance" in *Love Me or Leave Me,* or the small-town girl who's tougher than the feckless musician (played by Sinatra) she takes up with in *Young at Heart.*

You can see why Mike Nichols wanted to cast her as Mrs. Robinson in *The Graduate,* but you can also understand why Doris figured there was nothing for her in agreeing to it. I brought up the old Groucho Marx line: "I knew Doris Day before she was a virgin." She insisted it wasn't Groucho, preferring to attribute it to the musical misanthrope Oscar Levant. "That was such a stupid Levant joke," she said, "though it's very possible he didn't say it, either." Whether or not it's a fair assessment of her screen persona, there is a truth to the line: Before she was a Hollywood virgin, there was another Doris Day, the Doris Day who wed at seventeen and was brutally beaten on the second day of her married life by a psychotic husband whose reaction to her subsequent pregnancy was to shovel some illegal pills down her throat to force her to miscarry. He failed, and her only son, Terry, grew up to become, eventually, her record producer.

That first husband was the *Young at Heart* feckless-musician routine without the Hollywood gloss and Sinatra in the role: He was the trombonist in the band she was singing with. Her second spouse was a saxophonist, who offered a more stable home life, but in a rundown trailer park, not the picture-perfect picket-fence small-town idyll in which she passed her early movies. They split up, although they reunited for occasional bouts of wild sex. Her first husband blew his brains out in a car; her second she failed to recognize when she bumped into him on the street a few years back; and the third bilked her out of all her dough. (There was, briefly, a fourth, a head waiter who always gave Doris a complimentary doggie bag on her way out of the restaurant.) Surely, I suggested, that would dent your faith in all these boy-meets-girl movie plots and moon-June love songs?

"Well, as I always say," she chirped, "que sera, sera. Even before they ever wrote the song, that was my philosophy." She admitted that she regretted "most of my marriages," and you sense that it was not until very late that she enjoyed the domestic placidity that came so easily in her films. She told me she needs the dogs, but can do without a man. "A lot of women do," she said. "I'm doing just fine, thank you. I love being able to go to the supermarket. It's my favorite activity. But you should never go to the supermarket when you're hungry, Mark, because, if you do, you'll wind up filling three carts—or trolleys, as they say in Britain."

And so we talked about supermarkets for a while. At home in Carmel-by-the-Sea, Doris Day has finally become the girl next door.

Her son, Terry, was mostly raised by her mother, while Doris was on the road with the Les Brown band. But they were always close, especially after she packed in the hubby business for good, and he became her closest confidant—and the man behind her later and mostly unreleased recordings. A widely admired producer for the Byrds, the Mamas and Papas, and the Beach Boys (for whom he wrote the song "Kokomo"), Terry Melcher died of melanoma ten years ago, and in 2011 Doris picked out a few of the tracks he'd recorded with her in the Eighties and Nineties and put out a CD, *My Heart*. At eighty-seven, she became the oldest ever singer to have a UK Top Ten album of previously unreleased material.

Strange to hear Doris Day sing the Beach Boys song "Disney Girls," and Billy Preston's "You Are So Beautiful." I wonder what else she's keeping in the vaults. When we spoke by telephone, I told her that her version of "I Had the

Craziest Dream" was one of my favorite recordings, and it made me sad that she preferred walking shitsus and pushing supermarket carts, which anyone can do. "Oh, I might do some singing again," she said. "I sang at a Best Friends fundraiser we held at the house not long ago, and I was pretty pleased." And then came, as for Allan Carr at the Oscars, the inevitable letdown. "But I've been hoarse for months now. I have hundreds of trees and they're all live oaks, and, because of the pollen, it affects the voice."

"Really?" I responded, unable to suspend disbelief. "The trees have damaged your singing voice?"

"My doctors wouldn't dare blame it on my animals," she said, firmly, "so I've decided to blame it on the poor trees."

And over the telephone line, from far in the distance, Wesley, or possibly Buster, barked—up a wronged tree.

Happy ninetieth birthday, Doris. And here's to the next album.

THE SEVENTY-YEAR
ITCH

In 1996, The Daily Telegraph *in London gave me one of my best assignments—the chance to interview a living legend as she prepared to celebrate her seventieth birthday.*

The Daily Telegraph, May 31, 1996

SHE ARRIVES, AS ALWAYS, late but, when she does, every head turns: not because of that trademark lip-quiver in the smile or the breathless, girlish voice inquiring about her luncheon guest or the famous bosom (a little fuller) and the wiggling hips (a little fuller still), but because, for the first time in half a century, Marilyn Monroe's bleached blonde hair is once again a mousey brown.

"It's about closure; it's about letting go," she says, declining an aperitif. "It's all in the book." The book is *Norma Jean: The Child Inside,* by Marilyn Monroe (Lorelei & Lee, £15.99) and, as Oprah Winfrey writes in a perceptive introduction, "Before Roseanne, there was Marilyn." It's an exhaustive account of sexual abuse, abortions, drugs, and suicide attempts that has shocked the millions of Americans for whom the name Marilyn Monroe will always mean Glory Bea Barnes, Miss Ellie's love rival for Clayton Farlowe through eight smash seasons of *Dallas.*

On the jacket, a gauche teenager stares out, combing her thick, brown curls, in an early modeling assignment. "That's Norma Jean just before she bleached her hair and became Marilyn," says Miss Monroe. "It's taken me fifty years to pluck up the courage to dye my hair its natural color."

"You dye your hair its natural color?"

339

She ruffles her locks and laughs and, unusually, the still childlike voice has a faint rasp of world weariness. "Honey, I'm about to turn seventy. I could leave it white—when we did *Cocoon*, Jessica Tandy said I should and, God knows, she cleaned up. But to be confident enough to dye my hair the color it was before I started dyeing it is a big part of rediscovering who I am. You have to know where you've come from to find where you're going to. Besides, I've hated my hair ever since Elton."

"That would be your sixth husband?"

"Yeah. After all those father figures, I figured I'd try a younger man. When I'd come out of the bathroom with my old brown hairbrush sticking up out of the wavy peroxide, he used to say 'Ooh, what I'd give for a 99 from Mister Whippy.' Funny thing with these artistic types: they always want to talk dirty."

She kicks off her pumps, pulls her knees up and hugs her pedal-pushers—the pink and yellow checks that Elton claimed made him homesick for Battenberg cake. She stares into my eyes, draws down her upper lip, and purrs creamily: "As Marcel Proust, 1871 to 1922, said in *Du côté de chez Swann*, volume one, in the Scott-Moncrieff translation, 'Learning to love yourself is the greatest love of all.'"

"Are you sure?" I say. "It doesn't sound like Proust."

Momentarily, she panics, puts her spectacles on and fumbles through her index. Even at seventy, she packs well-thumbed copies of Proust and Whitman and Rilke, as if still craving the approval of an Elia Kazan or Arthur Miller. Only recently has she begun to find her own voice. Her next book will be a volume of New Age philosophy (*Crystals Are a Girl's Best Friend*), though neither that nor *Norma Jean: The Child Inside* seems to find much room for the movie career Miss Monroe used to have long before she fetched up in *Dallas*.

"I can't watch those early films anymore," she says. "That whole vulnerability thing—it makes me so angry. And anger is not where I reside."

"Where do you reside?" I ask.

"Palm Springs mainly, but I was speaking"—She exhales the next word breathily, as in her famous "Happy Birthday" greeting to President Nixon—*"metaphorically."*

The movies fizzled out after *The Graduate* flopped in 1968. "I blame myself," she says. "The director, Mike Nichols, wanted someone else but the studio forced me on him. It killed all our careers, but it was my fault. I still feel guilty about that boy—what was he called? Justin Hoffberg? He drops me a line every couple of years. Last I heard he was running a not-for-profit theatre in South Bend, Indiana. Could have been a big star."

"Oh, that's ridiculous," I say. "He was just a nerdy little shrimp."

"They wrote that song for me, you know. 'Boop-boop-be-doop Mrs. Robinson.... Where have you gone, Joe DiMaggio?' Yeah, tell me about it."

Her smile sags, and she falls silent for a moment, until the young waiter awkwardly hovering interrupts. "Miss Monroe, this is an honor. I loved you in *Mrs. Doubtfire*."

"That was Robin Williams, dear," she says. "I'll have a Caesar salad and the lobster."

"Which one?" He waves towards the tank.

"All of them."

"You're going to eat forty-seven lobsters?"

"Silly! I'm going to release them into the ocean."

"Like in *The Misfits*," I say, "where you try to save the wild horses from being captured and killed."

Since her character was written out of *Dallas*, when Clayton went off to find himself with Ray Krebbs, things haven't been easy. A cover version of "I Want Your Sex" by the Pet Shop Boys failed to re-ignite her singing career; her animal shelter was closed down, and her line of perfume, *Breathless by Marilyn*, was taken off the market after it was revealed that *eau de toilette* for the latter had been tested on raccoons from the former.

Then, in 1994, she was unceremoniously sacked four days before she was due to open in Andrew Lloyd Webber's *Sunset Boulevard*. "Andrew was so, y'know, goofy about it. He kept saying he couldn't hear the songs. But she was a silent film star, wasn't she? So he wouldn't have heard any songs, would he? I learnt that at the Actors Studio: sometimes the artist can see things the author's missed, and my take on the role was that a silent screen actress just wouldn't have been comfortable with the whole idea of singing. I met Gloria Swanson, and, believe me, she was no Ethel Merman...."

I ask the question everyone wants to put: "Have you had cosmetic surgery?"

She laughs and wrinkles her nose. "No," she declares, and stretches out her hands. "Eat your heart out, Queen Elizabeth!" Liver spots, but not many lines. "You can feel if you want to," she says, adjusting the silk clinging to her breasts. "I'm the last squishy star. They all have these hard bodies now."

She was *Playboy*'s first and most famous Playmate in December 1953 and reprised her performance for the twenty-fifth anniversary and again for the fortieth. "Do you want to know the secret?"

"Sure," I say.

"Always sleep in your bra. It preserves the muscle tone."

She's just sold the film rights to her book and passed the tip on to the actress who'll be playing young Marilyn, Kate Moss. ("My what?" said Kate.)

The waiter returns with the lobsters. "Just wheel the tank round by the car," she says. "You can put it on expenses, can't you?"

"Well, I'm not sure," I begin. But I know she's never had much money. Even in the Fifties, she never made more than $1,500 a week, and Jane Russell got paid five times as much for *Gentlemen Prefer Blondes*. Since then, she's compounded her problems by some ill-advised lawsuits. She sued Madonna, arguing that her "Material Girl" video amounted to the theft of her professional identity, and lost. Her publicist had warned me there's one area she won't discuss, but I can't resist bringing it up: her ongoing sexual harassment suit against President Clinton.

"Well, it's upsetting to me because I was one of his first supporters," she says, "long before Barbra or Fleetwood Mac. It was a big rally and I sang 'He's Just a Little Boy from Little Rock,' and you can imagine my shock when he comes up to me afterwards and goes"—the voice drops to a whisper—"'Say hello to a girl's best friend, baby. And I don't mean rhinestones.'"

I am, frankly, skeptical. "Oh, come on," I scoff. "This is the President of the United States we're talking about!"

"Well, he wasn't the first of those Hail-to-the-Chief boys to try it on with me."

"Really? Who else?"

"I'd rather not say."

"It was Nixon, wasn't it?"

"I'm not saying. But it was before Nixon."

"My God, Eisenhower!"

"I told you I won't say. But it was after Eisenhower."

"Good grief. LBJ?"

"Just drop it, okay?' And the girlish voice has a sudden flash of steel. So I move on. "What a life!" I marvel.

"Oh, silly!" she chides. "I'm just one of those old faces people look at in restaurants and airports because somewhere under the wrinkles they think they can see a young face they used to recognize. U wrote a song about me. 'And it seems to me you lived your life like a candle in the wind, never knowing who to cling to when the rain set in....'"

"That's very good," I say. "You should get him to record it."

"Oh, please. I told him I don't get the simile. I mean, a candle doesn't cling to you in the wind, does it? It would set your shirt alight. So he went off and composed a song about Judy Garland instead."

I remind her of some lines young Marilyn had written to herself almost half a century earlier: "There was something special about me and I knew what it was. I was the kind of girl they found dead in a hall bedroom with an empty bottle of sleeping pills in her hand."

She laughs, a big, full, throaty laugh. "Maybe it would have been better that way," she says, and points to a framed poster across the restaurant. "Like James Dean. He'll be in that T-shirt for eternity. D'you remember *The Seven Year Itch*? When it played New York, they had this fifty-foot blow-up on the front of Loew's State—me over the subway grating with the wind blowing the pleats of my skirt above the waist. I thought they'd never take it down."

The lips quiver playfully one last time and she begins to sing softly:

Men grow cold
As girls grow old
And we all lose our charms in the end …

"But to be one of the Poster People. That's forever."

XIV

LAST LAUGHS

JOKING ASIDE

National Review, June 6, 2011

I READ *The Joke*, Milan Kundera's first novel, when I was a schoolboy. Bit above my level, but, even as a teenager, I liked the premise. Ludvik is a young man in post-war, newly Communist Czechoslovakia. He's a smart, witty guy, a loyal Party member with a great future ahead of him. His girlfriend, though, is a bit serious. So when she writes to him from her two-week Party training course enthusing about the early-morning calisthenics and the "healthy atmosphere," he scribbles off a droll postcard:

> Optimism is the opium of the people! A healthy atmosphere stinks
> of stupidity! Long live Trotsky! Ludvik.

A few weeks later, he's called before a committee of the District Party Secretariat. He tries to explain he was making a joke. Immediately they remove him from his position at the Students Union; then they expel him from the Party, and the university; and shortly thereafter he's sent to work in the mines. As a waggish adolescent, I liked the absurdity of the situation in which Ludvik finds himself. Later, I came to appreciate that Kundera had skewered the touchiness of totalitarianism, and the consequential loss of any sense of proportion. It was the book I read on the flight to Vancouver, when *Maclean's* magazine and I were hauled before the British Columbia "Human Rights" Tribunal for the crime of "flagrant Islamophobia." In the course of a week-long trial, the best part of a day was devoted to examining, with the aid of "expert witnesses," the "tone" of my jokes.

Like Ludvik at the District Party Secretariat, we faced a troika of judges. Unfortunately, none of them had read Milan Kundera, or, apparently, heard of him. So immediately after my trial they ensnared a minor stand-up comic,

Guy Earle, who had committed the crime of putting down two drunken hecklers. Unfortunately for him, they were of the lesbian persuasion. Last month, he was convicted of putting down hecklers homophobically and fined fifteen thousand dollars. Mr. Earle did not testify at his trial, nor attend it. He lives on the other side of the country, and could afford neither flight nor accommodation. Rather touchingly, he offered to pay for his trip by performing at various comedy clubs while in town, before he eventually realized that no Vancouver impresario was going to return his calls ever again. Ludvik would have recognized that, too. Comrade Zemanek, the chairman of the plenary meeting that decides his fate, participated with him in earlier jests with the same girl, but he makes a brilliant speech explaining why Ludvik has to be punished, and everyone else agrees:

> No one spoke on my behalf, and finally everyone present (and there were about a hundred of them, including my teachers and my closest friends), yes, every last one of them raised his hand to approve my expulsion.

And so it went for Guy Earle, hung out to dry by his comrades at the plenary session of the Canadian Collective of Edgy Transgressive Comedians. I speak metaphorically. But, if you'd like something more literal, let's move south of the border. Recently, *Surgery News*, the official journal of the American College of Surgeons, published a piece by its editor-in-chief, Lazar Greenfield, examining research into the benefits to women of... well, let Dr. Greenfield explain it:

> They found ingredients in semen that include mood enhancers like estrone, cortisol, prolactin, oxytocin, and serotonin; a sleep enhancer, melatonin; and, of course, sperm, which makes up only one to five per cent. Delivering these compounds into the richly vascularized vagina also turns out to have major salutary effects for the recipient.

As this was the Valentine's issue, Dr. Greenfield concluded on a "light-hearted" note:

Now we know there's a better gift for that day than chocolates.

Oh, my. When the complaints started rolling in from lady doctors, *Surgery News* withdrew the entire issue. All of it. Gone. Then Dr. Greenfield apologized. Then he resigned as editor. Then he apologized some more. Then he resigned as president-elect of the American College of Surgeons. *The New York Times* solemnly reported that Dr. Barbara Bass, chairwoman of the department of surgery at Methodist Hospital in Houston, declared she was "glad Dr. Greenfield had resigned." But Dr. Colleen Brophy, professor of surgery at Vanderbilt University, said "the resignation would not end the controversy."

Dr. Greenfield is one of the most eminent men—whoops, persons—in his profession, and, when it comes to vascularized vaginas, he would appear to have the facts on his side. But, like Ludvik, he made an ideologically unsound joke, and so his career must be ended. An apology won't cut it, so the thought police were obliged to act: To modify the old line, the operation was a complete success, and the surgeon died.

Years later, Ludvik reflects on the friends and colleagues who voted to destroy him. I wonder if, in the ruins of his reputation, Dr. Greenfield will come to feel as Kundera's protagonist does:

Since then, whenever I make new acquaintances, men or women with the potential of becoming friends or lovers, I project them back into that time, that hall, and ask myself whether they would have raised their hands; no one has ever passed the test.

Who would have thought all the old absurdist gags of Eastern Europe circa 1948 would transplant themselves to the heart of the west so effortlessly? Indeed, a latter-day Kundera would surely reject as far too obvious a scenario in which lesbians and feminists lean on eunuch males to destroy a man for disrespecting the vascularized vagina by suggesting that semen might have restorative properties. "Give it to me straight, doc. I can take it"? Not anymore. Kundera's Joke is now on us.

THE PINKSHIRTS

The National Post, April 11, 2012

YOU GO AWAY for ten minutes, and come back to find there's a new acronym in town. "Dueling Queen's Park Protests Planned over GSAs," reports *Xtra*. "OECTA Comes Out in Favor of GSAs," reports *The Catholic Register*. "Obama Blames Bush for GSA Scandal," reports Fox News.

Honestly. Is there anything that isn't Bush's fault? No, wait. That last one turns out to be an American GSA—the Government Services Administration, the government agency that picks out the office furniture for the other government agencies and is currently under fire for flying itself to Vegas and throwing itself a lavish party with clowns (professional clowns, not just government bureaucrats) and a fortune teller, who curiously enough failed to foretell that the head of the agency would shortly thereafter lose her job. By contrast, Canada's GSA is the Gay-Straight Alliance. The GSA is all over the GTA (the Gayer Toronto Area), but in a few remote upcountry redoubts north of Timmins intolerant, knuckle-dragging fundamentalist school boards declined to get with the beat. So the Ontario Government has determined to afflict them with the "Accepting Schools Act."

"Accepting"? One would regard the very name of this bill as an exquisite parody of the way statist strong-arming masquerades as limp-wristed passivity were it not for the fact that the province's Catholic schools, reluctant to accept government-mandated GSAs, are proposing instead that they should be called "Respecting Differences" groups. Good grief, this is the best a bigoted theocrat can come up with?

Bullying is as old as the schoolhouse. Dr. Thomas Arnold, one of the great reforming headmasters of nineteenth-century England, is captured in the most famous novel ever written about bullying, *Tom Brown's Schooldays*, in what, by all accounts, is an accurate summation of his approach to the matter:

"You see, I do not know anything of the case officially, and if I take any notice of it at all, I must publicly expel the boy. I don't wish to do that, for I think there is some good in him. There's nothing for it but a good sound thrashing." He paused to shake hands with the master. . . . "Remember," added the Doctor, emphasizing the words, "a good sound thrashing before the whole house."

These days, a Thrashing Schools Act mandating Thrashing Out Differences groups across the province would be the biggest windfall for Chief Commissar Barbara Hall and her Ontario "Human Rights" Commission since the transsexual labiaplasty case went belly up.[1] Teachers are not permitted, in any meaningful sense, to deal with the problem of bullying. And, when you can't deal with a problem, the easiest option is to institutionalize it. Thus, today is the Day of Pink, "the international day against bullying, discrimination, homophobia and transphobia." Don't know how big it is in Yemen or Waziristan, but the Minister of Education for the Northwest Territories is on board, and the Ontario MPP Peggy Nash has issued her own video greeting for the day, just like the Queen's Christmas message: "Today's the day we can unite in celebrating diversity and in raising awareness. . . ."

So it's just like every other bloody boring day in the Ontario school system then?

Meanwhile, Cable 14 in Hamilton has been Tweeting up a storm: "National Day of Pink/Anti-Bullying Day is tomorrow. What will you be wearing?"

Er, I don't think I have a lot of choice on that front, do I? "For schools holding Anti-Bullying events in April, you still have time to order shirts at a discount." That's great news! Nothing says "celebrate diversity" like forcing

---

1   This was at the time of my own difficulties with the Ontario "Human Rights" Commission. A lady had gone to see a surgeon who specializes in labiaplasties for aesthetic reasons. When the doctor had discovered his would-be patient had been born a man, he declined to perform the labiaplasty on the grounds that, as a specialist in (biological) lady parts, he had no idea what he was getting into. So she took him to the HRC and made his life hell.

everyone to dress exactly the same, like a bunch of Maoists who threw their workers' garb in the washer but forgot to take the red flag out.

If you're thinking, "Hang on. Day of Pink? Didn't we just have that?" No, that was Pink Shirt Day, the last Wednesday in February. This is Day of Pink, second Wednesday in April. Like the King streetcar, there'll be another one along in a minute, enthusiastically sponsored by Scotiabank, Royal Bank of Canada, ViaRail, and all the other corporate bigwigs.

If you're thinking, "Hang on. Pink awareness-raising? Isn't that something to do with breast cancer?" No, that's pink ribbons. Unfortunately, all the hues for awareness-raising ribbons are taken: not just white for bone cancer and yellow for adenosarcoma, but also (my current favorite) periwinkle for acid reflux. We need to raise awareness of how all the awareness-raising ribbons have been taken, so anti-bullying groups have been obliged to move on from ribbons to shirts.

If you're thinking, "Hang on. That sounds vaguely familiar," it is. P. G. Wodehouse, *The Code of the Woosters* (1938):

> "Don't you ever read the papers? Roderick Spode is the founder and head of the Saviours of Britain, a Fascist organization better known as the Black Shorts...."
>
> "By the way, when you say 'shorts,' you mean 'shirts,' of course."
>
> "No. By the time Spode formed his association, there were no shirts left. He and his adherents wear black shorts."
>
> "Footer bags, you mean?"

Pink Shorts Day is the second Wednesday in October in the Northwest Territories.

Yes, there have been a small number of bullied teens driven to suicide, and these particular deaths are tragedies for the families involved that blow a great big hole in their lives that can never be repaired. But they are not a cause for wrongheaded public policy. Hard cases make bad law, and hard cases hijacked by social engineers, backed by make-work bureaucracies, and bankrolled by dimwit craven pandering boardroom patsies make bad law on a catastrophic scale.

According to the Toronto District School Board's own survey, the most common type of bullying is for "body image"—the reason given by 27 percent of high school students, 38 percent of grades seven and eight, and yea, back through the generations. Yet there are no proposals for mandatory Fat-Svelte Alliances or Homely-Smokin' Alliances.

The second biggest reason in Toronto schools is "cultural or racial background." "Cultural," eh? Yet there seems no urge to install Infidel-Believer Alliances in Valley Park Middle School's celebrated mosqueteria,[2] although they could probably fit it in the back behind the menstruating girls. So the pressure for GSAs in every school would seem to be a solution entirely unrelated to the problem. Indeed, it would seem to be a gay hijacking of the issue. Queer Eye for the Fat Chick. "But enough about you, let's talk about me."

What about if you're the last non-sexualized tween schoolgirl in Ontario? You're still into ponies and unicorns and have no great interest in the opposite sex except when nice Prince William visits to cut the ribbon at the new Trans-gendered Studies Department. What if the other girls are beginning to mock you for wanting to see *Anne of Green Gables* instead of *Anne Does Avonlea*? Is there any room for the sexual-developmentally challenged in the GSAs?

Why, of course! GSAs are officially welcoming of gays, straights, and even those freaky weirdy types who aren't yet into sexual identity but could use a helpful nudge in the right direction. "Advisors Say GSA Also for Straight Students," as the headline to a poignant story in yesterday's edition of the Pembroke Academy newspaper in New Hampshire puts it. The school-approved GSA began five years ago with an ambitious platform of exciting gay activities. "They had plans for group events, like bake sales and car washes, but they never came to pass," explained Ms. Yackanin, the social studies teacher who served as the GSA's first advisor.

---

2   See "How Unclean Was My Valley."

From a lack of gay bake sales and gay car washes, the GSA has now advanced to a lack of gays. "The students just stopped coming," said Mrs. McCrum, the new Spanish teacher who took over the GSA at the start of this school year.

This is the homophobic reality of our education system: a school gay group that has everything it needs except gays.

Ms. Yackanin is reported by the Pembroke Academy paper as "saying to heterosexuals that the GSA is a resource for the entire school community." C'mon, you guys, what's wrong with you? No penetrative sex with other boys is required, or even heavy petting. It's all about getting together in the old school spirit and organizing a gay car wash.

And now the model that has proved so successful at Pembroke Academy will be enthralling school-children from Thunder Bay to Moosonee. In Thomas Arnold's day, the object was to punish bullies, and teach their victims to stand up to them. Now a defensive and enfeebled educational establishment lets the bullies get on with it, and Dalton McGuinty's ministry has decided everyone else should be taught how to be victims—or, at any rate, members of approved victimological identity groups. Gays? Sure. Muslims? You betcha. Gay Muslims? We'll cross that Rainbow Bridge when we come to it. For the moment, let's stay focused: Bullying is merely the sharp end of "heterosexism," as the Ontario "Human Rights" Commission calls it. Chief Commissar Hall defines heterosexism as "the assumption that heterosexuality is superior and preferable," which will come as news to anyone who's had sex with me.

When you shrink from punishing the bullies (as our schools do), when you pursue phantom enemies (as our "human rights" nomenklatura do), when you use the victims as a pretext for ideological advancement (as the Ontario government is doing), all that's left is the creepy, soft totalitarian, collectivized, state-enforced, glassy-eyed homogeneity of "uniting to celebrate diversity" (in Peggy Nash's words).

So Canada will have GSAs from Niagara to Nunavut; and for the lonely and unsocial, the lumpy and awkward, real bullying will proceed undisturbed in the shadows; and ideologically-compliant faux-bullying will explode, as a generation of children is conscripted into a youth corps of eternal victimhood, alert to every slight, however footling. In New York, where children are bullied with gay abandon, the school board recently proposed banning from its tests fifty hurtful, discriminatory words such as "religious holidays," "birthdays," and "cigarettes." From such an environment come a cowed pliant herd and a cadre of professional grievance-mongers, but not a lot of functioning, freeborn citizens.

"Awareness-raising"? I think we need to raise awareness that, unless you've got the T-shirt concession, all these Pink Days are worthless crap that do nothing for the problem they claim to be addressing. If you've chanced to see me in person, you'll know I often wear a pink shirt (I may even wear one on stage in Toronto later this month). Like the country song says, "I Was Pink Shirt When Pink Shirt Wasn't Cool—Er, Mandatory." But, on Pink Shirt Day, I would wear mauve or turquoise or chartreuse or anything but pink, because, when the state is committed to coercing a ruthless conformity, that's the time to show that a flickering flame of the contrarian, iconoclastic spirit still flickers in the Canadian schoolhouse. You may get bullied for not wearing pink on the Day of Pink, but you'll feel better for it.

LITTLE STASI-ON-AVON

Maclean's, April 29, 2010

NOT LONG AFTER the fall of the Iron Curtain, I chanced to be in Hungary making a TV film co-produced by the BBC and MTV. Not the MTV of caterwauling rockers but MTV as in "Magyar Televízió"—their version of the BBC, although obviously nowhere near as monolithically left-wing. We spent the first few days in Budapest meeting our local contacts—producers, fixers, interviewees, all of whom were urbane Mitteleuropean charmers, and delightful company. We'd then go on to the next meeting, at which we'd be assured by György that, while József may on the surface seem urbane and charming, he'd spent the previous thirty years as an informant for the Ministry of the Interior. Moving on to our appointment with Gábor, we'd be told that it was the eminently civilized and amusing György who'd been the state informer for the past several decades. Needless to say, Viktor had much the same to say about Gábor, and Imre about Viktor.

The BBC lads found this most disquieting. They had no objection to Commies per se, being mostly the usual bunch of university Trots and Marxists themselves. But they disliked the idea of snitches, of never being able to be sure whether your neighbor or workmate wasn't sneaking to the authorities on your every casual aside. It offended against their sense of fair play; it wasn't cricket. I took a more relaxed view, having been on the receiving end of the famous British sense of fair play, not least in my dealings with the duplicitous bastards at the BBC. I figured sure, Gábor and Viktor and József and Imre and György and pretty much everyone else we ran into in that post-Soviet spring doubtless had their dark secrets, but under a totalitarian regime the state can apply all kinds of pressure those of us in free societies can scarce imagine. Who are we to judge?

Less than two decades later, something very odd has happened. The United Kingdom is not (yet) a totalitarian regime, yet huge numbers of Britons have in effect signed on as informers to a politically correct Stasi, and with far greater enthusiasm than Gábor and György ever did. Last year, David Booker was suspended from his job at a hostel for the homeless in Southampton after a late-night chat with a colleague, Fiona Vardy, in which he happened to reveal that he did not believe in same-sex marriage or in vicars being allowed to wed their gay partners. Miss Vardy raised no objection at the time, but the following day mentioned the conversation to her superiors. They immediately suspended Mr. Booker from his job, and then announced that "this action has been taken to safeguard both residents and staff."

That's good to know, isn't it? The hostel is run by the Society of St. James, which comes under the Church of England, which in theory holds exactly the same views on homosexuality as Mr. Booker. But, if in doubt, suspend. Six weeks ago, Roy Amor, a medical technician who made prosthetics for a company called Opcare, glanced out of the window at their offices at Withington Community Hospital, and saw some British immigration officials outside. "You better hide," he said to his black colleague, a close friend of both Mr. Amor and his wife. Not the greatest joke in the world, but the pal wasn't offended, laughed it off as a bit of office banter, and they both got on with their work. It was another colleague who overheard the jest and filed a formal complaint reporting Mr. Amor for "racism." He was suspended from his job. Five days later, he received an email from the company notifying him of the disciplinary investigation and inviting him to expand on the initial statement he had made about the incident. Mr. Amor had worked in the prosthetics unit at Withington for thirty years until he made his career-detonating joke. That afternoon he stepped outside his house and shot himself in the head.

The black "victim" of his "racism" attended the funeral, as did other friends. It is not known whether the creep who reported the racist incident did, nor whether the management who opened the (presumably still ongoing) investigation troubled themselves to pay their respects to an employee with three decades of service.

"You better hide, mate." What can we do to show racists like the late Roy Amor that they won't be tolerated in our tolerant society? Well, we can take early action. Fourteen-year-old Codie Stott asked her teacher at Harrop Fold High School if she could sit with another group to do her science project as in hers the other five girls all spoke Urdu and she didn't understand what they were saying. The teacher called the police, who took her to the station, photographed her, fingerprinted her, took DNA samples, removed her jewelry and shoelaces, put her in a cell for three-and-a-half hours, and questioned her on suspicion of committing a Section Five "racial public order offence." "An allegation of a serious nature was made concerning a racially motivated remark," declared the headmaster Antony Edkins. The school would "not stand for racism in any form." In a statement, Greater Manchester Police said they took "hate crime" very seriously, and their treatment of Miss Stott was in line with "normal procedure."

So what can we do to show racists like young Miss Codie Stott that racist remarks on the linguistic preferences of members of her school science project will bring the full force of the otherwise somnolent constabulary of Her Majesty's crime-ridden realm crashing down on her? Well, obviously, we need to start the Racism Watch far earlier. The government-funded National Children's Bureau has urged nursery teachers and daycare supervisors to record and report every racist utterance of toddlers as young as three.

Like what?

Well, for example, if children "react negatively to a culinary tradition other than their own by saying 'Yuk,'" that could be a clear sign that they'll grow up to make racist immigration gags like the late Roy Amor's. If we get all their names in a big government database by pre-kindergarten, it'll be much easier to keep tabs on them for the four or five decades until we drive them to suicide.

My British friends say of Mr. Amor, "Well, obviously, he was a little disturbed, he overreacted." No, it's the system that's disturbed. Look at it from his point of view: you've worked hard, been a model employee, for thirty years—and suddenly it's all over because of a single joke that didn't offend your black friend but only the white snitch who decided to get offended on his behalf. It wasn't Roy Amor who overreacted.

"It's an enormous tragedy and we are all in mourning," said Opcare's chief executive. But actually Roy blowing his head off works out pretty well from the company's point of view. They could have dismissed the racism complaint as a lot of hooey, but then who's to say the aggrieved complainant might not report them for "creating a racist work environment"? So they suspended Roy, investigated Roy, and probably would have fired Roy. And then he might have sued for wrongful dismissal and, even though no contemporary jurist would find in favor of such an obvious racist, just fighting the suit would rack up a six-figure legal bill. All in all, suicide's the most cost-effective option. Maybe more racist employees might consider it.

Earlier this month, Matthew Parris, a very squishy Tory gay, was called up by the BBC, Sky News, Channel 4, and many others anxious to send TV and radio crews round to his country place to record his reaction to a front-page lead in *The Observer*: "Secret Tape Reveals Tory Backing for Ban on Gays." As it turned out, the "ban on gays" was a bit oversold: the Shadow Home Secretary had been musing on distinctions in public accommodation between running a hotel on the High Street and a B&B out of your own home. Mr. Parris had no particular views on that one way or the other, but the "secret tape" bit prompted the following:

> There was also something unpleasantly Orwellian in the lip-smacking way in which my informants were telling me how Mr. Grayling had been recorded—caught—expressing his opinion. That Nineteen Eighty-Four feeling was reflected, too, in the un-self-aware failure of irony with which an *Observer* journalist referred to the view that Britain should not "tolerate" (his word) intolerance. Burn the bigots! To the tumbrels with zealots! Crack down on narrow-mindedness! No to the naysayers!

Droll, and very British—or it used to be. But in Little Stasi-on-Avon, where you can't make a joke in private conversation or say "Yuk!" in the nursery school lunch hour, the words of the French philosopher Alain Finkielkraut seem more pertinent: "The lofty idea of 'the war on racism' is gradually turning into a hideously false ideology," he said in 2005. "And this anti-racism will be for the twenty-first century what Communism was for the twentieth century: a source of violence."

I think back to those weeks in Budapest, and similar conversations in Berlin, Prague, and Bucharest, and I wonder whatever happened to that British sense of fair play.

But then, I suppose, the very concept is racist.

"THERE IS NO MORE MOLLY"

SteynOnline, September 20, 2010

TOO MANY PEOPLE in the free world have internalized Islam's view of them. A couple of years ago, I visited Guantanamo and subsequently wrote that, if I had to summon up Gitmo in a single image, it would be the brand-new copy of the Koran in each cell: To reassure incoming prisoners that the filthy infidels haven't touched the sacred book with their unclean hands, the Korans are hung from the walls in pristine, sterilized surgical masks. It's one thing for Muslims to regard infidels as unclean, but it's hard to see why it's in the interests of us infidels to string along with it and thereby validate their bigotry. What does that degree of prostration before their prejudices tell them about us? It's a problem that Muslims think we're unclean. It's a far worse problem that we go along with it.

Take this no-name pastor from an obscure church who was threatening to burn the Koran. He didn't burn any buildings or women and children. He didn't even burn a book. He hadn't actually laid a finger on a Koran, and yet the mere suggestion that he might do so prompted the President of the United States to denounce him, and the Secretary of State, and the commander of U.S. forces in Afghanistan, various G7 leaders, and golly, even Angelina Jolie. President Obama has never said a word about honor killings of Muslim women. Secretary Clinton has never said a word about female genital mutilation. General Petraeus has never said a word about the rampant buggery of pre-pubescent boys by Pushtun men in Kandahar. But let an obscure man in Florida so much as raise the possibility that he might disrespect a book—an inanimate object—and the most powerful figures in the western world feel they have to weigh in.

Aside from all that, this obscure church's website has been shut down, its insurance policy has been canceled, its mortgage has been called in by its bankers. Why? Why was it necessary or even seemly to make this pastor a non-person? Another one of Obama's famous "teaching moments"? In this case teaching us that Islamic law now applies to all? Only a couple of weeks ago, the President, at his most condescendingly ineffectual, presumed to lecture his moronic subjects about the First Amendment rights of Imam Rauf and his Ground Zero mosque. Where's the condescending lecture on Pastor Jones's First Amendment rights?

When someone destroys a bible, U.S. government officials don't line up to attack him. President Obama bowed lower than a fawning maître d' before the King of Saudi Arabia, a man whose regime destroys bibles as a matter of state policy, and whose depraved religious police forces schoolgirls fleeing from a burning building back into the flames to die because they'd committed the sin of trying to escape without wearing their head scarves. If you show a representation of Mohammed, European commissioners and foreign ministers stampede to denounce you. If you show a representation of Jesus Christ immersed in your own urine, you get a government grant for producing a widely admired work of art. If you insult Christ, the media report the issue as freedom of expression: A healthy society has to have bold, brave, transgressive artists willing to question and challenge our assumptions, etc. But, if it's Mohammed, the issue is no longer freedom of expression but the need for "respect" and "sensitivity" toward Islam, and all those bold brave transgressive artists don't have a thing to say about it.

Maybe Pastor Jones doesn't have any First Amendment rights. Musing on Koran burning, Supreme Court Justice Stephen Breyer argued:

> [Oliver Wendell] Holmes said it doesn't mean you can shout "fire" in a crowded theater.... Why? Because people will be trampled to death. And what is the crowded theater today? What is the "being trampled to death"?

This is a particularly obtuse remark even by the standards of contemporary American jurists. As I've said before, the fire-in-a-crowded-theatre shtick is the first refuge of the brain-dead. But it's worth noting the repellent modification Justice Breyer makes to Holmes's argument: If someone shouts fire in a crowded gaslit Broadway theatre of the Gay Nineties, people will panic. By definition, panic is an involuntary reaction. If someone threatens to burn a Koran, belligerent Muslims do not panic—they bully, they intimidate, they threaten, they burn, and they kill. Those are conscious acts, at least if you take the view that Muslims are as fully human as the rest of us and therefore responsible for their choices. Justice Breyer's remarks seem to assume that Muslims are not fully human.

More importantly, the logic of Breyer's halfwit intervention is to incentivize violence, and undermine law itself. What he seems to be telling the world is that Americans' constitutional rights will bend to intimidation. If Koran-burning rates a First Amendment exemption because Muslims are willing to kill over it, maybe Catholics should threaten to kill over the next gay-Jesus play, and Broadway could have its First Amendment rights reined in. Maybe the next time Janeane Garofalo goes on MSNBC and calls Obama's opponents racists, the Tea Partiers should threaten to behead a few people, and NBC's free-speech rights would be withdrawn.

But forget about notorious rightwing hatemongers like us anti-Obama types, and look at how liberal progressives protect their own. Do you remember a lady called Molly Norris? A cartoonist with *The Seattle Weekly*, she was shocked by the way Comedy Central had censored *South Park* after the usual threats from violent Muslims. So she proclaimed May 20 as "Everybody Draw Mohammed" Day. What was novel about this was that Ms. Norris is a liberal progressive, and therefore a rare, if not all but unique, example of a feminist leftie recognizing that the Islamic enforcers were a threat to her way of life. This was a very welcome development.

Unfortunately, Ms. Norris was not so much recognizing reality as blissfully unaware of it. When the backlash against her idea began, she disassociated herself from it and signed off with—Lord help us—a peace symbol. I dismissed Ms. Norris as (to rewrite Stalin) a useless idiot, and she wrote to *Mark's Mailbox* to object:

I agree with what you wrote. Mostly. But why do I have to carry all of the weight? Why won't others do their part and step forward? There is nothing stopping others from doing something positive!

I don't get it. It can be like a relay race, but it's easier to condemn and sound "right"—right?

Molly Norris

Seattle, Washington

Mark says: Well, you're not "carrying all the weight," are you? I mean, surely you can't be that self-absorbed, can you? There's a guy called Kurt Westergaard. He's a cartoonist, like you. Four and a half years ago, he drew the best and most provocative of the Mohammed cartoons. Since then, he has lived with explicit death threats, and in a house extensively remodeled to accommodate a safe room, to which he was obliged to retreat recently when an Islamic nutcase broke in and tried to kill him and his granddaughter. On top of that, he's just been involuntarily retired by his newspaper on "security grounds." You think he hasn't occasionally wished over the last half-decade that "others" would "do their part and step forward"? Other cartoonists maybe? Members of a profession (the media) that incessantly congratulates itself on its bravery, except on those rare occasions when it's actually called to display some....

Nobody asked you to cook up "Everybody Draw Mohammed" Day. You chose to do that—and, if you didn't understand what you were getting into, then where have you been the last nine years? Kurt Westergaard, who's 74, could have bailed after 48 hours and whined that it's all getting way more attention than he ever expected and drawn a picture of himself in a peace-sign T-shirt. But he didn't.

That's why we're all down on you. You took a bad situation and made it worse. You announced that at last there was a liberal progressive who was going to stand up to Islamic intimidation—and then you caved, in nothing flat. And even then I could have forgiven you, if it weren't for the final self-humiliating *coup de grâce* of your crappy peace-sign T-shirt. I'd love to have glimpsed the stage of the creative process at which you thought that would be just the ticket. Good luck betting your future on that clapped out obsolescent talisman.

I stand by what I wrote then, especially the bit about her crappy peace-sign T-shirt. Now *The Seattle Weekly* informs us:

> You may have noticed that Molly Norris' comic is not in the paper this week. That's because there is no more Molly.

On the advice of the FBI, she's been forced to go into hiding. If you want to measure the decline in western civilization's sense of self-preservation, go back to Valentine's Day 1989, get out the Fleet Street reports on the Salman Rushdie fatwa, and read the outrage of his fellow London literati at what was being done to one of the mainstays of the Hampstead dinner-party circuit. Then compare it with the feeble passivity of Molly Norris's own colleagues at an American cartoonist being forced to abandon her life: "There is no more Molly"? That's all the gutless pussies of *The Seattle Weekly* can say? As James Taranto notes in *The Wall Street Journal*, even much sought-after Ramadan-banquet constitutional scholar Barack Obama is remarkably silent:

> Now Molly Norris, an American citizen, is forced into hiding because she exercised her right to free speech. Will President Obama say a word on her behalf? Does he believe in the First Amendment for anyone other than Muslims?

Who knows? But listen to what President Obama, Justice Breyer, General Petraeus, and *The Seattle Weekly* are telling us about where we're headed. It is a basic rule of life that if you reward bad behavior, you get more of it. Every time Muslims either commit violence or threaten it, we reward them by capitulating. Indeed, Obama & Co. are now telling Islam, you don't have to kill anyone, you don't even have to *threaten* to kill anyone. We'll be your enforcers. We'll demand that the most footling and insignificant of our own citizens submit to the universal jurisdiction of Islam. So Obama and Breyer are now the "good cop" to the crazies' "bad cop." Ooh, no, I wouldn't say that if I were you, because my friend here is a little excitable, and you really don't want to get him worked up. The same people who tell us "Islam is a religion of peace" then turn around and tell us you have to be quiet, you have to shut up, because otherwise these guys will go bananas and kill a bunch of people.

While I was in Denmark, one of the usual Islamoloons lit up premalurely in a Copenhagen hotel. Not mine, I'm happy to say. He wound up burning only himself, but his targets were my comrades at the newspaper *Jyllands-Posten*. I wouldn't want to upset Justice Breyer by yelling "Fire!" over a smoldering jihadist, but one day even these idiots will get lucky. I didn't like the Danish Security Police presence at the Copenhagen conference, but I understood why they were necessary. No one should lose his name, his home, his life, his liberty because ideological thugs are too insecure to take a joke. But Molly Norris is merely the latest squishy liberal to learn that, when the chips are down, your fellow lefties won't be there for you.

✳   ✳   ✳

Four years later, there was not much left of "Everybody Draw Mohammed" Day, but there was even less of Molly Norris. As the website Blogwrath put it:

> *Because of the Muslim death threats, Molly Norris, who started the event, had to go into hiding and change her name. She disappeared completely and nobody knows whether she is dead or alive.*

Salman Rushdie was, with hindsight, fortunate in his timing. Had he written The Satanic Verses *twenty years later, no one would have published it. But, even if someone had, far fewer liberals (if any) would have spoken up on his behalf.*

And so it is that an American citizen has vanished from the face of the earth because she made a joke about Islam.

Hello, Molly?

THE UNSAFE SPACE

The Spectator, April 19, 2014

THESE DAYS, PRETTY MUCH every story is really the same story:

- In Galway, at the National University of Ireland, a speaker who attempts to argue against the BDS (Boycott, Divestment, and Sanctions) program against Israel is shouted down with cries of "F**king Zionist, f**king pricks.... Get the f**k off our campus."
- In California, Mozilla's chief executive is forced to resign because he once made a political donation in support of the pre-revisionist definition of marriage.
- At Westminster, the House of Commons Science and Technology Committee declares that the BBC should seek "special clearance" before it interviews climate sceptics, such as fringe wacko extremists like former Chancellor of the Exchequer Nigel Lawson.
- In Massachusetts, Brandeis University withdraws its offer of an honorary degree to a black feminist atheist human rights campaigner from Somalia.
- In London, a multitude of liberal journalists and artists responsible for everything from *Monty Python* to *Downton Abbey* sign an open letter in favor of the first state restraints on the British press in three and a quarter centuries.

- And in Canberra the government is planning to repeal Section 18C[1]—whoa, don't worry, not all of it, just three or four adjectives; or maybe only two, or whatever it's down to by now, after what Gay Alcorn in the Melbourne *Age* described as the ongoing debate about "where to strike the balance between free speech in a democracy and protection against racial abuse in a multicultural society."

I heard a lot of that kind of talk during my battles with the Canadian "human rights" commissions a few years ago: of course, we all believe in free speech, but it's a question of how you "strike the balance," where you "draw the line" … which all sounds terribly reasonable and Canadian, and apparently Australian, too. But in reality the point of free speech is for the stuff that's over the line, and strikingly unbalanced. If free speech is only for polite persons of mild temperament within government-policed parameters, it isn't free at all. So screw that.

But I don't really think that many people these days are genuinely interested in "striking the balance"; they've drawn the line, and they're increasingly unashamed about which side of it they stand. What all the above stories have in common, whether nominally about Israel, gay marriage, climate change, Islam, or even freedom of the press, is that one side has cheerfully swapped that apocryphal Voltaire quote about disagreeing with what you say but defending to the death your right to say it for the pithier Ring Lardner line: "'Shut up,' he explained."

A generation ago, progressive opinion at least felt obliged to pay lip service to the Voltaire shtick. These days, nobody's asking you to defend yourself to the death: a mildly supportive retweet would do. But even that's further than most of those in the academy, the arts, the media are prepared to go. As Erin

---

1   Section 18C of Australia's Racial Discrimination Act makes it unlawful to "offend, insult, humiliate or intimidate" people based upon their race, which, as tends to happen, is something of a term of art.

Ching, a student at sixty-grand-a-year Swarthmore College in Pennsylvania, put it in her college newspaper after being affronted by a visit to campus of a (stand well back) Christian conservative: "What really bothered me is the whole idea that at a liberal arts college we need to be hearing a diversity of opinion." Yeah, who needs that? There speaks the voice of a generation: celebrate diversity by enforcing conformity.

The examples above are ever-shrinking Dantean circles of Tolerance: At Galway, the dissenting opinion was silenced by snarling thugs baying four-letter words. At Mozilla, the chairwoman is far more housetrained: she issued a nice press release all about (per Miss Alcorn) striking a balance between freedom of speech and "equality," and how the best way to "support" a "culture" of "diversity" and "inclusiveness" is by firing anyone who dissents from the mandatory groupthink. At the House of Commons they're moving to the next stage: in an "inclusive culture" ever more comfortable with narrower bounds of public discourse, it seems entirely natural for dissenting voices to require state permission—"special clearance"—to speak.

At Brandeis University, we are learning the hierarchy of the new multiculti caste system. In theory, Ayaan Hirsi Ali is everything the identity-group fetishists dig: female, atheist, black, immigrant. If conservative white males were to silence a secular women's rights campaigner from Somalia, it would be proof of the Republican Party's "war on women," or the encroaching Christian fundamentalist theocracy, or just plain old Andrew Boltian[2] racism breaking free of its redoubt at the Melbourne *Herald Sun* to rampage as far as the eye can see. But when the sniveling white male who purports to be President of Brandeis (one Frederick Lawrence) does it out of deference to Islam, Miss Hirsi Ali's blackness washes off her like a bad dye job on a telly news anchor. White feminist Germaine Greer can speak at Brandeis because, in one of the more whimsical ideological evolutions even by dear old Germaine's standards, Ms. Greer feels that clitoridectomies add to the rich tapestry of "cultural

---

2   Mr. Bolt is the *Herald Sun* columnist who fell afoul of the Section 18 "hate speech" law referenced above.

identity": "One man's beautification is another man's mutilation," as she puts it. But black feminist Hirsi Ali, who was on the receiving end of "one man's mutilation" and lives under death threats because she was boorish enough to complain about it, is too "hateful" to be permitted to speak. In the internal contradictions of multiculturalism, Islam trumps all: race, gender, secularism, everything. So, in the interests of multiculti sensitivity, pampered upper-middle-class trusty-fundy children of entitlement are pronouncing a Somali refugee beyond the pale and signing up to Islamic strictures on the role of women.

That's another reason why Gay Alcorn's fretting over "striking the balance" is so irrelevant. No matter where you strike it, the last unread nonagenarian white supremacist Xeroxing flyers in a shack off the Tanami Track will be way over the line, while, say, Sheikh Sharif Hussein's lively sermon to an enthusiastic crowd at the Islamic Da'wah Centre of South Australia, calling on Allah to kill every last Buddhist and Hindu, will be safely inside it. One man's decapitation is another man's cultural validation, as Germaine would say.

Ms. Greer has reached that Circle of Tolerance wherein the turkeys line up to volunteer for an early Eid. The Leveson Inquiry declaration of support signed by all those London luvvies like Emma Thompson, Tom Stoppard, Maggie Smith, Bob Geldof, and Ian McKellen is the stage that comes after that House of Commons Science and Technology Committee—when the most creative spirits in our society all suddenly say: "Ooh, yes, please, state regulation, bring it on!" Many of the eminent thespians who signed this letter started their careers in an era when every play performed in the West End had to be approved by the Queen's Lord Chamberlain. Presented with a script that contained three "f**ks" and an explicit reference to anal sex, he'd inform the producer that he would be permitted two "crikeys" and a hint of heavy petting. In 1968, he lost his censorship powers, and the previously banned *Hair*, of all anodyne trifles, could finally be seen on the London stage: this is the dawning of the age of Aquarius. Only four and a half decades after the censor's departure, British liberals are panting for the reimposition of censorship under a new "Royal Charter."

This is the aging of the dawn of Aquarius: new blasphemy laws for progressive pieties. In *The New Statesman*, Sarah Ditum seemed befuddled that the "No Platform" movement—a vigorous effort to deny public platforms to the British National Party and the English Defence League—has mysteriously advanced from silencing "violent fascists" to silencing all kinds of other people, like a *Guardian* feminist who ventured some insufficiently affirming observations about trans-women and is now unfit for polite society. But, once you get a taste for shutting people up, it's hard to stop. Why bother winning the debate when it's easier to close it down?

Nick Lowles defined the "No Platform" philosophy as "the position where we refuse to allow fascists an opportunity to act like normal political parties." But free speech is essential to a free society because, when you deny people "an opportunity to act like normal political parties," there's nothing left for them to do but punch your lights out. Free speech, wrote *The Washington Post*'s Robert Samuelson last week, "buttresses the political system's legitimacy. It helps losers, in the struggle for public opinion and electoral success, to accept their fates. It helps keep them loyal to the system, even though it has disappointed them. They will accept the outcomes, because they believe they've had a fair opportunity to express and advance their views. There's always the next election. Free speech underpins our larger concept of freedom."

Just so. A fortnight ago I was in Quebec for a provincial election in which the ruling separatist party went down to its worst defeat in almost half a century. This was a democratic contest fought between parties that don't even agree on what country they're in. In Ottawa for most of the 1990s the Leader of Her Majesty's Loyal Opposition was a chap who barely acknowledged either the head of state or the state she's head of. Which is as it should be. Because, if a Quebec separatist or an Australian republican can't challenge the constitutional order through public advocacy, the only alternative is to put on a black ski-mask and skulk around after dark blowing stuff up.

I'm opposed to the notion of official ideology—not just fascism, Communism and Baathism, but the fluffier ones, too, like "multiculturalism" and "climate change" and "marriage equality." Because the more topics you rule out of discussion—immigration, Islam, "gender fluidity"—the more you delegitimize the political system. As your average cynical political consultant sees it, a commitment to abolish Australia's appalling Section 18C is more trouble than it's worth: you'll just spend weeks getting damned as cobwebbed racists seeking to impose a bigots' charter when you could be moving the meter with swing voters by announcing a federal program of transgendered bathroom construction. But, beyond the shrunken horizons of spinmeisters, the inability to roll back something like 18C says something profound about where we're going: a world where real, primal, universal rights—like freedom of expression—come a distant second to the new tribalism of identity-group rights.

Oh, don't worry. There'll still be plenty of "offending, insulting or humiliating" in such a world, as Ayaan Hirsi Ali and the Mozilla CEO and Zionists and climate deniers and feminist "cis-women" not quite *au courant* with transphobia can all tell you. And then comes the final, eerie silence. Young Erin Ching at Swarthmore College has grasped the essential idea: it is not merely that, as the Big Climate enforcers say, "the science is settled," but so is everything else, from abortion to gay marriage. So what's to talk about? Universities are no longer institutions of inquiry but "safe spaces" where delicate flowers of diversity of race, sex, orientation, "gender fluidity," and everything else except diversity of thought have to be protected from exposure to any unsafe ideas.

As it happens, the biggest "safe space" on the planet is the Muslim world. For a millennium, Islamic scholars have insisted, as firmly as a climate scientist or an American sophomore, that there's nothing to debate. And what happened? As the United Nations Human Development Programme's famous 2002 report blandly noted, more books are translated in Spain in a single year than have been translated into Arabic in the last thousand years. Free speech and a dynamic, innovative society are intimately connected: a culture that can't bear a dissenting word on race or religion or gender fluidity or carbon offsets is a society that will cease to innovate, and then stagnate, and then decline, very fast.

As American universities, British playwrights, and Australian judges once understood, the "safe space" is where cultures go to die.

XV

LENGTHENED SHADOWS

FOOTSTEPS IN THE
DESERT

National Review, February 25, 2013

IN A DISPUTE between Hamas and Fatah, it's tempting to take the old Kissinger line re the Iran Iraq War: It's a shame they can't both lose. But, in fact, only one side wins: In Gaza, al-Aqsa University has just announced that female students will be required to attend in proper Muslim garb from head to toe—i.e., the full body bag. At present, some still wear headscarf, trousers, and a long coat, but that's too revealing for the new Gaza, so time to get fitted for your burqa, niqab, or abaya. Al-Aqsa University is funded by the Palestinian Authority—that's Yasser Arafat's old Fatah—but it's controlled by Hamas. The higher-education minister, Ali Jarbawi, fumed impotently from Ramallah that the new dress code is illegal and must not be implemented, but the hard men on the ground in the Gaza Strip regard him as just another irrelevant member of a fading personality cult for a dead kleptocrat with a taste for Aryan rent boys.

And so it goes across the region: Regimes that represented nothing but their Swiss bank accounts have fallen, and in their stead arises the only alternative—an Islam purified by decades in opposition to the secularists and distilled to a scorching 175° proof. What else is left?

Some years ago, for a telly documentary, the BBC sent the novelist Lawrence Durrell back to Alexandria, the setting of his eponymous *Alexandria Quartet*, his "prose poem to one of the great capitals of the heart." Durrell had lived in Egypt during the war years, and did not enjoy his return. "The city seemed to him listless and spiritless, its harbor a mere cemetery, its famous cafés no longer twinkling with music and lights," wrote Michael Haag in

Alexandria, City of Memory. "His favorite bookshop, Cité du Livre on the rue Fouad, had gone, and in others he found a lamentable stock."

Only on the western fringe of the Ummah, in a few Moroccan redoubts, can you still discern the flickers of the way it was. Otherwise, to anyone who knew the "Muslim world" of the mid–twentieth century, today's Maghreb and Levant are dull places, drained of everything but Islam. And Durrell was returning in 1977: Another third of a century on, and Alexandria's stock is even more lamentable. Indeed, his cast of characters would be entirely bewildering to contemporary Alexandrians: an English writer (of course), a Greek good-time girl, a homosexual Jew, a wealthy Copt. In the old days, Alexandria bustled with Britons, Italians, and lots and lots of Greeks. All gone. So are the Jews, homo- and hetero-, from a community fifty thousand strong down to some four dozen greybeards keeping their heads down. I got an email a year or so back from the great-grandson of Joseph Cattaui, a Jew and Egypt's finance minister back in the Twenties: These days, the family lives in France—because it's not just that in Egypt a Jew can no longer be finance minister, but that in Egypt a Jew can no longer *be*. Now, in the absence of any other demographic groups to cleanse, it's the Copts' turn to be encouraged toward the exits—as in Tripoli and Benghazi it's the blacks'. In the once-cosmopolitan cities of the Arab world, the minority communities are confined to the old graveyards, strewn with garbage and broken headstones. Islam is king on a field of corpses.

Nowadays, for the cosmopolitan café society Durrell enjoyed, you have to go to the cities of multicultural Europe, where "diversity" is not a quirk of fate but the cardinal virtue. At Westminster, the House of Commons has just voted in favor of same-sex marriage. Almost simultaneously, a group calling itself the Muslim London Patrol posted a YouTube video of its members abusing a young man for "walking in a Muslim area dressed like a fag." Another Londoner is made to empty his beer can: "No drink in this area." An insufficiently covered woman is warned, "This is not so Great Britain. This is a Muslim area."

The "moderate Muslim" Maajid Nawaz writes in *The New York Times* that his youthful European-born coreligionists, back from Islamic adventuring during the Arab Spring, are anxious to apply the lessons learned abroad. The Danish group Kaldet til Islam (Call to Islam) has introduced "Sharia-controlled zones" in which "morality patrols" of young bearded men crack down on underdressed and bibulous blondes. In the Balearic Islands, Muslims have taken against the local meter maids, and forced the government to withdraw them. In the "Islamic Republic of Tower Hamlets"—the heart of London's East End, where one sees more covered women than in Amman—police turn a blind eye to misogyny, Jew-hatred, and gay-bashing for fear of being damned as "racist." Male infidel teachers of Muslim girls are routinely assaulted. Patrons of a local gay pub are abused, and beaten, and, in one case, left permanently paralyzed.

The hostelry that has so attracted the ire of the Muslim youth hangs a poignant shingle: The George and Dragon. It's one of the oldest and most popular English pub names. The one just across the Thames on Borough High Street has been serving beer for at least half a millennium. But no one would so designate a public house today. The George and Dragon honors the patron saint of England, and it is the cross of St. George—the flag of England—under which the Crusaders fought. They brought back the tale from their soldiering in the Holy Land: In what is now Libya, St. George supposedly made the sign of the Cross, slew the dragon, and rescued the damsel. Within living memory, every English schoolchild knew the tale, if not all the details— e.g., the dragon-slaying so impressed the locals that they converted to Christianity. But the multicultural establishment slew the dragon of England's racist colonialist imperialist history, and today few schoolchildren have a clue about St. George. So the pub turned gay and Britain celebrated diversity, and tolerance, and it never occurred to them that, when you tolerate the avowedly intolerant, it's only an interim phase. There will not be infidel teachers in Tower Hamlets for much longer, nor gay bars.

Meanwhile, the BBC reports that February 1 was the first World Hijab Day, in which non-Muslim women from fifty countries took a stand against "Islamophobia" and covered themselves to show how much they objected to society's prejudice against veiled women. From Gaza to Alexandria to

Copenhagen to London, I don't think we'll have to worry about that. As Balthazar, Lawrence Durrell's homosexual Jew, muses, "Narouz once said to me that he loved the desert because there 'the wind blew out one's footsteps like candle-flames.' So it seems to me does reality"—for the footsteps of Copts in Egypt, meter maids in Majorca, and gay pub-goers on the streets of the East End.

SEX AT SUNSET

National Review, November 11, 2013

TO WESTERN EYES, contemporary Japan has a kind of earnest childlike wackiness, all karaoke machines and manga cartoons and nuttily sadistic game shows. But, to us demography bores, it's a sad place that seems to be turning into a theme park of P. D. James's great dystopian novel *The Children of Men* Baroness James's tale is set in Britain in the near future, in a world that is infertile: The last newborn babe emerged from the womb in 1995, and since then nothing. It was an unusual subject for the queen of the police procedural, and, indeed, she is the first baroness to write a book about barrenness. The Hollywood director Alfonso Cuarón took the broad theme and made a rather ordinary little film out of it. But the Japanese seem determined to live up to the book's every telling detail.

In Lady James's speculative fiction, pets are doted on as child-substitutes, and churches hold christening ceremonies for cats. In contemporary Japanese reality, Tokyo has some forty "cat cafés," where lonely solitary citizens can while away an afternoon by renting a feline to touch and pet for a couple of companiable hours.

In Lady James's speculative fiction, all the unneeded toys are burned, except for the dolls, which childless women seize on as the nearest thing to a baby and wheel through the streets. In contemporary Japanese reality, toy makers, their children's market dwindling, have instead developed dolls for seniors to be the grandchildren they'll never have: You can dress them up, and put them in a baby carriage, and the computer chip in the back has several dozen phrases of the kind a real grandchild might use to enable them to engage in rudimentary social pleasantries.

P. D. James's most audacious fancy is that in a barren land sex itself becomes a bit of a chore. The authorities frantically sponsor state porn emporia promoting ever more recherché forms of erotic activity in an effort to reverse the populace's flagging sexual desire just in case man's seed should recover its potency. Alas, to no avail. As Lady James writes, "Women complain increasingly of what they describe as painful orgasms: the spasm achieved but not the pleasure. Pages are devoted to this common phenomenon in the women's magazines."

As I said, a bold conceit, at least to those who believe that shorn of all those boring procreation hang-ups we can finally be free to indulge our sexual appetites to the full. But it seems the Japanese have embraced the no-sex-please-we're-dystopian-Brits plot angle, too. In October, Abigail Haworth of *The Observer* in London filed a story headlined "Why Have Young People in Japan Stopped Having Sex?" Not all young people but a whopping percentage: A survey by the Japan Family Planning Association reported that over a quarter of men aged sixteen to twenty-four "were not interested in or despised sexual contact." For women, it was 45 percent.

The Observer seems to have approached the subject in the same belief as P. D. James's government porn stores—that it's nothing that a little more sexual adventurism can't cure. So Miss Haworth's lead was devoted to the views of a "sex and relationship counselor" and former dominatrix who specialized in dripping hot wax on her clients' nipples and was once invited to North Korea to squeeze the testicles of one of Kim Jong-il's top generals. So, as *The Observer* puts it, "she doesn't judge." Except, that is, when it comes to "the pressure to conform to Japan's anachronistic family model," which she blames for the young folks checking out of the sex biz altogether.

But, if the pressure to conform were that great, wouldn't there be a lot more conforming? Instead, 49 percent of women under thirty-four are not in any kind of romantic relationship, and nor are 61 percent of single men. A third of Japanese adults under thirty have never dated. Anyone. Ever. It's not that they've stopped "having sex"—or are disinclined to have hot wax poured on their nipples. It's bigger than that: It's a flight from human intimacy.

They're not alone in that, of course. A while back, I flew from a speaking engagement on one side of the Atlantic to a TV booking on the other. And backstage at both events an attractive thirtysomething woman made the same complaint to me. They'd both tried computer dating but were alarmed by the number of chaps who found human contact too much effort: Instead of meeting and kissing and making out and all that other stuff that involves being in the same room, they'd rather you just sexted them and twitpicced a Weiner-esque selfie or two. As in other areas, the Japanese seem merely to have reached the end point of western ennui a little earlier.

By 2020, in the Land of the Rising Sun, adult diapers will outsell baby diapers: The sun also sets. In *The Children of Men*, the barrenness is a medical condition; in real life, in some of the oldest nations on earth, from Madrid to Tokyo, it's a voluntary societal self-extinction. In Europe, the demographic death spiral is obscured by high Muslim immigration; in Japan, which retains a cultural aversion to immigration of any kind, there are no foreigners to be the children you couldn't be bothered having yourself. In welfare states, the future is premised on social solidarity: The young will pay for the costs of the old. But as the west ages, social solidarity frays, and in Japan young men aren't even interested in solidarity with young women, and young women can't afford solidarity with bonnie bairns. So an elderly population in need of warm bodies to man the hospital wards and senior centers is already turning to robot technology. If manga and anime are any indication, the post-human nurses and waitresses will be cute enough to make passable sex partners—for anyone who can still be bothered.

A STROLL AT TWILIGHT

From a speech in Boston,[1] October 10, 2010

A COUPLE OF months ago, I happened to be in Tangiers, in a fairly decrepit *salon de thé* off the rue de la Liberté in Tangiers, enjoying a coffee and a stale croissant grilled and flattened into a panini. What could be more authentically Moroccan? For some reason, the napkins were emblazoned with *"Gracias por su visita."*

And, while enjoying all this vibrant diversity, I chanced to remember yet another example of it—a recent headline from Canada's *Shalom Life*: "No Danger to the Jewish Cemeteries in Tangiers."

Apparently, the old Jewish hospital in this ancient port city had been torn down a couple of months back, and the Moroccan Jewish diaspora back in Toronto worried that the old Jewish cemetery might be next on the list. There are a lot of old Jewish cemeteries around the world, not a lot of new ones. Not to worry, Abraham Azancot assured *Shalom Life* readers: The Jewish cemetery on the rue du Portugal is perfectly safe. "Its sanctity has consistently been respected by the local government that is actually providing the community with resources to assist in its current grooming."

Sounds great. Being in the neighborhood, I thought I'd swing by and check out the "current grooming." It's kind of hard to spot unless you're consciously looking for it: two solid black metal gates off a steep, narrow street where the rue du Portugal crosses the rue Salah Dine, and only the smallest of signs to indicate what lies behind. On pushing open the gate and squeezing

---

1 At a meeting of CAMERA, the Committee for Accuracy in Middle East Reporting in America.

through, I was greeted by a pair of long underwear, flapping in the breeze. In Haiti, this would be some voodoo ritual, alerting one to go no further. But in Tangiers it was merely wash day, and laundry lines dangled over the nearest graves. If you happen to be Ysaac Benzaquen (died 1921) or Samuel Maman (died 1925), it is your lot to spend eternity with the groundskeeper's long johns. *Pace* Mr. Azancot, there is no sense of "sanctity" or "community": as the underwear advertises, this is no longer a public place, merely a backyard that happens to have a ton of gravestones in it. I use the term "groundskeeper," but keeping the grounds doesn't seem to be a priority: another row of graves was propping up piles of logs he was busy chopping out of hefty tree trunks. Beyond that, chickens roamed amidst burial plots strewn with garbage bags, dozens of old shoes, and hundreds of broken bottles.

It's prime real estate, with a magnificent view of the Mediterranean, if you don't mind the trash and the stench and the chicken crap, and you tiptoe cautiously round the broken glass. I wandered past the graves: Jacob Cohen, Samuel J. Cohen, Samuel M. Cohen.... Lot of Cohens here over the years. Not anymore. In one isolated corner, six young men—*des musulmans, naturellement*—watched a seventh lightly scrub a tombstone, as part of a make-work project "providing the community with resources to assist in its current grooming."

What "community"? By 2005, there were fewer than 150 Jews in Tangiers, almost all of them very old. By 2015, it is estimated that there will be precisely none. Whenever I mention such statistics to people, the reaction is a shrug: why would Jews live in Morocco anyway? But in 1945 there were some three hundred thousand in this country. Today some three thousand Jews remain—i.e., about 1 percent of what was once a large and significant population. That would be an unusual demographic reconfiguration in most countries: imagine if America's black population or Canada's francophone population were today 1 percent of what it was in 1945. But it's not unusual for Jews. There are cemeteries like that on the rue du Portugal all over the world, places where once were Jews and now are none. In the Twenties Baghdad was 40 percent Jewish, and Tripoli. But you could just as easily cite Czernowitz in the Bukovina, now part of Ukraine. "There is not a shop that has not a Jewish name painted above its windows," wrote Sir Sacheverell Sitwell, visiting the city in 1937. Not today. As in Tangiers, the "community" resides in the cemetery.

You can sense the same process already under way in, say, London, the thirteenth-biggest Jewish city in the world, but one with an aging population; and in Odense, Denmark, where last year superintendent Olav Nielsen announced he would no longer admit Jewish children to the local school; and in Malmö, Sweden, where a surge in anti-Semitism from, ahem, certain quarters has led Jewish residents to abandon the city for Stockholm and beyond. Soon Malmö will be just another town with an abandoned and decaying "old Jewish cemetery."

I was there a couple of weeks ago—sat and had a coffee in a nice little place in a beautiful medieval square, and fell into conversation with a couple of cute Swedish blondes. Fine-looking ladies. I shall miss Scandinavian blondes when they're extinct.

At dusk, and against their advice, I took a twenty-minute walk to Rosengård. As you stroll the sidewalk, the gaps between blondes grow longer, and the gaps between young bearded Muslim men coming toward you grow shorter. And eventually the last blonde recedes into the distance behind you, and there are nothing but fierce bearded men and the occasional covered woman. And then you're in the housing projects, and all the young boys kicking a soccer ball around are Muslim, and every single woman is covered—including many who came from "moderate" Muslim countries and did not adopt the headscarf or hijab until they came to Sweden. In progressive, post-Christian, swingin' Sweden, the veil is de rigueur for Muslim women. Increasingly, ambulances and fire trucks do not respond to emergency calls in Rosengård without police escort. The writ of the Swedish state does not really run.

Sweden is about as far as you can get from Israel, but, as in the Jewish state, they're trading "land for peace," even if they're not yet quite aware of it—and will likely wind up with neither. As I said, it's about a twenty-minute walk between downtown and Rosengård, as the Nordic blondes thin out and yield to the beards and hijabs. That's Europe's future walking towards you.

XVI

AGAINST THE GRAIN

DUTCH COURAGE

The Irish Times, June 7, 2004

ALL WEEKEND LONG, across the networks, media grandees who'd voted for Carter and Mondale, just like all their friends did, tried to explain the appeal of Ronald Reagan. He was "the Great Communicator," he had a wonderful sense of humor, he had a charming smile...self-deprecating...the tilt of his head....

All true, but not what matters. Even politics attracts its share of optimistic, likeable men, and most of them leave no trace—like Britain's "Sunny Jim" Callaghan, a perfect example of the defeatism of western leadership in the 1970s. It was the era of "détente," a word barely remembered now, which is just as well, as it reflects poorly on us: the Presidents and Prime Ministers of the free world had decided that the unfree world was not a prison ruled by a murderous ideology that had to be defeated but merely an alternative lifestyle that had to be accommodated. Under cover of "détente," the Soviets gobbled up more and more real estate across the planet, from Ethiopia to Grenada. Nonetheless, it wasn't just the usual suspects who subscribed to this feeble evasion—Helmut Schmidt, Pierre Trudeau, François Mitterrand—but most of the so-called "conservatives," too—Ted Heath, Giscard d'Estaing, Gerald Ford.

Unlike these men, unlike most other senior Republicans, Ronald Reagan saw Soviet Communism for what it was: a great evil. Millions of Europeans across half a continent from Poland to Bulgaria, Slovenia to Latvia, live in freedom today because he acknowledged that simple truth when the rest of the political class was tying itself in knots trying to pretend otherwise. That's what counts. He brought down the "evil empire," and all the rest is details.

At the time, the charm and the smile got less credit from the intelligentsia, confirming their belief that he was a dunce who'd plunge us into Armageddon.

Everything you need to know about the establishment's view of Ronald Reagan can be found on page 624 of *Dutch*, Edmund Morris's weird post-modern biography. The place is Berlin, the time June 12, 1987:

> "Mr. Gorbachev, tear down this wall!" declaims Dutch, trying hard to look infuriated, but succeeding only in an expression of mild petulance.... One braces for a flash of prompt lights to either side of him: APPLAUSE.
>
> What a rhetorical opportunity missed. He could have read Robert Frost's poem on the subject, "Something there is that doesn't love a wall," to simple and shattering effect. Or even Edna St. Vincent Millay's lines, which he surely holds in memory …
> Only now for the first time I see
> This wall is actually a wall, a thing
> Come up between us, shutting me away
> From you … I do not know you any more.

Poor old Morris, the plodding, conventional, scholarly writer driven mad by fourteen years spent trying to get a grip on Ronald Reagan. Most world leaders would have taken his advice: you're at the Berlin Wall, so you have to say something about it, something profound but oblique, maybe there's a poem on the subject.... Who cares if Frost's is over-quoted, and a tad hard to follow for a crowd of foreigners? Who cares that it is, to the casual (never mind English-as-a-second-language) hearer, largely pro-wall, save for a few tentative questions toward the end?

Edmund Morris has described his subject as an "airhead" and concluded that it's "like dropping a pebble in a well and hearing no splash." Morris may not have heard the splash, but he's still all wet: the elites were stupid about Reagan in a way that only clever people can be. Take that cheap crack: if you drop a pebble in a well and you don't hear a splash, it may be because the well is dry but it's just as likely it's because the well is of surprising depth. I went out to my own well and dropped a pebble: I heard no splash, yet the well supplies exquisite translucent water to my home.

But then I suspect it's a long while since Morris dropped an actual pebble in an actual well: As with walls, his taste runs instinctively to the metaphorical. Reagan looked at the Berlin Wall and saw not a poem-quoting opportunity but prison bars.

I once discussed Irving Berlin, composer of "God Bless America," with his friend and fellow songwriter Jule Styne, and Jule put it best: "It's easy to be clever. But the really clever thing is to be simple." At the Berlin Wall that day, it would have been easy to be clever, as all those Seventies détente sophisticates would have been. And who would have remembered a word they said? Like Irving Berlin with "God Bless America," only Reagan could have stood there and declared without embarrassment: "Tear down this wall!"

And two years later the wall was, indeed, torn down. Ronald Reagan was straightforward and true and said it for everybody—which is why his "rhetorical opportunity missed" is remembered by millions of grateful Eastern Europeans. The really clever thing is to have the confidence to say it in four monosyllables.

Ronald Reagan was an American archetype, and just the bare bones of his curriculum vitae capture the possibilities of his country: in the Twenties, a lifeguard at a local swimming hole who saved over seventy lives; in the Thirties, a radio sports announcer; in the Forties, a Warner Brothers leading man... and finally one of the two most significant presidents of the American century. Unusually for the commander in chief, Reagan's was a full, varied American life, of which the presidency was the mere culmination.

"The Great Communicator" was effective because what he was communicating was self-evident to all but our decayed elites: "We are a nation that has a government—not the other way around," he said in his inaugural address. And at the end of a grim, grey decade—Vietnam, Watergate, energy crises, Iranian hostages—Americans decided they wanted a President who looked like the nation, not like its failed government. Thanks to his clarity, around the world governments that had nations have been replaced by nations that have governments. Most of the Warsaw Pact countries are now members of NATO, with free markets and freely elected parliaments.

One man who understood was Yakob Ravin, a Ukrainian émigré who in the summer of 1997 happened to be strolling with his grandson in Armand Hammer Park near Reagan's California home. They chanced to see the former President, out taking a walk. Mr. Ravin went over and asked if he could take a picture of the boy and the President. When they got back home to Ohio, it appeared in the local newspaper, *The Toledo Blade*.

Ronald Reagan was three years into the decade-long twilight of his illness, and unable to recognize most of his colleagues from the Washington days. But Mr. Ravin wanted to express his appreciation. "Mr. President," he said, "thank you for everything you did for the Jewish people, for Soviet people, to destroy the Communist empire."

And somewhere deep within there was a flicker of recognition. "Yes," said the old man, "that is my job."

Yes, that was his job.

THE UNCOWARDLY LIONESS

Syndicated column, April 12, 2013

A FEW HOURS after Margaret Thatcher's death on Monday, the snarling deadbeats of the British underclass were gleefully rampaging through the streets of Brixton in South London, scaling the marquee of the local fleapit and hanging a banner announcing "THE BITCH IS DEAD." Amazingly, they managed to spell all four words correctly. By Friday, "Ding Dong! The Witch Is Dead," from *The Wizard of Oz*, was the Number One download at Amazon UK.

Mrs. Thatcher would have enjoyed all this. Her former speechwriter John O'Sullivan recalls how, some years after leaving office, she arrived to address a small group at an English seaside resort to be greeted by enraged lefties chanting "Thatcher Thatcher Thatcher! Fascist fascist fascist!" She turned to her aide and cooed, "Oh, doesn't it make you feel nostalgic?" She was said to be delighted to hear that a concession stand at last year's Trades Union Congress was doing a brisk business in "Thatcher Death Party Packs"—almost a quarter-century after her departure from office.

Of course, it would have been asking too much of Britain's torpid left to rouse themselves to do anything more than sing a few songs and smash a few windows. In *The Wizard of Oz*, the witch is struck down at the height of her powers by Dorothy's shack descending from Kansas to relieve the Munchkins of their torments. By comparison, Britain's Moochkins were unable to bring the house down: Mrs. Thatcher died in her bed at the Ritz at a grand old age. Useless as they are, British socialists were at one point capable of writing their own anti-Thatcher singalongs rather than lazily appropriating Judy Garland blockbusters from MGM's back catalogue. I recall in the late Eighties being at the National Theatre in London and watching the crowd go wild over Adrian Mitchell's showstopper, "F**k-Off Friday," a song about union workers getting their redundancy notices at the end of the week, culminating with the lines:

> I can't wait for
> That great day when
> F**k-Off Friday
> Comes to Number Ten.

You should have heard the cheers.

Sadly, when F**k-Off Friday did come to 10 Downing Street, it was not the Labour Party's tribunes of the masses who evicted her but the duplicitous scheming twerps of her own cabinet, who rose up against her in an act of matricide from which the Tory party has yet to recover. In the preferred euphemism of the American press, Mrs. Thatcher was a "divisive" figure, but that hardly does her justice. She was "divided" not only from the opposition party but from most of her own, and from almost the entire British establishment, including the publicly funded arts panjandrums who ran the likes of the National Theatre and cheerfully commissioned one anti-Thatcher diatribe after another at taxpayer expense. And she was profoundly "divided" from millions and millions of the British people, perhaps a majority.

Nevertheless, she won. In Britain in the Seventies, everything that could be nationalized had been nationalized, into a phalanx of lumpen government monopolies all flying the moth-eaten flag: British Steel, British Coal, British Airways, British Rail.... The government owned every industry—or, if you prefer, "the British people" owned every industry. And, as a consequence, the unions owned the British people. The top income-tax rate was 83 percent, and on investment income 98 percent. No electorally viable politician now thinks the government should run airlines and car plants, and that workers should live their entire lives in government housing. But what seems obvious to all in 2013 was the bipartisan consensus four decades ago, and it required extraordinary political will for one woman to drag her own party, then the nation, and subsequently much of the rest of the world back from the cliff edge.

Thatcherite denationalization was the first thing Eastern Europe did after throwing off its Communist shackles—although the fact that recovering Soviet client states found such a natural twelve-step program at Westminster testifies to how far gone Britain was. She was the most consequential woman on the world stage since Catherine the Great, and the United Kingdom's most important peacetime prime minister. In 1979, Britain was not at war, but as much as in 1940 faced an existential threat.

Mrs. Thatcher saved her country—and then went on to save an enervated "free world," and what was left of its credibility. The Falklands were an itsy bitsy colonial afterthought on the fringe of the map, costly to win and hold, easy to shrug off—as so much had already been shrugged off. After Vietnam, the Shah, Cuban troops in Africa, Communist annexation of real estate from Cambodia to Afghanistan to Grenada, nobody in Moscow or anywhere else expected a western nation to go to war and wage it to win. Jimmy Carter, a ditherer who belatedly dispatched the helicopters to Iran only to have them crash in the desert and sit by as cocky mullahs poked the corpses of U.S. servicemen on TV, embodied the "leader of the free world" as a smiling eunuch. Why in 1983 should the toothless arthritic British lion prove any more formidable?

And, even when Mrs. Thatcher won her victory, the civilizational cringe of the west was so strong that all the experts immediately urged her to throw it away and reward the Argentine junta for its aggression. "We were prepared to negotiate before," she responded, "but not now. We have lost a lot of blood, and it's the best blood." Or as a British sergeant said of the Falklands: "If they're worth fighting for, then they must be worth keeping."

Mrs. Thatcher thought Britain was worth fighting for, at a time when everyone else assumed decline was inevitable. Some years ago, I found myself standing next to her at dusk in the window of a country house in England's East Midlands, not far from where she grew up. We stared through the lead diamond mullions at a perfect scene of ancient rural tranquility—lawns, the "ha-ha" (an English horticultural innovation), and the fields and hedgerows beyond, looking much as it would have done half a millennium earlier. Mrs. T. asked me about my corner of New Hampshire (90 percent wooded and semi-wilderness) and then said that what she loved about the English countryside was that man had improved on nature: "England's green and pleasant land" looked better because the English had been there. For anyone with a sense of history's sweep, the strike-ridden socialist basket case of the British Seventies was not an economic downturn but a stain on national honor.

A generation on, the Thatcher era seems more and more like a magnificent but temporary interlude in a great nation's bizarre, remorseless self-dissolution. She was right and they were wrong, and because of that they will never forgive her. "I have been waiting for that witch to die for thirty years," said Julian Styles, fifty-eight, who was laid off from his factory job in 1984, when he was twenty-nine. "Tonight is party time. I am drinking one drink for every year I've been out of work." And when they call last orders and the final chorus of "Ding Dong! The Witch Is Dead" dies away, who then will he blame?

During the Falklands War, the Prime Minister quoted Shakespeare, from the closing words of *King John*:

> And we shall shock them: naught shall make us rue,
> If England to itself do rest but true.

For eleven tumultuous years, Margaret Thatcher did shock them. But the deep corrosion of a nation is hard to reverse: England to itself rests anything but true.

THE REFORMATION
OF MANNERS

Maclean's, March 19, 2007

"WILLIAM WILBERFORCE," WRITES Eric Metaxas in his book *Amazing Grace,* "was the happy victim of his own success. He was like someone who against all odds finds the cure for a horrible disease that's ravaging the world, and the cure is so overwhelmingly successful that it vanquishes the disease completely. No one suffers from it again—and within a generation or two no one remembers it ever existed."

What did Wilberforce "cure"? Two centuries ago, on March 25, 1807, one very persistent British backbencher secured the passage by Parliament of an Act for the Abolition of the Slave Trade throughout His Majesty's realms and territories. It's not that no one remembers the disease ever existed, but that we recall it as a kind of freak pandemic—a SARS or bird flu that flares up and whirrs round the world and is then eradicated. The American education system teaches it as such—as a kind of wicked perversion the Atlantic settlers had conjured out of their own ambition.

In reality, it was more like the common cold—a fact of life. The institution predates the word's etymology, from the Slavs brought from eastern Europe to the glittering metropolis of Rome. It predates by some millennia the earliest laws, such as the Code of Hammurabi in Mesopotamia. The first legally recognized slave in the American colonies was owned by a black man who had himself arrived as an indentured servant. The first slave owners on the North American continent were hunter-gatherers. As Metaxas puts it, "Slavery was as accepted as birth and marriage and death, was so woven into the tapestry of human history that you could barely see its threads, much less pull them out. Everywhere on the globe, for 5,000 years, the idea of human civilization without slavery was unimaginable."

I'm not sure whether *Amazing Grace* the movie is the film of the book or whether *Amazing Grace* the biography is the book of the film. But Metaxas's book does a better job of conveying the scale of the challenge than Michael Apted's film. The director of *Gorky Park* and 007's *The World Is Not Enough* and the ongoing "7 Up" TV documentaries, Apted has made a conventional period biopic—men in wigs sparring with each other across the floor of the House of Commons, some rather flat scenes with the little woman back home, the now traditional figure of the "numinous Negro" (in Richard Brookhiser's phrase), although for once he's not played by Morgan Freeman; and a lot of argument by empathy—the chains in which slaves are transported to the Indies being slapped down dramatically on the tables of London dining rooms. In between come irritating slabs of plonkingly anachronistic dialogue—Wilberforce has to choose between doing "the work of God or the work of a political activist"—and more subtly so: Pitt the Younger rebukes his friend with the words, "I warn you as your prime minister"—not a phrase the King's first minister would have used back then.

But the costume dramatics and the contemporary emotionalizing miss the scale of the abolitionist's achievement. "What Wilberforce vanquished was something even worse than slavery," says Metaxas, "something that was much more fundamental and can hardly be seen from where we stand today: he vanquished the very mindset that made slavery acceptable and allowed it to survive and thrive for millennia. He destroyed an entire way of seeing the world, one that had held sway from the beginning of history, and he replaced it with another way of seeing the world." Ownership of existing slaves continued in the British West Indies for another quarter-century, and in the United States for another sixty years, and slave trading continued in Turkey until Atatürk abolished it in the Twenties and in Saudi Arabia until it was (officially) banned in the Sixties, and it persists in Africa and other pockets of the world to this day. But not as a broadly accepted "human good."

There was some hard-muscle enforcement that accompanied the new law: the Royal Navy announced that it would regard all slave ships as pirates, and thus they were liable to sinking and their crews to execution. There had been some important court decisions: in the reign of William and Mary, Justice Holt had ruled that "one may be a villeyn in England, but not a slave," and in 1803 William Osgoode, Chief Justice of Lower Canada, ruled that the institution was not compatible with the principles of British law. But what was decisive was the way Wilberforce "murdered" (in Metaxas's word) the old acceptance of slavery by the wider society. As he wrote in 1787, "God almighty has set before me two great objects: the suppression of the slave trade and the reformation of manners."

The latter goal we would now formulate as "changing the culture"— which is what he did. The film of *Amazing Grace* shows the Duke of Clarence and other effete toffs reeling under a lot of lame bromides hurled by Wilberforce on behalf of "the people." But, in fact, "the people" were a large part of the problem. Then as now, citizens of advanced democracies are easily distracted. The eighteenth-century Church of England preached "a tepid kind of moralism" disconnected both from any serious faith and from the great questions facing the nation. It was a sensualist culture amusing itself to death: Wilberforce goes to a performance of *Don Juan*, is shocked by a provocative dance, and is then further shocked to discover the rest of the audience is too blasé even to be shocked. The Paris Hilton of the age, the Prince of Wales, was celebrated for having bedded seven thousand women and snipped from each a keepsake hair. Twenty-five percent of all unmarried females in London were whores; the average age of a prostitute was sixteen; and many brothels prided themselves on offering only girls under the age of fourteen. Many of these features—weedy faint-hearted mainstream churches, skanky celebs, weary provocations for jaded debauchees—will strike a chord in our own time.

"There is a great deal of ruin in a nation," remarked Adam Smith. England survived the eighteenth century, and maybe we will survive the twenty-first. But the life of William Wilberforce and the bicentennial of his extraordinary achievement remind us that great men don't shirk things because the focus-group numbers look unpromising. What we think of as "the Victorian era" was, in large part, an invention of Wilberforce which he succeeded in selling to his compatriots. We, children of the twentieth century, mock our nineteenth-century forebears as uptight prudes, moralists and do-gooders. If they were, it's because of Wilberforce. His legacy includes the very notion of a "social conscience": in the 1790s, a good man could stroll past an eleven-year-old prostitute on a London street without feeling a twinge of disgust or outrage; he accepted her as merely a feature of the landscape, like an ugly hill. By the 1890s, there were still child prostitutes, but there were also charities and improvement societies and orphanages. It is amazing to read a letter from Wilberforce and realize that he is, in fact, articulating precisely 220 years ago what New Yorkers came to know in the Nineties as the "broken windows" theory: "The most effectual way to prevent greater crimes is by punishing the smaller."

The Victorians, if plunked down before the Anna Nicole updates for an hour or two, would probably conclude we're nearer the 18th century than their own. A "social conscience" obliges the individual to act. Today we call for action all the time, but mostly from government, which is another way of excusing us and allowing us to get on with the distractions of the day. Our schoolhouses revile the Victorian do-gooders as condescending racists and oppressors—although the single greatest force for ending slavery around the world was the Royal Navy. Isn't societal self-loathing just another justification for lethargy? After all, if the white man is inherently wicked, that pretty much absolves one from having to do anything. And so the same kind of lies we told ourselves about slaves we now tell ourselves about other faraway people, and for the same reason: because big changes are tough and who needs the hassle? The hardest thing in any society is "the reformation of manners."

EVERYONE'S A CRITIC

THROWAWAY LINE

The Daily Telegraph, January 5, 1987

MOSS HART, THE American playwright, used to say that the most satisfying moment for a writer was when he had finished something and nobody had yet seen it. I agree. Nothing beats the exhilarating feeling of punching that last typewriter key.

Of course, one's happiness may be only fleeting. But, for the moment, there's no one around to say it stinks—or, worse, "I appreciate that it was only meant as a 'humorous' article, but I should point out that that type of bird is not, in fact, found in Western Samoa."

* * *

I'm not so sure I still agree with that Moss Hart line, and I do like to hear from Samoan ornithologists now and again. One of my favorites in that vein was prompted by a casual aside about the strange misapprehension of the British that the rest of the world wishes it had a health service just like theirs—with its two-year waits for hip replacement and C difficile–infested hospital wards and all the other delights. Here's what I wrote:

The Daily Telegraph, September 3, 1993

To any outsider, the capacity of the British for self-delusion is amazing.

"The National Health Service is the envy of the world": really? Maybe to a yak farmer in Bhutan, but not to anyone I've ever spoken to in Western Europe, North America, or Australia.

* * *

A couple of days later, the following missive appeared on our letters page:

Bhutan's health service better

SIR—Mark Steyn's off-the-cuff remarks about yak farmers in Bhutan being the only ones in the world to envy the NHS cannot be allowed to pass without comment.

Bhutan, although small and poor, has devoted a large proportion of its resources to provide free, comprehensive health care for its scattered population, including the yak farmers, who incidentally constitute a small minority of the population.

Starting from scratch in the Sixties, Bhutan had achieved 90 per cent coverage of primary health by 1991....

I may not be a "yak farmer" but I am a Bhutanese. I regret to say that my experience with the NHS has been disappointing. Both my parents-in-law, who are British citizens, have had to wait more than two years for operations, after being turned away several times for lack of hospital beds.

However basic the Bhutanese health service is, it has not yet come to this sorry state.

SONAM CHHOKI

Say what you like about Bhutanese yak farmers, but they don't have to worry about Obama tearing up their plans.

MY FAVORITE
WAHHABI

The Daily Telegraph, September 28, 2002

I AM SORRY to hear that Ghazi Algosaibi, Saudi Ambassador to the Court of St. James's, has been "recalled" to Riyadh. Like many *Spectator* readers, I enjoyed his recent laugh-a-minute interview with Boris Johnson, in which he demonstrated to Boris the best technique for lashing sodomites and adulteresses and gleefully mocked the idea that the west could transform Iraq into the kind of democracy where Boris would "inherit a safe seat in Basra South from Michael Heseltine."[1]

At this point, I should declare an interest. In the last year, among the torrent of dreary missives from leftie terror apologists accusing me of being a "hatemonger," Ghazi (as I like to think of him) was the only critic I looked forward to. It started quietly after one of my routine calls for the overthrow of the House of Saud. His Excellency wrote to *The Spectator* to say that "ever since Mark Steyn, maps at the ready, threatened to dismantle Saudi Arabia, our population has been living in a state of high anxiety and fear. Our children are having nightmares and our old men and women are quaking in terror. We promise," he added, to "drink our own oil," "teach nothing in our schools except pornography and devil worship, and refer to all Muslims, ourselves included, as either 'Islamofascists' or 'Islamabaddies.'"

Well, the following week I made some passing reference to "that famous Saudi sense of humour" and Dr. Algosaibi wrote back to mock another "riveting spectacle" by "Mark Steyn, the dismantler of sovereign nations and destabilizer

---

1   Boris Johnson, now the Mayor of London, had just "inherited a safe seat" at Henley-on-Thames from Michael Heseltine, and been elected to the House of Commons.

of whole regions"—which I liked so much I've had it put on my business cards ("Consultations by Appointment"). After the Saudi World Cup team lost eight–nil, I mused in this space on whether the entire squad were Mossad Jew infiltrators. His Excellency wrote to *The Telegraph* denying this "interesting theory" and offering the alternative claim that the U.S. team were knocked out by "a Wahhabi Islamofascist masquerading as a German player who used his terrorist head to score the goal."

A couple of weeks later, I wrote a column pronouncing Osama bin Laden dead. Ghazi responded by noting my "obsession" with "Osama bin Laden's 'trouser department.' Mr. Steyn is looking for a dirty bomb, and he is looking in the right place."

My obsession with Osama's trouser department is as nothing to Sheikh Algosaibi's obsession with me. Me in general, I hasten to add, not my trouser department. They're not big on that in Saudi, and I wouldn't want Ghazi landing back in Riyadh to find them sharpening the scimitar for him.

But, if you have to pick a London envoy to get into a feud with, I reckon I did better than Barbara Amiel with her French ambassador.[2] My guy's a non-stop laugh-riot: he could be the first Wahhabi to play the Catskills, which is more than you can say for the Saudis' oleaginous man in Washington, Prince Bandar.

But Ghazi's not just a comedian, he's also a poet. He wrote an ode to Ayat Akhras, a Palestinian teenybomber who detonated herself in a Jerusalem supermarket and took a couple of hated Jews with her. The ambassador was evidently smitten by "Ayat, the bride of loftiness." "She embraced death with a smile," he cooed.

"How come he's never written an ode to me?" I brooded bitterly. "Who do I have to blow up to get in an Algosaibi anthology?" The Foreign Office rapped him over the knuckles, but Ghazi stuck to his guns—or, rather, her

---

2   Miss Amiel had hosted a party at which the French Ambassador, M. Daniel Bernard, had opined that "all the current troubles of the world are because of that shitty little country Israel."

plastic explosives. He insisted that he personally would be honored to be a suicide bomber if he weren't so old and out of shape.

This struck me as a pretty feeble excuse. I mean, how fit do you have to be to strap on a Semtex belt and waddle into a pizza parlor? The talk in the diplomatic corps is that that's why Ghazi was recalled. Alternatively, he was doing so much shtick in *The Spectator,* Crown Prince Abdullah has finally twigged he's Jewish.

After that hilarious interview with Boris, I suggested to Dan Colson, the Telegraph Group's executive supremo, that we hire Dr. Algosaibi and alternate him as a columnist with me—one of those Point-Counterpoint deals, Infidel & Believer, Whacko & Wahhabi, that kind of set-up. But a couple of days later it was announced that King Fahd had appointed him Minister of Water—which, on closer inspection, turns out mostly to involve being Minister of Sewage. It's a sad day when an offer of a *Telegraph* column isn't competitive with manning the Sewage Department in Riyadh. Ghazi issued a statement saying he accepted his new gig "with humility and a deep sense of responsibility." Like his incendiary heroine "the bride of loftiness," he embraced the sewage portfolio with a smile.

I don't know whether Boris has yet introduced the lash to the Speccie office but, judging from Thursday's *Telegraph* column, he's pretty much signed on to the Algosaibi line on Iraq. Who says ambassadors have no impact? As for me, I'll miss the old suicide-bomber groupie, but I'm keeping his name in the Rolodex. Of all the A-list Saudis I know, he's the one with the most effluents in government circles.

✳　✳　✳

A couple of days later The Telegraph *published the following letter:*

Sir—Mark Steyn was kind enough to greet my appointment at what he calls the Ministry of Sewerage in his usual, charming manure of speaking (Comment, Sep 28). I would like to inform him that our treatment plants will always be ready to receive the literary outpourings emanating from his most humane soil.

    Ghazi Algosaibi

    Minister of Water and Electricity

    Riyadh, Saudi Arabia

Ghazi's replacement as ambassador in London was the deeply sinister Prince Turki, a classmate of Bill Clinton at Georgetown and former head of Saudi intelligence. And His Highness was no barrel of laughs. "The arrogance of Mark Steyn knows no bounds," he huffed after one column. "With his imperialist pen he would like to wipe my country off the map." I read it and re-read it, but I couldn't spot any wit or wordplay, and I felt an odd sense of loss.

Not long afterwards, Sheikh Algosaibi sent me a book—a slim, rather limpid novel he'd written called A Love Story. On the inside was written:

    To Mark,

    Ambivalently,

    Ghazi

That's my all-time favorite book inscription. He wrote many novels, and a memoir of his time in government, Yes, (Saudi) Minister!, which is a lot funnier than The Audacity of Hope or It Takes a Village. Most of his books were at one time or another banned in his native land: The House of Saud found Ghazi an indispensable diplomat and technocrat, but the playfully subversive themes of his literary side were less welcome. He died of cancer in 2010, and for me a little bit of the fun went out of our civilizational death-match. I wish he were around for me to send this book to:

    To Ghazi,

    Ambivalently,

    Mark

OF ALL THE GIN JOINTS IN ALL THE TOWNS IN ALL THE WORLD...

The Canadian blogger Kathy Shaidle wrote of the piece that follows:

"Can we build a special museum just to put this Mark Steyn post in?

Stick it in a fancy gold frame and surround it with red velvet ropes?

Almost too amazing to be real."

*Well, nobody offered the money for the museum and the velvet ropes, so
I'd thought I'd stick it in a book. And yes, it's amazing but it's true.
I believe there are just shy of twenty thousand municipal entities in the
United States. How hard can it be to pick three random all-American towns
that one effete Canadian writer would never have set foot in?
Harder than you'd think....*

The Corner, September 20, 2011

OVER AT *The Hill,* the daily newspaper covering Congress, Bernie Quigley
notes a spate of similarly-titled apocalyptic tomes:

Several recent books see the end coming. John Birmingham's *After America*: Fighter bombers rushing at us on the cover. You get the picture. Paul Starobin's *After America: Narratives for the Next Global Age*: Planet of the Apes with nerds instead of apes. Be afraid. But not that afraid. Mark Steyn's *After America: Get Ready for Armageddon*: Self-explanatory. Andrew Breitbart said, "May puke I'm so happy." Meaning he liked it.

These books see America as an idea rather than a place because the authors don't understand place and have probably never been to an American place they were inclined to stay in. They would get a rash in real places like Tobaccoville, N.C., Haverhill, N.H., or Luckenbach, Texas, where Waylon, Willie and the boys hang.

There are arguments to be made against my book, but that's probably not the one to hang your hat on. As it happens, the Steyn global corporate headquarters are located in Woodsville, which is a *quartier* of the town of… Haverhill, New Hampshire. My *Corner* posts are filed from Haverhill. My *National Review* columns are filed from Haverhill. My fabulous hair for tonight's *O'Reilly Factor* was coiffed by Amanda, my Haverhill hairdresser. I'll be guest-hosting *The Rush Limbaugh Show* live from Haverhill this Friday, and, if Mr. Quigley cares to swing by the studio, I promise to do the show naked so he can observe that I have no rash.

Better luck next time, genius.

* * *

Bernie Quigley never took me up on my offer. As to his other rash-inducing "real places," Luckenbach, Texas, is a ghost town (population: 3) and Waylon, Willie and the boys don't hang there, because Waylon Jennings is dead and, even when he wasn't, never set foot in the joint. But, if all it takes to be authentically American is to record a song about a place you've never been to, I'm happy to do "Luckenbach, Texas" on my next album.

LAYING IT ON THE LINE

In 2000, a few weeks before that year's presidential election, running out of cheap Alec Baldwin jokes (he'd promised to leave the country if Bush won) and in need of a bit of filler to pad out the page, I wound up accidentally inaugurating what became a quadrennial tradition. Here's how I ended that column.

The National Post, September 21, 2000

ONE OF THE peripheral reasons Dubya will triumph on November 7 is that he has no interest in Hollywood celebrities. Still, on the matter of his self-removal, I think Alec Baldwin shows great courage. Following last week's prediction that Bush would win with around 380 of the 538 electoral college votes, I see that several readers have written in to query my sanity. So, while I'm at it, let me make another prediction: Bush will win the debates—at least in the political sense of improving his position as a result of his performance. Go ahead, scoffers, scoff your scoffiest. "Al Gore will win," wrote Alan Rutkowski on Monday's letters page. "When he does, will Mr. Steyn turn in his political pundit's badge?"

I'll do better than that, man. If Bush loses, I hereby pledge that I will kill myself live on the Internet.

Er, okay, maybe not. Being a corpse would severely impact on my earning potential, though apparently it's no obstacle to holding down a columnar gig at *The Globe and Mail.* But I think Mr. Rutkowski makes a good point—that the sage whose wisdom is unheeded ought, like Alec Baldwin, to depart the scene. It would be ridiculous to continue posturing as an incisive analyst of

U.S. affairs once I have been exposed as a complete buffoon. So I'm happy to assure readers that, if my prediction of a Bush victory is wrong, I will refrain from writing on U.S. politics in *The National Post* for the entire duration of a Gore presidency.

And now, if you'll excuse me, I have to get on with my application for *National Post* ballet critic.

* * *

A few weeks later, we were plunged into the hell of dimpled chads, recounts, and Supreme Court decisions—none of which I'd had an inkling of when I breezily put my job on the line. Notwithstanding that that was a closer shave than I'd anticipated, four years later I did it all over again— this time across the Atlantic:

The Irish Times, October 11, 2004

IT WAS SOBERING, on reading the recent flurry of letters in this newspaper under the heading "Balancing the U.S. Debate," to discover that it was this column that had single-handedly unbalanced it. "If Steyn represents the American right, where is the spokesperson for the American left?" demands Conor McCarthy of Dun Laoghaire. The hitherto perfectly poised seesaw of press coverage of the United States is apparently all out of whack because my corpulent column is weighing down one end while on the other up in the air are the massed ranks of *Irish Times* correspondents, RTE, the BBC and 97 percent of the European media class, plus Anthony O'Halloran, who opined in these pages a few days ago that "anyone who cares to visit a small town in the Midwest will encounter what can only be described as ultra-right-wing thinking." Prof. O'Halloran didn't cite any examples of this "ultra-right-wing thinking," secure in his assumption that most readers would know the sort of thing he had in mind.

As the ne plus ultra of unbalanced right-wing thinkers, it's not for me to suggest how the U.S. debate might be balanced in these pages. I have only one theory on column-writing, which is this: at a certain basic level, a columnist has to be right more often than not, otherwise the reader (I use the singular advisedly) is just wasting his time. If I were Robert Fisk, the famed foreign correspondent with decades of experience in the Muslim world, I'd be ashamed to leave the house. Sample Fisk headlines on the Afghan War: "Bush Is Walking into a Trap," "It Could Become More Costly than Vietnam." Sample insight on the Iraq War: when the Yanks announced they'd taken Baghdad International Airport, Fisky insisted they hadn't and suggested they'd seized an abandoned RAF airfield from the Fifties by mistake. It's this kind of unique expertise that has made him so admired around the world, not least in Ireland.

By contrast, readers of this column may have gained the impression that George W. Bush will win the presidential election on November 2. If he doesn't, I shall trouble readers of this newspaper no further. It would be ridiculous to continue passing myself off as an incisive analyst of U.S. affairs after I've been exposed as a deluded fool who completely misread the entire situation. In the bright new dawn of the Kerry Administration, you'd deserve better. If that's not an incentive for Irish citizens to smuggle a few illegal campaign contributions the Senator's way, I don't know what is.

But, if, on the other hand, Bush is re-elected, I make one small request of the Irish and European media: you need to re-think your approach to this Presidency....

If Kerry wins, I'm outta here. If Bush wins, eschewing lazy European condescension for the next four years would be the best way of "balancing the U.S. debate."

✳ ✳ ✳

The rapturous reception from Dublin readers rejoicing at the impending demise of my career was so heart-warming that I thought I might as well do it in London, too:

The Spectator, October 30, 2004

USUALLY AFTER MAKING wild predictions I confidently toss my job on the line and say, if they don't pan out, I'm outta here. I've done that a couple of times this campaign season—over Wes Clark (remember him?)—but it almost goes without saying in these circumstances. Were America to elect John Kerry president, it would be seen around the world as a repudiation not just of Bush and of Iraq but of the broader war. It would be a declaration by the people of American unexceptionalism—that they are a slightly butcher Belgium; they would be signing on to the wisdom of conventional transnationalism. Having failed to read correctly the mood of my own backyard, I could hardly continue to pass myself off as a plausible interpreter of the great geopolitical forces at play. Obviously that doesn't bother a lot of chaps in this line of work—Sir Simon Jenkins, Robert "Mister Robert" Fisk, etc.,—and no doubt I could breeze through the next four years doing ketchup riffs on Teresa Heinz Kerry, but I feel a period of sober reflection far from the scene would be appropriate. My faith in the persuasive powers of journalism would be shattered; maybe it would be time to try something else—organizing coups in Africa, like the alleged Sir Mark Thatcher[1] is alleged to have allegedly done; maybe abseiling down the walls of the presidential palace and garroting the guards personally.

But I don't think it will come to that. This is the 9/11 election, a choice between pushing on or retreating to the polite fictions of September 10. I bet on reality.

* * *

Reality isn't the sure bet it once was. Do you remember the afternoon of the 2004 election? A flurry of leaked "exit polls" showed John Kerry cruising to victory.

---

1   Sir Mark, the son of Margaret Thatcher and brother of my old pal Carol Thatcher, had been arrested in South Africa for his role in an attempted coup in Equatorial Guinea. He was subsequently convicted, fined three million rand, and received a four-year suspended sentence.

Across the pond, it was late evening and the traditional election night party at the U.S. embassy in Grosvenor Square was in full swing when news of the impending Kerry presidency came through. My Fleet Street comrade Peter Oborne contemplated the implications of this bright new dawn:

> *Not long before midnight on Tuesday, a mood of dogmatic certitude overcame the throng of British MPs, ministers and journalists assembled at the traditional election-night party at the American embassy in Grosvenor Square. We knew that John Kerry had won, and dismissed with knowing contempt the warnings of our hosts—whose election, after all, it was—that it was far too early to tell.*
>
> *A delicious report went round that shares in Halliburton, the construction company associated with Vice-President Dick Cheney, had crashed on Wall Street shortly after 4 p.m. local time, in reaction to the first unofficial exit polls. One lonely Foreign Office official, along with Bruce Anderson, the political columnist, challenged the prevailing mood....*
>
> *The rest of us spent two or three carefree hours, while we imagined the consequences of a Kerry victory: rapprochement between America and the rest of the world; reconciliation between Tony Blair and the Labour Party; the resignation of Mark Steyn.*

But, like Houdini, I escaped yet again. I'm less optimistic than I used to be, and offering to resign if my prediction of total civilizational collapse doesn't come to pass doesn't have quite the same ring. And on most of the big questions these days I'd be very happy to be proved wrong.

ACKNOWLEDGMENTS

THESE COLUMNS ORIGINALLY appeared in the following publications: *The American Spectator, The Atlantic Monthly, The Chicago Sun-Times*, Britain's *Daily Telegraph, Sunday Telegraph*, and *The Independent, The Irish Times, Maclean's*, Canada's *National Post*, America's *National Review, The Spectator* in the United Kingdom and Australia, *The Wall Street Journal*, and Canada's *Western Standard*.

I would like to thank the editors at the respective titles: R. Emmett Tyrrell Jr., Wlady Pleszczynski, and Marc Carnegie at *The American Spectator*; Cullen Murphy at *The Atlantic*; Steve Huntley at *The Chicago Sun-Times*; Charles Moore, Dominic Lawson, Sarah Sands, Martin Newland, Sarah Crompton, Mark Law, and Anna Murphy at *The Telegraph*; Tom Sutcliffe at *The Independent*; Peter Murtagh at *The Irish Times*; Ken Whyte and Dianne de Gayardon de Fenoyl at *Maclean's*; Natasha Hassan, John O'Sullivan, and Ruth-Ann MacKinnon at *The National Post*; Rich Lowry and Jay Nordlinger at *National Review*; Boris Johnson, Liz Anderson, Stuart Reid, Tom Switzer, and the late Frank Johnson at *The Spectator*; Max Boot, James Taranto, and Tunku

Varadarajan at *The Wall Street Journal*; and Ezra Levant and Kevin Libin at *The Western Standard*.

I would also like to thank Conrad Black and Dan Colson who ran the newspaper group that operated several of the above titles and many others in which I had the honor to appear. A large number of the pieces here appeared in multiple publications on multiple continents, from *The Ottawa Citizen* to *The Jerusalem Post*, *The Australian*, and all the way to *Hawkes Bay Today* in New Zealand, with a tweak here and a tweak there en route. So I've picked the version I like best and occasionally, no disrespect, put back a line or two that the fine ladies and gentlemen listed above in their wisdom chose to excise.

I am also indebted to readers in America, Canada, Britain, Australia, Europe, Asia, and elsewhere whose comments, questions, historical tidbits, and occasional insults prompted many of the columns.

I would like to thank Marji Ross, Harry Crocker, and their colleagues at Regnery for their enthusiasm and encouragement. And I'd be completely lost without my trusty sidekicks over the years—Chantal Benoît, Tiffany Cole, Katherine Ernst, and Moni Haworth—who've put up with a lot of pacing the floor an hour before deadline and all the usual hair-tearing.

I thank my beloved daughter Ceci for permission to include her Memorial Day poem. On the day she was born, I got a bit bored during a somewhat protracted labor and started writing a column for *The Telegraph*. So literally her first sight of this world was me typing away. If what goes around comes around, I'll look up from my deathbed and see her live tweeting it.

INDEX

20th June Group, 136

24 Sussex Drive, 169

1984 (Orwell), 114

A

ABC network, 41–43, 181

Abdullah (crown prince of Saudi Arabia), 407

Abdullah (king of Jordan), 212

Abingdon, 279

abortion, 65–66, 311, 315–17, 339, 374

Act for the Abolition of the Slave Trade (United Kingdom), 397

Adams, John, 151, 236

Advocate, The, 312

Afghanistan

Communists in, 395

Taliban in, 184, 191–92, 226, 283

Three Cups of Tea and, 142

war, 194–201, 204, 242, 247, 283, 362, 413

winter in, 181–85, 187

Afghan National Army, 196

African-Americans, 28, 48, 101, 160, 163

After America (Birmingham), 410

After America: Get Ready for Armageddon (Steyn), x, 317, 410

After America: Narratives for the Next Global Age (Starobin), 410

Agence France-Presse, 181

AIDS, 55, 259

Aitkenhead, Decca, 156–58

Akhras, Ayat, 406

Albrechtsen, Janet, 12

Alcohol, Tobacco, and Firearms (ATF), 75, 97

Alexander, Lamar, xiii

Algosaibi, Ghazi, 405–8

Almaleki, Noor, 225–26

al-Qaeda, 183, 187, 190, 203, 210–12, 263, 283–84

Alzheimer's disease, 318

Amazing Grace (Metaxas), 397–99

Amazon (company), 290–91

America Alone: The End of the World as We Know It (Steyn), x, 315

America, American. *See also* United States, U.S.

  bureaucracy of, 105–8, 119

  coffee culture of, 6–8

  constitutional rights in, 363–64

  crime rates in, 69–72

  culture of, xv–xvi, 19, 28–30, 43, 79–83, 143, 235, 251, 256, 264, 266, 271, 302–3, 312, 366, 368, 391, 410

  decline of, 19, 46, 144, 410

  demographics of, 26, 43, 280, 291–92, 294–97, 302, 313, 315, 385–86

  differences with other countries, 79–82, 112, 118–19

  drones and, 202–4

  economy of, 44–47, 261

  financial policies of, 118

  as former British colony, 158, 160–61, 397

  founding of, 151

  hegemony of, 10–11, 196–97, 246–47

  immigration in, xi, 105–8, 143, 160–65, 315

  liberal criticism of, 135, 180, 184–85, 187, 189–90, 213, 225, 247–48

  media in, 40–43, 153, 207, 224, 264–65, 394

  military engagements of, 194–201, 203–4, 209–13, 242

  police power in, 91–102

  politicians in, xiv, 33–34, 88, 143, 152, 154, 170–73, 389–92, 414

  race relations in, 161–64

  relationship with other countries, 44, 46–47, 167, 189–90, 193, 205–8, 330–31, 415

  Steyn as immigrant in, xvii, 10, 409

  theatre in, 128–33

  World War II and, 10–11

American College of Surgeons, 348–49

American Dream, 164, 297

American Spectator, The, 2, 6, 67

Amiel, Barbara, 406

Amman, 209, 212, 379

Amor, Roy, 358–60

"Ana wa Laila," 254

Anglicanism, Anglicans, 162, 228, 301–2

Anglo-French settlement of 1922, 210

Anwar, Jawed, 230, 232

Apted, Michael, 398

Aravamudan, Gita, 316

Archbishop of Canterbury, 301–2
Arnold, Thomas, 351, 355
Assads, the, 151, 193
Associated Press (AP), 181
Ataka ("Attack" political party), 259
Atlantic, The, xi, 328
Attenborough, David, 329
Audacity of Hope, The, 408
Austin Powers, 7
Austin Powers, International Man of Mystery, 63
Australia, 9, 14, 54, 80, 90, 198, 297, 302, 370, 372–74
    media in, 67
    relationship with America, 330–31
    relationship with Britain, 158, 166–69
    Steyn and, xvii, 11–12, 332, 403
Australian, The, xviii, 328
Australia Zoo, the, 328, 332
Austrian Freedom Party, 258, 260
"Autumn Leaves," 373
Awlaki, Abdulrahman al-, 202–3
Awlaki, Anwar al-, 202–3
Axworthy, Lloyd, 181, 185

B
Baath, 211, 247, 373
"Baby, It's Cold Outside," xviii
Baez, Joan, 263
Baghdad, 53, 212, 385
Baghdad International Airport, 413
Baldwin, Alec, 411

Baldwin, Thomas, 318
Bandar, Prince, 406
Barack on Broadway, 171
Barbie, xi, 223–27
Barfield, Deborah, 181
Barlow, Tony, 310
Barnum, P. T., 324
Barre, VT, xi, 81–82
Barry, Marion, 162, 164
Barrymore, Drew, 33–34
Bart, Lionel, 55
Battle of the Atlantic, 11
Bauer, Gary, xiii
BBC, x, 6, 36,
    news, x, 36, 116, 181–82, 187, 247, 360, 379, 412
    television programs, 6, 109, 135, 151, 329, 334, 357, 360, 377
BBC2, 129, 136
BBC World Service, 253–56
Beach Boys, the, 251, 337
"Beautiful Dreamer," 238–39
Beckel, Bob, 294, 296
Belafonte, Harry, 163
Belgium, Belgians, 12, 37, 100, 138, 158, 190, 206, 244–46, 258, 262, 297, 414
"Believe," 254
Bell, Alexander Graham, 6
Belloc, Hilaire, 197
Benghazi, 206–8, 378
Bennett, Catherine, 154
Bergman, Ingrid, x, 312
Berlin, Germany, 12, 132, 224, 361, 390

Berlin, Irving, 164, 235–36, 245, 270, 391

Berlin Wall, the, 390–91

Best, Shirley, 68

Beverly Hills, 170

Bezos, Jeff, 290–93

Bhutan, Bhutanese, 403–4

Biden, Joseph, 27, 29

Big Government, 19, 26, 79, 81, 144, 293, 297, 304

Bingham, Mark, 180

bin Laden, Osama, 172, 180, 192, 198, 208, 406

Birmingham, John, 410

black flics, 186

Blair, Tim, 33, 176, 224

Blair, Tony, 67, 107, 115, 154, 157, 169, 193, 280, 285, 307, 415

Blanchett, Cate, 32–33

Blazing Cat Fur, 230

Bloomberg, Michael, 210

Bloomberg News, 86

"Blues in the Night," 271

Blunt, James, 279, 281

Bobos in Paradise: The New Upper Class and How They Got There, 8

Bobrow, Martin, 318

Boehner, John, 47

Bolivia, 12

Bond, James, 123–27, 244

Booker, David, 358

Book of Spies, The, 125

Boreman, Linda. *See* Lovelace, Linda

Boston Globe, The, 98, 181, 314

Boston Herald, The, 27

Bradley, James, 93, 95–96

Bragg, Melvyn, 135–37

Breyer, Stephen, 363–67

Britain, British, 34, 105, 190, 293

   biological experiments in, 317–19

   crime rates in, 67–72

   criticisms of, 136–40, 154, 157, 254

   cultural differences with the U.S., 23, 79–80, 96, 132–33, 161–63, 189–90, 198–99, 280

   culture of, 23, 84, 86, 130–33, 157, 310–12, 357–61, 372, 403

   demography of, 231, 378–80

   economy of, xvi, 92

   empire of, 10–11, 141, 157–58, 160–65, 195, 199, 209, 256, 265, 302, 398

   European Union and, 258–62

   Margaret Thatcher's legacy in, 393–96

   media of, 35, 106, 153, 175, 223, 369

   military engagements of, 180

   politicians of, xiv, 40, 102, 112, 135, 389

   slavery and, 397–400

   sovereigns of, 89, 154, 166–69

   Steyn and, xvii–xviii, 414–15

   surveillance in, 112–16

   theatre in, 128–31

   third sector in, 280

   weather in, 186–88

   welfare in, 282–84

   in World War II, 10–11, 201

British army, 201

British Columbia "Human Rights" Tribunal, 347

British Imperialism, 165. *See also* Britain, British: empire of

British National party, 258, 260, 373

British police, the, 68–70, 112–16, 137, 359, 379

British Union of Fascists, 260

Broadway, 31, 128–33, 205, 270–71, 324, 364

Brokaw, Tom, 181

Brokest Nation in History, xi, 82, 119

Brookhiser, Richard, 398

Brophy, Colleen, 349

Brown, Amos, 179–80

Brown, Gordon, 260

Browning, Tod, 324–27

Brown, Jerry, 295

Brussels, 198, 226, 244, 247

"brutal Afghan winter," the, 181–85, 187

"brutal Cuban winter," the, 186–90

Bucharest, 361

Buckingham Palace, 166–67, 176

Budapest, 259, 357, 361

Bulgaria, 259, 261, 389

Bulgarian National Patriotic Party, 259

Burchill, Julie, 279

Burger, Warren, xiii

Burlington Free Press, The, 25

burqas, xi, 115, 220–25, 377

Bush Administration, the, 11

Bush, Barbara, 42

Bush, George H. W., 5, 42, 92

Bush, George W. "Dubya," 14, 147, 166, 171, 191, 193–95, 212, 331, 351, 411–14

Bush, Jeb, 155

BuzzFeed, 142–43

Byrd, Robert C., 197

Byrds, the, 337

C

Cabaret, 12, 131

Cairo, 206, 225, 231

California, 86, 89, 152, 237, 295, 310, 312, 333, 336, 339, 392

Caliphate, the, 213

Caliphate State, 284

Cambodia, 395

Campbell, Colleen Carroll, 315–16

"Camptown Races," 235, 237

Canada, 14, 54, 109–10, 118, 223, 399
 culture of, 79–80, 351, 355–56
 demography of, 12, 302, 316
 economy of, xvi, 297
 government services in, 225–26
 human rights commissions in, 259, 370
 Indians in, 285–89
 media in, 152–53, 166, 181–82, 191, 256, 384, 409
 military of, 10–11, 198, 246
 monarchy and, 151, 156, 166–69
 Muslims in, 224–25, 228–32

politics in, xvii, 79, 102, 135, 167–69, 190–91

Steyn and, xvii–xviii, 110–11, 409

weather in, 182–85

World War II and, 10–11

Capitol Police, 101–2

Carey, Miriam, 101–2

Caribbean, the, x, 156–57, 161–64, 187, 195

Carter, Jimmy, 63, 389, 395

Casino Royale, 123–27

Castro, Fidel, 263

CBC network, 286

CBS network, 42–43, 96, 211

CCTV, 112–16

Central America, 296–97

CFL light bulbs, 14–15

Chang and Eng (Siamese twins), 324–27

Chappaquiddick, 176

Charter of the Forest, 89–90

Cheney, Dick, 211, 247, 415

Cher, 254

Cherokee tribe, 27–31, 142–43

Chicago Sun Times, The, xvii, 240

Chiluba, Frederick, 157

"chimeras," 317

Chrétien, Jean, 102, 169, 286

Christie, Chris, 82

Christmas, xvi, 51–54, 84, 130, 152, 156, 180, 273, 332, 352

Church of England, the, 358, 399

Churchill, Winston, 281

Civil War, 34, 87, 160, 236–37, 242

Clark, Wes, 414

Clinter, Billy (satirical name of fake character), 146–47

Clinton, Hillary Rodham, 41, 107, 145–47, 155, 206–7, 268, 307, 314–15, 362

Clinton, William "Bill," x–xi, xiv, 4–5, 62–66, 71, 96, 160, 175, 264, 307, 342, 408

clones, 305–8, 312–13

Clooney, George, 171

Clooney, Rosemary, 335

CNN, 141, 192

Cocoon, 340

Code of the Woosters, The, 353

Cohen, Laura Rosen, 224

Cold War, the, 125, 196–97, 201, 265

Cole, Natalie, 36

Collins, Phil, 67, 72

"combat risk," 62, 65

Coming of Age, the, 319

Coming Apart (Murray), 301

Comita, Jenny, 32

commencement, 23–25

Communism, Communists, 5, 91, 97, 115, 180, 265, 267, 347, 361, 373, 389, 392, 395

Conservative Party (Britain), the, xiv, 71, 92

conservatives (generally), xiv–xv, 136, 329, 331, 389

conservatives (U.S.), 10, 26, 30, 62, 142–43, 193, 371

culture and, xiii, 246, 294–95, 302

constitutional monarchy, 169

Continent, the, xiv, 7, 10, 80, 82, 114, 118, 224, 260–61, 284

    Muslims and, 192, 231

Cook County, 314

Coolidge, Calvin, xii, 155, 295–96

Côte d'Ivoire, 34

Couric, Katie, 224, 241

Cowger, Scott, 15

Crazy for You, 128–133

crime rates. *See under* America, American; Britain, British

Crocodile Hunter, the, 328–32

Cromwell, Oliver, 116

Crosby, Bing, 239, 272

Crow, Sheryl, 33–35, 239

Cruise, Tom, 68–69

cultural eclipse, 11, 13

cultural genocide, 287

Curly Fry Lightbulb, 14, 17–19. *See also* CFL light bulb

"cybrids," 317

Cypher, Julie, 312

D

Dacopa, 6, 8

Daffy Duck, xvi

Daily Express, The, 116

Daily Mail, The, 110, 152, 223, 260, 317

Daily Telegraph, The, ix, xvii, 23, 36, 145, 156, 179, 217, 282, 305, 339, 403, 405

Daily Telegraph, The (Australia), 176, 224

Damascus, 212

Darcy (character in *What Women Want*), 59–60

Daschle, Tom, 175–76

Davis Inlet, 285–89

Davis, Jefferson, 241

"Day after Day," 335

Day, Doris, 60, 333–38

"Daydream Believer," xi

Dean, Howard, 82, 292

debt ceiling (U.S.), 44, 46

debt (U.S.), x, 7–8, 44–46, 304, 317

Dees-Thomases, Donna, 41–43

Defense of Marriage Act, xiv

Deming, NM, 99–102

democracy, xiv, 113, 262, 370, 405

Democratic National Committee (DNC), 87

Democratic Party, Democrats, xi, 27–28, 41, 46, 63, 89, 153, 172, 175, 242, 294, 296–97, 314–16

demographics, 11

    of America, 294–96

    of China, 315

    demographic decline of West, x, 12, 35, 157, 192, 304, 316, 383

    of Japan, 381

    of Tangiers, 385

Dempsey, Martin, 206–7

Dent, Grace, 154

De Palma, Brian, 247

DeParle, Jason, 296–97

Department of Environmental Protection (Maine), 15–19
Department of Indian Affairs (Canada), 289
détente, 190, 389, 391
Deutsche Welle, 210
Diaz-Balart, Mario, 89
Diaz, Cameron, 33
"Dil Dil Pakistan," 254, 256
"Ding Dong! The Witch Is Dead,"393, 396
Disney World, 187
diversity
    absurdity surrounding, 27–31, 228–29, 303, 352–53, 355, 371, 374
    dangers of, 230–31, 312, 378–79
    at Harvard Law School, 27–28
    the Queen and, 156–58
Dixie Chicks, the, 263
Dole, Bob, xiii, 3
Dole, Elizabeth, xiii
"Don't Tread on Me," 79, 83
Dornan, Bob, xiii
Downton Abbey, 281, 291, 369
Dreams from My Father, 26, 142–43
Drewitt, Barrie, 310
drones, 173, 202–4, 212, 290–93
Drug Enforcement Administration (DEA), 93–98
Duchess of Windsor, 31
Dukakis, Michael, xii
Duke of Edinburgh, 166–67, 246, 283
Duke of Windsor, 31
Durbin, Dick, 247

Dutch (Morris), 390
Dylan, Bob, 32, 249–52, 253

E

Earle, Guy, 347–48
East Anglia, 67
Eastern Europe, 136, 349, 389, 391, 395
East Midlands, 395
Eckert, David, 99–100, 102
economy, the
    of America, 172, 212, 290, 293, 296–97
    of Britain, 394–96
    global, 261, 319
Edison, Thomas, 14
Educating Rita, 130
Education of Little Tree, The, 142
Egypt, xviii, 157, 208, 232, 377–78, 380
Eighties, the, xiii, 59, 101, 337, 393–94
Ekland, Britt, 67
Electric Prunes, the, 251
'Elf 'n' Safety, 84–86. *See also* Health & Safety
Ellis, Angela, 223–24
Ellis Island, 164
Energy Independence and Security Act, 14
Equal Employment Opportunities Commission, 30
Etheridge, Melissa, 312–13
Europe, 80, 100, 109, 130, 157, 303, 363, 403
    Big Government in, 79, 81, 261, 317

Communists in, 190

demographics of, x, 192, 231–32, 295, 304, 317, 378, 383, 386

economies of, xvi, 118, 261, 284, 304, 317

forms of government in, 151, 158, 261, 296, 304, 317

relationship with America, 196, 246, 254, 413–15

European Parliament, 258–59, 261–62

European Union, the, 14, 259–60

euro zone, the, 118

evil empire, the, 389

F

Facebook, xiv, 171

Fain, Sammy, 239

Falklands, the, 395

Falklands War, 395–96

Faludy, George, 223

Farooq, Nada, 13

Fast & Furious, 143

FATCA Act, 118

Fatwas, 134, 138, 366

Federal Reserve, the, 46

Feinstein, Dianne, 180

Female Eunuch, The, 67

female genital mutilation, 219, 362

feminism, feminists, 60, 316, 349–50, 364, 369, 373–74

   in America, xi, 62–66, 334, 336

   in Australia, 67, 329, 371

   in Canada, 231

   in London, 217

   Muslims and, 304

Ferdinand, Franz, 180

Ferraro, Geraldine, 314

Fifties, the, 45, 126, 163, 226, 335, 342, 413

Fire Island, NJ, 41, 307

First Amendment, the, 363–64, 355. *See also* freedom of speech

Fish, Michael, 186–87

Fisk, Robert, 413–14

Fleet Street, xvii, 32, 100, 125, 153, 187–89, 280, 366, 415

Fleming, Ian, 123–27

Flemish Interest political party, 258

Flight 93, 180, 197

Fluke, Sandra, 144

folk songs, 237, 250–51, 266

Fonda, Jane, 3

Food and Drug Administration (FDA), 1, 110, 119

"Fools Rush In," 272

Foreign Office, the, 406, 415

Foreign Terrorist Tracking Task Force, 108

forelocks, 154, 168

For Fatherland and Freedom Party, 258

Foster, Jodie, 312

Foster, Stephen, 235–39

Fox News, 42, 294, 351

Fragments: Memories of a Wartime Childhood, 142

France, French, 10, 80–81, 100, 158, 198, 211, 232, 258, 262, 318, 378

Franklin, Benjamin, 151, 155

Frayling, Christopher, 334, 336

Freaks, 325–27

freedom of speech, 65, 135, 138, 157, 207, 316, 364, 366, 370–74

"Free Iraq," 209, 213

Frey, James, 141

Friedman, Thomas, 201

Front National (French political party), 258, 262

Frost, Robert, 390

Fry, Stephen, 130

"F**k-Off Friday," 394

fundraisers, 153, 170–73, 205, 307, 338

Furst, Alan, 125

Furuya, Fusa, 319

G

Garfield, James, 33–34

Garofalo, Janeane, 364

gay marriage, xiii–xiv, 258, 301, 358, 370, 373–74, 378

gays, xv, 24, 41, 72, 143, 180, 260, 301–3, 360. *See also* gay marriage; homosexuals

bullying of, 354

children and, 309–11

persecution of, 92, 157, 159, 180, 225, 230, 232, 379–80

Gay-Straight Alliances (GSAs), 351–55

genocide, 287, 295

George III (king), xv, 155, 160

George, Prince, 151

Georgetown Law School, 143–44

Germany, Germans, 46, 80, 115, 118, 151, 179–80, 186, 198, 223, 227, 245, 302, 335

demographics of, 12, 35

under the Nazis, 138–39, 201

Gershwin brothers, the, 128–30

Gershwin, Ira, 270–72, 275

Gibson, Mel, 58–61

GI Joe, 198, 223, 244–48

Gila Regional Medical Center, New Mexico, 99

Gilbert, John, 240

Gilbey, Deena, xi, 105–8

Gilbey, Paul, 105–8

Girl Crazy, 130–31

Giuliani, Rudy, 82, 241

Glasgow, Scotland, 153, 182

Global Integrated Joint Operating Entity, 198–99, 244

"global upheaval," 192

Globe and Mail, The, 286, 411

Glover, Stephen, 187

Glyn, Noah, 31

"God Bless America," 240, 391

Goldberg, Jonah, 30, 290

Golden Age, The, 32

Goldwyn, Sam, 164

"Goody Goody," 274

GOP, the, xv, 44, 294, 297. *See also* Republican Party

Gore, Al, 1, 32–33, 43, 242, 411–12

Gorky Park, 398

Government Services Administration (GSA), 351

government shutdown, 87–90

Graduate, The, 336, 441

Graham, Sylvester, 4

Gramm, Phil, xiii

Granite State, the, xii, 79, 100, 117. *See also* New Hampshire

Grant, Caroline, 241

Grant, Turner, 240

Greater Manchester Police, 116, 359

Greater Romania Party, 258

Great Escape, The, 117

Great Satan, the, 193, 254

Great War, the, 180, 240, 245, 296

Greece, Greek, 118, 164, 378

Greeley, CO, xviii

Green Cards, 106–8, 117

Greenfield, Lazar, 348–49

Green, Michael, 67

Greenwoods, the, 310–11

Green Zone, the, 53, 170, 302

Greer, Germaine, 67, 72, 329, 371–72

Grenada, 195, 389, 395

Groskop, Viv, 154

Ground Zero, 108, 179–80

Ground Zero mosque, the, 363

Guantanamo, 188–89, 362

Guardian, The, 35, 38, 154, 156–58, 187, 279–80, 309, 329, 373

Guatemala, 142, 191

Guess Who's Coming to Dinner?, 163

Gulf War I, 62, 162, 195

Gulf War II, 195

H

Haden-Guest, Anthony, 55–57

Hall, Barbara, 229, 231, 352, 355

Halliburton, 247, 415

Hammerstein, Oscar, 270

Hamza, Abu, 284

Hamzi, Salem al-, 108

"Hard Rain's A-Gonna Fall, A," 251

Harper's, 2

Harrison, David, 9, 12–13

Harrow, 279, 281

Harry Potter series, 145

Hart, Lorenz, 270

Hart, Moss, 403

Harvard Law Review, The, 28

Harvard Law School, 27–31, 92

Harvard University, xvii, 314

Hasselhoff, David, 219

Hatch, Orrin, xiii

Haverhill, NH, xi, 410

health care, xvi, 100, 290, 292, 297, 404

Health & Safety, 84, 86. *See also* 'Elf 'n' Safety

Hedda Gabler, 32

Heidenry, John, 55, 57

Henry III, 89

Hidalgo County, NM, 99, 102

hijabs, 225–26, 316, 379, 386

Hill, The, 409–10

Hill, Anita, 62–63

Hilliard, Bob, 239

Hilton, Daisy, 324–27

Hilton, Violet, 324–27

Hindu Kush, the, 182, 192, 303

Hispanics, 29, 58, 79, 292, 294–96, 302

Holder, Eric, 143

Hollywood, 11, 32–33, 56, 67, 73, 126, 170, 245–48, 272, 325, 336, 381, 411

Holm, Paul, 180

Holocaust, the, 143, 287

Home Office, the (Britain), 70

homophobia, homophobics, xiv, 156–58, 231, 304, 331, 348, 352, 355

homosexuals, xiii, 156–57, 230, 232, 259–60, 301, 304, 358, 378, 378. *See also* gays

Hope, Bob, xii, 325, 335

Horse Whisperer, The, 246

Houghton, Katharine, 164

House of Representatives, the, 14

Howard, John, 167, 331

Huang Shuzheng, 318

Hudson, Rock, 60, 335–36

Hugo, Victor, 55

humanitarians, 183–85

Hungary, Hungarian, 164, 258–59, 305, 357

Hunter, Will, 92–98

Hunt, Helen, 59–61

Hunt, Marsha, 219

Hussein, Saddam, 168, 209–11, 241

I

Ibrahim, Samira, 203

"I Dream of Jeanie with the Light Brown Hair," 235

"If I Had a Hammer," 265–66

Ignatieff, Michael, xvii–xviii, 135

"I Had the Craziest Dream," 337–38

Ilayaraja, 254

"I'll Be Seeing You," 239

Independent, The, xi, 129, 132, 134, 154, 184

Independent Magazine, The, 137,

India, 158, 163, 164, 198–99, 201, 209, 255, 256, 287, 302, 314–16

Indians (America), 27. *See also* Cherokee tribe

Innu community, the, 285–89

INS, 105–8

Internal Revenue Service (IRS), 91, 153

Iraq, 185, 200, 255
    ISIS and, 209–13
    liberation of, 209, 407
    war in, 62, 192, 194, 241–42, 247, 413–14
    war with Iran, 134–35, 377

I, Rigoberta Menchú, 142

Irish Times, The, xviii, 389, 412

Iron Curtain, the, 357

Irwin, Steve, 328–32

Irwin, Terri, 332

Islam
    dress mandated by, 225–26
    factions within, 192–93
    growth of, 192, 231–32, 377–79
    political correctness and, 230–32, 261, 363–65, 370–74

relationship with the West, 203, 207–8, 228–31, 284, 295, 362, 365–68, 377–79

Sharia law and, 134, 362–63, 379

theology of, 230, 374, 377

"Islamic State of Iraq and Syria" (ISIS), 210–12

Islamophobia, 206–7, 223, 231, 347, 379

Italy, Italian, 12, 80–81, 118, 151, 164, 198, 251, 378

"(I took a trip on a train and) I Thought about You," 271–72

"It's Magic," 334

It Takes a Village, 408

J

Jackson, Glenda, 217

Jackson, Jesse, 101, 162–64

Jagger, Mick, 56, 219, 279–80

Jalalabad, 184–85, 246

Jamaica, 123, 156–58, 160–65, 230

Japan, Japanese, 12, 88, 90, 141, 158, 198, 201, 219, 316–19, 381–83

"Jeepers Creepers," 272

Jenkins, Simon, 414

Jews, 142, 157–58, 163–64, 203, 221, 232, 250, 259, 378–80, 384–86, 392, 406

Jim Crow, 242

Jobbik (political party), 258–59

Jobseeker's Allowance, 282, 284

Johannesburg, South Africa, 36

Johnson, Boris, 405, 407

Johnson, Brian D., 246

Joke, The (Kundera), 347–50

Jonas, George, 223

Jones, Paula, x, 62

Jordan, 147, 200, 209–12

"Julia" (Obama administration campaign ad), 26, 30

Juno Beach, 10

K

Kabul, Afghanistan, 182, 184–85, 189, 194

Kallawayan people, the, 12

Kandahar, 182, 187, 197, 199, 231, 362

Kan, Naoto, 319

Kaplan, Muhammed Metin, 284

Kate, Princess, 152–54

Kato, Sogen, 319

Kauffman, Hattie, 42

Kaus, Mickey, 46, 180

Kazan, Elia, 340

Kelly, Lorraine, 219

Kelly, Megyn, 211

Ken (of Barbie and Ken), 224–25

Kennedy, Anthony, xv

Kennedy, Edward "Ted," 174–76, 247

Kennedy, John F., 33, 180, 328

Kerry, John, ix–xii, 203, 413–15

Kerry, Teresa Heinz, xii, 414

Keyes, Alan, xiii

Khomeieni, Ayatollah, 85, 134, 136

Kim family, the, 151

Kinder Eggs, 109–11
King John (Shakespeare), 396
King, Larry, 331
Knight Bachelors, 140
Knight Commanders, 140
Kopechne, Mary Jo, 176
Kopp, Nancy, 314
Koran, the, 189, 362–64
Korean War, 195, 197
Krauthammer, Charles, 296
Krugman, Paul, 45–46
Ku Klux Klan, 241–42
Kundera, Milan, 347, 349–50

L

Labour Party (Britain), 115, 128, 136, 217, 260–62, 285, 308, 394, 415
"Land of Hope and Glory," 23
Langley Park, MD, 296
Laster, James B., 194–95
Last Party: Studio 54, Disco, and the Culture of the Night, The, 55
Las Vegas, NV, 58, 205, 208, 268, 351
Late Show, The, 42, 135
Latin America, xv, 109, 191, 281, 296
Latvia, 258, 389
"Laura," 272
"leading from behind," 195
Lee, Pamela (Anderson), 3, 249
left, leftists, left-wing, xiv, xvi, 128, 134, 137–38, 141, 157, 179, 261, 265, 297, 302, 357, 364, 367, 393, 405, 412
lesbians, 311–13, 348–49

Letterman, David, 42, 206
Levant, the, 210, 378
Levant, Oscar, 336
Lewinsky, Monica, ix, 65
Liberal Party (Canada), xvii, 134–35, 169, 286
liberals, liberalism, 134, 226, 301
  in America, 31, 43, 143, 225, 247, 291, 301, 304, 316, 364–68
  in Canada, 286–87
  culture and, xiii–xv
  in Europe, 258, 369, 372
Liberia, 34
Libya, 195, 200, 207–8, 379
Lileks, James, 266
Lily Allen, 279
Limbaugh, Rush, 19
Lincoln, Abraham, 33, 240, 242, 307
Living History (Rodham Clinton), 145, 147
Living Tongues Institute for Endangered Languages, 9
Loewenstein, Antony, 11–12
Logan, Kate, 25
London School of Economics, 279
Longman, Phillip, 316
Los Angeles, CA, xvii, 152–53, 171, 232
Los Angeles Times, The, 181
Lovejoy, Charles, 240–41
Lovelace, Linda, 56
Love Me or Leave Me, 336
Lover Come Back, 336
Love Story, A, 408
Loving v. Virginia, 302

Luckenbach, TX, 410
Ludvik (character in *The Joke*), 347–49

M

Magati Ke tribe, the, 9–12
Magna Carta, 89, 287
mail fraud, 97–98
Mail on Sunday, The, 189
Major, John, 161–62
malaria, 187–88
Malaysia, 158
Mamas and Papas, 337
Manhattan, NY, 31, 55, 170, 325
Marshall, Nick (protagonist of *What Women Want*), 58–61
Martin, Ricky, xiv, 171
Martin, Tony, 68–69
Martin, Trayvon, 29, 101
Marx, Groucho, 336
Marxists, 261, 291, 314, 357
Mary II (queen). *See* William and Mary
Massa, Gilary, 316
McCarthyism, 97
McCarthy, Jenny, 3
McCarthy, Joseph, 190
McGuinty, Dalton, 355
McKinley, William, 33
McMillan, Kate, 226
media, the. *See under* America, American; Australia; Britain, British; Canada; United States, U.S.
Medicare, 8

memoirs, 27, 29, 141–44, 145, 161, 408
Memorial Day, 240, 242–43, 314
Me and My Girl, 128–30
Mercer, John Herndon "Johnny," 270–75
meritocracy, 154
Metaxas, Eric, 397–99
Meyers, Nancy, 58–61
Michael, Princess, 219
Microsoft, 1, 200
Midnight in the Garden of Good and Evil, 270
Mihdar, Khalid al-, 108
Mikhalkov, Sergei, 267–69
Miles, Sarah, 32
militarization of the police, 91. *See also* paramilitarization of the bureaucracy
Millay, Edna St. Vincent, 390
Millennials, 290
Miller, Arthur, 340
Miller, David, 170
Million Little Pieces, A, 141
Million Mom March, xi, 40–43
minimum wage, the, 290–91, 303
Mirror, The, 189
Miss World, 217
Mitchell, Adrian, 394
Mitchell, William, 6
Modern Family, 304
Moi, Daniel arap, 157
monarchy, 31, 89, 151–54, 166–74, 176
Monbiot, George, 35, 38
"Monica's dress" column (Steyn),

Monkees, the, ix–x

Monroe, Marilyn, xvi, 339–44

Montreal, 111, 117, 284, 287–88

Mooney, Chris, 30

"Moon River," 270–75

Moore, Demi, 306

Moore, Susan, 282–84

Morris, Edmund, 390

Mortenson, Greg, 142, 198–99

Morvai, Krisztina, 259

Moscow, 124, 395

Mosimann, Anton, 67

Mosley, Oswald, 260

mosquitoes, 187–88

Mounties, 69, 102, 229

Mount Rushmore, 88

Moussaoui, Zacarias, 284

"Move Over, Darling," 334

Mrs. Robinson (character), 336, 341

Mugabe, Robert, 36, 46, 156–57, 159, 294

multiculturalism, 156–58, 199, 229, 232, 255–56, 283–84, 296, 304, 331, 370–73, 378–79

Murdoch, Rupert, 42, 167

Murphy, Ryan, 170

Murrah Building, 179

Murray, Charles, 293, 301

Museveni, Yoweri, 157

Mushuau people, 285–87

Muslim, The, 230

Muslim Brotherhood, the, xviii

Muslim Community Affairs Unit (Los Angeles), 232

Muslims, 138, 212, 283, 355, 405, 413
  in Australia, 331
  in Canada, 13, 228–32
  in Europe, 192, 231–32, 304, 378–79, 383, 386
  and the West, 203, 362, 374
  women and, 220, 224–32, 316, 362, 364–68, 377, 379

My American Journey (Powell), 160

My Heart, 337

"My Old Kentucky Home," 235

"My Sharia Amour," 218, 220–21

N

NAFTA, 100

Napolitano, Janet, 110, 202

Nash, Peggy, 352, 355

National Children's Bureau, 359

National Day of Pink, the, 352

National Front (France), 258

National Geographic, 9, 11

National Health Service, the (NHS), 304, 403–4

national interest, 197–200

nationalization, xvi, 395

National Mall, the, 87, 89

National Movement for the Salvation of the Fatherland, 259

National Oceanic and Atmospheric Administration, 119

National Park Service (NPS), 87–90

National Post, The, xviii, 40, 73, 75, 105, 166, 181, 229, 249, 253–54, 267, 351, 411–12, 417–18

National Public Radio (NPR), 143, 181, 203, 331

National Review, 6, 31, 79, 84, 117, 119, 151, 174, 191, 193–94, 263, 279, 317, 347, 377, 381, 410

National Review Online, 119, 193

National Rifle Association (NRA), 43, 73–74, 92, 183

nation-building, 199, 201

"Nation Once Again, A," 254–57

Native Americans, 27, 29, 31

Natuashish, 285–86, 288–89

Nazi Germany, 138–39

NBC network, 41–43, 181, 364

"Nelly Was a Lady," 237

Neville, Stuart, 114

Newfoundland, 10

New Hampshire, xi–xii, xvi, 24, 69–70, 79, 86–87, 94, 100, 117, 166, 182, 186, 240, 243, 292, 354, 396, 410

New Labour Party, 308

Newsday, 181

New York, xvii, 2, 26, 46, 56, 73–75, 86, 116, 128–29, 134, 161, 171, 182, 235, 237–38, 242, 249–50, 255, 270–71, 343, 356, 400

New York City, NY, 2, 86, 161

New Yorker, The, 195, 255, 400

New York Post, The, 171

New York Sun, The, xvii, 263

New York Times, The, xvii, 29, 31, 42, 62, 73, 129, 201, 203, 232, 250, 296, 349, 378

Nichols, Mike, 336, 341

Nigeria, 46, 217, 232, 295

Nightline, 181

Nineties, the, x, 97, 109, 131, 318, 326, 329, 334, 337, 400

niqabs, 377

Nkomo, Joshua, 294

non-governmental organizations (NGOs), 36, 280

NORAD, 110

Norquist, Grover, 294, 296

North Korea, 109, 112, 151, 382

Nujoma, Sam, 157

O

Obama Administration, 143, 297

Obama, Barack, xi, xiv, 8, 26–27, 30, 45–6, 81, 89, 100, 141, 143–44, 152–54, 160, 170–73, 194–95, 203, 208, 211–13, 225, 263, 290, 293, 297, 304, 314, 351, 362–64, 366–67, 404

Obamacare, 100, 143, 171, 290–91, 293, 304

Obama, Michelle, 154, 203

Obamaphones, 293

Objective: Burma, 11

Oborne, Peter, 415

O'Brien, Soledad, 141

Observer, The, 360, 382

Occupy Wall Street, 263

Ockrent, Mike, 128–33

O'Halloran, Anthony, 412

"Oh! Susanna," 235–37, 334

Oklahoma, 28, 31, 63, 179

Oklahoma City bombing, 179

"Old Black Joe," 237

Old Faithful, 88

"Old Folks at Home (Swanee River),
The," 235

Old Labour, 115, 128

Oliver!, 55

"Ol' Man River," 235

Olson, Ted, 302–3

Omari Abdul Aziz al-, 108

Omar, Mullah, 183, 191–92, 197

"On the Atchison, Topeka and the
Santa Fe," 271

Ontario Human Rights Commission,
229, 352, 355

Opcare, 358, 360

Oregonian, The, 181

Orwell, George, 113–14, 116, 360

Osgoode, William, 399

"Our Day Will Come," 239

out-of-wedlock births, xiii, 302, 304,
312, 313

P

Pakistan, 138, 181, 184, 208, 226, 232,
254–56

Palmer, Alasdair, 187

paramilitarization of the bureaucracy
91, 117–19

Parker, Sarah Jessica, 172

Parliament (Britain), 102, 199, 397

Parliament (Canada), 102

Parris, Matthew, 187, 189–90, 360

Passion Play, 130

Paul, Rand, 202

PBS, 188

Pearl Harbor, 10, 180, 246

Pelosi, Nancy, 89, 91

Pembroke Academy, 354–55

Peter, Paul, and Mary, 263, 266

Petraeus, David, 198–99, 362, 366

Pet Sounds, 251

Pfizer, 1

Philips, Bilal, 230, 232

Pillow Talk, 336

Pink Shirt Day, 353, 356

Pinter, Harold, 135–36

Pisgah Inn, 87

Podhoretz, John, 193

Poitier, Sidney, 163–64

Poland, Polish, 212, 270, 389

political correctness, 199–201, 358

"Pomp and Circumstance," 23

"Pooyum Nadakkuthu Pinchum Nadakkuthu," 254, 256

Porter, Cole, 31 270, 273, 275, 323–24

potpourri, xvi, 1, 51–54

Powell, Alma, 161

Powell, Charles, 162

Powell, Colin, 158, 160–65, 247

Powers, Austin, 7, 59, 63, 316

Powers, Kirsten, 294

Pow Wow Chow, 28, 30, 31

Prague, 361

Previn, André, 334

Producers, The, 128

progressives, 26, 226, 316, 364

Proust, Marcel, 340

"PS I Love You," 274

Q

Qaddafi, Muammar, 195

Qatada, Abu, 284

"Quantum of Solace" (Fleming), 124

Quayle, Dan, 314

Quebec, 7, 100, 109, 111, 117–18, 124, 182, 191, 202, 287–88, 292, 373

Queen, the, 31, 96, 101, 140, 153–54, 156, 158, 161, 165–70, 173, 176, 239, 246, 279, 324, 328, 352, 372, 381

Quigley, Bernie, 409–10

Qutb, Sayyid, xviii

R

Radiohead, 279

Radosh, Ron, 263–65

"Rakkamma Kaiya Thattu," 254

Ramadi, 209–12, 246

Rather, Dan, 42–43

Ravin, Yakob, 392

Reagan, Ronald, 5, 294–95, 389–92

"Reetu Haruma Timi," 254

Reno, Janet, 96

Renton, Alex, 184

Republican Brain, The, 30

Republican Party, the, xiii, 46, 295, 371. *See also* GOP, the

republicans, xv, 1, 44, 153–54, 168–70, 294–97, 389

"Return to Me," 251

"Return of Patriarchy, The," 316

right, right-wing, xiv, xvi, 2, 30, 81, 141, 146, 296, 304, 412–13

"right to choose, the," 65, 311, 314–16

Rise of the Planet Apes, 318

Rodham, J. K. (satirical name of invented author), 145–47

Rome, 34, 119, 397

Romney, Mitt, xiii, 207, 294

Ronell, Ann, 235

Rowling, J. K., 145

Royal Family, the, 152, 154, 167, 169

Ruby Ridge, 92, 94

Rumsfeld, Don, 189, 247

Running Down Broadway (Ockrent), 129

Rushdie, Salman, 134–40, 366–67

Rush Limbaugh Show, The, 15, 410

Rutba, 200, 209–12

Rutkowski, Alan, 411

Ryan, Paul, 44, 47

Ryan's Daughter, 32

S

Saher, Kazem al-, 254–55

Salem witch trials, 190

same-sex marriage. *See* gay marriage

Sandwich, England, 1

San Francisco, 179–80, 199

Sarkozy, Nicolas, 318

Satanic Verses, The (Rushdie), 135, 138, 367

Saudi Arabia, 107, 109, 230, 363, 398, 405, 408

Savannah, GA, 270, 272

Saving Private Ryan, 11, 246

Sawyer, Diane, 41, 241

Scandinavians, 302

Schmidt, Helmut, 190, 289

Scott, Ridley, 67, 72

Second Amendment, the, 82

Secret Service, 101–2

Seeger, Pete, 263–66

September 11, 2001, attacks, 105–8, 192–93, 195, 197, 203, 224

Sergeant Pepper, 251

Seventies, the, 32, 55–57, 60, 89, 92, 188–89, 226, 272, 295, 301, 335, 391, 394, 396

Seven Year Itch, The, 343

sexual harassment, 62–64, 66, 227, 342

sexuality, xv, 55–57, 301–4, 310, 381–83

Shaidle, Kathy, 228, 409

Shakespeare, William, 64–65, 287, 396

Sharia law, 134, 217–21, 379

Sharpton, Al, 101, 162

Shelton, Robert, 250

Shepard, Matthew, 225

Sherborne, 279

Shop-A-Sponger Hotline, 282, 284

Siamese twins, 323–27

Sierra Leone, 34

Silva, Daniel, 112, 114, 115

Simmonds, Rita, 68

Sinatra, Frank, 58–59, 170, 209, 249, 253, 274, 334, 336

Singapore, 158

Sixties, the, 12, 40, 55, 58, 60, 97, 163, 189, 219, 226, 249–50, 253, 256, 302, 398, 404

Slate, 180

slavery, 156, 163, 316, 397–400

Slovak National Party, 258–59

Slovenia, 80, 389

Smith, Andreas Whittam, 140

Smith, Ben, 142

social liberalism, 304

social mobility, 281, 303

Social Security, 26, 293

Society of St. James, 358

sodomy, xiii, 156

Somalia, 195, 369, 371

Sopranos, The, 251

South Bank Show, The, 136

South Park, 329, 364

Soviet national anthems, xvi, 267–69

Soviet Union, the, 10, 43, 93, 124, 197, 261, 267, 293, 357, 389, 393, 395

Spain, 118, 176, 261, 374

Speaking Truth to Power, 64

Spectator, The, 58, 62, 91, 160, 186, 190, 369, 405, 407, 414, 417–18

"Spring, Spring, Spring," 272–73

Springsteen, Bruce, 251, 263

Spy Who Loved Me, The, 124

Starbucks, 2, 6, 8

Stark (old POW camp), 186

Starobin, Paul, 410

Steinem, Gloria, 12, 62–66

Stevens, Chris, 207–8

Stevens, Scott, 91–92, 96–97

Stewart, Dave, 251

Stewart, Martha, 52

Stewart, Rod, 192, 250

St. Louis Post-Dispatch, The, 315

Stone, Oliver, 245

Stott, Codie, 359

Streisand, Barbra, 132, 171, 307, 312

Stroman, Susan, 128

Studio 54, 55–56

Styne, Jule, 391

"Summer Wind," 273

Summit of the Americas, 191, 193

Sun, The, 282

Sunday Telegraph, The, 40, 92, 182, 309, 417

Sunnis, 209–13

Sunni Triangle, the, 209, 211

Supreme Court, the, xiii, 100, 144, 202, 302–3, 363, 412

Surgery News, 348–49

Swarthmore College, 9, 370, 374

SWAT, 102, 119

Sydney Conservatorium of Music, 11

Syria, 151, 173, 210–12

T

Taliban, the, xviii, 180, 184, 189, 191–92, 224, 226, 283–4

Talk Show with Clive James, The, 136

Tancredo, Tom, xiii

tax rates, 394

Taylor, Alastair, 282

Tebbit, Norman, 135, 137–39

Telegraph Group, the, 407

Telemundo, 208

Tennyson, Alfred Lord, 258

Te'o, Manti, 44

terror, terrorism, 106–8, 189, 203, 203–4, 223, 283–84, 301, 314, 405–6

Terry (son of Doris Day), 336–37

Thapa, Arun, 254

Thatcher, Margaret, 132, 134–38, 162, 393–96, 414

Thatcher, Mark, 414

Third Reich, 30, 118, 139

third sector, the, 280

Third Way, the, 285

Third World, the, 190, 197

Thirumalai Chandran, 254

This Day, 217

Thompson, Fred, 9–11

Thompson, Tommy, xiii

Thomson, Alice, 187–88

Three Cups of Tea, 142, 198–99

"Times They Are A-Changin', The," 251

Tobaccoville, NC, 410

Toledo Blade, The, 392

Tom Brown's Schooldays, 351

Tora Bora, 192

Toronto Star, The, 228, 286

torture, 126, 141, 189, 199

totalitarian, totalitarianism, 140, 180, 261, 264, 347, 355, 357

traditional marriage, 301–3

traffic signs, 79–83

Trebil border, 209, 211

Trenton, Ontario, 152

trillion-dollar coin, the, 44–46

Trippin', 33

Trudeau, Pierre, 190, 289

True Finns party, 258

Truman, Harry S., 170, 173, 265

TSA, the, 79, 119

Turner, Anthea, 67

U

U2, 251

U-571, 11

Ukraine, Ukrainian, 91, 385, 392

UN 2002 Arab Development Report, 226

Unicef, 181

Union Jack, the, 10

Union of Patriotic Forces, 259

United Kingdom, the, 67, 71, 112–13, 151, 165, 260, 262, 358, 295, 417

United Kingdom Independent Party (UKIP), 262

United Nations (UN), 37, 183–84, 192, 19, 198, 219, 226, 259, 374

United States, U.S., 4, 23, 34, 20, 109, 198, 207–8, 281, 295, 303, 312, 332, 398, 406, 409

crime rates in the, 69–70, 80–81

culture of the, 2–3, 81, 246, 284

economy of the, 44–47, 118–19

government of the, 90–91, 95, 101, 105–6, 111, 117–19, 167, 169, 225, 363

hegemony of the, 196

immigration in the, 105–7, 202, 297

media in the, xi, 40, 42, 44, 194, 411–13

military engagements of the, 62, 181, 184–85, 188–95, 197, 209, 244–45, 247, 362, 395

politicians of the, xii–xiv, 44, 101, 141–43, 152, 160, 172, 174, 225, 342, 362

relationships with other nations, 44, 200, 212, 412, 415

taxes in the, 199

in World War II, 10

University of Minnesota, 250

U.S. border, 7, 100, 108–11, 117, 143, 202, 232, 348

U.S. Congress, 1, 3, 27, 44, 59, 65, 70, 89, 96, 101–2, 203, 393, 409

U.S. Customs and Border Protection, 109

U.S. Department of Homeland Security, 105, 109, 111

U.S. Immigration office, 297

U.S. News & World Report, 15

USSR, 112, 264
U.S. State Department, 46, 107, 191, 206
Uzbekistan, 184, 255

V

Vaidyanathan, R., xvi
Valley Park Middle School, 228, 231–32, 354
"Vande Mataram," 254, 256
Vardy, Fiona, 358
Vargas, Elizabeth, 41
Variety, 244
Vermont, xi, 3, 7, 24–25, 81–82, 92–98, 109, 111, 117, 155, 202, 255, 258, 292
Viagra, xvi, 1–5
Vidal, Gore, 309
Vietnam War, 195, 246, 391, 395, 413
Visa Express, 107
Vital Signs, 254

W

Waco, 92, 94, 96–97
Wall Street Journal, The, 1, 55, 366, 417–18
Warren, Elizabeth, 27–31
Washington, DC, 10, 40, 42, 264, 314, 373
Washington Post, The, 10, 40–42, 264, 314, 373
Watergate, 391

"Way You Look Tonight, The," 235
Weekly Standard, The, 292
Weiner, Anthony, 154, 383
Weisenthal, Joe, 44, 46
Welby, Justin, 301
Weldon, Fay, 135–36
Wendy's, xii
west, the, xvi, 38, 143, 318, 349, 395, 405
    Cold War and, 190
    decline of, xvi, 13, 35, 143, 158, 283, 383
    Muslims and, 192, 203, 225
western civilization, xviii, 11, 35, 366
Western Standard, The, 285–86, 417–18
West Indies, the, 156, 203, 398
What Wild Ecstasy: The Rise and Fall of the Sexual Revolution, 55
What Women Want, 58, 60
"When the World Was Young," 273
"Where Have All the Flowers Gone?," 263, 266
White Christmas, 245
White Mountain Militia, the, 91–92
"white vote," 294
Whiting, Margaret, 335
Wilberforce, William, 397–400
Wilders, Geert, 261
Wilkomirski, Binjamin, 142, 144
William III (king). *See* William and Mary
William and Mary, 399
William, Prince, 152, 170, 229, 354
Williams, Zoe, 280

Wilson, Pete, xiii

Wilson, Woodrow, 296

"Wimoweh (The Lion Sleeps Tonight),"
    263

Windsor, Elizabeth, 42, 167. *See also*
    Queen, the

Wintour, Anna, 172

Withington Community Hospital, 358

Wodehouse, P. G., 353

Wolfe Tones, The, 254, 257

Woodsville, NH, 24, 410

Working Woman, 64

World Is Not Enough, The, 398

World Summit, 36

World Trade Center, 105, 108, 179–80

World Trade Center, 245–46

World War II, 196, 201

Worstall, Tim, 280

Worsthorne, Peregrine, 92–93

Zimbabwe, 46, 157, 94

Zimmerman, George, 29–30

"Zip-a-Dee-Doo-Dah," 272

Y

Yank, The Army Weekly, 245

Yawaru tribe, the, 9, 12

Yemen, 202–3, 206, 231, 290, 352

Yes, (Saudi) Minister! (Algosaibi), 408

Young at Heart, 336

Young, Michael, 154

Z

ZANU-PF, 294

ZAPU-PF, 294